intel®

U.S. and CANADA LITERATURE ORDER FORM

AF877601

NAME: ______________________________

COMPANY: ______________________________

ADDRESS: ______________________________

CITY: ____________________ STATE: ________

COUNTRY: ______________________________

PHONE NO.: (   ) ____________

ORDER NO.	TITLE	QTY.		PRICE		TOTAL
			×		=	
			×		=	
			×		=	
			×		=	
			×		=	
			×		=	
			×		=	
			×		=	
			×		=	
			×		=	

Subtotal ________

Must Add Your Local Sales Tax ________

Include postage:
Must add 15% of Subtotal to cover U.S. and Canada postage. (20% all other.) → Postage ________

Total ________

Pay by check, money order, or include company purchase order with this form ($100 minimum). We also accept VISA, MasterCard or American Express. Make payment to Intel Literature Sales. Allow 2-4 weeks for delivery.

☐ VISA ☐ MasterCard ☐ American Express Expiration Date ________

Account No. ______________________________

Signature ______________________________

Mail To: Intel Literature Sales
P.O. Box 7641
Mt. Prospect, IL 60056-7641

International Customers outside the U.S. and Canada should use the International order form on the next page or contact their local Sales Office or Distributor.

For phone orders in the U.S. and Canada
Call Toll Free: (800) 548-4725

Prices good until 12/31/91.
Source HB

intel®

INTERNATIONAL LITERATURE ORDER FORM

NAME: ______________________________

COMPANY: ______________________________

ADDRESS: ______________________________

CITY: ______________ STATE: ________ ZIP: ________

COUNTRY: ______________________________

PHONE NO.: ( )

ORDER NO.	TITLE	QTY.		PRICE		TOTAL
			×		=	
			×		=	
			×		=	
			×		=	
			×		=	
			×		=	
			×		=	
			×		=	
			×		=	
			×		=	

Subtotal ________

Must Add Your Local Sales Tax ________

Total ________

PAYMENT

Cheques should be made payable to your ***local*** Intel Sales Office (see inside back cover).

Other forms of payment may be available in your country. Please contact the Literature Coordinator at your ***local*** Intel Sales Office for details.

The completed form should be marked to the attention of the LITERATURE COORDINATOR and returned to your ***local*** Intel Sales Office.

intel®

Intel Corporation is a leading supplier of microcomputer components, modules and systems. When Intel invented the microprocessor in 1971, it created the era of the mircromputer. Today, Intel architectures are considered world standards. Whether used in embedded applications such as automobiles, printers and microwave ovens, or as the CPU in personal computers, client servers or supercomputers, Intel delivers leading-edge technology.

COMPONENTS QUALITY AND RELIABILITY

1991/92

About Our Cover:

Thinkers, inventors, and artists throughout history have breathed life into their ideas by converting them into rough working sketches, models, and products. This series of covers shows a few of these creations, along with the applications and products created by Intel customers.

Intel Corporation makes no warranty for the use of its products and assumes no responsibility for any errors which may appear in this document nor does it make a commitment to update the information contained herein.

Intel retains the right to make changes to these specifications at any time, without notice.

Contact your local sales office to obtain the latest specifications before placing your order.

The following are trademarks of Intel Corporation and may only be used to identify Intel products:

> 287, 376, 386, 387, 486, 4-SITE, Above, ACE51, ACE96, ACE186, ACE196, ACE960, ActionMedia, BITBUS, COMMputer, CREDIT, Data Pipeline, DVI, ETOX, FaxBACK, Genius, i, ↑, i486, i750, i860, ICE, iCEL, ICEVIEW, iCS, iDBP, iDIS, I²ICE, iLBX, iMDDX, iMMX, Inboard, Insite, Intel, int$_{e}$l, Intel386, int$_{e}$lBOS, Intel Certified, Intelevision, int$_{e}$ligent Identifier, int$_{e}$ligent Programming, Intellec, Intellink, iOSP, iPAT, iPDS, iPSC, iRMK, iRMX, iSBC, iSBX, iSDM, iSXM, Library Manager, MAPNET, MCS, Megachassis, MICROMAINFRAME, MULTICHANNEL, MULTIMODULE, MultiSERVER, ONCE, OpenNET, OTP, Pro750, PROMPT, Promware, QUEST, QueX, Quick-Erase, Quick-Pulse Programming, READY LAN, RMX/80, RUPI, Seamless, SLD, SugarCube, ToolTALK, UPI, VAPI, Visual Edge, VLSiCEL, and ZapCode, and the combination of ICE, iCS, iRMX, iSBC, iSBX, iSXM, MCS, or UPI and a numerical suffix.

MDS is an ordering code only and is not used as a product name or trademark. MDS® is a registered trademark of Mohawk Data Sciences Corporation.

CHMOS and HMOS are patented processes of Intel Corp.

Intel Corporation and Intel's FASTPATH are not affiliated with Kinetics, a division of Excelan, Inc. or its FASTPATH trademark or products.

Betascope is a registered trademark of Twin City Testing Co.

Surfscan is a trademark of Tencor Instruments Co.

Additional copies of this manual or other Intel literature may be obtained from:

Intel Corporation
Literature Sales
P.O. Box 7641
Mt. Prospect, IL 60056-7641

THE CHAIRMAN'S VIEW OF QUALITY

Intel is engaged in a quality revolution. Quality has always been important at Intel, but over the last few years we've dedicated ourselves more than ever before to permeating our workforce with two key concepts: customer satisfaction and continuous improvement.

The purpose of this handbook is to serve as reference for the quality and reliability of Intel's products, technologies and management systems.

To date, our devotion to customer satisfaction and continuous improvement has garnered us the honor of being rated number one, number two or excellent in quality by 90 percent of our major customers. This *quality Vendor Of Choice* rating is very important to us, and we won't be satisfied until it's 100 percent.

It takes an extensive effort to achieve the required quality, but we know of no other way to succeed. Semiconductor technology continues to increase in complexity at a faster pace than ever before. The 486™ microprocessor has four times the transistors as the 386™ microprocessor and nine times as many as are in the 286 microprocessor—a nine-fold increase in five short years. As our products get more powerful and designers incorporate more system functions in them, quality and reliability become more important than ever. In many applications component failure just cannot be tolerated.

Why they almost never fail is part of the story we have to tell here. The first chapters give an overview of our quality philosophy, systems and standards. The second half of the book provides more specifics and technical details. This two-part structure, together with a detailed table of contents and comprehensive index, should help you find the information you need.

Intel is committed to be your *Vendor Of Choice*. Through a process of continuous improvement we expect to meet your ever-increasing demands for quality products and services.

Gordon E. Moore
Chairman of the Board

CUSTOMER SUPPORT

INTEL'S COMPLETE SUPPORT SOLUTION WORLDWIDE

Customer Support is Intel's complete support service that provides Intel customers with hardware support, software support, customer training, consulting services and network management services. For detailed information contact your local sales offices.

After a customer purchases any system hardware or software product, service and support become major factors in determining whether that product will continue to meet a customer's expectations. Such support requires an international support organization and a breadth of programs to meet a variety of customer needs. As you might expect, Intel's customer support is extensive. It can start with assistance during your development effort to network management. 100 Intel sales and service offices are located worldwide – in the U.S., Canada, Europe and the Far East. So wherever you're using Intel technology, our professional staff is within close reach.

HARDWARE SUPPORT SERVICES

Intel's hardware maintenance service, starting with complete on-site installation will boost your productivity from the start and keep you running at maximum efficiency. Support for system or board level products can be tailored to match your needs, from complete on-site repair and maintenance support to economical carry-in or mail-in factory service.

Intel can provide support service for not only Intel systems and emulators, but also support for equipment in your development lab or provide service on your product to your end-user/customer.

SOFTWARE SUPPORT SERVICES

Software products are supported by our Technical Information Service (TIPS) that has a special toll free number to provide you with direct, ready information on known, documented problems and deficiencies, as well as work-arounds, patches and other solutions.

Intel's software support consists of two levels of contracts. Standard support includes TIPS (Technical Information Phone Service), updates and subscription service (product-specific troubleshooting guides and; *COMMENTS Magazine*). Basic support consists of updates and the subscription service. Contracts are sold in environments which represent product groupings (e.g., iRMX® environment).

NETWORK SERVICE AND SUPPORT

Today's broad spectrum of powerful networking capabilities are only as good as the customer support provided by the vendor. Intel offers network services and support structured to meet a wide variety of end-user computing needs. From a ground up design of your network's physical and logical design to implementation, installation and network wide maintenance. From software products to turn-key system solutions; Intel offers the customer a complete networked solution. With over 10 years of network experience in both the commercial and Government arena; network products, services and support from Intel provide you the most optimized network offering in the industry.

CONSULTING SERVICES

Intel provides field system engineering consulting services for any phase of your development or application effort. You can use our system engineers in a variety of ways ranging from assistance in using a new product, developing an application, personalizing training and customizing an Intel product to providing technical and management consulting. Systems Engineers are well versed in technical areas such as microcommunications, real-time applications, embedded microcontrollers, and network services. You know your application needs; we know our products. Working together we can help you get a successful product to market in the least possible time.

CUSTOMER TRAINING

Intel offers a wide range of instructional programs covering various aspects of system design and implementation. In just three to ten days a limited number of individuals learn more in a single workshop than in weeks of self-study. For optimum convenience, workshops are scheduled regularly at Training Centers worldwide or we can take our workshops to you for on-site instruction. Covering a wide variety of topics, Intel's major course categories include: architecture and assembly language, programming and operating systems, BITBUS™ and LAN applications.

PREFACE

Intel began publishing a Components Quality and Reliability Handbook in 1985. The initial goal was to provide an overview of the technical considerations of integrated circuit design and manufacturing. Intel's philosophy and approach to quality and reliability management was discussed to a lesser extent.

The 1991 edition places more emphasis on the way Intel manages quality and reliability and addresses the basic technical considerations as they apply to today's technologies. A survey conducted as part of the planning for this edition showed that users requested a more accessible handbook. We have added an Index and a hierarchical Table of Contents to meet this need.

ORGANIZATION OF THE HANDBOOK

Intel's quality system closely follows a component product's life cycle, beginning with development and continuing through manufacturing (see the following figure).

The handbook is divided into four major sections. The first is an overview of "Intel's Quality Culture" (Chapter 1). Intel's quality management philosophy, tools and business systems are presented.

The second section contained in Chapter 2, "Customer Quality Support System," explains the many programs available to support our customers' quality needs.

The next section describes Intel's quality systems in terms of a product's life cycle. Chapter 3, "Design and Development Systems," discusses Intel's process, product and package certification procedures. Chapter 4, "Manufacturing Systems," describes the

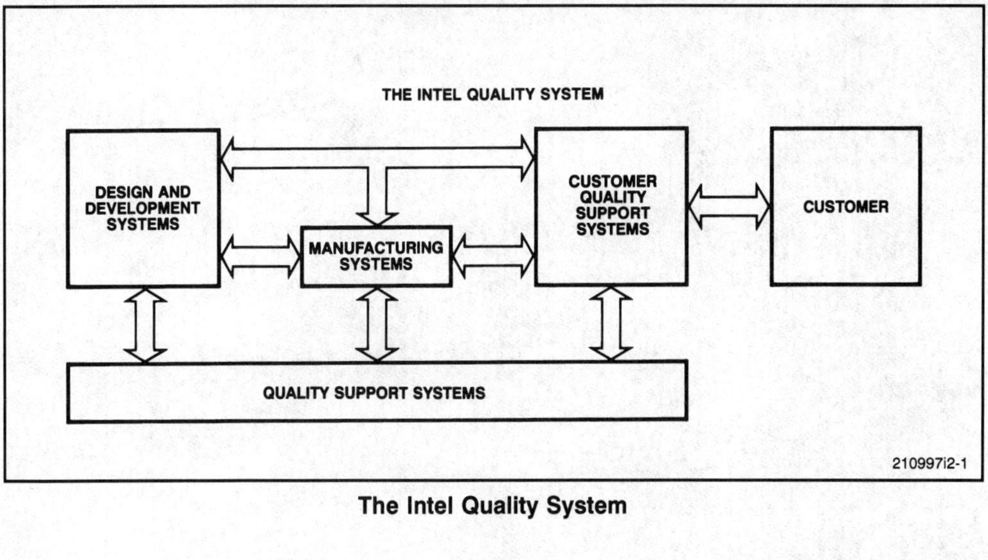

The Intel Quality System

manufacturing environment and the production management tools used to build high quality and reliable components. Chapter 5, "Quality Support Systems," provide an overview of internal procedures which reinforce continuous improvement.

The fourth section (Chapters 6 through 9) provides increased detail about specific systems and tools used by the Quality and Reliability organization. These chapters supplement the first three sections with data and explanations to use as a reference if more detail is desired. The major elements are Process Technology (6), Reliability Measurements (7), Process Reliability/Failure Mechanisms (8) and Failure Analysis/Analytical Techniques (9). Information in these chapters has been revised and updated for current technology.

Glossary

GL

Index

IN

Related Readings

REL

TABLE OF CONTENTS

CHAPTER 8 **Page**
PROCESS RELIABILITY/FAILURE MECHANISMS

CHAPTER 9
FAILURE ANALYSIS/ANALYTICAL TECHNIQUES

Figures

Figures

Figures

Figures

Figures

Tables

Tables

Intel's Quality Culture 1

CHAPTER 1 **Page**
INTEL'S QUALITY CULTURE

CHAPTER 1
INTEL'S QUALITY CULTURE

1

INTRODUCTION

Intel's Approach to Quality in Products and Services

At Intel, we know that customer satisfaction and continuous improvement are more than just important; they are the keys to success. That's why the concepts of customer satisfaction and continuous improvement are at the very root of our culture and our quality vision. Our quality framework focuses on building in quality, which leads to customer satisfaction and customer-defined quality levels. This framework (Figure 1-1) supports our corporate objective to be our customer's *Vendor Of Choice*.

Within this quality framework, Intel's culture promotes an environment where excellence is expected and dedication to quality results is a daily routine, along with teamwork, openness and hard work. The continuous improvement philosophy promotes ongoing improvements in our processes and systems with customers, suppliers and employees.

Intel's quality framework emphasizes developing and enhancing partnerships with our customers and suppliers. As an example, Intel was ready with the introduction of the first one-million-transistor microprocessor, the i860™ processor, to address our customers' increasingly demanding applications. Likewise, the popular X86 family of microprocessors and the 80960 family of embedded controllers provide high performance in applications requiring extremely fast response.

Another example of Intel's continuous improvement and customer orientation is our on-time delivery performance, measured as Intel Commit Date (ICD). In 1985, Intel considered our delivery on time if product was shipped 14 days ahead or seven days after the committed shipping date. In 1987, our customers indicated that a 21-day window was not acceptable and Intel tightened the window to seven days ahead and four days late. Late in 1987, Intel took the customer-oriented approach of measuring on-time deliveries against the specific customer-defined expectation. With this approach, the average delivery window again tightened, to seven days ahead and zero days late. By the end of 1989, the average window had narrowed, again, to five days ahead and zero days late. In the 1990s, the ICD delivery window average is heading toward three days ahead and zero days late. See Figure 1-2 for the ICD chart.

Intel's Total Quality Evolution

In the early days, businesses focused on developing new technologies and meeting quantity demands. Today, there is just as much emphasis on quality; customers insist on it. For example, one to five percent defect rates were standard in the semiconductor industry a decade ago. Today, defect rates are measured in defects per million (DPM).

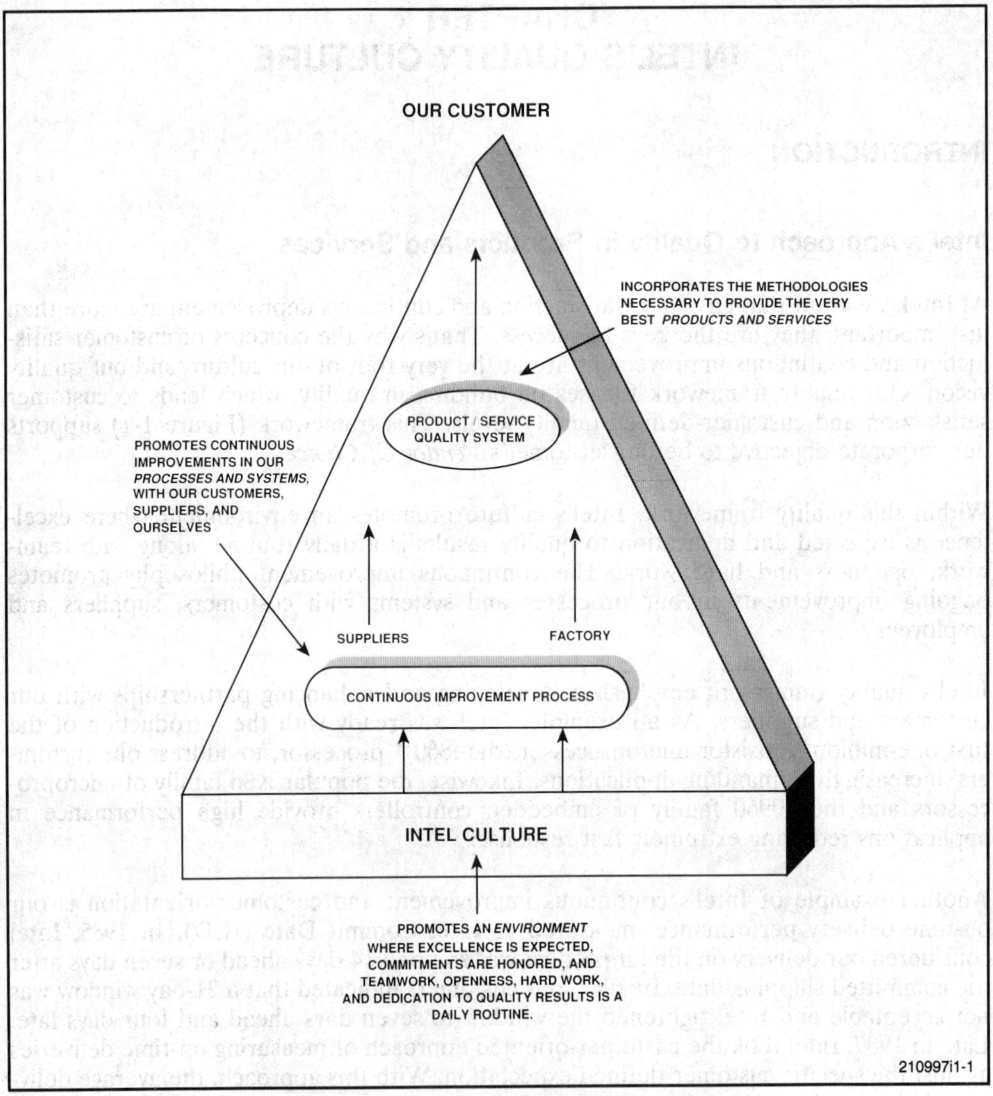

Figure 1-1. Intel Quality Framework

Thanks to a rigorous process of feedback, control and steady improvement in both process and product, Intel, in 1990, consistently offers a defect rate of less than 250 DPM (0.025%). That's a far cry from our 20,000 DPM (2%) level in the late 1970s and a sure sign of Intel's customer orientation and commitment to quality. The 1990s will demand zero defects. Figure 1-3 shows the quality evolution. Figure 1-4 shows component DPM levels.

Not surprisingly, Intel's total quality evolution has required continuous improvement and continuously refocusing and redeploying resources.

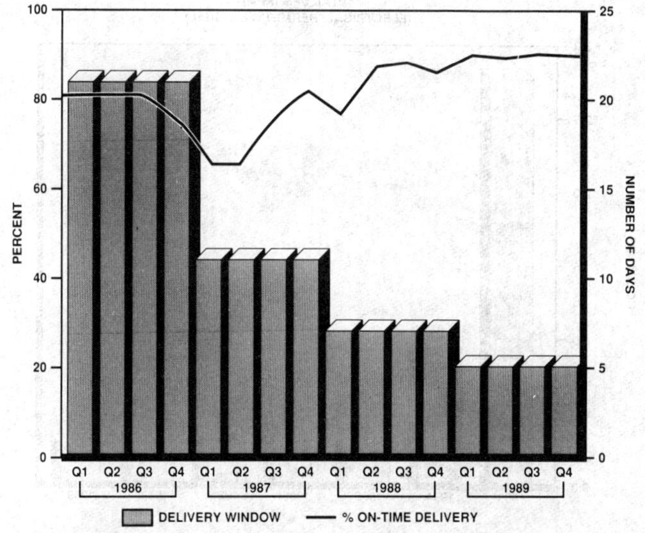

Figure 1-2. ICD Delivery

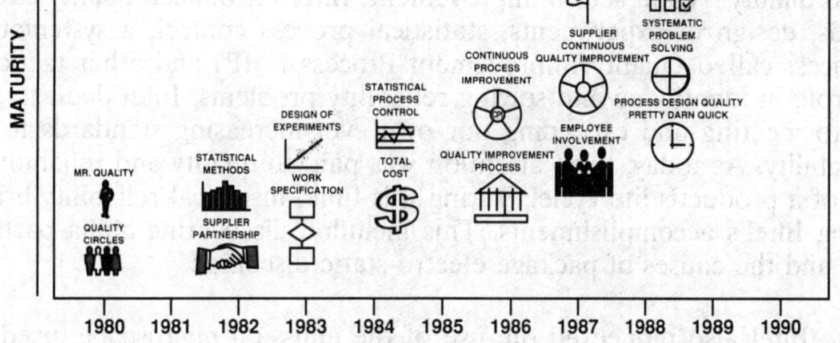

Figure 1-3. Intel's Total Quality Evolution

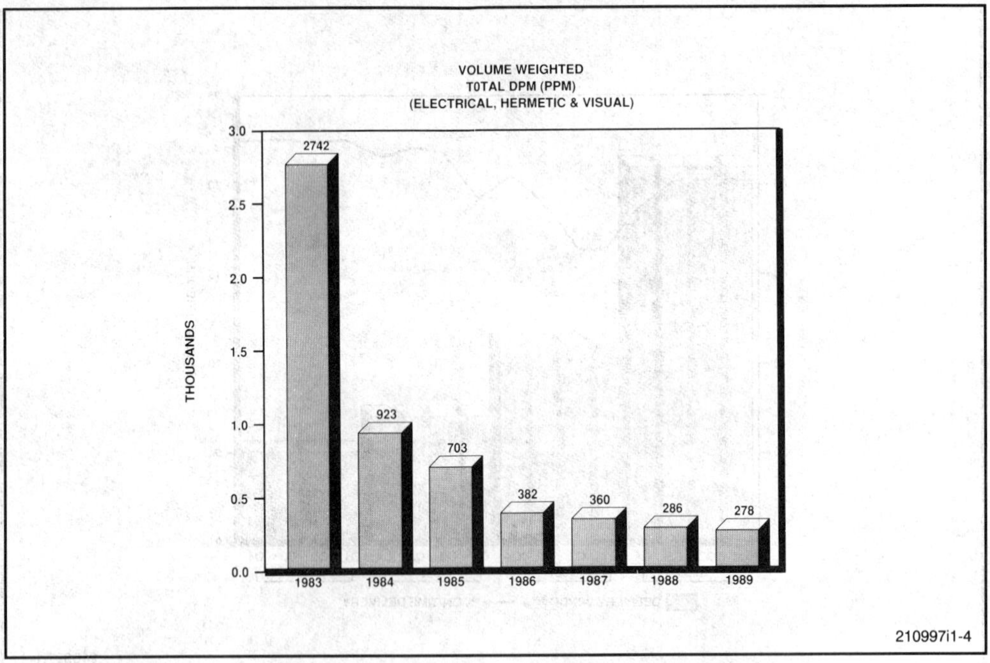

Figure 1-4. Component DPM (PPM) Levels

Consider that during the 1970s, Intel's sights were set on technology leadership. In fact, 16 of the 22 major breakthroughs in microelectronic technology during this time were Intel's. Among these was our 1971 introduction of the microprocessor, which revolutionized computing tasks. Intel's development of the first powerful microprocessors and advanced memories also led to the introduction of the personal computer and its dramatic impact on today's world. During this time, the emphasis was placed on manufacturing yields and product reliability. Along with improving yields, DPM levels declined and Intel failures in time (FIT) rates improved as well as the goals. (See Figure 1-5.)

With the 1980s, Intel's focus expanded to include emphasis on manufacturing leadership and process quality. Again set on improvement, Intel introduced quality circles, statistical methods, design of experiments, statistical process control, a systematic problem-solving process called Quality Improvement Process (QIP) and other tactics. Playing a dominant role in identifying and solving reliability problems, Intel dedicated significant resources to meeting and exceeding our own ever-increasing standards for integrated circuit reliability. As today, keen attention was paid to quality and reliability criteria in all phases of a product's life cycle. During this time, historical reliability breakthroughs were among Intel's accomplishments. This included discovering alpha particle-induced soft errors and the causes of package electro-static discharge.

In addition, Intel also pioneered the use of the emission microscope, used to discover the sources of latchup, understand electrostatic discharge and study various circuitry. Intel also led the way in dynamic fault imaging, used to trace error sources in integrated circuits.

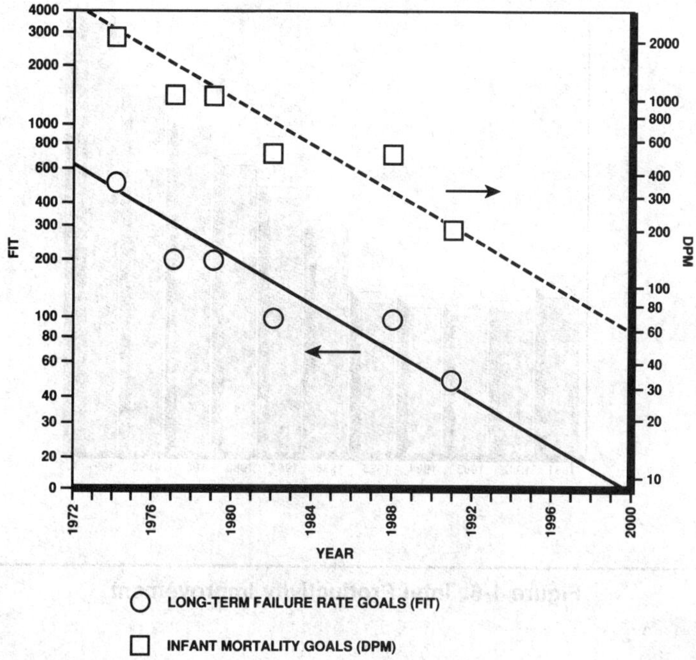

Figure 1-5. Trends in Reliability Goals

An ever-strong and innovative force in the electronics industry, Intel continues on its improvement path in the 1990s. Today, Intel is focused on total quality leadership, encompassing not only technological and manufacturing quality but people quality as well. Marking this new focus are healthy increases over the past years in productivity per employee and revenue per employee. (See Figures 1-6 and 1-7.) Indeed, our revenues per manufacturing employee doubled from 1984 to 1988. Thanks to such increases, Intel is able to improve its cost performance, ultimately benefiting our customers.

INTEL'S STRATEGY FOR TOTAL QUALITY LEADERSHIP

Definition of Total Quality

Intel defines total quality by three high-level attributes. The first attribute expands the view of quality to cover more than just outgoing products and services. Quality also applies to the process used to make products or provide services, as well as to the people involved in those processes.

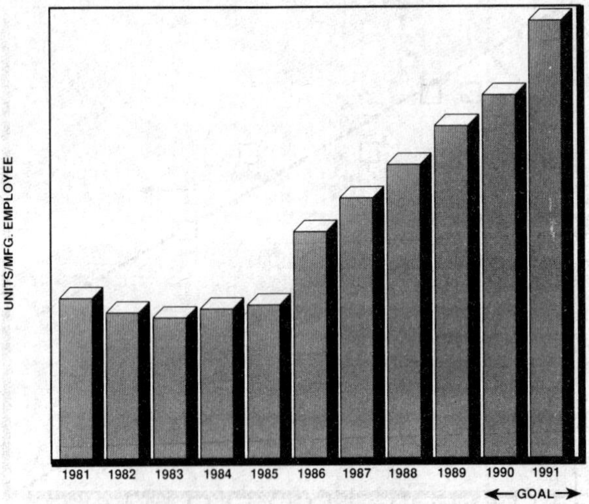

210997i1-6

Figure 1-6. Intel Productivity Improvement

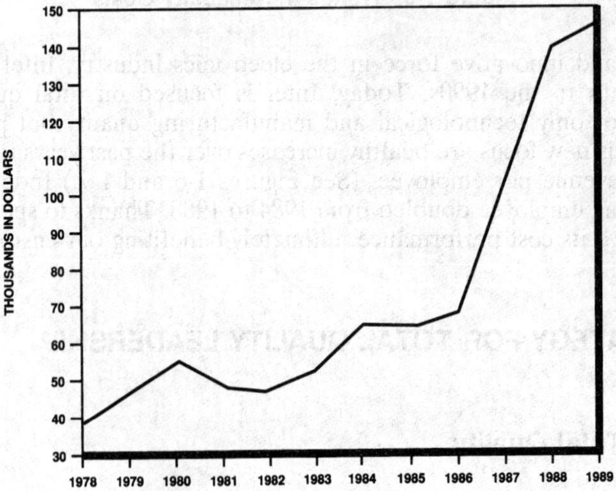

210997i1-7

Figure 1-7. Revenue Per Employee

With this in mind, Intel works to continuously control and improve our processes, the systems and methods used to produce products. Rather than focus on detecting and removing defects after the product is made, emphasis is placed on process quality, improving the production and process with the goal of preventing defects before they occur.

In addition to process improvement, Intel is actively engaged in people improvement. Employees at all levels are provided with education, training, the tools and the time to improve their jobs and the way they produce a product, whether that product is a highly complex microprocessor or a monthly report.

The second attribute of Intel's total quality commitment is a customer orientation. Employees at all levels are fine-tuning their skill at determining customers' needs and doing what's needed to meet and exceed those needs. To make this a reality, employees recognize that their co-workers are also their customers who depend upon them to provide quality work. In short, customer satisfaction drives every activity.

Finally, quality is a priority at the highest levels. Our executives embrace and act on the fundamental premise that total quality is Intel's number-one business objective.

Under this new mindset, aspects such as developing and introducing new products, exploring new technology and fulfilling production needs are not displaced. Rather, these objectives are more efficiently and consistently met when emphasis is placed on quality. The result is a reduced cost of doing business accompanied by an increase in satisfied customers.

Intel Cultural Changes Required for Total Quality

Intel's total quality environment fosters more effective management. Intel managers are instructed and encouraged to make quality their first priority.

Putting customer satisfaction as a top priority is another key management principle. In this area, Intel is proud of its product quality rating as number one, number two, or excellent by more than 90 percent of our major accounts worldwide. This selection as our customer's *quality Vendor Of Choice* is testimony to Intel's ongoing efforts to provide outstanding quality. (See Figure 1-8.)

Managers are also responsible for providing, optimizing long-term and short-term efforts, managing by facts, building trust and focusing on continuous process improvement. The results of this management philosophy are direct and measurable.

For example, a process quality focus has led to numerous achievements, including a 50 percent cut in average component design time – from more than 80 weeks in 1986 to 40 weeks in 1989. We have also dramatically reduced process introduction time. See Figure 1-9 for the average component design time.

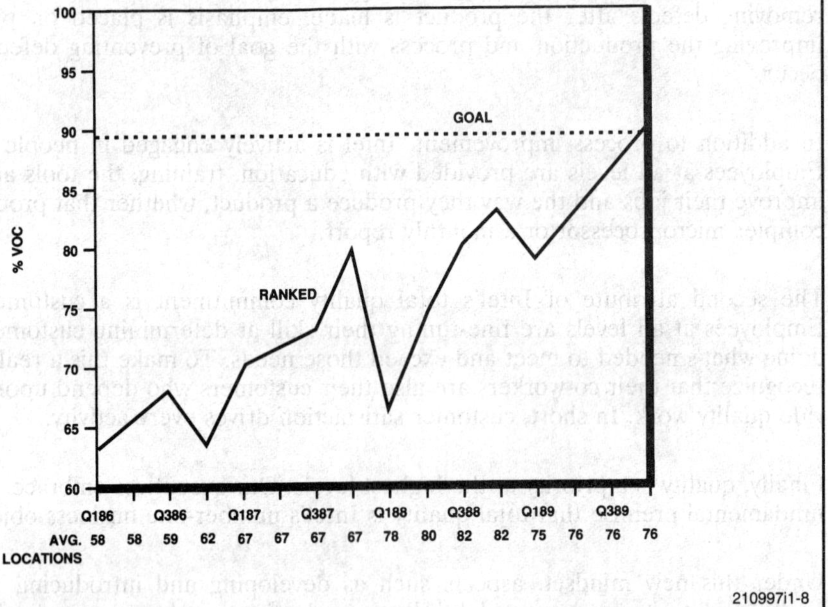

Figure 1-8. Vendor Of Choice Worldwide Quality and Reliability

Paramount to managing more effectively is a sincere respect for and investment in our people. With Intel's evolution toward a total quality environment has come a vital emphasis on providing training and education. In fact in 1989, we spent nearly 5 percent of our annual payroll for training. This is more than three times the national average.

Playing a key role in meeting Intel's training and educational needs is Intel University – our internal training structure that delivers training in such areas as interpersonal skills, customer support, information management and design methodologies. University attendees also learn about the development of individual training plans and Intel's commitment to continuous improvement and customer satisfaction.

Career Liink – which stands for Leverage Intel and Individual Needs and Knowledge – is another Intel program for investing in our people. Under this program, employees work with their managers to assess their skills, values and future.

Complementing Intel's investment in employees is our recognition of employee achievement. One such tool of recognition is the Intel Achievement Award. Once called the Individual Achievement Award, this coveted honor has been renamed to reflect not only the unique contribution made by teams, but the complex nature of our business. Solving today's problems often requires the insight, resources and creativity of more than one individual, leading to teams that are often cross-functional, cross-organizational and multilevel in composition. Figure 1-10 shows the achievement award graph.

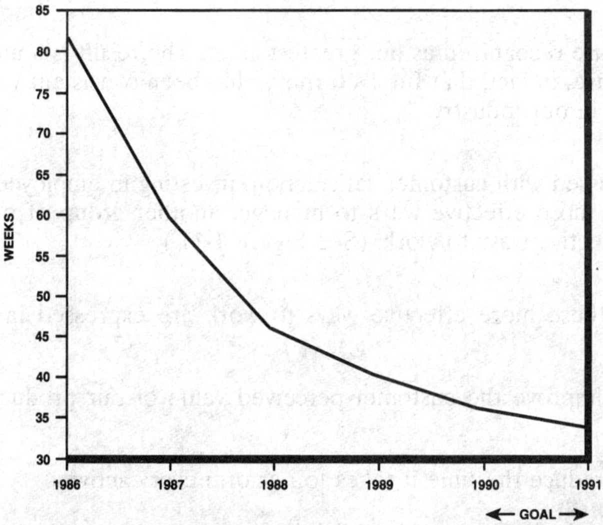

210997i1-9

Figure 1-9. Average Weeks from Definition to Sample Component Design Time

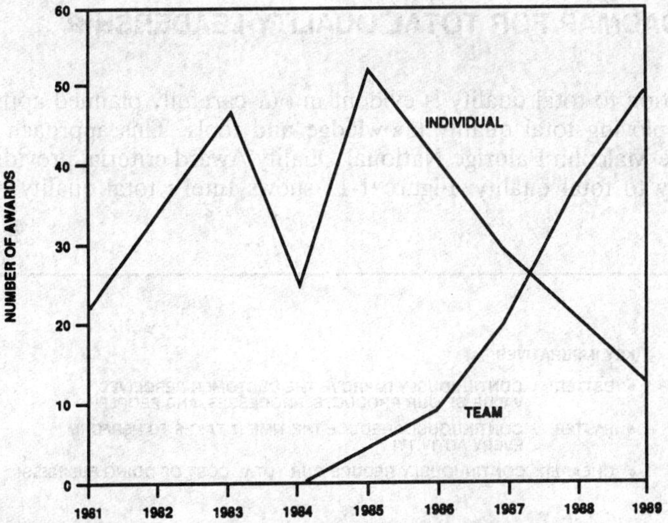

210997i1-10

Figure 1-10. Intel Achievement Awards

In addition to awards, Intel maintains a competitive and comprehensive benefits program and incentives for quality performance such as cash bonus, stock and profit-sharing programs.

Intel employees are recognized as our greatest asset. The result is a unique and positive culture – so positive, in fact, that Intel's turnover has been consistently lower than that of other companies in our industry.

While being obsessed with customer satisfaction, investing in employees and other principles encourage more effective ways to manage, another group of principles seeks to develop more effective ways to work. (See Figure 1-11.)

For employees, these more effective ways to work are expressed in three Intel total quality actions:

- Continuously improve the customer-perceived value of our products, processes and people.
- Continuously reduce the time it takes to perform every activity.
- Continuously reduce our total cost of doing business.

For both managers and non-managers, each of these principles or actions reflect the goal of continuous improvement, or what has been summed up as working to be "better, faster and cheaper." Ultimately, being better, faster and cheaper satisfies our customers.

INTEL'S ROADMAP FOR TOTAL QUALITY LEADERSHIP

Intel's dedication to total quality is evident in our carefully planned approach to developing and deploying total quality knowledge and tools. This approach is strategically mapped to the Malcolm Baldrige National Quality Award criteria, providing guidance in Intel's journey to total quality. Figure 1-12 shows Intel's total quality implementation roadmap.

KEY IMPERATIVES:

- BETTER: CONTINUOUSLY IMPROVE THE CUSTOMER-PERCEIVED VALUE OF OUR PRODUCTS, PROCESSES, AND PEOPLE!
- FASTER: CONTINUOUSLY REDUCE THE TIME IT TAKES TO PERFORM EVERY ACTIVITY!
- CHEAPER: CONTINUOUSLY REDUCE OUR TOTAL COST OF DOING BUSINESS!

210997i1-11

Figure 1-11. Key Imperatives

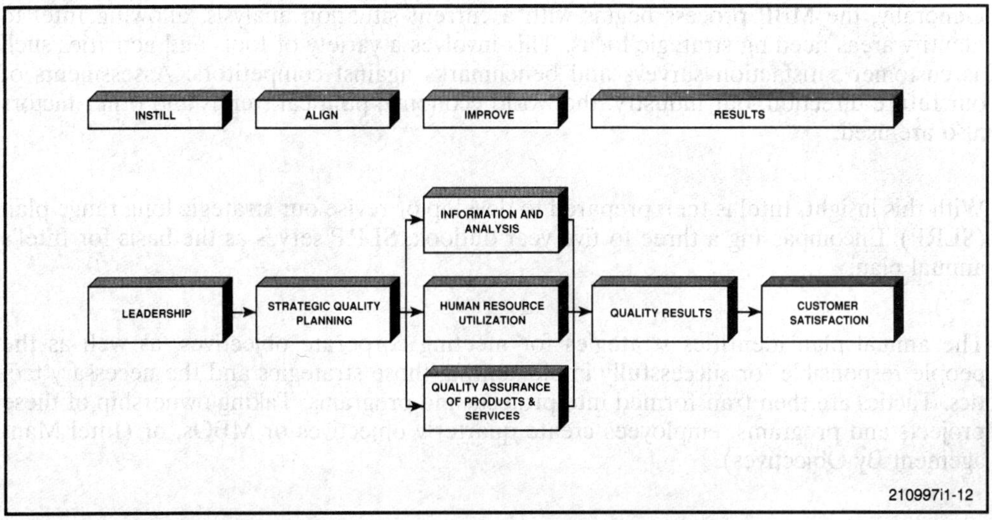

Figure 1-12. Total Quality Implementation Roadmap

Leadership

The first part of our approach – or our roadmap – is leadership. Basically, this calls for instilling within managers not only an understanding of what total quality is, but what behaviors and actions are needed to make total quality a reality. Top management has established an environment built on customer focus and continuous quality improvement. Managers then define appropriate values and systems conducive to a total quality environment.

To help our managers understand and implement our quality goals, we have a special quality leadership series, presented to individuals or small groups of executives and managers. It consists of courses like "What is Total Quality?" and "Quality Leadership: Personal Commitment Series." This training helps provide managers with the framework for creating a total quality environment.

Strategic Quality Planning

The second part of Intel's quality roadmap, strategic quality planning, requires integrating a strategic quality planning system into typical business planning activities. In other words, planning for quality improvement is a normal part of both short- and long-term planning efforts. Furthermore, quality priority is equal to or higher than other business planning objectives.

This is accomplished through Management by Planning (MBP), a planning process that aligns the resources necessary to achieve Intel's business improvement objectives down to the project level. Encompassing long-range, annual and individual planning processes, MBP has been taught to senior executives at Intel, who then deploy it throughout their organizations.

Generally, the MBP process begins with a current situation analysis, allowing Intel to identify areas needing strategic focus. This involves a variety of tools and activities such as customer satisfaction surveys and benchmarks against competitors. Assessments of our future direction, our industry, the world economy, political trends and other factors also are used.

With this insight, Intel is then prepared to develop or revise our strategic long range plan (SLRP). Encompassing a three to five year outlook, SLRP serves as the basis for Intel's annual plan.

The annual plan identifies strategies for meeting corporate objectives, as well as the people responsible for successfully implementing those strategies and the necessary tactics. Tactics are then transformed into projects and programs. Taking ownership of these projects and programs, employees create quarterly objectives or MBOs, or (Intel Management By Objectives).

Through this planning sequence – current situation analysis, strategic long-range planning, annual planning and employees' MBOs – Intel's MBP process ensures that individual employee planning impacts our corporate business objectives. This is possible because plans are nested vertically in the organization and resources are aligned cross-functionally to achieve our objectives by optimizing the interfaces between organizations.

What about funding and resources for those projects? Under Intel's MBP process, projects are funded according to zero-based-budgeting principles. Specifically, projects are prioritized and the available resources (in terms of dollars and people) are allocated only to the most important. This funding method, combined with specific planning processes, allows MBP to align the resources necessary to achieve Intel's business objectives down to the project level.

Information and Analysis

The third aspect of a quality roadmap is a comprehensive quality management data system. We collect volumes of quality data throughout our operation so we can track quality problems and fix them as quickly as possible.

We use a seven-step method to solve and document quality problems, as shown in Figure 1-13. A standardized format allows process improvement teams to benefit from one another's work.

Other tools in the information and analysis area include check sheets, pareto chart analysis, fishbone diagrams, histograms, trend charts and gantt charts. More advanced tools include design of experiment, basic statistics and graphs, process capabilities, critical path analysis, PERT charts, matrix diagrams, force field analysis and more.

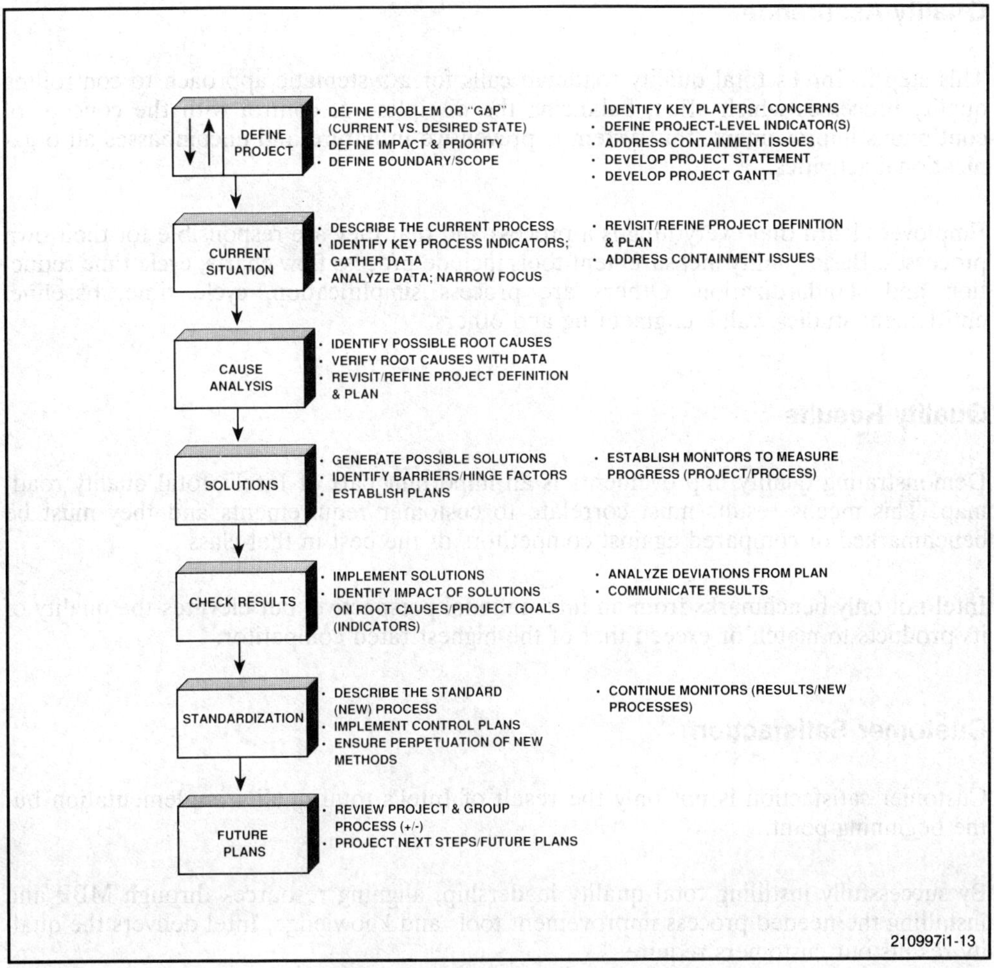

Figure 1-13. Seven Step Method

Human Resource Utilization

We made a deliberate, ongoing investment to upgrade both the skills and knowledge of our employees, managers and non-managers alike. Intel Achievement Awards, Intel University and other programs are examples.

To improve team effectiveness we offer, training in such subjects as meeting skills, the stages of team development, brainstorming and team leadership. At a more advanced level, employees can learn facilitation skills, effective meeting skills and contracting. Basic training is also provided in the customer focus area, emphasizing the importance of how to work with customers. Central to this training is the understanding that each person's work or output is used by a customer in the customer's quality process. Advanced customer focus training includes exploring customer surveys and Quality Function Deployment (QFD).

Quality Assurance

This step in Intel's total quality roadmap calls for a systematic approach to controlling quality processes which affect balancing the discipline of control with the concept of continuous improvement, this system is preventive in nature and encompasses all organizational activities.

Employees learn that everything is a process and that they are responsible for their own processes. Basic quality measurement tools include process flow charts, cycle time reduction and standardization. Others are process simplification, cycle time, baseline/entitlement studies, value engineering and others.

Quality Results

Demonstrating quality improvements is an important part of Intel's total quality roadmap. This means results must correlate to customer requirements and they must be benchmarked or compared against competitors or the best in that class.

Intel not only benchmarks from an international perspective, but elevates the quality of its products to match or exceed that of the highest rated competitor.

Customer Satisfaction

Customer satisfaction is not only the result of Intel's total quality implementation but the beginning point.

By successfully instilling total quality leadership, aligning resources through MBP and installing the needed process improvement tools and knowledge, Intel delivers the quality results our customers require.

Also key to customer satisfaction is regular customer feedback. We listen to our customers constantly and feed this information back into our quality systems to continue meeting and exceeding their requirements. (See Figure 1-14.)

INTEL'S QUALITY ORGANIZATION

Introduction

The quality assurance function is implemented at two levels in Intel: at the corporate, or cultural, level and at the product level. Intel's Quality Technology Department takes care of the first, Intel's Components Quality and Reliability organization focuses on the second.

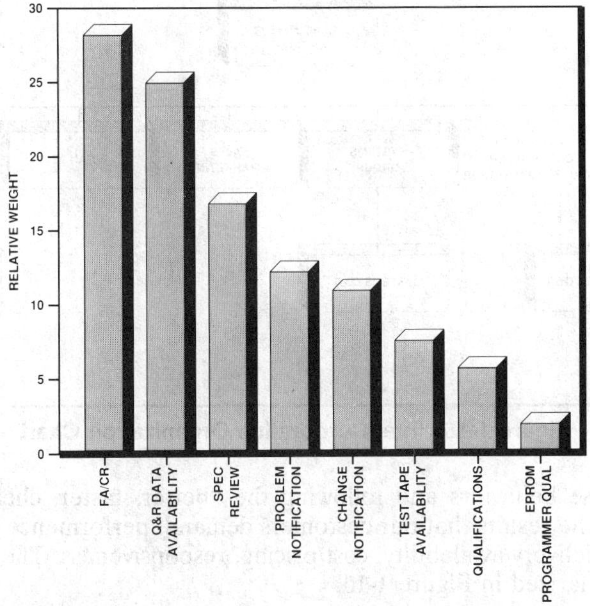

210997i1-14

Figure 1-14. Service and Support Systems Impacting Quality VOC Plan 1990 Worldwide

Intel's Corporate Quality Structure

Reporting directly to the executive office, Intel's Quality Technology Department is chartered with helping Intel management create a total quality environment. (See Figure 1-15.) This environment provides the means to improve our business performance as reflected in our mission and values: customer orientation, quality risk taking, results, discipline and a great place to work.

In order to achieve this total quality environment, employees are encouraged to adopt and practice the following seven total quality behaviors:

- Make quality your first priority
- Become obsessed with customer satisfaction
- Optimize long-term and short-term efforts
- Be process focused
- Speak the facts
- Build trust
- Respect and invest in people

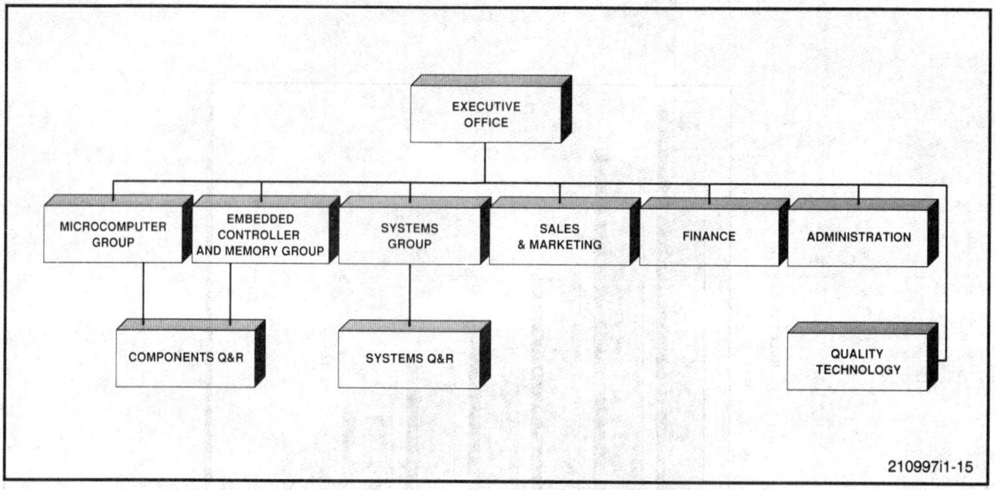

Figure 1-15. Intel Corporation Organization Chart

By exhibiting these behaviors and following the "better, faster, cheaper" philosophy, Intel can achieve the results that our customers demand: performance solutions, product quality, support, delivery/availability, cost/pricing, responsiveness. The Intel Total Quality system is summarized in Figure 1-16.

The Quality Technology Department works hand in hand with Intel's operational world to develop and deploy a corporate-wide total quality system. A senior management-level steering committee provides strategic direction and directs the overall efforts of two groups: the statistical council, which provides strategic direction for the application of statistics within Intel and the extended staff.

The extended staff consists of senior-level quality improvement professionals within Intel. Matrixed to the Quality Technology Department and the operational departments they represent, these professionals have a dual reporting structure. Providing a vital link to Intel's day-to-day business, they direct the development and deployment of total quality systems and methods.

In addition to the extended staff and statistical council, Intel employs an international network of quality improvement professionals and practicing statisticians to facilitate the implementation of quality improvement and statistical processes. This network provides ongoing feedback to the extended staff and statistical council.

The Quality Technology Department works to standardize quality improvement processes throughout the corporation, jointly develop total quality-related training courses and provide senior management coaching. The Quality Technology Department also promotes corporate awareness of total quality through internal magazines, videos, special events and other media.

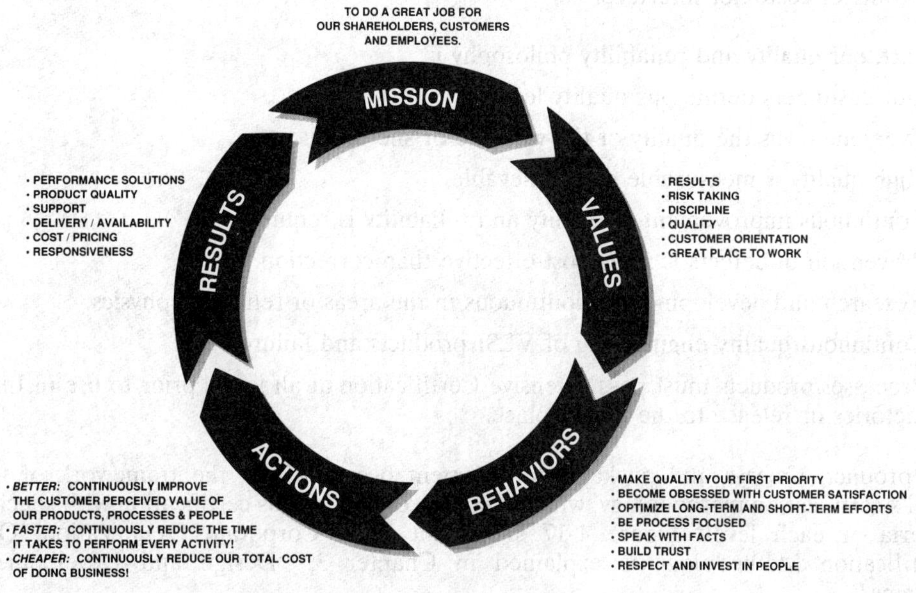

Figure 1-16. Intel's Total Quality System

Intel's Components Quality

Intel's Component Quality and Reliability organization is a vital part of our total quality environment. Its mission is to continuously improve the satisfaction of both internal and external customers with Intel products and services. This mission calls for close partnerships with Intel's development groups, factories, business units and sales/marketing groups.

Intel's Quality and Reliability group is dedicated to making Intel the *Vendor Of Choice* for quality, the Quality and Reliability group as a partner of choice with internal customers and Intel a workplace of choice for employees.

Integrating quality into day-to-day operations and driving quality ownership back to the source is the strategic quality objective of Components Quality and Reliability. The organization's core values are:

1. Consistency in policies and procedures.

2. Focus on reliability fundamentals.

3. Providing a progressive analytical capability.

4. Unity of customer interface.

In part, our quality and reliability philosophy is:

- Our customers define our quality levels.
- Everyone owns the quality of the work he or she produces.
- High quality is measurable and achievable.
- Continuous improvement of quality and reliability is required.
- Prevention of defects is more cost-effective than correction.
- Research and development is continuous in the areas of reliability physics.
- Continuous quality engineering of VLSI products and failure.
- Processes/products must pass extensive Certification at all levels prior to use in Intel factories or release to the marketplace.

All product, process and package development occurs within the framework of the Intel's certification methodology, which emphasizes continuous certification with specific criteria at each level. Figure 1-17 shows the Intel Corporate Organization. Our Certification Methodology is explained in Chapter 3, "Design and Development Systems."

The Quality and Reliability organization is functionally aligned with our individual business focus groups: product development, manufacturing and sales and marketing. See Figure 1-18 for Intel's Quality and Reliability Organization.

Serving as the primary customer interface, Intel's Sales and Marketing arms include a sales force, local sales office support and factory support. The parallel Quality and Reliability organization, staffed by customer quality engineers, provides a communication channel for quality and reliability issues between customers and Intel factories. The result is a readily accessible point of contact for customers, who otherwise would have to

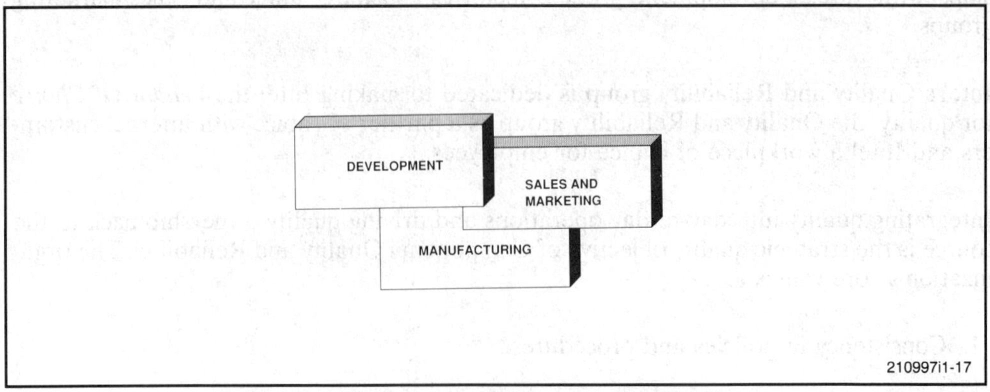

Figure 1-17. The Intel Corporate Organization

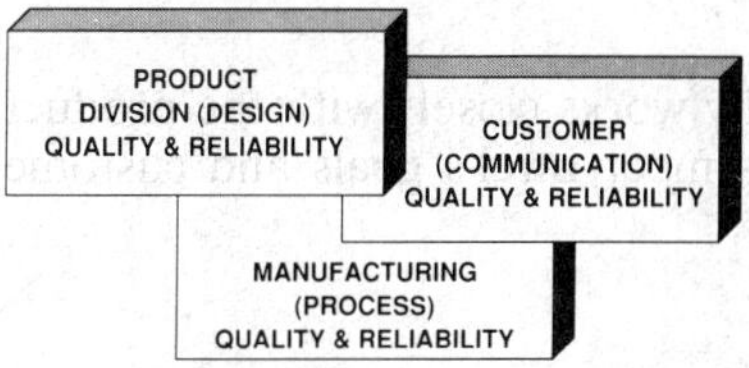

Figure 1-18. The Intel Q&R Organization

deal with a complex matrix organization. The Customer Quality and Reliability organization also maintains a hotline for customers with questions about Intel quality systems. For more information on this function, see Chapter 2.

Intel's manufacturing organization includes wafer fabrication, assembly, high-volume testing and all technology development of both processes and packages. Geographically dispersed, this organization has wafer fabrication facilities at six U.S. sites and in Israel, assembly locations and manufacturing test facilities in the U.S., Malaysia and the Philippines and technology development at two U.S. sites. Additionally, design centers are located in five U.S. sites, Japan and Israel.

Not surprisingly, the manufacturing Quality and Reliability organization is also dispersed. At each manufacturing site, a Quality and Reliability staff monitors quality, provides feedback to manufacturing and technology development and participates in problem-solving. These local Quality and Reliability organizations report jointly to local site management and the Quality and Reliability management. This matrixed relationship provides the flexibility to meet local needs while maintaining policy consistency through central organization. The activities of local quality and reliability organizations are discussed in more detail in Chapter 2, "Customer Quality Support System," Chapter 3, "Design and Development Systems" and Chapter 4, "Manufacturing Systems."

The third major functional group at Intel, product development, consists of various product divisions. These groups are responsible for product development, product marketing and start-up manufacturing for new products. Intel's component product divisions are all headquartered in the U.S., as indicated below:

Microcomputer Products	Santa Clara, California
Memory Products	Folsom, California
Microcontroller Products	Chandler, Arizona

Product development is supported by the third arm of the Q&R organization, Division Q&R. Again, the Division Q&R organization is geographically dispersed to correspond to the divisions it supports and also reports into both local site management and central Q&R management.

Division Quality and Reliability works closely with the product design and development teams to assure that products meet Intel's goals and customers' quality and reliability expectations.

CONCLUSION

Intel's evolution towards total quality is guided by customer satisfaction and continuous improvement – deeply rooted in Intel culture. Highlighting this evolution is an ongoing series of improvements in Intel products, processes and people.

Using the Malcolm Baldrige National Quality Award has a blueprint, we are achieving quality results and satisfied customers.

Customer Quality Support System

2

2

CHAPTER 2 **Page**
CUSTOMER QUALITY SUPPORT SYSTEM

CHAPTER 2
CUSTOMER QUALITY SUPPORT SYSTEM

2

INTRODUCTION

Intel's efforts towards total quality leadership in products and service are driven by a central, uncompromising objective: to make Intel and our customers successful. The ultimate goal of our diverse quality efforts is to increase our customers' competitiveness and reduce their cost of doing business with us. Intel strives to respect the values and views of its customers, clearly understand and respond to their needs, and communicate mutual intentions and expectations. Figure 2-1 shows how the Customer Quality Support Systems relate to Intel's overall quality system. To serve our customers' increasing market demands, Intel uses a multi-channeled communication network as illustrated in Figure 2-2.

Intel has implemented this network in all our geographic locations – North America, Japan, Asia Pacific, Europe and the intercontinental market to provide the same level of service to all customers. This is crucial for multinational customers who compete globally and insist on one level of service. Intel also customizes its service to meet local needs. Intel's Field Sales Engineers (FSEs) and Field Application Engineers (FAEs) are in constant contact with our customers, soliciting feedback on service perception and product requirements.

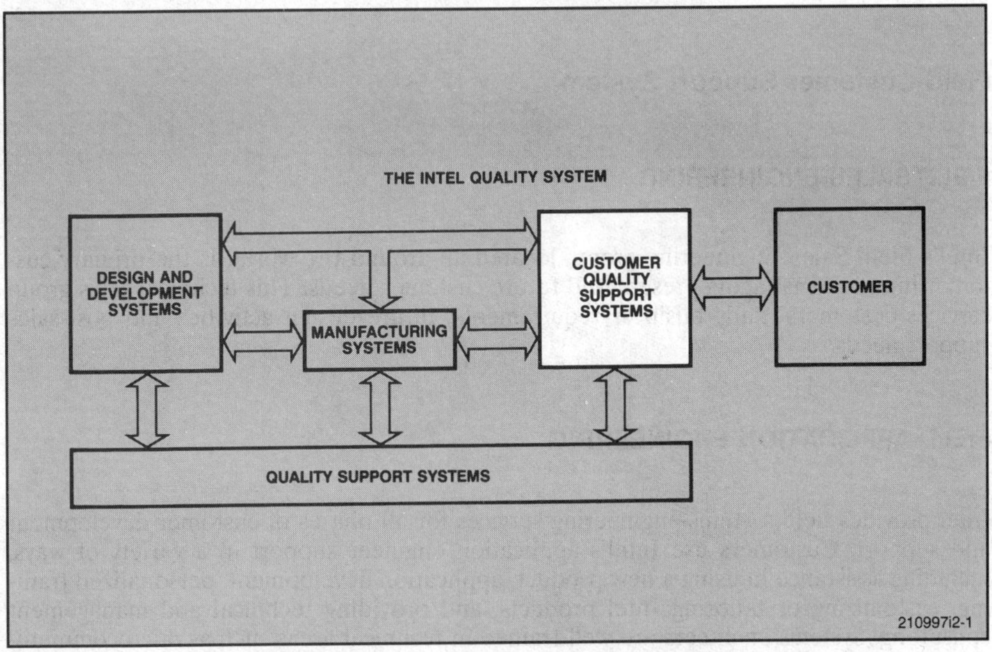

Figure 2-1. Intel Quality System Diagram

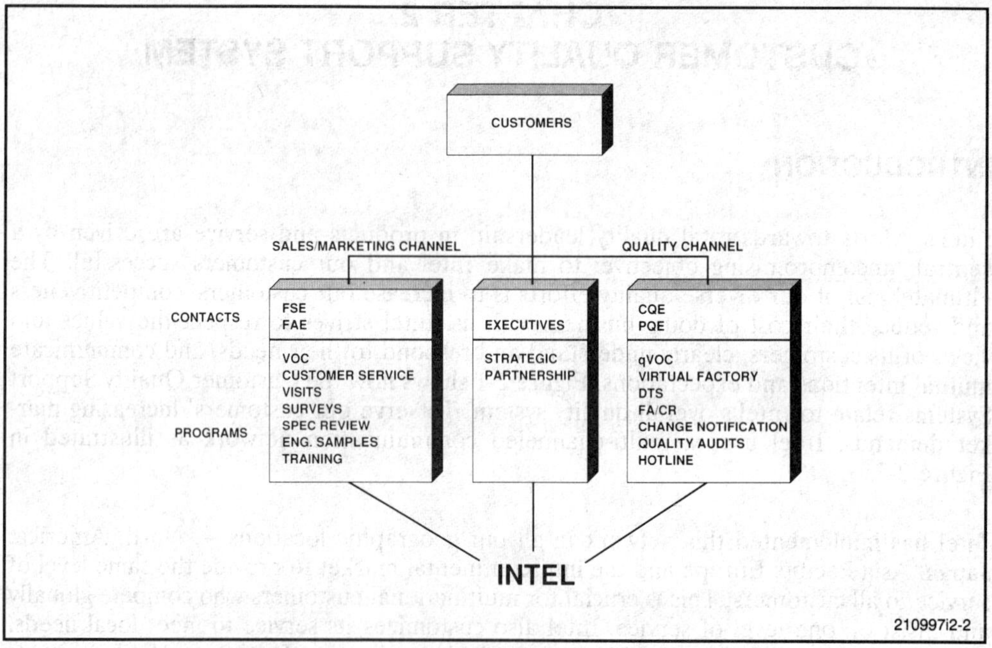

Figure 2-2. Customer Communication Network

SALES/MARKETING CHANNEL

Field Customer Support System

FIELD SALES ENGINEERING

Intel's Field Sales Engineering group, located all around the world, is the primary customer interface managing present and future customer needs. This technical sales group services customers' daily business requirements, future design activities and post-sales support needs.

FIELD APPLICATION ENGINEERING

Intel provides field systems engineering services for all phases of customer development and support. Customers use Intel's application engineer support in a variety of ways, including assistance in using a new product, application development, personalized training, customizing or tailoring Intel products, and providing technical and management consulting. Systems engineers are well trained in technical areas such as microcommunications, real-time applications, embedded microcontrollers and network services.

Support Programs

ENGINEERING SAMPLES

Engineering samples of new devices and design changes are available to customers for evaluation. These samples provide customers with tools for end product design and development activities. Customer feedback provides Intel with detailed information for further component evaluation and enhancements. In turn, our field sales engineers use the wealth of customer knowledge to improve existing products and enhance future designs.

SPECIFICATION REVIEW ADMINISTRATION

Since Intel customers may require products and/or services that differ from Intel's standard products or services, we have a Specification Review Administration (SRA). Customers present special requirements to us and the SRA reviews them to ensure that they are met. When a specification is received, the SRA determines which require special processing and, once approved, provides the proper instruction to the appropriate Intel organizations.

An important element of Intel's documentation system is the Special Specification (S-Spec). S-Specs direct Intel manufacturing sites to modify standard products to meet special customer requests. S-Specs might pertain to testing, marking or packing.

INTEL DISTRIBUTORS

Also covering the globe is the Intel distributor network, another valuable resource for customers. Intel distributors, thoroughly trained in the application of Intel products, provide a full range of sales, application development and customer services. They maintain product literature, time and place inventory, value-added services such as programming, product seminars and system integration, and customer support.

PRODUCT LITERATURE

A toll-free literature number provides 48-hour turnaround for documentation and literature on Intel products, including data sheets, application notes, customer training information and other documents. To place an order or join Intel's literature update service, simply follow the instructions on the inside front cover of this handbook, or contact your local sales office.

CUSTOMER TRAINING

Intel offers a broad spectrum of lab-intensive, in-depth workshops covering various aspects of system design and product implementation. Workshops are scheduled regularly at Intel Training Centers around the world and at customer sites. Intel's major course categories include microprocessors and microcontrollers, operating systems and programming, local area networking, and office automation. A complete description of the training courses offered is available through Intel Literature.

VENDOR OF CHOICE PROGRAM (VOC)

Intel established the *Vendor Of Choice* program in the mid-1980s to improve our response to our customers' needs in the areas of delivery, product quality, technical support, business relationships and cost-competitiveness. Intel's goal is to be ranked the number-one or number-two supplier or rated as excellent for the products and services we provide. This rating is done by customers using their own rating systems, not ours. Intel then reviews these ratings to focus on improvement.

Another method of obtaining information about customer needs is Intel Customer Forums. These are face-to-face interviews with customers held approximately every two years and conducted by Intel's field and factory interview team. The interview questionnaire covers 26 different business topics and includes questions to determine Intel's relative quality performance. Customers are asked to respond to topics ranging from pricing process/performance, product availability, product quality/reliability, delivery criteria/performance, shipping services and sales service. The results are entered into Intel's Strategic Long Range Plan process to generate improvements to our products and services.

QUALITY CHANNEL

Customer Quality Support System

CUSTOMER QUALITY AND RELIABILITY GROUP

To maintain customer service excellence throughout a varied customer base and product line, Intel has a Customer Quality and Reliability Engineering Group (CQ&R). This group gives customers easy access to Intel on product quality matters. They are responsible for understanding customers' quality and reliability requirements and expectations, resolving customer quality issues, disseminating this information to appropriate Intel organizations, recommending standard and uniform quality and reliability goals based on customer expectations, and defining and driving Intel's quality systems to achieve the required quality. The Customer Quality and Reliability Group also provides Intel Quality System presentations, audits all our factories for conformance to Intel requirements, assists with customer audit evaluations, performs failure analysis and device correlation, analyzes returned materials, drives quality program implementation, and recommends quality and reliability standards for the entire product line. In this way, Intel makes the customer an important link in the manufacturing process.

Customer Quality Engineers

Customer Quality Engineers (CQEs) reside in the quality support centers and are the Intel interface on all quality and reliability issues. Customer Quality and Reliability Engineers transfer Intel quality and reliability information generated by Intel's design, development, manufacturing and support systems to the customer and, conversely, receive and disseminate customer information to Intel.

The Customer Quality Engineer periodically holds formal reviews with the customer, in which the customer provides his assessment of the quality and reliability of Intel's components and services. The Customer Quality Engineer develops programs to enhance or improve the product quality and services to meet the customer's needs. Customer Quality Engineers manage quality systems information, quality program management, device qualification information, quality and reliability monitor data, customer audits, and other customer support issues.

Product Quality Engineers

Also residing in the support centers are Product Quality Engineers (PQE), responsible for product failure analysis, device correlation, resolving test correlation issues, providing engineering analysis expertise and resolving other quality issues of a technical nature. These product-specific technical engineers ensure technical product customer support through the FA/CR (Failure Analysis/Correlation Request) system.

Support Programs

"VIRTUAL FACTORY"—TOTAL PRODUCT QUALITY SUPPORT

CQ&R uses the "virtual factory" model to provide total product quality support to our worldwide customers. This model says that customers throughout the world should be serviced as if they are dealing directly with local factory personnel. Figure 2-3 illustrates this.

Intel has six major quality support centers worldwide, in Europe, Japan, Far East and three in North America. The "virtual factory" charter is to provide total factory-like response to any customer worldwide on quality-related problems and processes with the objective of making and maintaining Intel as the *Vendor Of Choice* for quality. Intel has staffed and equipped all its quality support centers with the latest testing and analytical equipment – each has over $10 million in equipment alone. With customer requirements changing rapidly and requiring faster response time, our next major step is to have regional support centers nearer our customers' factories. This will allow even faster response to meet just-in-time manufacturing quality-related needs. Figure 2-4 illustrates Total Quality Support.

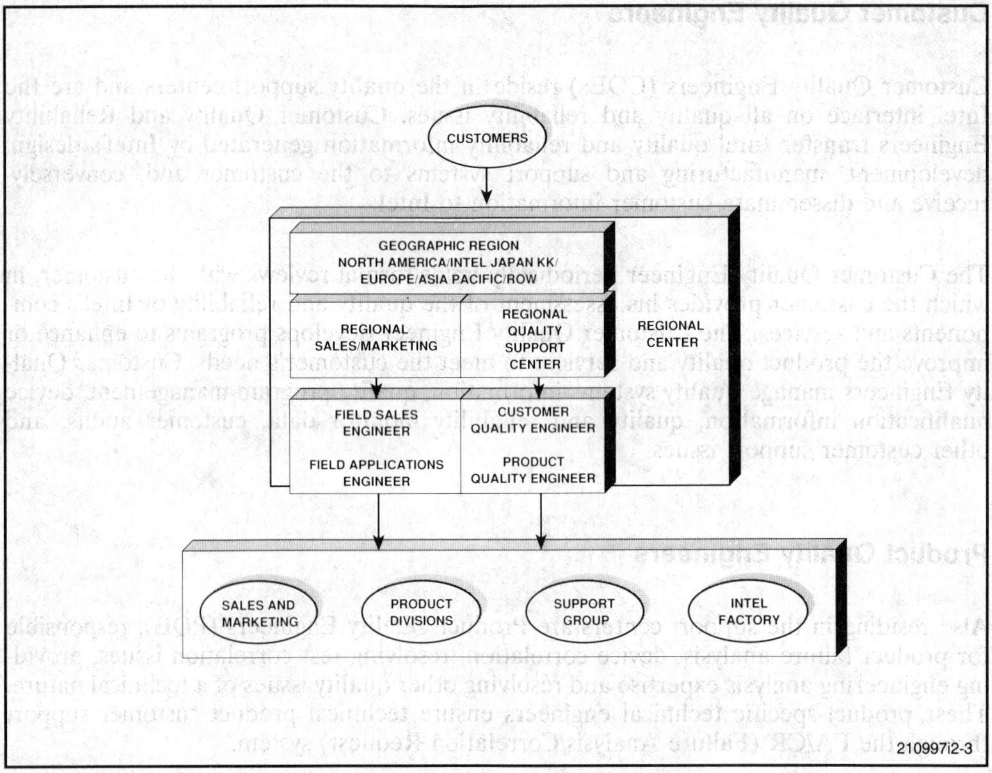

Figure 2-3. Intel's Geographic Support Model

FAILURE ANALYSIS/CORRELATION REQUEST (FA/CR) SYSTEM

Intel's Failure Analysis/Correlation Request (FA/CR) system handles technical issues or questions that arise from the use of Intel's components. The FA/CR system addresses two areas:

1. Failure analysis of devices that fail to meet (or are perceived as failing to meet) agreed-upon customer expectations for quality or reliability.

2. Correlations for customers who experience incoming inspection failures, device qualification or applications problems.

The majority of questions that arise involve differences between the customer's and Intel's methods used for device qualification and manufacture. When these differences are determined, the results are reviewed and correlated with the customer and Intel and may result in changes to Intel qualification, process or tests.

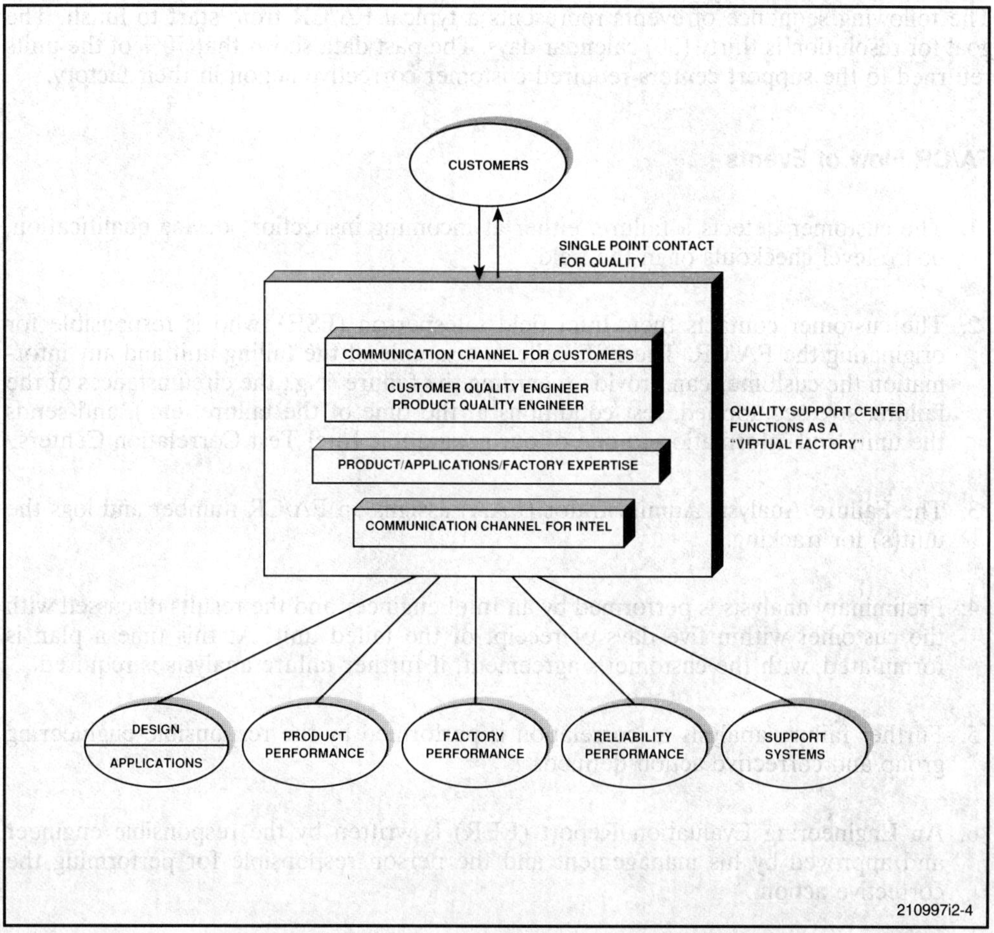

Figure 2-4. Total Quality Support "Virtual Factory"

The other major issue addressed by FA/CRs is devices that appear not to meet quality and reliability expectations. In the case of large-scale random logic devices, Intel defines a complete reliability test as a sequence that allows devices to operate in the customer's system without failing in that application.

The tools at the disposal of the PQE resolving such FA/CRs include, but are not limited to, stuck at 1/0 fault grading, knowledge of the customer's application, adding features to the design for testability, characterizing the device to determine marginalities, and complex failure analysis equipment. The final test programs usually combine all the above tools and techniques, along with the experience and judgment of the design and test engineers. The FA/CR system encourages the customer to return a product sample with a complete description of the problem.

The following sequence of events represents a typical FA/CR from start to finish. The goal for resolution is thirty (30) calendar days. The past data shows that 70% of the units returned to the support centers required customer corrective action in their factory.

FA/CR Flow of Events

1. The customer detects a failure, either at incoming inspection, device qualification, board-level checkouts or in the field.

2. The customer contacts their Intel field salesperson (FSE), who is responsible for originating the FA/CR. The FSE collects a sample of the failing unit and any information the customer can provide regarding the failure (e.g., the circumstances of the failure, stresses applied, test conditions at the time of the failure, etc.), and sends the units and information to one of our geographic Intel Test Correlation Centers.

3. The Failure Analysis Administrator (FAA) assigns an FA/CR number and logs the unit(s) for tracking.

4. Preliminary analysis is performed by an Intel engineer and the results discussed with the customer within five days of receipt of the failed unit. At this time a plan is formulated, with the customer's agreement, if further failure analysis is required.

5. Further failure analysis or correlation is performed by the responsible engineering group and corrective action defined.

6. An Engineering Evaluation Report (EER) is written by the responsible engineer and approved by his management and the person responsible for performing the corrective action.

7. The report is discussed with the customer and the customer's agreement sought. If the customer disagrees, the FA/CR remains open until further analysis is performed.

8. Once the customer is in agreement with the analysis and corrective action (if required), the FA/CR is closed and the corrective action tracked against the commitment made to the customer.

9. The customer receives a written report documenting the failure, the analysis, and any corrective action.

Since it is vital that the customer work with Intel engineers in arriving at a solution to the problem, the customer is encouraged to furnish as much information as possible regarding the failure and circumstances surrounding the observed failure. Intel Test Correlation Centers depend on engineers in the divisions and off-shore test and assembly sites to help analyze and define corrective actions and on the manufacturing sites to implement the corrective actions.

QUALITY QUESTION LINE

The Customer Quality and Reliability Engineers manage a Quality Question Line at the corporate headquarters in Santa Clara, California, to provide quick answers to quality questions. A factory-based quality engineer is available to answer questions about Intel's complete quality system covered within this handbook. The Quality Question Line (see Figure 2-5) is managed from 8:00 A.M. to 5:00 P.M. Pacific Standard Time by quality engineers trained to answer questions regarding Intel's Quality Systems.

QUALITY VENDOR OF CHOICE

It is Intel's goal to be chosen as our customers' *Vendor Of Choice* in quality, reliability, engineering, delivery and customer services. To this end, Intel tracks customer ranking data, customer-perceived defects per million, failure analysis and correlation indicators, delivery, and engineering performance indicators. Intel actively reviews these indicators on an ongoing basis and defines action plans to enhance or improve performance. Intel wants to be rated number one or excellent by all its customers. As shown in Chapter 1, Figure 1-8, 90 percent of Intel's customers consider our quality and reliability number one, two or excellent. Intel also actively participates in a variety of customer quality improvement programs and vendor rankings and ratings.

QUALITY AUDIT DEPARTMENT

The Customer Quality and Reliability Group maintains a Quality Audit Department that acts on behalf of customers to satisfy their audit requirements. In addition to the audit function, this group also completes quality surveys requested by customers. Due to Intel's large customer base, a structured guideline exists for scheduling and planning customer audits. Figure 2-6 details this procedure.

The purpose of the audit scheduling procedure is to plan and organize customer audits and deal effectively with the audit workload conflict inside Intel. The audit scheduling process works best in an eight-week timeframe, from initial notice to actual audit date. Because of Intel's self-audit system, our plants are continuously involved in self audits and customer audits. The results are fed back into Intel's continuous improvement response process.

QUALITY QUESTION LINE

(800) 852-2040

210997i2-5

Figure 2-5. Quality Question Line

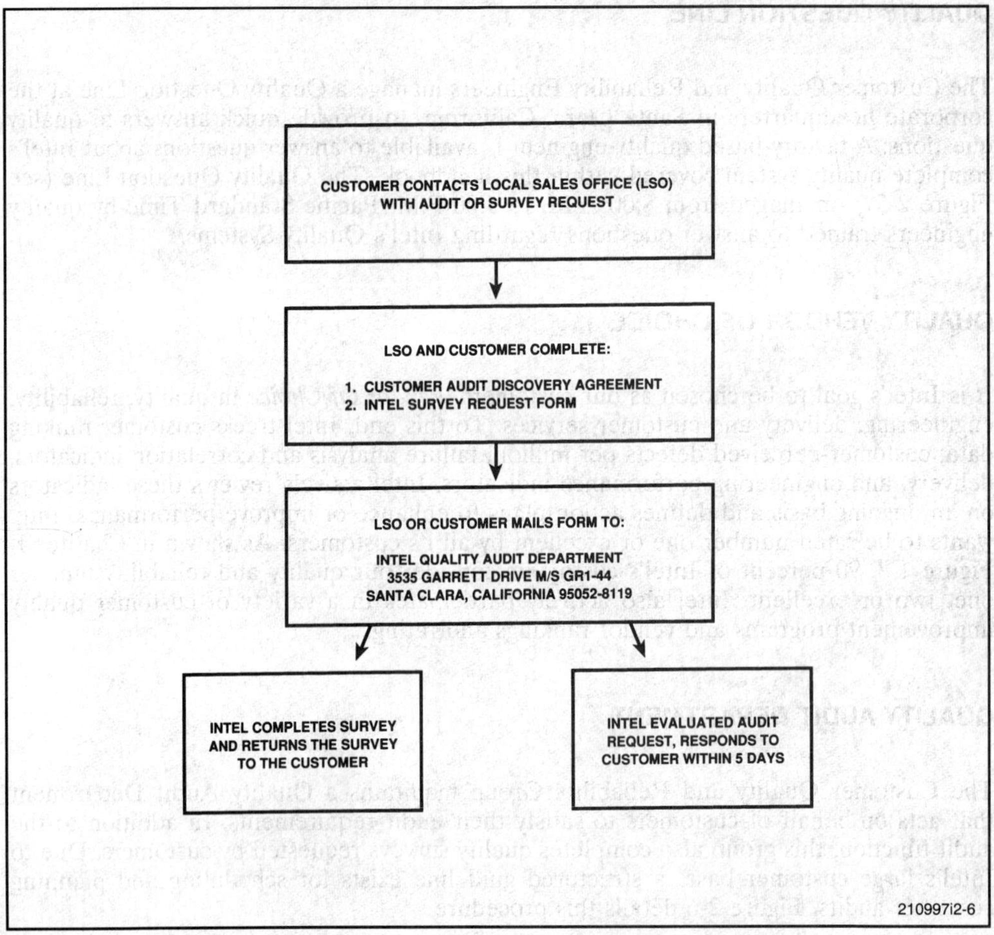

Figure 2-6. Customer Quality Survey/Audit Scheduling Flow

Intel encourages customers to become familiar with Intel's self-audit system and to work with the Quality Audit Department to meet their quality management objectives. Intel's audit system is described fully in Chapter 5.

MILITARY CUSTOMER QUALITY ENGINEERING

Due to the demanding requirements placed on military products, a comprehensive military customer quality program exists at Intel. Through constant communication and feedback between supplier and vendor, problems are identified and rapidly solved. For this reason, Intel's Military Q&R Group runs a high-level customer quality program, which includes direct phone contact between Intel Military Quality Engineers and customers, monthly data exchanges to identify problems, and quarterly quality management reviews to ensure progress is being made on ongoing quality improvement programs.

DOCK-TO-STOCK PROGRAM

The increasing complexity of modern integrated circuits devices has greatly increased the cost in time, equipment, and personnel required for testing to today's high quality standards. At the same time, the drive to Just-in-Time manufacturing and reduced time to market creates pressure to reduce bottlenecks. By taking advantage of Intel's Dock-to-Stock program, an increasing number of our customers are able to reduce or eliminate their incoming quality inspection procedures and reliability testing programs for Intel products they have certified. Routine, detailed reports are provided based on Intel's final quality assurance inspections and comprehensive reliability monitoring program. As shown in Figure 2-7 there are currently 177 products and 70 major customers worldwide actively participating in the Dock-to-Stock program. The number of customer locations participating increases monthly.

The Customer Qualification Data Pack provides the customer with specific process, package and product manufacturing information necessary to eliminate stress testing. The complete data pack, available through a local Intel sales office, includes process and package characteristics, electrical test information, and product qualification information.

Intel's Dock-to-Stock program has made it easier, faster and less expensive for the customer to integrate Intel's product line into his own.

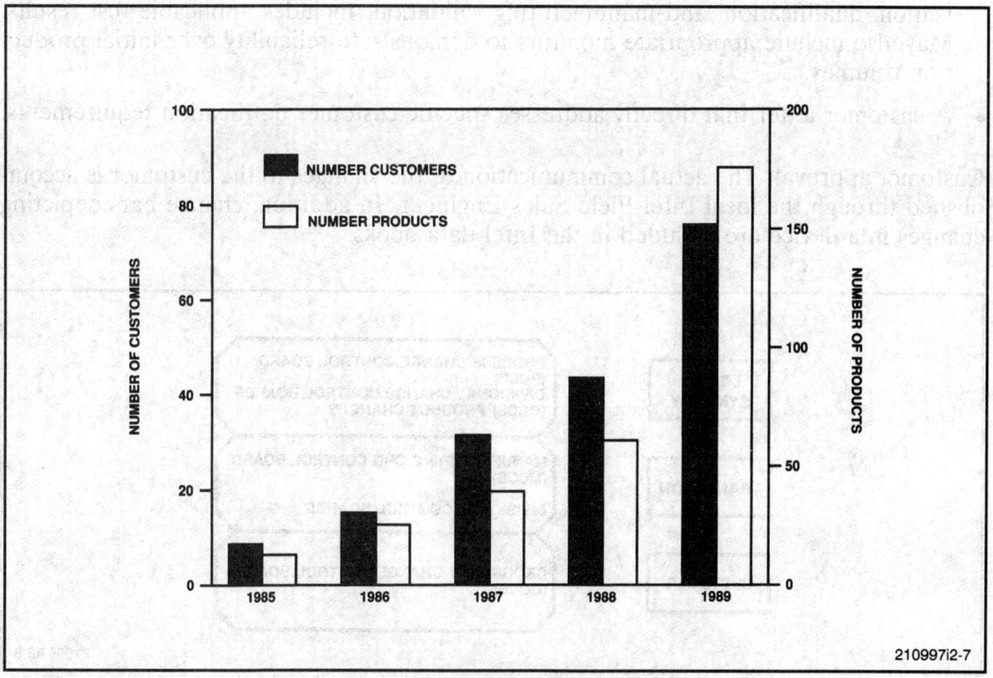

Figure 2-7. Dock-to-Stock Performance

CHANGE NOTIFICATION

To fully meet the customers' requirements for change notification, Intel has developed a fully documented change notification network. This network consists of local groups chartered to document the change; a central group which provides a bridge from manufacturing (the Technology and Manufacturing Group) to the product division (the Components Group); and the Intel Marketing Operation Geographies, which link Intel and the customer. Figure 2-8 shows the change notification information flow.

The customer receives formal change notifications through the local Field Sales Engineer. The Intel Change Notification Package is centered around a technical white paper that includes the following information:

- Name of change.
- Description of change (a summary paragraph explaining the change. Also details of the change with comparisons to previous process or product which is being changed and/or replaced).
- Reason for change (including potential benefits to the customer).
- Products affected by the change (lists specific package, device, and stepping combinations that will be affected by the change).
- Concerns and considerations (details the possible concerns and risks. Describes what elements of the characterization and/or qualification plan address those concerns).
- Reliability data (summary of reliability tests performed or planned in the characterization, qualification, and manufacturing validation. Includes applicable test results. May also include appropriate monitors to demonstrate reliability over initial production volumes.
- A customer letter that directly addresses specific customer notification requirements.

Customer approval: The actual communication of the changes to the customer is accomplished through the local Intel Field Sales Engineer. In addition, change bars depicting changes in a device are included in the Intel data books.

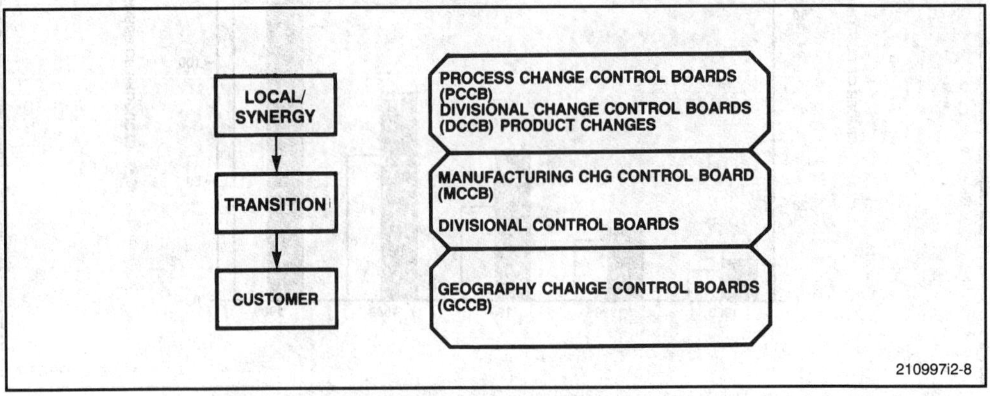

Figure 2-8. Change Notification Information Flow

CONCLUSION

The Intel Customer Support System effectively utilizes the information from Intel Quality Design and Development Systems, Manufacturing Systems and the Support Systems to provide quality products and services to customers. The Field Customer Support, the Customer Quality Support and the Customer Support Services Systems work together to provide a complete support system for our customers. The local sales and applications engineers, as well as a worldwide network of distributors, are available to support a wide variety of customer business requirements. The Customer Quality and Reliability Group manages a variety of quality programs and maintains a question line to answer any questions regarding the Intel quality system.

Currently, over 90 percent of the customers who participate in the *Vendor Of Choice* Program consider Intel quality as number one, two or excellent. In 1989, Intel received several awards commending our product quality and services. These awards are very much appreciated and convey the value of close Intel-customer partnership. Customers continue to participate in our Dock-to-Stock program in ever greater numbers and use our quality and reliability data to certify products. Overall, the Intel quality system provides customers with superior quality products, information and services.

Design and Development Systems 3

CHAPTER 3 **Page**

DESIGN AND DEVELOPMENT SYSTEMS

CHAPTER 3
DESIGN AND DEVELOPMENT SYSTEMS

INTRODUCTION

The Quality and Reliability (Q&R) organization has subgroups whose main responsibilities are to support Intel's development efforts. This involves new fabrication technologies, new assembly processes, packages and product designs. As these development areas vary greatly, so do the requirements for the Q&R groups supporting them. There are three main areas of expertise in the Q&R subgroups: fabrication process reliability, assembly process/package reliability and product reliability. These Q&R groups are responsible for working with their particular development teams to ensure that quality and reliability issues are addressed early in the development cycle. The goal is to be proactively involved, so the impact to introduction schedules and customer expectations is minimized.

3

Figure 3-1 shows a diagram of the Intel quality system.

DESIGN QUALITY FUNCTION DEPLOYMENT

As part of our Total Quality effort Intel has begun to use Quality Function Deployment (QFD) in product definition. Quality Function Deployment is a tool or mechanism whereby the needs, wants and quality requirements of the customer are heard in the definition phase of a product and carried through to the final manufactured product. QFD takes the exact words of the customer, commonly known as "customer murmurs," and provides a structured means for evaluating proposed product features in light of those views.

The final output from a QFD project is a series of matrix charts that correlate customer wants and supplier capabilities (see Figure 3-2). The charts themselves are not the end

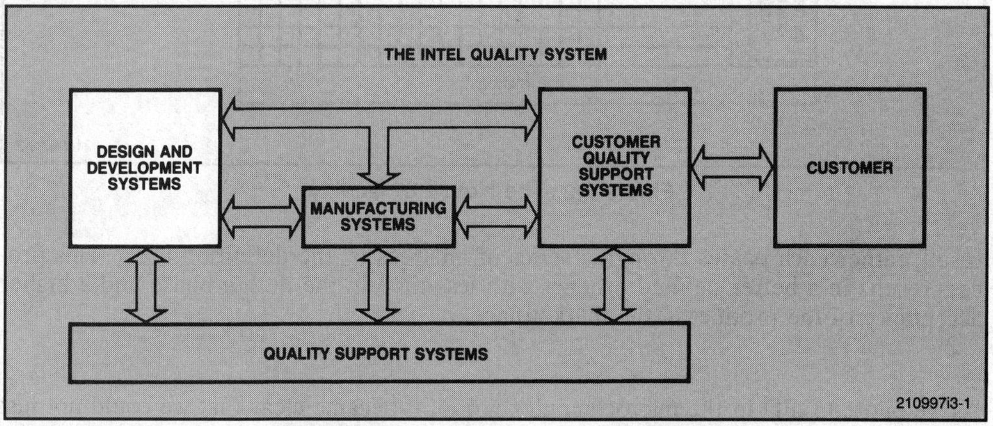

Figure 3-1. Intel Quality System Diagram

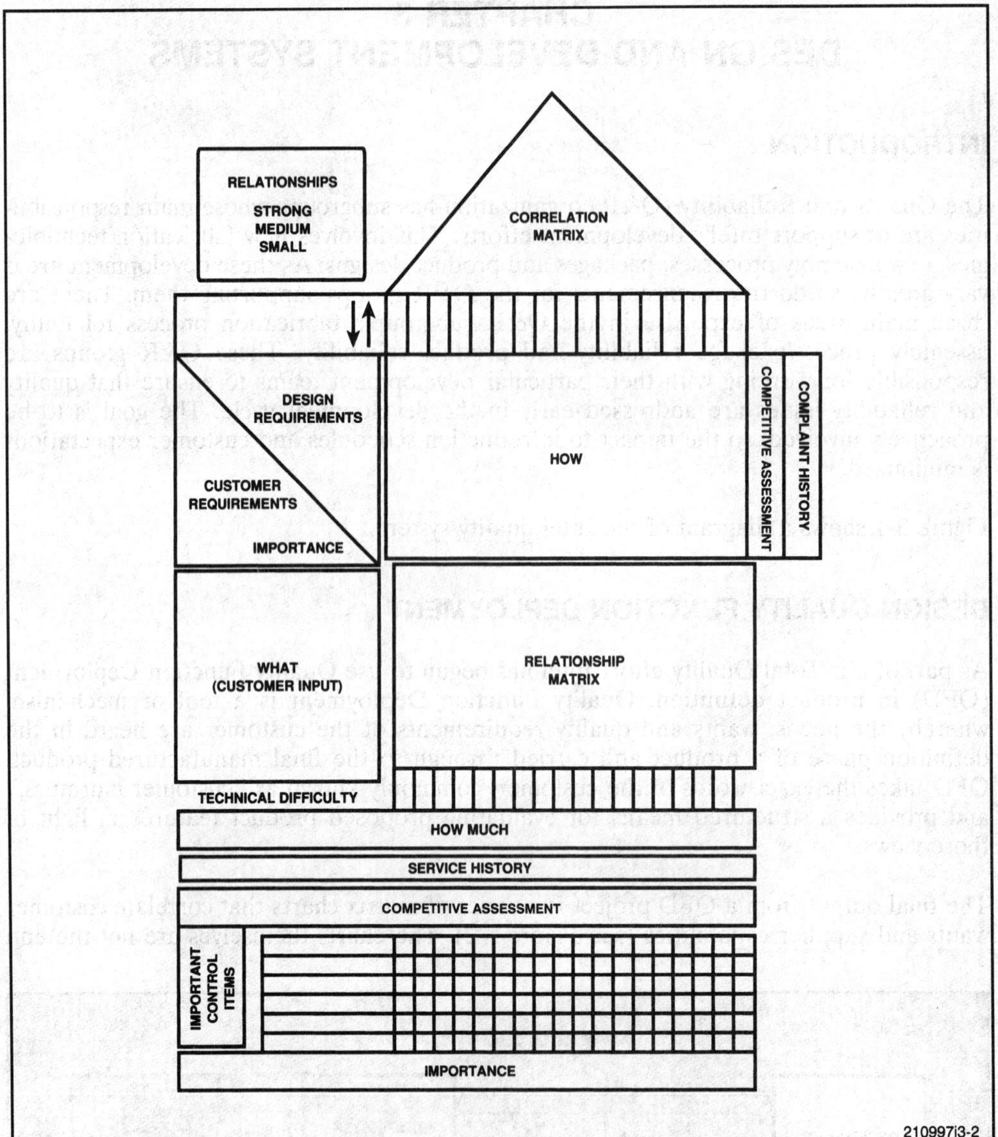

Figure 3-2. The House of Quality

result; rather each passes through a series of analyses by the definition team. This process results in a better defined product with less time in the design phase and a higher acceptance of the product in the marketplace.

As we piloted QFD in the microcomputer group, it became clear that we could not just look at one specific product without trying to understand the entire system that the product would need be working within. We found that by understanding the entire customer system we could solve other problems that occurred when customers connected our products with other products. We, therefore, extended our QFD design methodology to entire customer systems, when possible (see Figure 3-3).

DESIGN FOR MANUFACTURABILITY

Design for Manufacturability (DFM) is a design approach that combines new product/process design features with the manufacturing capabilities and requirements in order to shorten the time to market, reduce the product cost and increase its reliability. The manufacturability requirements (process window, number of different process steps, equipment capability, test time etc.), are considered early in the design phase and integrated into the design guidelines.

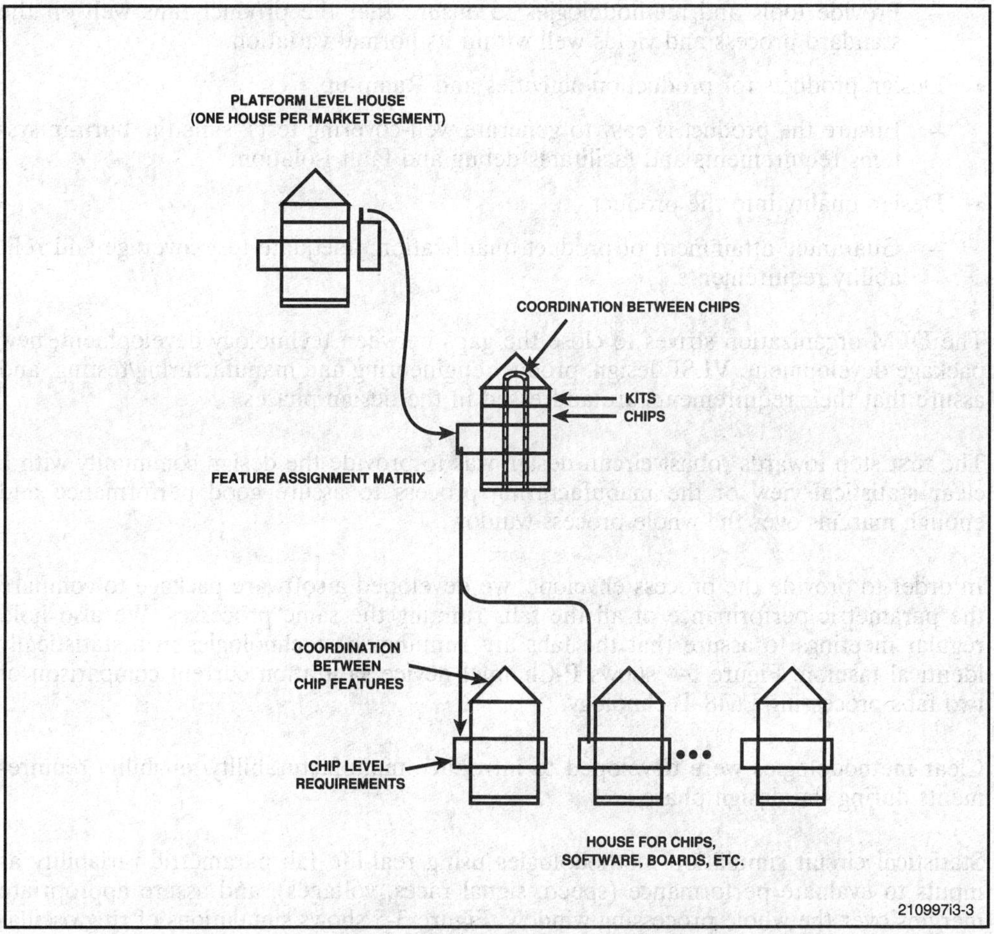

Figure 3-3. Design from the Broadest Possible Perspective

Implementing DFM requires a change of mindset to realize that a product design is complete only after the product is introduced to high-volume manufacturing at a low cost.

Multidisciplinary teams are the key factor for successful DFM. Integrating product engineers and test engineers into the chip design groups (so that their requirements will be considered early in the product definition and early design stages), integrating fab process engineers into the technology development teams (to better consider fabrication aspects during process development), integrating assembly engineers into the design CAD and new package development groups (to better manifest assembly requirements and gain better assembly process windows), are only a few examples of the high benefits associated with this concept.

Intel's Design for Manufacturability addresses three main areas:

- Design products for the fabrication process
  - Provide tools and methodologies to ensure that the product runs well on the standard process and yields well within its normal variation.
- Design products for production activities and Ramp-up
  - Ensure the product is easy to generate well-covering tests, suits the burn-in systems requirements and facilitates debug and fault isolation.
- Design quality into the product
  - Guarantee attainment of product qualification, adequate test coverage and reliability requirements.

The DFM organization strives to close the gaps between technology development, new package development, VLSI design, product engineering and manufacturing/testing, and assure that their requirements are addressed in the design phases.

The first step towards robust circuit design was to provide the design community with a clear statistical view of the manufacturing process to assure good performance and enough margins over the whole process window.

In order to provide the process envelope, we developed a software package to compare the parametric performance of all the fabs running the same processes. We also hold regular meetings to assure that the fabs are running the technologies in a statistically identical fashion. Figure 3-4 shows P-Channel device saturation current comparison of two fabs processing P648 Technology.

Clear methodologies were developed to introduce manufacturability/reliability requirements during the design phase.

Statistical circuit simulation methodologies using real-life fab parametric variability as inputs to evaluate performance (speed, signal races, voltages), and assure appropriate margins over the whole processing window. Figure 3-5 shows simulations of ring oscillator using statistical file simulation.

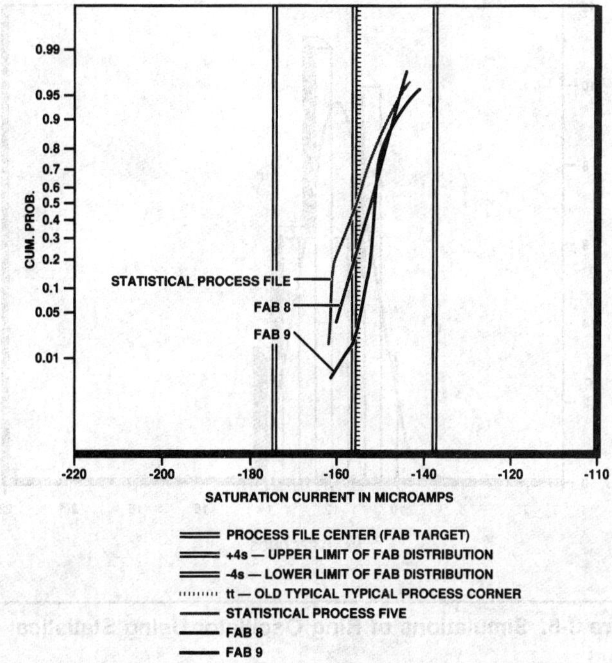

Figure 3-4. Fab-to-Fab, Fab-to-Statistical Process Saturation Current Comparison

We use an electronic rule checker (ERC) – a CAD tool that automatically identifies design methodology violations on a circuit schematic. ERC assures that the whole development group is not violating pre-defined methodologies. A special module verifies that there are no violations of hot electron design restrictions.

Another key factor for a successful DFM is that design engineers have a clear understanding of manufacturing requirements. Cross-training between the two organizations is ongoing, and career job enrichment programs (integrating manufacturing people into the design community) are under evaluation.

Present and Future trends at Intel in DFM include:

- **DFM Layout**. We are moving towards a set of layout rules that accounts for manufacturability requirements (defect immunity), in addition to the standard design rules.
- **Design for Testability.** Our major focus is to push testability considerations into the early phase of the design to allow us to develop high-quality tests before first silicon.
- **Design for Burn.** We are working to integrate some burn-in solutions on silicon.
- **Physical CAD Tools Algorithms.** We are working to better integrate fab requirements in our layout CAD tools.

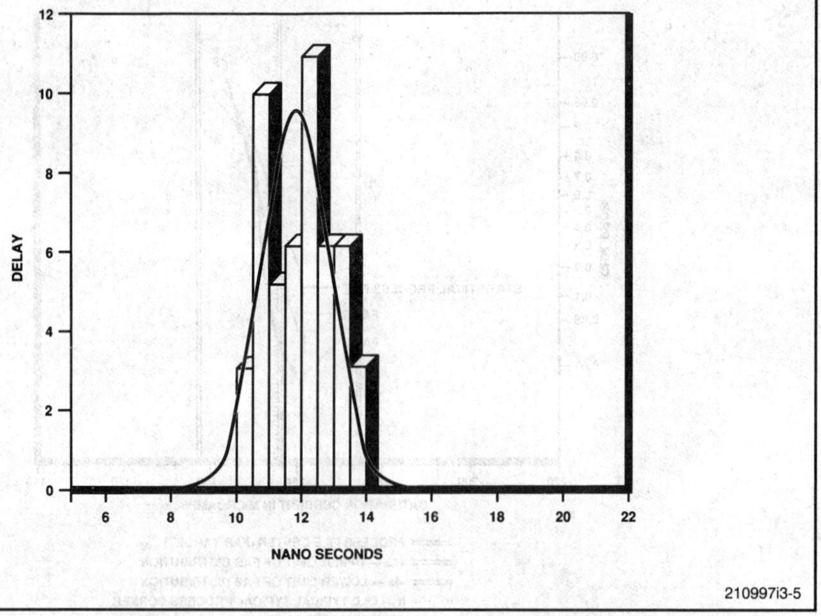

Figure 3-5. Simulations of Ring Oscillator Using Statistical File

The DFM organization strives to close the gaps between the different disciplines (technology development, new package development, VLSI design, product engineering, manufacturing and testing), and assure that their requirements are addressed in the design phases.

CERTIFICATION METHODOLOGY

The certification methodology for getting new processes, packages and products into production continues to evolve and improve. With an emphasis on continuous improvement, Intel continues to focus on customer feedback for improvements to our process, package and product development systems.

Manufacturability

In addition to the quality and reliability requirements that are the main ingredients of process, package and product certification plans, manufacturability requirements are a consideration. Manufacturability requirements cover both design and execution and include a number of indicators: critical-step process control capability, line yield, die yield, in-line and end-of-line monitors.

Including these manufacturability requirements in our certification methodology has resulted in a better integration of our Q&R and engineering development teams.

Proactive Engineering

Certifications continue to emphasize proactive engineering early in the development cycle. When problems show up late in the development cycle, product introductions can be delayed, affecting customer commitments and creating crises for the development team. Therefore we strive to anticipate problems before they arise. The more we concentrate on problem detection and resolution in the beginning, the more likely it is we will have a smooth transition into manufacturing and that customer commitments will be met.

Continuous Information

Rather than gather reliability data on a fixed number of production lots, Intel performs continuous certification throughout the development cycle.

Material from the very first fabrication runs pass through the same stresses that mature runs pass through. The idea is to start gathering information as quickly as possible.

In summary, Intel's certification methodology is a result of a desire to make manufacturability a part of the design effort and make the certification effort continuous. What follows are the internal requirements of our certification methodology. The details of the actual certification procedures are discussed in the process, package and product sections.

Certification Methodology System

The overall certification system integrates process, package and product certifications, understanding that the product's reliability is dependent on the reliability of the fab and packaging processes that built it. Therefore, we certify products in tandem with our fab and packaging processes to assure that there are no product sensitive reliability failure modes.

Yield, quality and reliability improve as a new product, process or package matures. Uncertainty decreases in both a statistical and a general sense. As a tool for both Intel management and our customers, we have partitioned this continuous improvement into four discrete steps to provide a shorthand way of communicating the level of quality and reliability a product, process or package has achieved. Certification level IV is the lowest level of certification and is the level at which product is available to customers for prototyping. Level I means that the product has achieved our goals for quality and reliability.

PROCESS DEVELOPMENT

Introduction

The development of a new wafer fabrication process is the responsibility of Intels' Technology Development organization and its associated Reliability Engineering group. The development activity is driven by a need to reduce chip cost, increase chip performance or increase chip functionality. Since there are a number of ways to achieve these goals, the team has to determine the approach that optimizes all variables. Whatever trade-offs are made, the result has to satisfy an internal or external customer need, and the process has to be transferable into production.

The transfer of any process into production requires that the process be capable of hitting the target performance goals, be cost-effective and manufacturable, and meet the corporate reliability requirements. What follows is the procedure that the Technology Development and Quality and Reliability groups use to produce a fabrication technology that satisfies both our customers' needs and our internal requirements.

Process Reliability Engineering

The Process Reliability group has the responsibility of ensuring that new technologies are reliable, meaning there are no intrinsic wearout mechanisms, the defect densities are enough to allow efficient and economical manufacturing, and the layout and circuit design rules provide sufficient margins to guarantee reliable operation throughout the life of the product.

Most device performance improvements, cost reductions, and design functionality increases are possible because of the continually shrinking geometries of new technologies. However, this scaling is limited by several things. Lithography constraints such as equipment and photoresist capabilities determine the amount of transistor scaling that can take place (see Table 3-1).

Reliability constraints also have a significant impact on the amount of scaling that can take place (see Table 3-2). Reliability is affected by scaling, because scaling gives rise to larger current densities, higher chip temperatures and higher electric fields during device operation.

The process reliability engineer must have an understanding of reliability failure mechanisms. Overall, the Process Reliability group focuses on wearout prevention, determination of reliability-related layout design rules, reliability analysis of device structures and materials, latent defect density characterization control and screening, and fundamental studies of failure physics.

3

Table 3-1. Impact of Ideal Scaling on Device Dimensions and Materials Parameters

Scaling Factor K>1 Dimension		Ideal Scaling
Channel Length	l_E	1/K
Channel Width	Z_E	1/K
Gate Oxide Thickness	t_{OX}	1/K
Field Oxide Thickness	t_{FOX}	1/K
Junction Depth	X_J	1/K
Contact Dimension	A	1/K
Line Width	W	1/K
Metal Thickness	t	1/K
Material Parameters		
Substrate Doping N_A		K
Field Implant Dose		K^2 or 1 Depending on voltage scaling

Table 3-2. Impact of Dimensional Scaling from Table 3-1 on Device Electrical Parameters. The Cases for Both Scaled and Unscaled Supply Voltage are Shown.

Shrink Factor K>1 Electrical Parameter	Ideal Scaling	
Supply Voltage	**1/K**	**1**
Device Current *1	$1/\sqrt{K} - 1/K$	K−1
CMOS RMS Current/Contact/Line	$1/\sqrt{K}$**	K**
Metal Current Density J_M	$K^{1.5}$	K^3
Contact Area Current Density J_C	$K^{1.5}$	K^3
Oxide Storage Cap C_{OX}	1/K	1/K
Oxide Storage Charge Q_{CRIT}	$1/K^2$	1/K
Oxide Field E_{OX}	1	K
Junction Capacitance C_J	1/K	$1/K^{1.5}$
Junction Storage Charge	$1/K^2$	$1/K^{1.5}$
Power Dissipation per Gate	$1/K^{1.5}$	K
Gate Delay τ_D	$1/K^{1.5}$	$1/K^2$
Delay X Power	$1/K^3$	1/K

* Saturated Velocity Case: Term on Right is for Saturation Limit
** Improved Performance: Duty Cycle = Constant

Pre-Certification Requirements

Before a new process technology can be certified, a number of activities must be completed. First the Technology Development (TD) group works on a plan for examining the process modules. This plan looks at material composition uniformity, required thickness, and machine operating parameters. Test structures are designed to examine various technology features and determine performance tradeoffs. The Process Reliability group identifies the potential reliability concerns and determines how they are going to evaluate them.

The goal here is to get some process performance data and feedback on the reliability fundamentals so we can determine whether or not the new technology is feasible. If it is, a preliminary set of design rules is drafted so a process certification vehicle can be designed. This vehicle might not be a marketable product. Its primary function is to serve as a yield and reliability vehicle; therefore, it is designed to be easy to test and failure-analyze.

At this point we have some feasibility data, a potential certification vehicle, test structures for evaluating reliability and process module performance, and process and reliability performance goals. Next, a process certification plan is written. We are now ready to begin the four levels of process certification.

Certification Level IV

The most critical reliability activity in Level IV concerns fundamental wearout failure mechanisms. The mechanisms of general concern are:

- Contact and metallization electromigration
- Threshold voltage stability
- Oxide wearout
- Hot electron and hole injection induced shifts
- Moisture performance

Wearout mechanisms, by nature, are difficult to test on actual product. Since the product doesn't function properly under the high temperature, voltage or current that these mechanisms require to be observed, special test structures are needed. However, a great deal of understanding of reliability physics and the actual circuit layout and operating conditions is needed to relate the accelerated data to how the product will perform in actual use. Since wearout prevention can often have a major impact on the design rules for follow-on products, these studies are run as early as possible.

Since the wearout studies are ongoing during this stage, it is unlikely that the process or design rules are frozen. The process modules are still being characterized for possible improvement. The lead product reliability and yield data are limited but sufficient to determine progress on the technology learning curve.

Prototype shipments are released if the new technology:

- Has no wearout issues (or there is a plan for addressing them)
- Has reasonable yields and product reliability as judged by the learning curve
- Is actively improving open issues on the process modules and design rules

Certification Level III

During certification Level III, the lead vehicle is used to characterize and improve the process. In-line process monitors are used to monitor key parameters, and the process is optimized to raise the capability of the individual process steps. Test structures are used to do this for device characteristics. Much emphasis is placed on optimizing the process for yield enhancement.

More fabrication lots of the lead vehicle are run through the product reliability stresses in order to gather some statistically significant reliability data. All failing devices are subjected to failure analysis to determine the root cause and the corrective actions so the process can be improved. At this point we have a lot of information to suggest that the process will be able to meet the requirements for the next level. Before leaving Level III, the process must meet the following requirements:

- Wearout issues are resolved.
- The process is fairly stable.
- The process is under statistical process control.
- All changes are managed through the Process Change Control Board (PCCB) as part of the change control system. (See Chapter 5 for a full discussion of change control.)
- Infant mortality fallout is known and screenable.
- The production burn-in is defined.
- The long-term failure rate meets the learning curve goals.
- There is a written plan for continuous improvement.
- Reliability and manufacturability monitors are in place.

It is during this level of the certification plan that non-prototype units are shipped. The process is fairly stable. The device and reliability performances are meeting our goals, although extra screening might be in use until the root causes are fixed. Change control is through the Process Development Team which also acts as the Process Control Board (PCCB). In general, the process is not fully certified, because we have not completed all the reliability testing nor have all the manufacturability issues been resolved.

During this period and continuing into Levels II and I, the certification methodology is continuously generating reliability and manufacturability data. As we gather more data, our confidence in the quality and reliability of the material goes up, and we begin to ship more early material to our customers. As with any customer shipments, regardless of our own internal certification status, this early material has to meet the customers requirements.

Certification Level II

At this level of certification the reliability stresses are complete and demonstrate that the process is reliable. The process is stable except for the ongoing continuous improvement work that the manufacturing process engineering group is doing. All changes are fully under the control of the Process Change Control Board (PCCB). The reliability monitor program is active and fully supported.

The technology is reliable and manufacturable. It now falls under the responsibility of the manufacturing fabrication site. How manufacturing certifies change is covered in the next chapter.

Product shipments have no internal restrictions on volume as they do at Levels IV and III. It is during this period and the previous one that our customers start their own qualifications.

Certification Level I

This level of certification is characterized by only a few traits. There are no inherent reliability issues. Level I processes meet Intel's quality, reliability and manufacturability goals. The process has no inherent instabilities and is under full statistical process control (SPC). There is an actively supported reliability monitor program that drives continuous improvement. This program affects not only the engineering and manufacturing areas of fab but periodically requires improvements in design, test and assembly.

Summary

The four-level certification methodology works for new technologies if the pre-certification groundwork is thorough and the concept of continuous improvement a reality. The success of products following the lead vehicle product is dependent on having a reliable and manufacturable process. Intel's process certification methodology includes some key highlights: the emphasis on proactive, anticipatory engineering early in the development cycle; joint ownership of certifications; and continuous improvement certifying, ramping production and making customer shipments.

PACKAGE DEVELOPMENT

Introduction

As silicon technology advances and more complex designs are created, there is a continuing demand for new packages and assembly processes. The performance requirements for these packages and assembly processes have become very complex and demanding. Electrical performance is so critical that the package's electrical parasitics have become a major factor in determining how well a device performs. A package must meet rigorous specifications for inductance and capacitance in order to support the increased speed requirements of new product designs. The heat dissipation requirements of the larger devices is driving the development of special package designs and assembly processes with improved thermal performances. In addition, mechanical requirements are becoming more demanding and complex as users are requiring smaller packages with increased numbers of leads.

There are other demands on new packages and assembly processes as customers' manufacturing techniques change. One example is surface mounting, which is a method of attaching the finished product to a circuit board. This technique places great demands on both thermal and mechanical capabilities of the package.

Intel uses one of two advanced manufacturing modules for developing new packages, materials and assembly processes: the Plastic Advanced Manufacturing Module (PAMM) and the Ceramic Advanced Manufacturing Module (CAMM). These modules are "mini" assembly lines with limited capacity and are used to determine feasibility of, develop, characterize and certify new processes, packages and/or materials. Initial production is performed using the AMM during the certification process. Extra controls and monitors are used to gather data needed for certification and to determine manufacturability. When sufficient data from monitors and stress testing are available and the package, materials and/or process is considered manufacturable, production is transferred to a standard assembly site.

Package Reliability Engineering

The package development efforts and goals are basically the same as those of the new technology development team. The goal is to produce a reliable, manufacturable product that meets our customers' needs for functionality, performance and cost. The reliability engineer's responsibility is also the same: produce an inherently reliable product.

The main characteristic of an inherently reliable package is no intrinsic wearout problems. The wearout issues are attacked with the same method: understand the failure mechanisms, learn which package or assembly process parameters affect the wearout mechanisms, learn how the product design and layout affect the wearout mechanisms, and then make the necessary changes to the package, device design, fabrication process or assembly process to eliminate the wearout problem.

The wearout failure mechanisms for packages can be separated into three main environmental causes: mechanical stresses, thermal stresses and chemical stresses. Individually or in combination, they produce a number of failure mechanisms:

- Die cracking (mechanical and thermal)
- Package cracking (mechanical and thermal)
- Corrosion failures (mechanical and chemical)
- Bond failures (mechanical and thermal)
- Lead quality/integrity (mechanical and chemical)
- Thin film cracking (mechanical and thermal)

While there are many similarities between the process and package development areas, the package-assembly reliability engineering goal of eliminating all reliability problems is very difficult to attain. In fact, a more reasonable goal is to keep the wearout mechanisms under control. This situation is the result of a number of factors.

First, wearout mechanisms are observed throughout the life of the package. Wearout mechanisms increase over time. For process evaluations, these are rarely seen in the product stress environments because they have an immeasurably low failure rate in early life, and the product cannot be stressed sufficiently in a reasonable amount of time to observe them in later life. For packages, these wearout mechanisms are evaluated on the finished product using industry-standard environmental stresses. These environments can stress the finished product to fail in a reasonable time period. So the issue isn't whether the product fails, but how long it takes to fail. The challenge for the reliability engineer is to determine how to push out the observable start of the wearout failures.

Second, the direction of new technologies and designs towards larger chips, more complex topographies, smaller packages, higher lead counts and plastic packages is reducing the reliability performance margins. Initially, it could force the manufacturer to make one reliability tradeoff for another until a non-compromising solution can be implemented. One real example is using copper leads to improve power dissipation but losing margin on lead fatigue performance. In actuality, the new technologies and designs are requiring that a number of performance and reliability trade-offs be balanced in order to meet internal and external customers' needs.

Third, the package is generally the last part of a finished product to be developed. Despite programs that use test chips to evaluate new packages and assembly processes, the finished product is still a part of the development work. Furthermore, the time required to make a package change is usually much longer than it takes to modify the wafer process or make a design change. A second issue is that sometimes an improvement in package performance requires either circuit design or wafer fabrication changes. The time to modify a packaged unit is generally months. Since this delay could be detrimental to Intel and its customers, much effort is expended relating the stress data to the actual use performance.

Last, the package reliability performance issues are almost always related to an industry-standard environment that is highly accelerated compared to the normal operating conditions of most applications. The industry standards are not the issue, since we strive to meet the performance requirements on all packages. The issue is that when the package performance of new products pushes the margins or falls short of the requirements, there is not enough information to know whether this is also a problem of the application environment.

Pre-Certification Activity

When a new product is developed, the design team defines package requirements and performance targets and gives them to the Package Development group. These consist of yield targets, cost goals, electrical and thermal performance requirements, quality and reliability requirements and specific customer requirements. The idea for a new package or assembly process is derived from the details of the new product. The package or assembly process idea is worked up in more detail by using knowledge from the literature, equipment and material vendors, competitive analyses, and past experience.

The first goal of the package development team is to determine whether the new package or assembly process is feasible. They run a matrix of equipment, material and process parameters to determine if there is a combination of these that will satisfy the product requirements. Once the feasibility has been demonstrated, a number of activities needs to be completed before moving into certification.

The first critical activity is a design rule check. There are specific design rules for Intel chips based on historically determined requirements for bond pad layout, die placement, and maximum and minimum die sizes. There are additional design rules for some unique problems, such as thin-film cracking. The check is to verify that the up-front engineering work among the product designers, assembly engineers, manufacturing engineers, fabrication process engineers and the reliability engineers was successful.

The second step is to focus on the electrical, thermal, mechanical and materials requirements. The product, as well as the package, must be characterized. This is accomplished using the actual product, other products or special test chips. The later activity involves special structures on a test chip that are designed to be extra sensitive to particular problems, such as thin-film cracking, die cracking and corrosion.

The third step is to make sure that the package and product designs are going to be manufacturable and reliable. We do this by developing a full understanding of the important process variables and their effect on quality, reliability, yields, defect rates, and manufacturability. This understanding includes process variable windows (optima and tolerances) and the interactions of the various packaging process modules.

By the time the characterization and feasibility work is completed, there will be enough information to define the following:

- Quality inspection gates
- Procurement specifications for materials
- Critical process monitors, including sample plans

The pre-certification information is enough to make a decision on whether or not to proceed with the certification of the new package.

Certification Level IV

At the first stage of the certification process (Level IV), major reliability and manufacturability issues are addressed. This activity takes place in one of two advanced manufacturing modules. Since the process is still in the development stage, changes can be made to the package and/or process.

During this activity the use of non-standard materials, processes or process flows is permitted, since the major intention is to determine reliability and manufacturing limitations. The material can be built on an engineering build kit or a prototype build kit since it is not production material.

The reliability issues and manufacturing issues have to be understood, and there has to be a plan for addressing them. This means that sufficient data exists on the suspected wearout mechanisms to determine whether or not there is a major problem. It also means that enough material has been run through the manufacturing line to determine whether there are major issues. For any detected issues, there has to be a corrective action plan in progress before moving on to the next certification level.

The only material released to customers during Level IV are prototype shipments. This is because the package and assembly process are not finalized, and the plans to address the reliability and manufacturability issues have not been completed.

Certification Level III

At this stage in the certification process, there is sufficient reliability data on the package and the product to indicate that there are no catastrophic reliability problems. This data is intended to show that the design is basically sound. Any early-life reliability issues can be minimized, in the short term, through screens. The assembly process is fairly stable. Changes to the process or piece parts are controlled by the Product Development Team (PDT). There is a complete set of reliability and manufacturing monitors in place showing that the process is meeting the performance goals and that it is in control. The specifications for materials, manufacturing and shipment are all in place. This means that non-standard materials, processes and process flows are no longer permitted, and the production build kit has to be on line. It is during this phase that the package/product can be transferred to a standard production line from the PAMM or CAMM line.

It is during Level III that the first production revenue shipments can be made. There is a high degree of confidence that customer reliability requirements can be met and that the product will satisfy performance and manufacturing needs. Since changes are not controlled through the MCCB, the necessity and method of customer notification is determined by the PDT.

Certification Level II

It is during Level II of the certification process that reliability and manufacturability are demonstrated. The reliability stresses have been completed and meet customer requirements, although some screens or gates might still be necessary. If the package and/or process has not previously been transferred from the AMM to a standard assembly line it is now transferred. Changes to the process/piece parts are now controlled by the MCCB. The manufacturability monitors show that the process is in control and that it meets our requirements. The data that supports these conclusions is taken on large samples of production material over time. This is consistent with our continuous certification methodology which requires that a large part of the material shipped during Level III be sampled to gather the data for the decision to certify Level II.

Full production shipments are made with no restrictions imposed by Intel. Once Level II work has been completed, the package is considered transferable to other manufacturing sites. Since changes are controlled through the MCCB, any changes need to involve customers.

Certification Level I

When a package attains Level I, it means it is reliable and the assembly process is stable. In addition, systems need to be in place for maintaining reliability and manufacturability, such as SPC, package reliability monitors, in-line and end-of-line process monitors and product monitors.

Another unique requirement for attaining Level I is that there has to be a plan for continuous improvement. This program is not just limited to production indicators like yield, cost, throughput times and equipment uptime but includes anything that impacts the package or assembly process performance or goals. Initially, it involves using the reliability monitors to provide feedback for reducing failures or increasing reliability performance margins. These efforts might lead to corrective actions in the product design or the fabrication process.

There are separate efforts ongoing in the design and process world to improve the product's performance; these might impact the assembly process. Materials people are continuously working to improve the quality of piece parts, chemicals and other materials to reduce cost, improve performance and improve manufacturability.

PRODUCT DEVELOPMENT

Introduction

The development cycle for products parallels that of packages and processes. The development team's major goals are to design a product that meets the functionality and performance targets, doesn't create a need to modify the process or package, and has quality and reliability consistent with the lead vehicle. As with all of the development efforts discussed in this chapter, the goal is a manufacturable, reliable product that satisfies customer needs.

Fault Grading

Testing every transistor in a complex random logic circuit is a difficult thing to do. There are computer programs and automatic test case generation tools that perform some of the checking, but none check 100 percent of the transistors. Because an untested, defective transistor may cause failure in some applications, it's important for us to test as thoroughly as possible. We do this by using extensive computer simulations in a process called fault grading. It's a vital part of Intel's component quality system.

The fault grading activity begins during product design, when design engineers generate test vectors as part of their logic design. As each design block is complete, the designer writes the accompanying test vectors. He runs a fault-grading exercise on the block, designing additional test vectors for any untested transistors detected. Designs are not considered complete until their test vectors are completed and pass the fault-grading program.

Fault grading consists of running a defect-free logic model using a test case as input. The output of this simulation, called the defect-free response, is stored. Next, one transistor in the model is changed to represent a random manufacturing defect. The test case is again used as an input and a simulation of the defective logic model run.

This time-consuming process repeats for every transistor in the circuit. If a product has 275,000 transistors, the simulation must be run 275,001 times.

After a complete fault simulation, the design team has a complete list of all untested transistors and can begin the task of writing additional test cases to improve fault coverage.

When we do discover a defective unit, we fix the problem and add appropriate test cases to eliminate that defect from all future units. Fault grading allows us to proactively track down untested transistors before they ever show up in customer applications.

Product Reliability Engineering

The product reliability engineer has overall responsibility for the reliability of the finished product, although process reliability engineers handle most process issues, and package reliability engineers handle most packaging issues. This allows the product reliability engineer to concentrate on two areas: design and test. Another responsibility of the product reliability engineer is product failure analysis. This is not only useful in resolving reliability problems but also in helping the development team resolve product yield and performance issues. Additional responsibilities involve making sure that special customer requirements are implemented in the certification plans and that the customers continue to receive reliability support on the product after it is certified.

Pre-Certification

Reliability engineers are engaged in a number of activities that minimize reliability and quality problems during the design process. The first of these is to make sure the same design rules were followed by both process and packaging design teams. Second, any known reliability problems that are design-induced are addressed. Third, we make certain that the latest design rules for improving latch-up and electrostatic discharge (ESD) are implemented. We are aided in all these efforts by a database of product attributes that help us identify which product attributes we need to focus on in terms of reliability concerns.

The reliability engineer also proactively tests the product to maximize the likelihood of a successful certification. The design engineer will design the chip so that it can be tested by functional areas. The reliability engineer then makes sure that all nodes of the chip are tested properly. The reliability engineer's knowledge of test ensures that reliability electrical screens and margin tests are included in the production electrical tests. It's also useful in addressing customer quality concerns.

Certification Level IV

For a new product design with a certified process and package, the first thing to resolve is the soundness of the design. This concern is addressed through an activity called design verification. The purpose is to make sure that the finished product meets the functional requirements, including marginal parameters and worst-case alternatives for temperature and/or power supplies. The product must also meet the data sheet specifications at three temperature conditions (cold, room and hot).

Because we are using a certified process and package, there are generally no wearout issues. The biggest potential issue is a missed design detail or a defect problem aggravated by the design. These are easily detectable in the early life of the product. For this reason, a dynamic burn-in is required on all early material until there is sufficient data to show that it is not needed.

For customers with aggressive time-to-market goals, we'll ship Level IV product as prototype units. In these cases, it is almost certain that these products will progress to levels II and I certification.

In addition to the issues discussed above, the following activities must also be completed before the product is certified at Level IV:

- The design, manufacturing, system and reliability verification plans have to be written and approved.
- The electrostatic discharge (ESD) and latch-up evaluations have to be performed.
- Manufacturing specifications have to be on line.
- Systems for shipping revenue material need to be in place.
- The test program has been released to manufacturing.

- The product is under the Divisional Change Control Board (DCCB) for stepping changes.
- A plan for continuous improvement into the next certification level must exist.

Certification Level III

To obtain a Level III certification the following things must have been done:

- There is sufficient reliability data to show that we are going to meet the Level II requirements.
- The manufacturing, system, and reliability verifications have progressed as planned.
- The manufacturing system continues to put all the operating and shipping specifications in place.
- Changes are controlled through the Product Development Team.

Shipments continue, but they are no longer for prototypes; they are considered production shipments. However, Intel imposes volume restrictions for Level III revenue shipments. Customers are performing their own qualification exercises, so Intel provides a white paper that provides all the internal certification data we used to grant Level III certification.

Certification Level II

At this level, the environmental stress tests are complete, reliability requirements have been met, verification plans have been completed, test programs are final and the manufacturing systems and specifications are in place. The MCCB and DCCB are reviewing and approving all changes. Except for a few in-process qualifications that customers are running, all the customer documentation is completed. Test improvements will continue to be made as customer and manufacturing issues arise and as efforts are made to improve test coverage, reduce test time and improve product quality performance.

Certification Level I

A Level I certified product meets all of Intel's quality reliability and manufacturability goals and is put on a continuous improvement plan that focuses on the processes and packaging. Occasionally there are variations. However, most problems at this stage are fixed by making an improvement to the process or package.

Summary

As with all development and certification efforts, the goal for Product Development is to transfer into production a reliable, manufacturable product that meets our customers' needs. The emphasis is on anticipating, detecting and resolving as many issues as possible, as early in the certification process as possible.

In general, production shipments are limited by the rate at which reliability data can be gathered to show that the development project is reliable. For processes and packages, this is generally months. Once the actual certification begins, the shipments of reliable material are usually limited only by manufacturing capabilities.

CAD TOOL DEVELOPMENT

Intel's innovation in process and products is supported by the industry's latest development tools. In fact, increased product complexity is made possible, to a large extent, by the increased capability of the tools that we use to design them. Intel has made the investments necessary to ensure that these tools are in place as they are needed.

While the growth in VLSI product complexity as measured by transistor count is staggering (see Figure 3-6), the growth in tool capability has outpaced it. One indicator of how rapidly Intel's CAD (computer-aided-design) capability has grown is seen in the increase in computer cycles used by a typical development team from the start of a product development project to initial mask generation (see Figure 3-7).

The increase in computer usage is growing much faster than the increase in the number of transistors, while the increase in actual design engineers is minimal. If one compares the 80286 design effort to the 80486 design effort, there is an 8X increase in transistors, only a 2X increase in design engineers, but a 135X increase in computer usage. CAD tools have more than kept pace with the increase in complexity, and this is one of the key reasons Intel is able to produce high-quality designs at an ever-increasing pace.

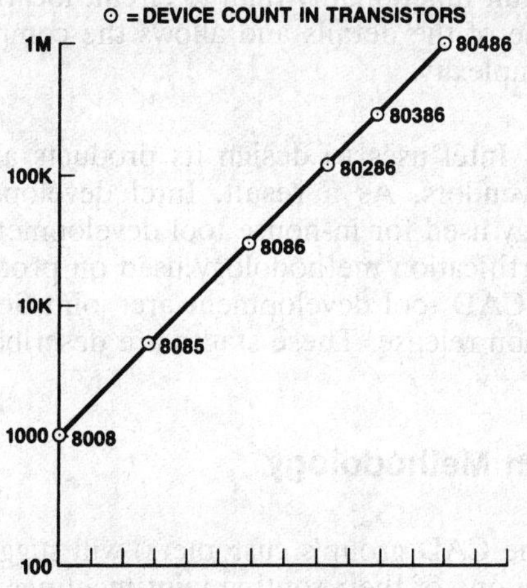

Figure 3-6. Increase in Product Device Count

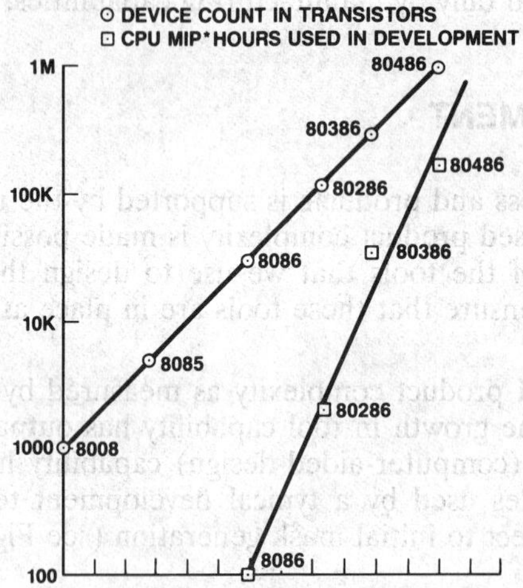

Figure 3-7. Increase of Computer Time Used to Develop Products Relative to Device Count

A recent example of a tool that gives component designers tremendously expanded capability is the auto-place and router. This tool allows the computer to interconnect circuits much faster and with fewer errors than an engineer can, thus allowing the engineer to pay more attention to circuit functionality than to circuit location on the die. Auto-place and route automates some of the details and allows the computer to partially compensate for the increased complexity.

The state-of-the-art tools Intel uses to design its products are generally not available from commercial CAD vendors. As a result, Intel develops most of its CAD tools in-house. The methodology used for in-house tool development shows remarkable similarity to the four-level certification methodology used on products, processes and packages. The four levels for CAD tool development are: joint development, alpha release, beta release and production release. These stages are described below.

CAD Tool Certification Methodology

Periodically, designers (the CAD group's customers) will suggest an idea for a new tool or a new capability during one of their routine joint meetings. A CAD engineer formalizes the idea into a proposal that details the desired capabilities and savings to the designers in terms of time, layout area, circuit performance, etc., as well as tool development costs and schedules. The proposal is then evaluated by senior members of both the CAD and design groups who decide whether or not to fund the development. Once funded, a product in design is selected as a joint development partner. This is to ensure that the tool development stays on track to meet the designer's needs.

During the joint development phase, the team actually uses initial versions of the new tool on real product design. However, since the tool is not finalized and changes are at the discretion of the development team, no other products are allowed to use it. Only the joint development product is at risk if the tool fails to meet the needed capabilities.

Once development reaches a point where any further changes are expected to be minor, alpha testing begins. Usage of a tool with alpha status is restricted to a very few products, often only one. Development efforts focus on fixing bugs and correcting any misinterpretations in the detailed functionality. Changes to the tool are no longer only at the discretion of the development team. The alpha testing concludes with a report detailing how well the tool met the initial objectives and performance goals and a list of problems that must be corrected before entering beta status.

Once beta status is reached, the new tool is very stable. Documentation (users' manuals, application notes, etc.) and training materials and courses are finished during this stage. Tool usage by several products is encouraged. Tool development engineers are available to work with and train the beta users as needed, and any final changes to the tool's functionality are completed. The beta test concludes with a report similar to the alpha test report but in much more detail and with much more actual performance data.

After a successful beta test, the tool is granted production status. Once production status is granted, changes to the tool can only be made by starting the entire process over with a formal proposal detailing the new capabilities to be added, followed by joint development, alpha testing and beta testing. It should be noted that while the new version of the tool is being developed, the current production version remains unchanged. The new version is not released to production until alpha and beta testing demonstrate compatibility with designs using the current version.

CAD Quality Systems

CAD tools must be matched to the processes with which they are used. In the example of the auto-place and router, the rules used to lay out circuit interconnects vary from process to process. If a new process is developed with different rules, the auto-place and router will need tuning to work efficiently.

In the previous tool development example, the CAD tool developer worked jointly with a product design engineer to reach an optimum mix between tool application flexibility and tool usage complexity. The product design engineer wants the tool to minimize many less important low-level details while maximizing flexible control over the critical performance trade-off details. Those low-level details, however, are only less important when the tool is tuned to the process. This situation often necessitates that the tool development engineer has a second joint development partner, the process designer.

When the first version of a CAD tool is developed, or when an existing tool is certified for use with a new process, the process development engineers must be part of the joint development team. The process engineers ensure that the tool designers have made valid assumptions on how the process details interact, and they work to guarantee that optimal combinations of these details are incorporated into the tool. In parallel, the process engineers also develop a good understanding of the limitations of the CAD tools. They are then able to modify the process development so that the CAD tools work more effectively.

The process designers are also responsible for creating design rules for new CAD tools. Because a computer program can check these design rules quicker and more accurately than can be done manually, these rules are always written for computer usage. Rules must therefore be described in terms that can be converted into computer programs. Sometimes it even becomes necessary to change the process to ensure that the design rule check can be automated. In all cases the goal of the development team is to maximize the usefulness of the CAD tool without over-compromising the actual design or process.

Product Simulation

Product simulation is a powerful tool for developing high-quality, complex designs. Early in the design cycle, simulation is necessary to ensure that product functionality is correct. Later in the design cycle, simulation is necessary to ensure that product performance goals are met. A design that performs the wrong functions perfectly is as undesirable as a design that is logically correct but has unachievable system timing requirements. Functional simulation and performance simulation are both used in developing product designs, but each has different modeling requirements.

The first requirement for simulation is that a description of the product functionality requirements be given to the design team. The designers then begin development by translating the functionality description into a high-level simulation language. This high-level description is a computer program, commonly called a product behavioral model. The design team uses this to run simulations of product behavior after the design is finished. Thus it is possible to detect incorrect functionality very early in the development cycle and to change how the product implements its functions without scrapping expensive detailed transistor and logic circuit design.

As portions of the high-level model are proven correct, they are translated into a more detailed lower-level logic design. As detail is added, the computer model grows larger and more complex. The cost of developing the model increases, as does the computer time needed to run it and the time required to review the results. Thus, a hierarchical approach to running the more detailed simulation becomes important.

Since the high-level model and the detailed model are required to have identical functionality, the lower-cost high-level model can be used to create the test cases for each piece of the more detailed logic model. A test case is created by recording all the signals running to and from a portion of the high-level model, and playing back these signals to the detailed logic-level piece. In this manner, the detailed logic-level pieces are simulated one at a time, greatly reducing simulation costs and focusing the designers' attention on the specific logic of interest.

As blocks of detailed logic are proven correct, they are turned into even more detailed transistor circuits. At this point, product performance now enters the picture, and it becomes necessary to measure the speed of the transistor circuits.

It is during the speed performance analysis and simulation that the tuning between the CAD tools and the process really becomes critical. If tools are not properly matched to the process, the performance of the transistors will not meet product performance specifications. The sooner the mismatch is detected, the sooner we are able to recover and minimize lost time and opportunity. If the mismatch is missed during the simulation, the device/process optimization is lost and could result in program delays as a result of inconsistent manufacturing or product performance.

Accurate speed simulations cannot be performed until transistor-level circuits are designed, laid out and interconnected. These speed simulations are only accurate if the CAD tools that analyze the layout and extract the parametric information are properly aligned to the process. Careful comparison between the performance of the first product designed on a process and the performance projected by the simulators must be made by the process development engineers and the CAD tool developers. Any discrepancies must be corrected before additional products are developed.

During the higher levels of simulation, it is necessary to estimate what the speed performance will be once the transistors are designed. The logic-level model is changed, based on these estimates, to reduce or eliminate rework after the transistors are through layout and accurate speed simulation is achieved.

Change Management

Tuning CAD tools to match new processes requires careful change management. Because these tools are already tuned to existing, active processes, we need to make sure that changes made to adapt tools to new process do not adversely impact their use on existing processes. To this end, all CAD tools must pass a test suite after any change; new tests may be added, but old tests are not removed.

If a tool undergoes a major enhancement, new tests are created to demonstrate the new features. If features were removed, then tests which are no longer valid are also removed. The new tests are added to the regression test suite and are always run after any change to the tool.

Another instance for change comes as a response to bug reports from the tool users. Once the bug is identified, a test case is generated to demonstrate the bug. The same test case is used to demonstrate the fix after the code is modified. The test case is added to the regression suite to ensure future bug fixes do not reintroduce old bugs.

After enhancements or changes, an independent group runs the test cases and verifies results. The new version of the tool is released for alpha testing by one design team. After a successful alpha test, the tool is released for beta testing by several design teams. After successful completion of beta testing, the tool is rotated into the production release area, and the old version is archived.

Summary

CAD tools are an integral and rapidly growing part of Intel's emphasis on innovative products and processes. There are a number of quality systems (tool-to-process matching, change management, simulations, fault grading and Intel's certification methodology) that are aimed at continuous quality improvement in our CAD tool development, in product design and in customer service.

CONCLUSION

The emphasis of this chapter has been on the process that Intel uses to develop new processes, packages and products and transfers them into production. Intel's certification methodology was discussed with the main emphases on doing as much anticipatory problems solving as possible, as early in the development cycle as possible and on using a continuous improvement approach throughout the certification process. Manufacturability requirements are a part of all certifications, as are change control and customer requirements, in addition to the standard quality and reliability requirements.

Manufacturing Systems 4

CHAPTER 4 **Page**
MANUFACTURING SYSTEMS

CHAPTER 4
MANUFACTURING SYSTEMS

INTRODUCTION

The Manufacturing Quality and Reliability (Q&R) organization has three main functions:

- Certifying all process/package changes
- Monitoring existing processes/packages
- Problem solving

The main emphases of the Q&R group are on continuous improvement, protecting the end user and protecting the factory.

What follows is a discussion on incoming materials control, equipment qualifications, process/package certifications (with emphasis on manufacturability and reliability performance) and process control (manufacturing and reliability monitors, problem solving, change control and audits).

The certification of new technologies, new assembly processes and new packages is a joint activity between the technology development teams and special subgroups in the Quality and Reliability organization (as described in Chapter 3). This chapter also deals with certifications involving the transfer of previously certified processes and packages to new manufacturing sites and with certifications involving changes to existing processes and packages. These certifications are a joint activity between the Manufacturing and Quality and Reliability groups. The end result is a process or package that exceeds both internal and external customer reliability and manufacturability performance needs.

Figure 4-1 shows the Intel quality system diagram.

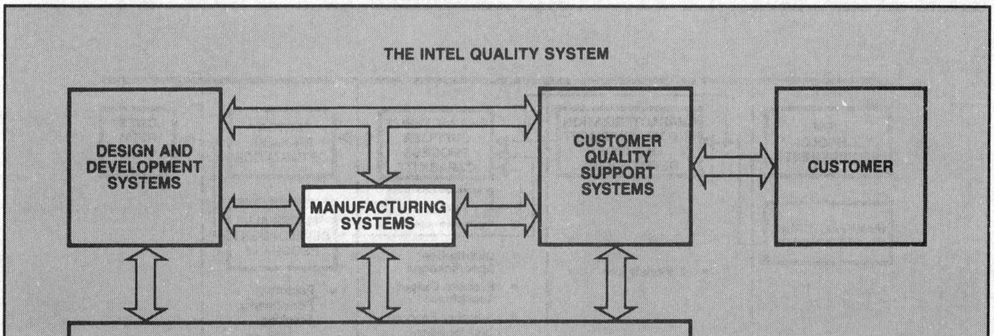

Figure 4-1. The Intel Quality System Diagram

INCOMING MATERIALS CONTROL

All materials used in the manufacturing process are under incoming materials control. Wafer fabrication materials (silicon, masks, chemicals, gases and quartzware) and assembly materials (lead frames, ceramic tops/bases, bonding wire, etc.) quality is managed through fabrication and assembly organizations whose responsibilities include materials quality improvement, materials technology and procurement. The integration of these activities is essential to assure materials are available which meet ever more stringent process requirements.

The quality improvement methodology applied by Intel to meet the current and future materials requirements is embodied in Intel's Supplier Continuous Quality Improvement (SCQI) program and includes:

1. The development of a strong customer-supplier relationship for strategic materials.
2. The use of distribution specifications and Cpk's (process capability indices).
3. The implementation of continuous process/system improvements.

The overall materials process flow is illustrated in Figure 4-2. The materials requirements are initially defined by technology and manufacturing needs. Measurement capability and correlation with the supplier are subsequently established. With that completed, supplier process and product capability are determined and variables-based specifications developed consistent with the technologies and manufacturing requirements.

Incoming production materials are monitored by reviewing vendor product parameter distribution data on a statistical basis or, where not available, by review of Certificates of Conformance (C of Cs) based on limit specifications. C of Cs are documents that state the specific lot of materials meets/specifications based on measurements made by the supplier. Audits of supplier manufacturing facilities are conducted on a regular basis.

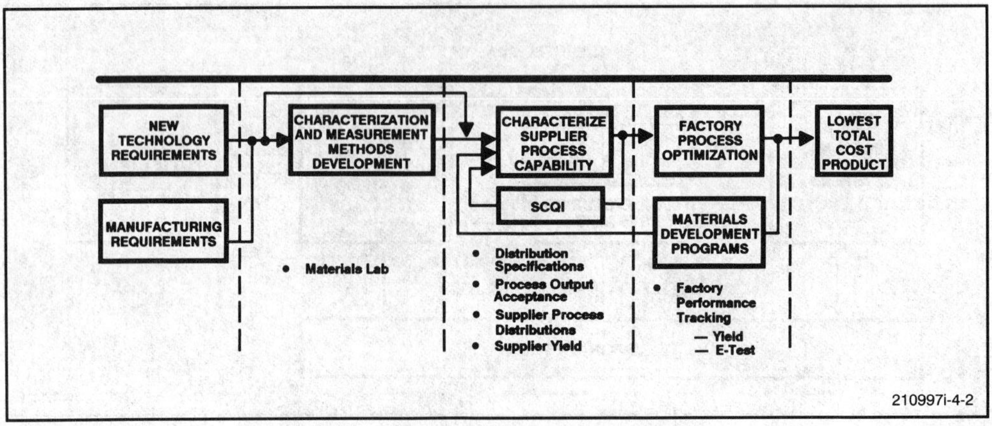

Figure 4-2. Materials Process Flow

The possibility of discrepant materials always exists. In the event the discrepant material is identified, a Material Review Board (MRB) is held with representatives from Materials QC, Technology, Procurement and Manufacturing. This board determines whether reliability or manufacturing risks will result from using this material. Vendor corrective actions are sought regardless of whether or not the material is fit for use in order to make improvements on subsequent deliveries.

EQUIPMENT QUALIFICATION

The introduction of a new piece of manufacturing equipment begins in the corporate group chartered with qualifying new equipment. The manufacturer's specs are validated and a manufacturability exercise is run. If the equipment meets the requirements for manufacturability, it is sent to a production area, which acts as a beta site. Only after passing the beta site criteria is the equipment disseminated to other sites.

The extensiveness of the beta site criteria depends on the process step for which the equipment is designed (e.g., lithography, etch, bonding). Each of these processes requires a certain performance (e.g., alignment, etch angle, bond strength), which forms part of the qualification criteria. Generally, qualification involves establishing machine control limits, in-line control criteria and finished product performance criteria (yields, speed, reliability, etc.).

The newer the piece of equipment the more likely it is that in-line and end-of-line product monitors will be used. As our knowledge base increases, the sample size and frequency are reduced and the equipment variables themselves are used as monitors.

The procedure for adding additional pieces of existing equipment (for increased capacity) is simpler than adding new equipment but is basically the same. The first step is to make sure that the new piece of equipment behaves like the existing equipment. Both configuration and performance must be the same. These matches are made by looking at test wafers, running in-line monitors and evaluating finished product. The analysis also usually involves visual checks, critical dimension checks and scanning electron microscope (SEM) cross sections. Typically, there is no need to verify product reliability, as machine characterization, process characterization and end-product performance are adequate.

Any time a new piece of equipment is placed on the manufacturing floor, the frequency and sample size of the standard monitors are increased until machine performance is equivalent to existing equipment. Afterwards, performance is controlled through statistical process control (SPC) monitoring.

PROCESS AND PACKAGE CERTIFICATION METHODOLOGY

The Quality and Reliability (Q&R) organization's role in supporting manufacturing continues throughout the lifetime of the process. Once new processes and packages are developed and certified as reliable and manufacturable, all subsequent changes are controlled, with emphasis on reliability and manufacturability through the Manufacturing and Quality and Reliability organizations. Since all certifications have requirements for reliability and manufacturability performance, all certification exercises are a joint effort between the Quality and Reliability and Manufacturing groups.

The certification exercise is a parallel activity rather than the traditional one where the Q&R group only assesses the reliability of the finished product after Manufacturing has produced the material. In this parallel effort, the Q&R group and the manufacturing group work together on all aspects of the process using a continuous four-level certification methodology (discussed in Chapter 3). Once the four levels of reliability and manufacturability are attained, the process or package is considered fully qualified and the continuous certification activity is continued throughout the life of the package or process as part of Intel's quality improvement process (QIP).

Continuous Certification

Both the fabrication and assembly groups use what is referred to as a continuous certification methodology, which consists of four distinct levels. Whether we are certifying a new process/package or a change to an existing process/package, the continuous certification methodology prevails. The goal is to certify the process or package using a learning-curve approach, as shown in Figure 4-3, with each of the four levels of certification being achieved only when certain manufacturability and reliability goals are reached.

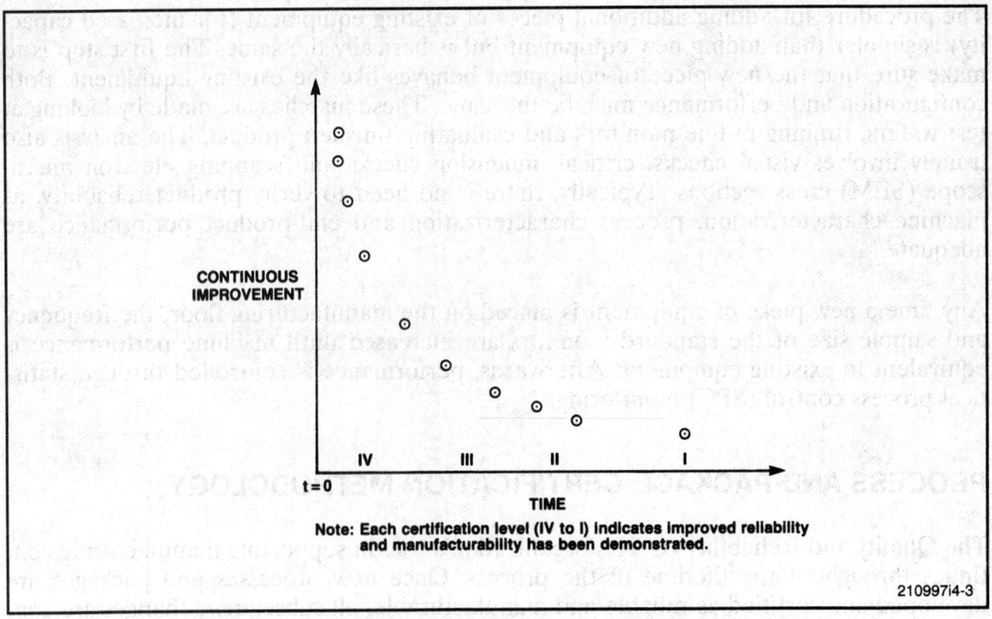

Figure 4-3. Reliability/Manufacturing Learning Curve

As customer needs (reliability, availability, performance, etc.) are often a factor in determining the usefulness of a given product, there are often various points on the learning curve where qualification might be granted by a particular customer (typically these correspond to points in Intel's Level III or Level II certifications). However, full qualification (Level I certification) is reached only when results are sufficiently down the reliability and manufacturing learning curve to meet Intel Q&R goals.

The continuous certification methodology results in the quality improvement process (QIP) starting at the introduction of a new process or package rather than after it reaches an advanced certification level. In traditional qualification procedures, manufacturing lines sit idle while process or package engineers debug the process or resolve pre-production package issues and later sit idle again while the Q&R group executes the qualification stresses. Once qualified, the volume is ramped and problems that were hidden in the smaller sample sizes of the qualification exercises now emerge.

With the continuous certification methodology, materials are continuously running through production. Feedback is sought from all areas, with emphasis on constantly measuring key parameters (in-line monitors, sort-class yields and performance, reliability performance, etc.). Quite often, the resulting data dictate that changes are needed. The result might be that none of the material produced up to that point is saleable; in fact, the basic premise of this methodology is that early materials are produced with the sole purpose of identifying problems. With the emphasis on information-gathering and feedback, the factory concentrates on problem-solving before shipping material.

While continuous certification takes more time, in the long run it allows for a faster and smoother production ramp in the factory. Problems are found early while volumes are low and impact to the factory and customers is minimal. A cooperative relationship among Engineering, Production and Reliability makes the transition to continuous quality improvement easier.

In summary, continuous certification literally monitors a process or package into existence, with each level of certification determined by customer needs and our position on the learning curve with respect to device performance, reliability and manufacturability. Additional details on this methodology are discussed later in this chapter.

PROCESS AND PACKAGE CERTIFICATION DETAILS

Manufacturability

One of the most important objectives in certifying a new process/package or process/package change is demonstrating that the change is manufacturable as well as reliable. This is achieved through a close working relationship among product engineers, process/package engineers and the production group. New processes or packages and changes to existing processes or packages are characterized at the critical processing steps for capability and for their ability to stay in statistical process control within the process module or assembly requirements. By determining what the process is capable of and by measuring how well it can stay in control, the factory is able to determine what additional controls, if any, are required and what additional engineering work is needed to make the process or package consistently manufacturable.

Through this characterization (involving process and assembly in-line performance, final device yields and performance, production's ability to show process repeatability, etc.), the critical process control parameters are determined before the process or package enters production.

Because this process is continuous, certification is never completely finished. Efforts to improve module performance, assembly processing, yields and ease of manufacturing are ongoing. Critical process controls are improved or changed as we become more knowledgeable about the factors impacting desired performance outcomes.

The continuous certification methodology has enabled Intel to meet a certain level of manufacturability before entering a full production ramp and has allowed us to ascertain whether or not a process or package is capable of being improved to a manufacturing level consistent with the long-term plan for production volumes.

Reliability

The second key aspect in process or package certifications is reliability performance. There are three stages to a reliability certification: device/package fundamentals, product performance and documentation.

Device/Package Fundamentals

During this phase, we demonstrate that there are no long-term wearout failure mechanisms that will impact customer failure rates during the useful life of the product. Conventional product qualification exercises rarely detect such problems.

For die-related issues, electromigration, hot electron degradation and threshold stability are evaluated on special test structures at accelerated conditions to measure process capability. Subsequent monitoring of these variables can take place by repeating the tests at periodic intervals. The biggest drawback to these monitors is that they do not provide feedback as quickly as is desirable. Too much material is produced during the intervals between these monitors to keep current on the long-term reliability performance. Therefore, other process monitors are used as an indirect method of monitoring for long-term reliability. These include specific metal monitors (step coverage, metal defects, undercut angles and more) and impact ionization currents for hot electron monitoring.

Since indirect monitors are not easily correlated to the fundamental reliability issue of concern – particularly in the case of electromigration, where many variables determine final performance – the original certification tests are repeated periodically to verify that the reliability performance still meets requirements. These tests also serve as a method of determining whether the indirect monitors are effective. This relationship is reviewed periodically, with more emphasis placed on monitoring reliability at critical factory process steps than on finished product.

For package certifications, the fundamentals testing includes stresses like bond strength, die-attach strength and package integrity testing, all of which are stressed through destructive testing. These tests are often added as part of the production process control monitors to provide almost immediate feedback to the manufacturing line. Efforts to relate these results to particular machine monitors is ongoing, as the goal is to control processes at their sources.

There are also a number of periodic package monitors (temperature cycling, mechanical shock, centrifuge, etc.) that measure the effectiveness of in-line monitors. They also provide information to address customer application requirements for package performance.

Device and package fundamentals testing is critical, because problems with poor reliability due to any of these causes is usually not screenable or reworkable. Thus, the sooner such problems are detected, the more Intel minimizes the impact to the factory and the customer.

Fortunately, significant performance changes are required before a problem impacts customers and such changes are typically detected by the in-line monitors. Nearly all device and package reliability parameters have significant margin built into their performance requirements to prevent reliability problems from occurring at a customer site.

Product Performance

The manufacturability and reliability fundamentals parts of the overall certification process describe a number of proactive things that manufacturing and reliability do to ensure successful certifications of new processes, packages or process/package changes. However, it is the finished product that must demonstrate required levels of reliability and manufacturability before any level of certification is granted. What follows are the methods used to maximize the likelihood that products meet desired reliability and manufacturability goals.

As with new processes and packages, new products follow a continuous certification methodology. The product learning curve is usually an extension of the learning curve resulting from the process and assembly continuous improvement efforts. Periodically, however, a design change must be made to allow further progress on the learning curve. As design changes can cause great delays, much effort is expended up front to minimize their occurrence.

DESIGN RULE REVIEWS

During new process development, design rules for product performance and reliability are determined by the technology development team and supplied to the product designers. The design rules are as comprehensive as possible, based on prior experience with other packages and technologies. However, as new product designs are developed, problems may arise that the design rules didn't anticipate. In such cases, either the design rules must be altered or the manufacturing process improved to eliminate the problem.

During process fundamentals testing (electromigration, hot electron degradation, etc.), the design rules are checked again. Based on the module performance, certain design margins will be required to meet corporate long-term reliability goals. This second check is critical, since the technology development design rules are based on what the process is designed to do, while the reliability inputs are based on how the process actually performs. The same is true for package design rules. As dice get larger, joint efforts between design and packaging are required to maximize product and package performance.

Because of the impact of design on product reliability, quality and reliability engineers have an opportunity to contribute to the design process. Over the years, a number of reliability-specific issues have been identified and a reliability checklist compiled that spells out things that need to be included or excluded from the design. Q&R inputs are again verified at the final design approval meeting, where the reliability engineer is part of the sign-off team.

TEST PROGRAM REVIEW

Another reliability check occurs in product test programs. Certain reliability screens are implemented during electrical testing, either during wafer-sort testing or finished product testing. These screens include margin screens, such as for guardbanding charge-loss performance on EPROMs and defect screens, such as a high-voltage cell stress to screen out weak oxides. As the use of such screens is based on a continuous learning process, test programs are periodically modified to improve them. Each test change must go through a test program review, which requires a final approval meeting where Q&R is a part of the sign-off team.

RELIABILITY CERTIFICATION

As the preceding discussion demonstrates, the quality and reliability organization does a number of things to maximize the likelihood of timely, non-interrupted progress through the four levels of certification. The Q&R group is involved in design, package and process development, manufacturing, test and any activity that can contribute to improved product reliability.

The ultimate measure of success, however, is how well the final product performs on reliability testing. Despite the many reliability checks made during design, manufacturing and test, a successful product certification (Level II or I) does not always result. This is why a final reliability certification by the Q&R group is still highly important.

Reliability certification exercises are necessary to validate that the process/package/product is reliable. They also provide us with an excellent learning tool as an integral part of Intel's quality improvement process (QIP).

Product certification is comprehensively outlined in a corporate specification. The list of possible stress environments is extensive and only rarely used in its entirety; however, it serves as an excellent checklist for designating reliability requirements for all finished products.

Since many of these requirements have been met previously by existing products or packages, usually only the differences are evaluated. For example, a process change to an oxide doesn't require a full package stress certification or moisture test but only those stresses that show the effect of the new oxide process. The decision as to which tests are run depends on the change being certified. Another factor in choosing the stress environments comes from our Manufacturing Change Control Board (the MCCB is a central group responsible for coordinating factory changes with our customers). Since customer concerns and qualification requirements are pertinent to our certification decisions, the reliability and engineering groups submit the proposed certification plan to the MCCB to solicit feedback from our customers. Any customer concerns or issues are addressed through a subsequent modification to the certification plan.

The goal of the Q&R organization is to find and resolve the majority of the reliability problems before the product certification exercises are run. Because this stage is late in the certification process, finding problems here is disruptive to the factory flow and to our customers' expectations on certified product deliveries. We believe that a product certification should serve as a validation of engineering and manufacturing work; it should not be a method for finding problems. While there is still a need for product certifications, it is our goal to learn from product certification problems and push this knowledge back to the design, manufacturing and test areas. The emphasis is on good engineering rather than putting the final product through extensive certification exercises.

Documentation

After all certification work is completed, we generate a comprehensive data package. This package includes a description of the change, the benefits or purpose of the change and the plan for justifying and qualifying the changes and the certification data. The certification data might consist of an monitor trend if the change is minor and confined to a single area. If the change is major, the data package might be extremely comprehensive, including in-line module data, SEM cross sections, comparative yield data, product reliability stress data and long-term reliability studies of electromigration and hot electron performance.

The data package is given to the MCCB, which relays pertinent information to customers.

PROCESS CONTROL

Fabrication and assembly processes are controlled through five major activities: statistical process control, manufacturing process monitors, reliability process monitors, change control and a comprehensive auditing program.

Statistical Process Control (SPC) in Manufacturing

Intel utilizes Statistical Process Control as one aspect of total quality management. The success of SPC as a tool is measured by the reduction of variability of significant (key) parameters for all manufacturing and job processes/products. Intel's SPC implementation, begun in the early 1980s, was initially focused on training classes and the engineering application of SPC tools such as control charts, parameter characterizations, correlation studies and design of experiments. In the later 1980's, SPC training became wide spread. SPC was successfully applied to manufacturing process control with the emphasis on product characteristics and the recognition of out-of-control situations. Reduction in variability gains were evident. The current focus of improvement is on SPC applications for process parameters and automation of data collection and analysis. The future focus will be on process input parameters and automation of reactions to significant SPC trends. The main SPC management indicators are percentage of parameters in statistical control and the percentage of key parameters with capability values (Cpk) greater than 1.0, 1.33 and 2.0. Intel's strategic SPC objectives by year are:

1990 A system is in place for identifying significant product characteristics and process parameters. All significant product characteristics are well within specification limits and the variability is decreasing. Most process parameters have been identified and characterizations are underway.

1991 Characterizations/capability studies are completed for all significant process variables. Process control systems are in place and most process parameters are "capable" (Cpk greater than 1.33). Variability has been significantly reduced on all process parameters.

1992 All process parameters are well understood (characterized), "in statistical control" and "capable." Systematic improvements occur rapidly and variability is increasingly difficult to measure and assess. Some real-time automated process controls are being established. Process/product parameter relationships have been established between wafer fab, sort, assembly, test and support organizations.

SPC tools and techniques are applied at Intel to design and manufacture quality, reliability and customer satisfaction into our products and services. Most of these SPC applications occur in three basic areas:

- Product/process design, development and validation
- Manufacturing/job process control
- Continuous improvement of products and services

SPC in Product/Process Design, Development and Validation

At Intel, we work with our internal and external customers to identify key parameters and goals that need to be controlled so that our processes efficiently produce products and services that are reliable and of the highest quality. To support our customers' quality, cost, functionality and time-to-market requirements, the development of our products, services and processes must be predictable and statistically accurate. The output from the development cycle must work the first time. Manufacturability of products and quality production of services starts with statistical-based design and development of processes and process control capability.

Significant parameters for all manufacturing processes are defined and developed to meet statistical capability criteria prior to volume production. Products are designed using the same significant process parameters for product computer simulation to ensure customer and manufacturing specifications are met. Closed-loop SPC design of experiments is used in concert with advanced computer process modeling tools and correlation of process parameters to design parameters. This serves to validate/update the computer product design models and keep them in sync with the manufacturing process.

A pyramid approach to technology development and qualification is used to ensure that each building block is sound before it is integrated into a higher level of complexity, as shown in Figure 4-4.

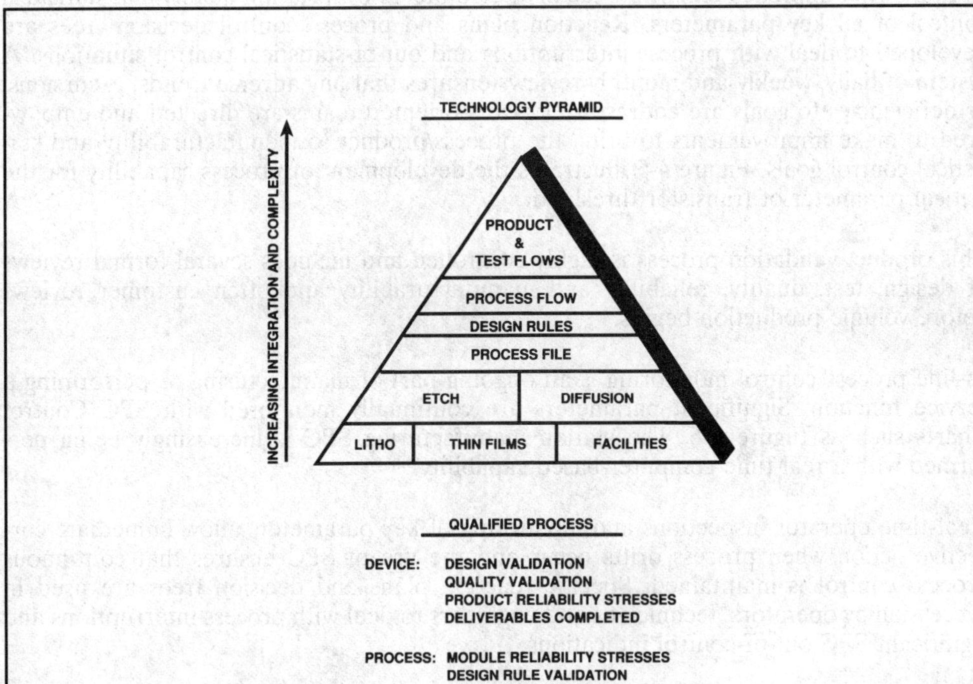

Figure 4-4. Technology Pyramid

Product Development Teams (PDTs), including engineering, manufacturing, marketing and design, are used from the beginning of lead product development to build this technology development pyramid on sound, statistically valid data. The PDT defines and validates product specifications and design targets, develops statistical process/product control capabilities and ensures that the process/product certification plan for product introduction satisfies all customer and internal standards. The plan details criteria for quality, reliability and manufacturing requirements that must be statistically demonstrated prior to customer shipments and prior to transfer to manufacturing. The certification plan also details product monitoring strategies, failure analysis capabilities and statistically-verified measurement capabilities that must be in place prior to shipment of significant volumes.

SPC in Manufacturing/Job Process Control

The Process/Product Development Team (PDT) stays with each new process/product through transfer to manufacturing until process control, high volume and yield targets have been achieved. The selection of significant process/product parameters for statistical control is completed and detailed Process/Product Control Plans are documented. A station owner approach empowers factory personnel to own station quality and statistical control of all key parameters. Reaction plans and process control decision trees are developed to deal with process interruptions and out-of-statistical-control situations. A system of daily, weekly and monthly reviews ensures that any adverse trends, excursions, or deficiencies to goals are addressed. Process-oriented teams are directed and empowered to make improvements to bring the process/product to manufacturability and statistical control goals. Figure 4-5 illustrates the development of process capability for the critical parameter of transistor threshold.

This product validation process is highly controlled and includes several formal reviews of design, test, quality, reliability and manufacturability and often customer reviews before volume production begins.

In-line process control monitoring is an ongoing part of manufacturing or performing a service function. Significant parameters are continually monitored with SPC Control Charts such as Figure 4-6. The station manufacturing SPC is increasingly being performed with a real-time computer-based capability.

Real-time operator inspections and monitoring of key parameters allow immediate corrective action when process drifts occur and the use of SPC ensures that continuous process control is maintained. Specific reaction plans and decision trees are used in succession by operators, technicians and engineers to deal with process interruptions and significant SPC out-of-control indications.

SPC in Continuous Improvement of Products and Services

As part of the PDT review process described above, and in production as an ongoing manufacturing improvement activity, Intel uses statistical analysis to evaluate each process step and its process control design to identify opportunities for process control

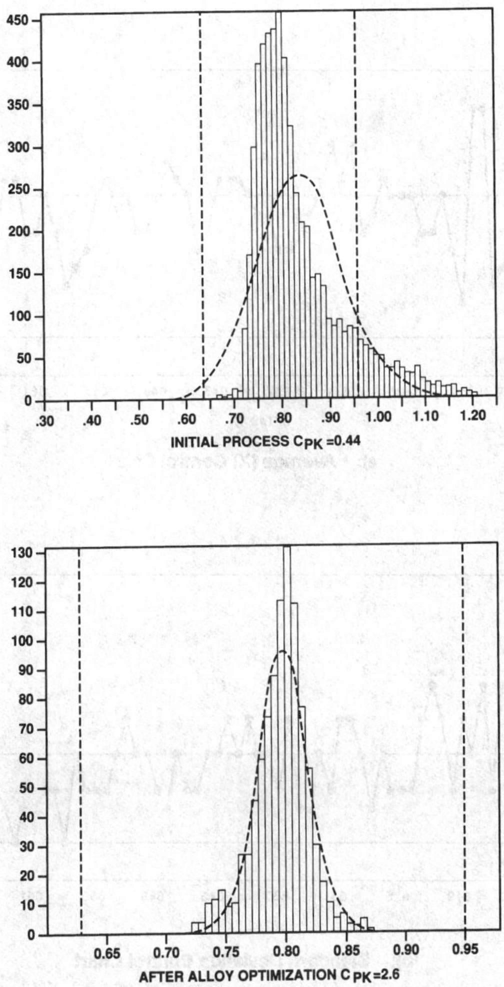

Figure 4-5. Improvement in Transistor Threshold C_{PK}

improvement. Opportunities for improvement are identified using customer feedback, competitive analysis, identification of the sources of variation in the manufacturing process and targets for world-class levels of quality, reliability, yields and throughput time. A key approach is cause-effect analysis (Ishikawa or fishbone diagram, Figure 4-7), which ensures that the root cause of a problem or the variation under attack is addressed and corrected.

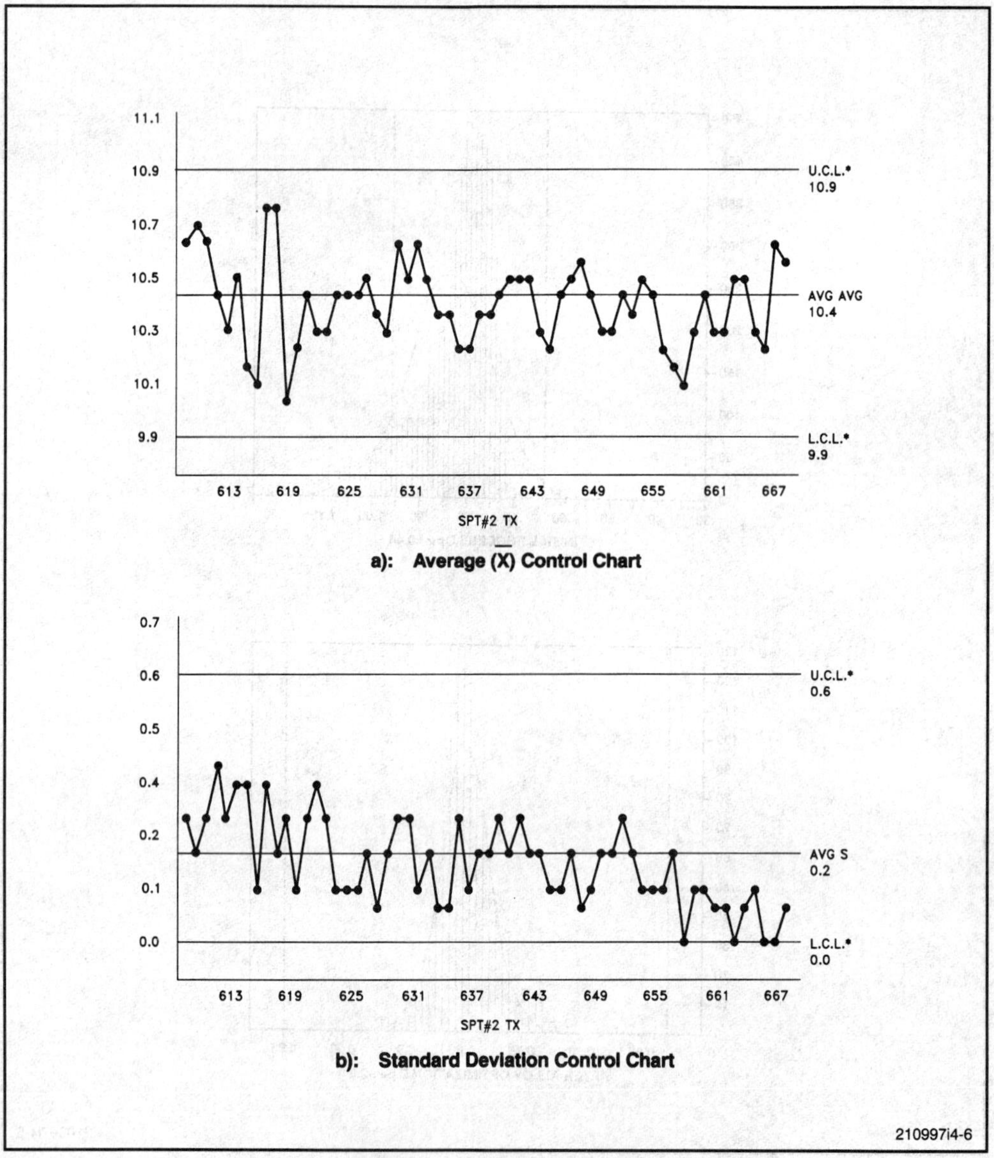

Figure 4-6. Control Charts

Intel's continuous improvement efforts are based on a structured problem-solving methodology that has been taught to the majority of employees allowing cross-functional teams to quickly form and address problems with a common approach and language. Statistical tools are an important part of these continuous improvement methodologies. Methods for improvement and optimizing processes vary from simple graphs to sophisticated statistical techniques. Pareto analysis and, if needed, statistical experimental design are used to pinpoint the root cause of a process variation or problem. Examples

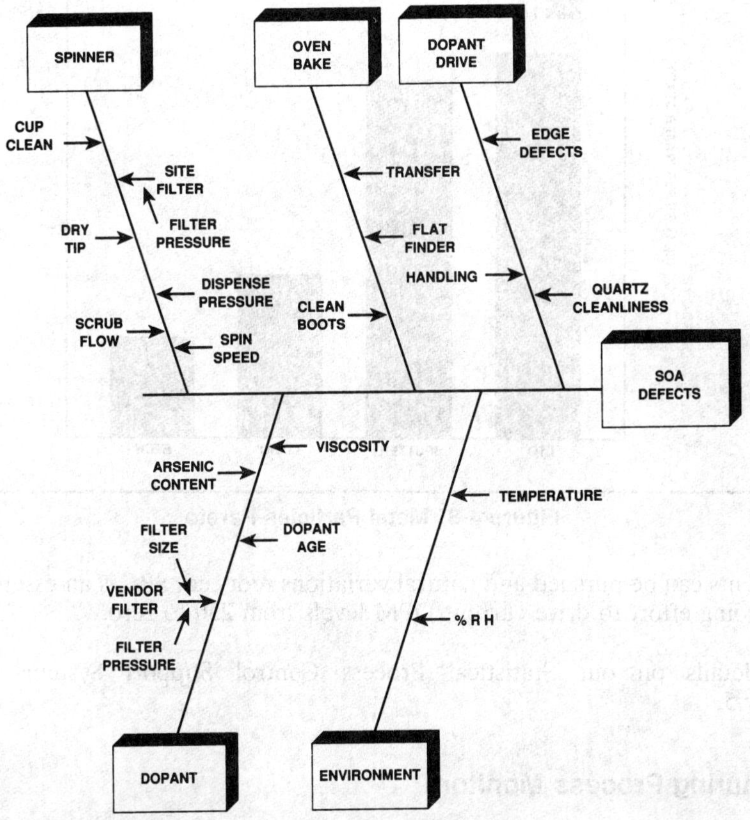

Figure 4-7. Example of Ishikawa Diagram

of commonly used techniques include trend charts, process flow charts, scatter diagrams and response surface analysis. The Technology Developments Yield Culture Steering Committee and the Manufacturing Process/Product Engineers continually focus on defect reduction and process margin improvement. Figure 4-8 is an example of a Pareto chart used to analyze the yield impact of metal particles from various process steps.

Intel emphasizes training in statistics, statistical process control, structured problem solving and team building. Each factory has a statistician on staff to assist employees in methods of analysis and experimental design, to identify root causes for problems and process variations and to correctly perform applied statistics such as distribution theory, confidence limits, correlation analysis and multivariate analysis. These statistical tools and resources are used at Intel to break processes or problems down, to isolate sources of variation and to identify the hidden variables in a stable process, so that continuous

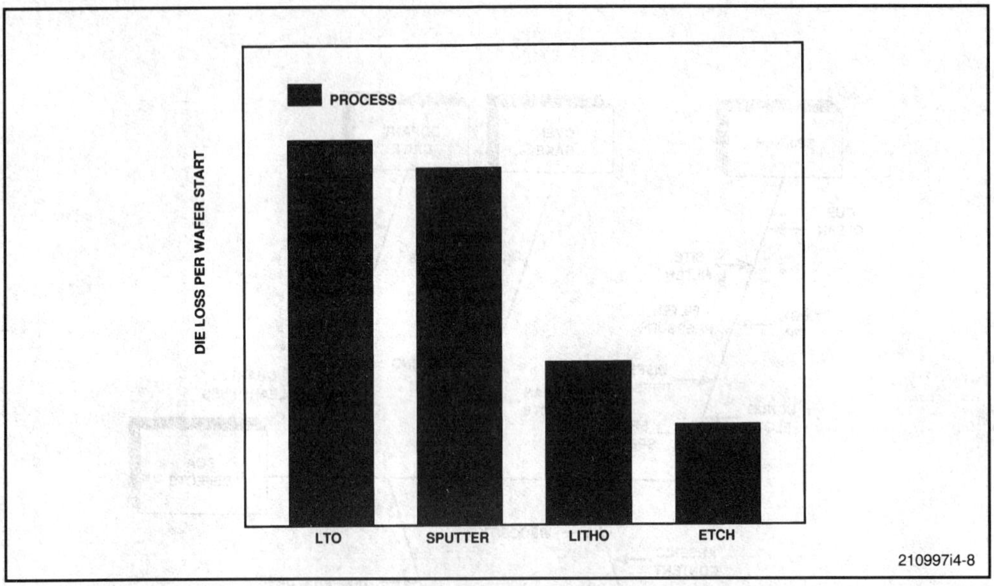

Figure 4-8. Metal Particles Pareto

improvements can be pursued and natural variations reduced. SPC is an essential part of Intel's ongoing effort to drive current DPM levels from 250 to zero.

Further details on our Statistical Process Control Support Systems are given in Chapter 5.

Manufacturing Process Monitors

Manufacturing monitors are used extensively to control various fabrication and assembly processes. Each process step has a number of monitored variables. For a bonding operation they might include machine controls (power, pressure, time, frequency, etc.) and finished product monitors (bond pulls, thermal cycling, etc.). For a photoresist development step, these variables might be equipment-related (develop volume, water pressure, spin speed, etc.) and inspections-related (amount of residual resist, levels of contamination, etc.). Anything that might affect the final product's general performance or factory flow is monitored.

Since processes, equipment and products are constantly changing, the monitoring program is also constantly changing. Our ongoing learning changes the way we monitor our fab and assembly processes. Sometimes a monitor is eliminated because it is no longer generating useful information, or it is replaced by a more effective monitor. Other times, monitors are added to address problems that existing monitors are missing.

The goal for all our manufacturing monitors is to operate under statistical process control (SPC). In Intel factories, SPC is more than just a method for plotting data; it is a feedback system designed to provide information to engineering and manufacturing on how processes are running so that problems can be identified and corrective action taken. When negative trends are spotted, corrective action is taken to get the process back in control. When positive trends are noted, the cause of the shift is examined to learn how it can be made a permanent part of the process and maintained under SPC. The SPC program is changing constantly as we learn which variables are most critical and as we develop corrective actions to process control excursions.

Reliability Monitors

A third set of process control monitors is reliability monitors. Some reliability monitors are a subset of manufacturing monitors and are referred to as process reliability monitors. They are executed in-line or at the end of the line in either wafer fabrication or assembly. The rest of the reliability monitors come from the reliability certification exercises. These include the fundamental wearout stresses, which are typically run on special test structures, and the environmental stresses, which are used to measure reliability performance on the finished product.

The establishment of manufacturing and in-line/end-of-line reliability monitors is part of the certification procedure. This means that a process or package is not certified at any of the four levels unless the critical manufacturing and reliability monitors are defined and in place.

Monitor frequency is high at the beginning of a fab or assembly process when volumes are low and customer impact is minimal. Information needs to be gathered at a rapid rate to correct problems early. As the fab or assembly process matures and a baseline of reliability and manufacturability data is compiled, monitor frequency and sample sizes are reduced.

This pattern parallels the continuous certification methodology learning curve. Early in the process the curve is the steepest, with performance changing rapidly as more is learned about the process. Because of this rapid change, we need a great deal of real-time data to determine our position on the curve. As the process matures and stabilizes, the learning curve flattens, indicating that change is taking place much more slowly. In this region, monitor frequency and sample size needs are reduced but not eliminated, since continuous quality improvement is in effect throughout the lifetime of all processes.

END-OF-LINE RELIABILITY MONITOR PROGRAM

Reliability is designed into each component Intel manufactures. From the time the design is put to paper, stringent reliability standards must be met at each step.

Designing in reliability is only the beginning. Ongoing tests are conducted to provide additional assurance that the processes continue to perform as designed.

Intel's Reliability Monitor Program is a proven tool designed to accomplish three primary objectives:

1. Ensure in-line control systems are effective
2. Provide customer data for assurance
3. Detect major reliability failure excursions

Over one half million units per year are tested through various stresses in the End of Line Reliability Monitor Program.

A standard set of reliability stresses are used to generate data to evaluate Intel's processes and packages. These tests are listed in Table 4-1. This table also shows the purpose and conditions of each test.

Table 4-1. Reliability Stresses

Stress	Purpose of Test	Typical Test Parameters	Sample Frequency/Stress Family
High Temperature Operating Life (HTOL)	Determine major changes in device and process infant mortality levels.	125°C @ maximum Vcc for 168 hours -Continuous Bias Applied	Monthly/Fab Process Family
Extended Life Test (ELT)	Determine device and process durability to electrical and thermal stresses for long periods of time.	125°C at maximum Vcc for 1000 hours -Continuous Bias Applied	Monthly/Fab Process Family
Steam	Test moisture resistance and integrity of plastic packages.	121°C @ 15 psi for 168 hours	Monthly/Fab Process Family Quarterly/Assembly Package Family
Temperature Humidity (85/85)	Evaluate moisture resistance of die in plastic packages under high temperature and high humidity.	85°C @ 85% R. H. for 1000 hours -Continuous Bias Applied	Quarterly/Fab Process Family Assembly Package Family
Temperature Cycling	Detect mechanical reliability problems and thin film leakage caused by temperature change.	Condition B - −55°C to 125°C air to air Condition C - −65°C to 150°C air to air per MIL-STD 883C, Method 1011	Quarterly/Fab Process Family Assembly Package Famiily
High Temperature Reverse Bias (HTRB)	Evaluate DC program or DC erase type failure mechanism, charge pulled onto the floating gate from the substrate or charge pulled off the floating gate to the select gate.	125°C @ 7.5 to 8.5V (array stress) for 168 hours	Quarterly/Fab Process Family (memory devices)
Bake	Assess electron charge retention in the floating gate of an EPROM cell and thermally activated process related fail mechanisms.	140°C for 1000 hours - Plastic 250°C for 500 hours - Ceramic	Quarterly/Fab Process Family (memory devices)

RELIABILITY MONITOR PROGRAM STRUCTURE

Fabrication Process Families

Intel's fabrication processes are grouped into families according to similarities in process and reliability characteristics and by fabrication facility. One or more products within these fabrication process families (FPF) are selected as monitor vehicles. These products are chosen using several criteria, such as high reliability stress sensitivity, ease of failure analysis and consistent production volume. This careful selection of FPF monitor products provides excellent fab process monitor coverage.

Assembly Package Families

Package types are grouped into families the same as FPFs. Package characteristics and assembly location are the primary considerations. Two major categories Plastic and Ceramic packages are identified. These categories are additionally divided by cavity type, frame type, lead type, die attach method, etc. to form the complete set of Assembly Package Families (APF). Each APF encompasses one or more lead counts.

All APF's are monitored once per quarter using a standard set of reliability tests. Each lead count within the APF is monitored at least yearly.

SAMPLE PLANS

Sampling plans have been designed to detect major failure excursions. A three level plan is used. Type I is reserved for process and package families that exhibit a high degree of stability and conformance to process reliability targets. The sample plan is designed so that very few failures are expected and response to failures is quick.

Monitor Type II is used with processes which meet all reliability goals but show a generally higher defect level than Type I processes. These processes are operating closer to the reliability targets and require increased sampling sensitivity. Some very low level of failures are generated by this plan. Reaction limits and response plans are defined to quickly identify valid process excursions.

Type III is used for production qualified products and processes which may require additional stress data to provide a reliability baseline with a good degree of confidence. It is a short term plan designed to assist in the evaluation of process control, capability and stability studies. Higher sample sizes or increased frequencies are used. A certain level of failures is expected in order to measure the defect rate being studied.

CONTROL LIMITS

Control limits and reaction plans are defined for each sampling level. Certain products also have individual control limits established. The reaction plans are designed to quickly validate the failure(s), identify the extent and effect on product field reliability, determine and fix the root cause of the failure.

Customer Assurance Data

Reliability data generated by the End of Line Reliability Program is available through various Intel reports and data summaries such as the EPROM Reliability Data Summary (RR-35G).

Manufacturing Change Control Boards

A fourth process control mechanism is the Manufacturing Change Control Board (MCCB). The MCCB's main function is to communicate factory changes to our customers and to provide feedback to the factory on customer concerns, issues or requests with the proposed changes. It also has the responsibility for approving the changes.

While the MCCB is the main change control body for Intel, there are other change control boards that are used to control change within smaller groups but whose output is still subject to MCCB approval. These include the Process Change Control Boards (PCCBs) which each manufacturing facility uses to control process and package changes and the Divisional Change Control Boards (DCCBs) which control design/testing changes. The entire system is defined in Chapter 5.

To show how such change control boards are used as a part of Intel's control system, the PCCB will be described. While the MCCB is primarily a vehicle for letting customers know about process changes and relaying their concerns back to the factory, the PCCB is designed to control changes within the manufacturing plant. All process changes have to go through the PCCB. The PCCB members include the managers from Process Engineering, Product Engineering (yields), Manufacturing and Reliability plus the plant manager and the site statistician.

Desired changes must be submitted to the PCCB with a certification plan. A document controlled specification provides the standard requirements for the documentation that is needed to submit a change for consideration before the certification effort begins. Depending on the nature of the change, the certification exercise could be minimal or quite extensive. Whether major or minor, all proposed changes must address all the sections contained in the PCCB change specification. This ensures a degree of consistency in all changes and ensures that the potential issues have been addressed. Once the PCCB approves of the change plan, the MCCB is notified of the proposed change so that it can provide information to and seek feed back from affected customers. Once the certification requirements are met and the PCCB approves of the change, the MCCB is notified of a successful certification and provides the documentation necessary to fulfill customer information needs.

At each PCCB, efforts are ongoing to improve the engineering work and thought that goes into process changes. As with most improvement programs, the PCCB involves continuous learning. It is resulting in better discipline in engineering decisions and a better understanding of how to control change.

Audits

The fifth process control mechanism at Intel is our auditing activity. There are three types of audit programs: self-audits, internal or corporate audits and customer/military audits. Audits help control the factory by identifying discrepancies through the use of specifications and identifying issues that might result in misprocessing. Intel's audit systems are discussed in detail in Chapter 5.

SUBCONTRACTING

Intel uses the services of subcontractors to perform some or all of the manufacturing process, including wafers, assembly or unit manufacture.

The use of subcontractors allows Intel to continue supporting customers' needs beyond the lifecycle of a product at Intel and/or improve availability by developing external manufacturing facilities. Both strategies allow Intel to focus its engineering and production talents on newer technologies and products.

The products manufactured by unit or wafer contractors include NMOS EPROM products, NMOS and CMOS microcontrollers, microprocessor products and peripherals. Assembly subcontracting includes many products for increased capacity and; in some cases, provides enhancements to Intel's package portfolio.

In selecting subcontractors Intel evaluates the potential supplier from both a business and a technical standpoint. Only suppliers who measure up to Intel's high standards are qualified to manufacture products bearing Intel's logo. The quality and support systems of each supplier, while not exactly like those at Intel, are expected to deliver the same high level of results that Intel's customers expect. To that end, Intel spends a great deal of energy to assure that our suppliers' internal systems and processes measure up to our standards. Examples of supplier systems inspected include: FA/CR, change control, dock-to-stock. In cases where these systems do not exist or need improvement, Intel brings the suppliers up to Intel standards.

We then perform product and process qualifications for each supplier that measures up to our screening. These qualifications are run jointly with the supplier supplying the data and Intel making the final judgement. All such transfers are cleared through Intel's change control board, since they represent changes in manufacturing sites. Intel is always in the decision loop on each qualification, assuring that the product manufactured by the subcontractor meets the same level of quality and reliability as one from an Intel factory.

Ongoing monitor and audit programs assure that the product quality and reliability do not degrade over time. Suppliers provide regular reports of manufacturing indicators and Intel reviews them to assure that continuous improvement is a way of life at the subcontractors. We hold regular meetings with each supplier to review results and goals and workout problems.

As a result of this program, Intel has been able to extend the life of many products, increase the availability of others and add packages to the Intel package portfolio and improving overall customer support without compromising product performance.

CONCLUSION

The quality and reliability group's involvement with manufacturing processes is a proactive one that continues throughout the life of the fab or assembly process. Every effort is made to ensure that new processes and packages make a smooth transition through the four levels of certification. The major emphasis is on a continuous certification methodology that maintains a proactive effort on reliability and manufacturability improvements. The certification exercises are designed to address the potential and real problems as early in the process as possible. By doing this, we maximize our likelihood for success and minimize any negative impact to our customers.

An equally important activity that Q&R is involved with is process control. There is a heavy emphasis on both reliability and manufacturing monitors that starts early in the certification process and is maintained throughout the life of the process. While the nature of many of the monitors is to create reactive responses to the data, the program itself is proactive. Furthermore, through continuous learning the monitors themselves are being modified to be more like leading indicators than lagging ones.

In general everyone involved in the certification of manufacturing changes is striving to make continuous improvement a way of life. Exceeding our customers' expectations is our ultimate goal.

Quality Support Systems 5

CHAPTER 5 **Page**
QUALITY SUPPORT SYSTEMS

CHAPTER 5
QUALITY SUPPORT SYSTEMS

INTRODUCTION

The systems discussed in this chapter are not exclusively aimed at either Intel manufacturing or our customers but rather are basic to the concept of a total quality system. They fill the gaps between our major quality and reliability programs in design and development, manufacturing and customer support and serve to link these major systems as an integrated whole. See Figure 5-1, for the Intel Quality System.

Intel support systems are divided into three categories: change management systems, quality management systems and process control management systems.

Change management systems assure that manufacturing changes are reviewed methodically and decisions made conscientiously about notifying customers. The actual notification process is discussed in Chapter 2.

Quality management systems include Intel's extensive auditing systems and its Material Review Board (MRB) activities.

Process control management systems include our statistical process control (SPC) activities, document control, calibration of measurement systems, traceability and data systems.

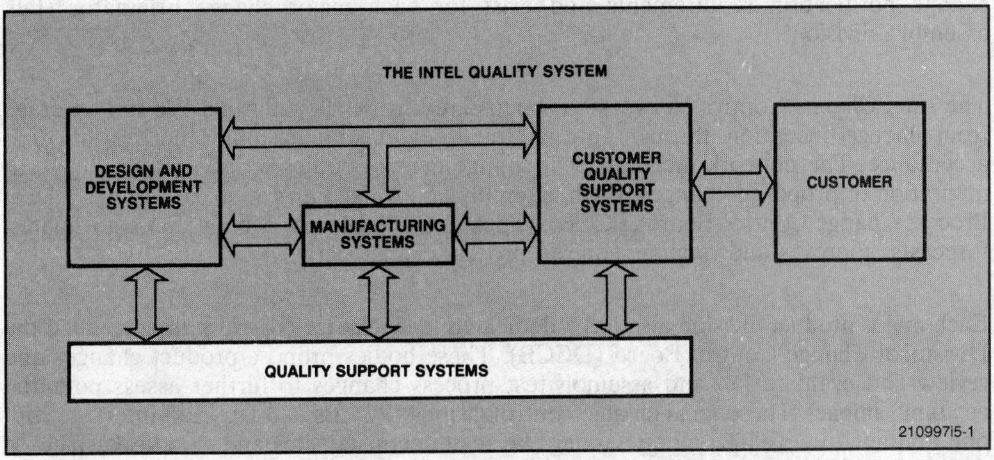

Figure 5-1. The Intel Quality System

CHANGE MANAGEMENT SYSTEMS

To address customer concerns and contractual obligations with regard to process and product change control, Intel has developed a Change Control System. Its purpose is to ensure that Intel customers are not adversely impacted by any Intel-generated process or product changes. This system is also responsible for ensuring that customers are given adequate notice and sufficient information to fully address any concerns caused by these changes.

Change Control Procedures

The Intel Change Control System is based on a set of change classification definitions. These definitions are guidelines to assess potential impacts on the customer base and to allow proper forecasting of customer response timing. The change classification definitions address three types of changes:

Class I. Major changes that require customer notification and could result in a customer qualification.

Class II. Major changes that require customer notification but for which we anticipate customers will accept Intel qualification data.

Class III. Minor changes with no customer impact, therefore requiring no customer notification.

The system has also defined change classification matrices as further guidelines to assist local bodies in properly applying the change definitions to each product or process change. These matrices have been constructed based on customer inputs regarding change notification requirements and exist for each major change originator (fab, assembly, division).

The Intel Change Control Network has been carefully developed to ensure full coverage from change inception through internal qualifications to customer notification and acceptance. The network includes local change control bodies which initiate the documentation of proposed changes. Each assembly and wafer fabrication facility has a local Process Change Control Board (PCCB), which is the local factory body that coordinates, forecasts, approves and reports required process change activity.

Each major product division also has a dedicated local change control function called the Divisional Change Control Board (DCCB). These bodies propose product changes and review and evaluate fab and assembly/test process changes to further assess potential customer impact. These local change control groups (PCCBs and DCCBs) interface with one another to develop synergy among the manufacturing sites and to address factory/division-specific change issues.

All these activities report into a centrally controlled Manufacturing Change Control Board (MCCB), which facilitates the internal (divisional and factory) and external (customer) notification of all process and product changes. The MCCB is ultimately responsible for ensuring that each of the network components has properly documented and communicated the change information fully and accurately. It reviews all change packages and makes the final judgement on change notification requirements.

Once the change package has cleared the internal Change Control Network, it is forwarded to the appropriate Intel marketing geography through a Geography Change Control board (GCCB). The GCCB is ultimately responsible for communicating the proposed product or process change to our customer base and seeking final customer approval. Once this approval is obtained (or specific issues worked further), the GCCB closes the notification loop by informing the MCCB which, in turn, gives the change originator permission to implement the change. (See Figure 5-2.)

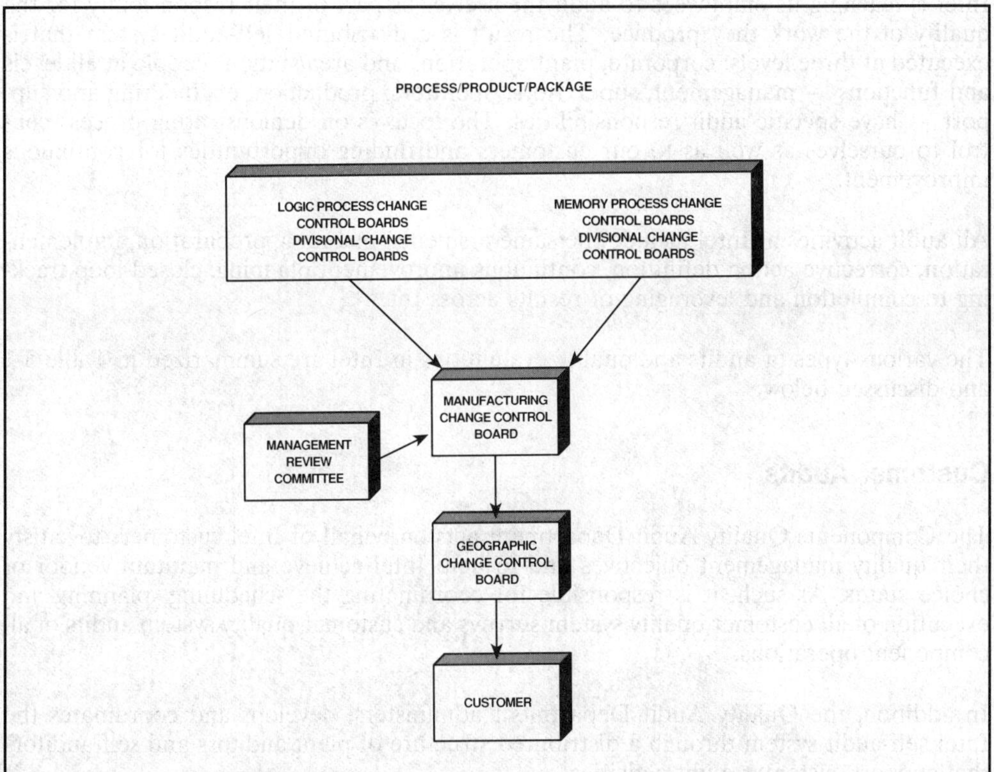

Figure 5-2. Change Control Information Flow Model

The Change Control MRC (Management Review Committee) consists of senior management representatives from Manufacturing, each major division Quality and Reliability and Sales and Marketing. The MRC serves as a guiding force for continuous improvement in the system and as an escalation path to top-level management.

QUALITY MANAGEMENT SYSTEMS

Intel's Quality Management Systems consist of an extensive auditing system and Material Review Board (MRB) activities.

Audits

The dictionary definition of audit is "... to examine with intent to verify." Intel's extensive audit system forms a key part of our quality improvement process. All Intel audits include quality evaluations conducted in the spirit of continuous improvement, as well as verifying compliance to specifications.

Intel is teaching its employees to audit themselves as part of their responsibility for the quality of the work they produce. The result is a distributed self-audit system that is executed at three levels: corporate, plant/operations and area/station. People at all levels and functions – management, supervisors, operators, production, engineering and support – have specific audit responsibilities. The focus is on demonstrating process control to ourselves as well as to our customers and finding opportunities for continuous improvement.

All audit activities at Intel include the same elements: planning, preparation, implementation, corrective action definition, continuous improvement planning, closed-loop tracking to completion and leveraging of results across Intel.

The various types of audits and quality evaluations in Intel are summarized in Table 5-1 and discussed below.

Customer Audits

The Components Quality Audit Department acts on behalf of Intel customers to satisfy their quality management objectives and to help Intel achieve and maintain vendor of choice status. As such, it is responsible for coordinating the scheduling, planning and execution of all customer quality system surveys and customer quality system audits of all component operations.

In addition, the Quality Audit Department administers, develops and coordinates the Intel self-audit system through a distributed structure of plant auditors and self auditors that support customer audit activities.

The customer support aspects of customer audit scheduling, customer technical visits and customer quality surveys are described in Chapter 2.

Table 5-1. Intel Audit Systems Functions

Type of Audit	Scope/Site	Frequency	Auditors
Customer Vendor Of Choice Audits	Quality Systems Audits of Intel Operations	By Customer and Plant Agreement	Customer Quality Auditors
Plant/Operation Level Self Audits	All Wafer Fab, Assembly and Test Manufacturing and Support Operations	Once per Quarter	Self Audit Area Teams. Plant Auditors and Management
Corporate Q&R Operations Audits	All Wafer Fab, Assembly, and Test Manufacturing and Support Operations	Once per Year	Intel Components Auditor
Corporate Contracting Audits	All Intel Wafer and Unit Contracting Operations	Once per Year	Intel Components Auditor
Corporate Military Audits	All Military/B/JAN/ Wafer Fab, Assembly, Test and Contracting Operations	Once per Year	Intel Military/ Components Auditor
Customer Military Audits	Military Test/Assembly Operations by Product	Per Contract Agreement	Customer Military Auditors
CSC/JAN Product Audits	All Intel JAN Wafer Fab, Assembly and Test Operations	Per Contract Agreement	DESC Auditors
Internal Customer/ Supplier Audits	Customer/Supplier Relationships and Processes Internal to Intel	Senior Management Initiated	Senior Manager Customer/Supplier Partners
Mr. Clean Environment Audits	All Intel Facilities	Typically Once per Quarter	Operations and Facilities Managers
Intel Supplier Continuous Quality Improvement Audits	All Direct Material Suppliers	From Six Months to Two Years by Performance	Intel Commodity and Quality Engineering Specialists
Process Certification Audits	Quality Systems/ Manufacturing Operations	As Needed to Certify Processes	Customer Auditor
MIL and Commercial Distributor Audits	Quality Systems and Facilities	Once Per Year	Third Party

5

Self-Audit System

Intel's distributed self-audit system revolves around a strong self-audit concept owned by the individual manufacturing plants and operations. The plant/operation is divided into self-audit areas by process or station. A self-audit team, comprised of various functional content experts, audits each self-audit area on a quarterly basis.

A plant auditor/coordinator administers the self-audit system in each operation, trains the self auditors, consolidates corrective action plans, issues quarterly reports to the Corporate Component Quality Audit Department and tracks corrective actions and continuous improvement line items to completion. These plant auditors are trained and guided by the corporate component auditors and the site Q&R organization. They coordinate and host all customer quality system audits in their operation.

Factory working teams of plant, operations and auditors meet regularly to share information and methods for leveraging audit results across Intel.

Intel's self-audit system has led to an increased level of integrity and openness about problem reporting without fear of management punitive action. Teamwork and continuous process improvement are our goals.

Component Operations, Military and Contracting Q&R Audits

The Corporate Component Q&R Quality Audit Department, along with the Military Q&R and Components Contracting Q&R organizations, administers the Intel corporate Q&R audits. These are required at least once a year in every Intel component manufacturing location and operations, including component contractors.

The corporate component Q&R audits are detailed quality system and customer and military requirement audits performed by the corporate components/military auditors. In addition, they perform a quality evaluation of the local self-audit system and its performance, examine specific items from an Intel continuous quality improvement viewpoint and gather and share information for leveraging improvements across Intel.

As part of the operations audits, all Intel military manufacturing operations are audited for compliance with both customer and governmental military requirements. The Components auditors act as the government auditors from the Defense Electronic Supply Center (DESC) would in verifying that all program requirements are met. Several Intel plants have been certified to produce military/B-grade product or have been certified by DESC to produce JAN (Joint Army Navy) product under the rigid government audit standard MIL-M-38510/XXX. The Intel auditors work closely with the local Defense Contract Administration Services (DCAS) representatives and military customers to verify that Intel meets or exceeds all federal and customer requirements for military products.

Management Quality Audits

Management quality audits are a key part of the Intel audit system. They provide management leadership and demonstrate commitment to the continuous quality improvement process. There are three types of management audits at Intel: management self-audits, internal customer/supplier partnership quality audits and Mr. Clean audits.

MANAGEMENT SELF-AUDITS

As part of each operation's self-audit system, the most senior management staff in each plant conducts management self-audits of their own organization. These audits typically occur quarterly and provide leadership, communication, direction and leverage to the self-audit system in each operation.

INTERNAL CUSTOMER/SUPPLIER PARTNERSHIP QUALITY AUDITS

These audits constitute a practical way for senior management to evaluate the quality of service between internal Intel organizations. Pairs of senior managers having a customer/supplier relationship within Intel, initiate a joint quality evaluation of their shop floor processes to enhance their relationship. These audits serve to identify continuous improvement opportunities and demonstrate management leadership and commitment for making the customer/supplier partnership concept part of our quality culture.

MR. CLEAN AUDITS

From Intel's inception, a clean and disciplined work environment has been an important part of our culture. Senior managers share the role of Mr. Clean, a site-level inspector who, accompanied by facilities and building managers, regularly evaluates every Intel building for cleanliness, neatness, safety and repair status. Conditions in every area of every building are evaluated according to a common standard. A report is issued quantifying variances and assigning corrective actions. The objective is to ensure a safe, pleasant, trouble-free environment that is conducive to producing superior quality work and defect-free products.

Supplier Quality Audits

Intel depends heavily on its suppliers and expects them to have continuous quality improvement processes of their own, stressing commitment, teamwork and attention to detail. Supplier Quality Audits are conducted with all direct material suppliers, with the objective of assessing the suppliers' quality systems, process control capability and product quality.

More complex supplier quality survey audits are conducted as part of Intel's Supplier Continuous Quality Improvement (SCQI) program described in Chapter 4. SCQI is a comprehensive partnership with key suppliers that includes a total commitment to continuous quality improvement, quality planning, statistical process control, production performance, quality data, product quality, delivery, costs and supplier quality assessment.

Supplier quality audits focus on guaranteed integrity of all materials supplied to Intel.

Conclusion

The comprehensive Intel Audit System provides continuous measurement of total quality and continuous improvement in all aspects of the manufacturing process. Intel's distributed self-audit system is unique in the industry. The systematic, disciplined methodology continually improves Intel's ability to design, manufacture, supply and support the highest quality products. Positive audit results demonstrate Intel employees' commitment to continuously improve our process control and product quality.

Material Review Board

Intel's Material Review Board (MRB) is an internal quality control function, convened to make consensus decisions on misprocessed material/product and discrepant raw materials. Its purpose is to prevent or eliminate the impact of all non-conforming material on Intel's customers.

MRB membership varies by function, product and problem situation, with representation required from manufacturing, engineering, planning and Q&R. Responsibilities include problem definition, containment, issue resolution, material disposition and short-term corrective action.

The MRB process begins by addressing (in parallel) problem definition, quarantining all affected material and initial containment actions required such as a product-hold notice to appropriate locations worldwide. The next step is a containment plan that documents the actions and ownership required to resolve the material disposition issues and any short-term corrective actions. The MRB tracks these actions to successful conclusion and appropriate material disposition (e.g., special screening or scrap and replace).

A final MRB report is written and distributed for follow-up. All actions must be completed or transferred to a permanent organization/owner. Long-term follow-up actions may be required, such as root cause analysis and a permanent fix. These reports form a permanent reference for future excursion management and problem resolution.

The MRB reports and results are utilized to define and drive continuous improvements in several ways. They are followed up on in quarterly factory self-audits and annual corporate audits. They are reviewed regularly for trends that point to fundamental improvements required and factored into Intel's continuous improvement plans for excursion prevention.

PROCESS CONTROL MANAGEMENT SYSTEMS

Statistical Process Control Support System

The Intel Quality Technology department provides formal support for SPC Education, Training and Tool Development for all organizations. A partial listing of the SPC Training Curriculum and SPC Tools supported is shown in Table 5-2. A wide range of topics for Quality and Process Improvement are supported, including problem-solving, team effectiveness, customer focus, process control/management and analytical tools as well as statistical tools.

Document Control

Intel has an extensive documentation system for document control and engineering change control to incorporate external and internal customer requirements on quality assurance, assessment and improvement into our operations. The document control system at Intel deals with the specifications that represent the cumulative technical know-how of design, development and manufacturing activities.

Like the geographically dispersed organizations that it supports, the Document Control Centers (DCs) are located at all Intel facilities. Components Document Control (CDC) provides guidelines for the approximately 30 satellite document control centers on minimum requirements for controlling and handling Intel documents. Each local DC then augments those with additional requirements specific to their respective organizational and customer needs. CDC acts as a centralized focal point for developing, implementing, standardizing and controlling Intel specifications worldwide. (See Figure 5-3.)

Table 5-2. SPC Training Curriculum Examples

Courses	Length
Basic Statistics	24 Hours
Using Control Charts	8 Hours
Designing and Implementing Process Control Systems	24 Hours
Managing Process Control Systems	4 Hours
Design of Experiments I/II	60 Hours
Basic Improvement Tools	16 Hours
Measurement Capability Studies	16 Hours

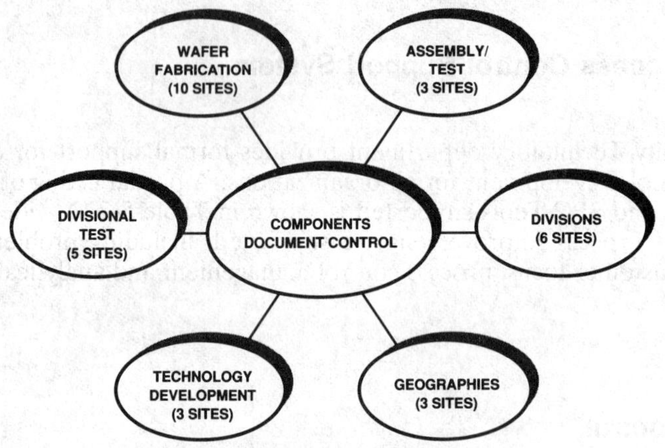

Figure 5-3. Components Document Control Organizational Structure

DOCUMENT CATEGORIES

Intel uses three major documentation systems:

1. Document Control for engineering specifications (process/product/procedure)
2. Customer Specification Review and Special Specs (S-Specs)
3. Intel Policies and Procedures (IPPs)

Engineering Specifications contain the knowledge about products and processes and represent engineering know-how. These documents are further divided into requirements documents, which are common to all sites and procedural documents, which are generally site-specific. It is the responsibility of the document originators to assure that the specified procedures meet the requirements and that the specification does not overlap or leave gaps. Document Controls' responsibilities include indexing, distributing, archiving, maintenance, reviewing and change management of these documents.

Special Specifications (S-Specs) are used to incorporate special customer requirements into products and/or services. Customer Specification Review interprets special customer spec requirements, generally test and finish operations, which are the result of negotiations between Intel and its customers. S-Specs guarantee that customer requirements are documented and always take precedence over the standard Intel specs.

S-Specs also define products that do not meet all of the data sheet parameters or limits. This situation often occurs with new products where the design is not yet fully functional but is sufficiently functional to allow the customers to begin development and prototyping work. They are generally limited to situations where the need for the product outweighs the need for meeting all of the specified limits. These S-Specs are cancelled as soon as a full spec product is available.

Intel Policies and Procedures System (IPPs) deals with purely administrative specifications; there are no technical documents within the IPPs. IPP administrative documents cover such areas as purchasing (not detailed part specs), finance and human resources. IPPs are managed by a corporate organization.

Another document control activity at Intel is the technical libraries at all domestic sites. These libraries provide a broad variety of technical publications and are a resource for all employees. Library materials include technical and managerial books, periodicals, published papers and reports, conference proceedings, etc. All are computer-indexed for easy access. The libraries also index and archive internal technical reports and memos.

Equipment Calibration

Calibration is the process of comparing test and measurement instruments of unknown status to well-defined standards of known accuracy to detect, eliminate by adjustment and report any variations in accuracy or capability. Calibration provides two major benefits: it allows confident use of instruments by minimizing the associated uncertainties; and it fulfills requirements for traceability to recognized national standards.

The primary function of Intel's calibration program is to ensure measured integrity of any instrument that provides quantitative or quality data concerning Intel products. The program includes all disciplines involving measurement mechanical, electrical, electronics and physical measurements. The policies of this program are designed to meet the requirements of MIL-STD-45662A and those of major customers. Accuracy and repeatability of measurements is assured by maintaining traceability to national standards, naturally occurring physical phenomena, ratio types of calibrations, or to industry consensus standards where no recognized national standard exists.

Calibration of test or inspection equipment directly affects outgoing product quality. The calibration system must provide for the prevention of inaccuracies by ready detection of deficiencies and timely positive action for correction. Through the periodic calibration of test equipment, drift or failure patterns can be recognized and corrected before the unit can introduce inaccuracies into product design, fabrication, assembly or final testing prior to shipping.

A network of primary and secondary laboratories (located at all major Intel sites around the world) provides the calibration service to maintain cost-effective and accurate measurements. Quality Assurance ensures that all inspection and test equipment used in the manufacturing and acceptance of product is under calibration control at all times.

5

This network maintains or has access to primary and secondary standards for measuring voltage, current, resistance, frequency, mass, light intensity and dimensional parameters. Each site tracks calibrated equipment, schedules calibration and maintains equipment histories. Each equipment user has the responsibility of ensuring that his equipment is calibrated. Conformance to calibration schedules and recall systems are each department's responsibility.

Proper use of the calibration service ensures that all measuring and test equipment meets specified tolerance. Drift, inaccuracies and out-of-tolerances found in equipment are compensated for or corrected. Written notification is required if a significant out-of-tolerance condition is found. Reports of calibration results are available at the certifying facility.

CALIBRATION TRACEABILITY

An unbroken chain of traceability links all inspection and test instruments through Intel standards laboratories to the National Institute of Standards and Technology (NIST) (formerly National Bureau of Standards), acceptable international standards or natural physical constants. (See Figure 5-4.)

Components test systems used to measure conformance of product or process to Intel specifications have a documented history of certification, tracing measured accuracies through a hierarchy of support equipment and standards.

For example, voltage comparator measurements made in device test systems are calibrated by the systems calibration group using a voltmeter. The voltmeter is calibrated by the Standards Lab using secondary voltage standards. The secondary voltage standard is calibrated with standard cells, which are traceable to the National Institute of Standards and Technology (NIST). Frequency and time intervals are derived from comparing the phase of an Intel standard frequency (10 MHz) to the phase of a signal broadcast from NIST, resulting in an accuracy of a few parts in a hundred billion. This standard frequency is then compared to the time base in frequency and time interval counters. Some measurement parameters, such as gauge blocks, are checked against vendor standards that are traceable to NIST.

A few measurement parameters are referred to as physically reproducible phenomena. For example, a triple-point cell is used as the reference point for temperature measurements. This standard triple point (the temperature at which water is in equilibrium as a liquid, gas and solid), is agreed to be within 0.01°C of the freezing point of water.

Reference to ratio types of calibrations involves the comparison of relative values of two or more devices without regard to their absolute values. For example, a typical application could include the use of voltage dividers whose ratios may be established without knowing the ohmic value of the resistors.

Where no recognized national standard is available, consensus standards are used. This can be an artifact or process that is used as a de facto standard by agreement of the contractor.

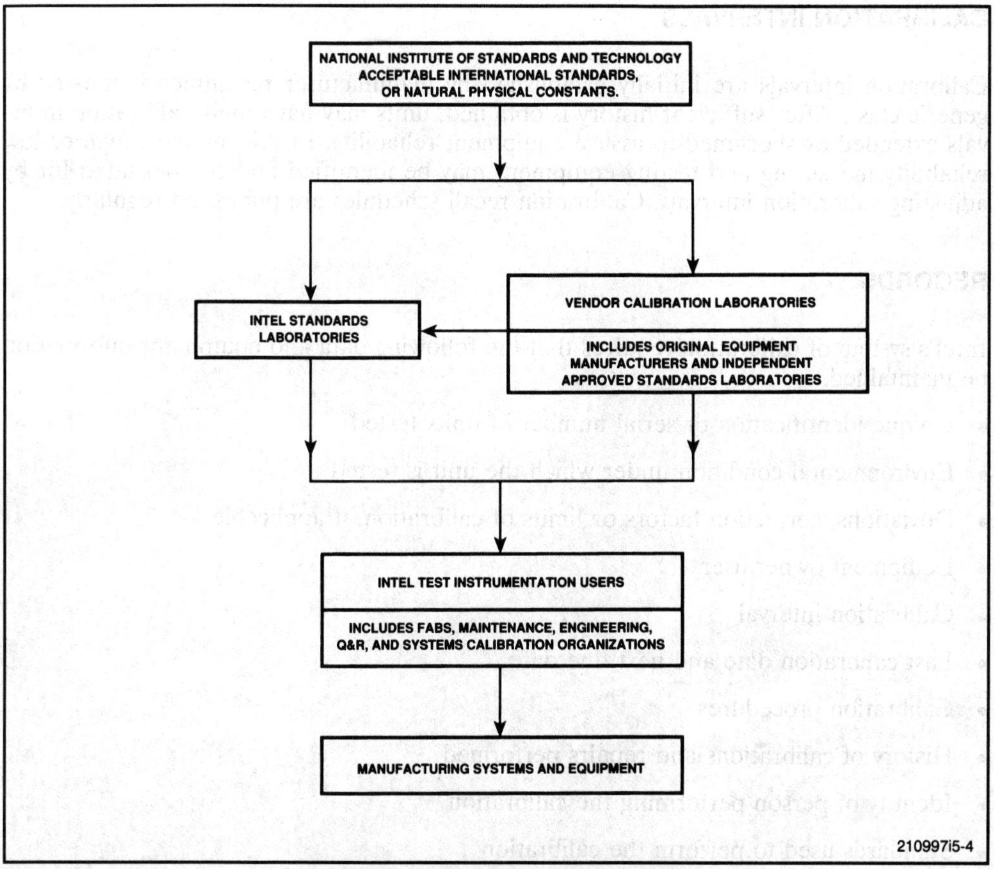

Figure 5-4. Intel's Traceability Chain

Table 5-3. Calibration Parameters

DC Voltage	Capacitance	Length
AC Voltage	Frequency	Mass
Current	Radiation	Pressure
Resistance	Temperature	Vacuum
Inductance	Light Intensity	Flow

CALIBRATION CAPABILITY

Measurement requirements for Intel calibration facilities are tailored to meet the specifications of each site. Due to different testing requirements, each calibration facility has a range of secondary standards designed to meet the equipment owner's needs. To maintain cost effectiveness some calibrations are done off-site at another Intel location or vendor calibration laboratory. Calibration for the following parameters can be obtained by all site calibration facilities, as shown in Table 5-3.

CALIBRATION INTERVALS

Calibration intervals are initially established by manufacturer recommendations or by generic class. After sufficient history is obtained, units may have their calibration intervals extended or shortened to assure equipment reliability. In this manner, high or low reliability measuring and testing equipment may be identified and compensated for by adjusting calibration intervals. Calibration recall schedules are published regularly.

RECORDS

Intel's system of calibration requires that the following data and equipment information be maintained.

- Unique identification or serial number of units tested
- Environmental condition under which the unit is tested
- Deviations, correction factors or limits of calibration, if applicable
- Equipment owner/user
- Calibration interval
- Last calibration date and next due date
- Calibration procedures
- History of calibrations and repairs performed
- Identity of person performing the calibration
- Standards used to perform the calibration

CALIBRATION LABELING

Labeling serves several functions in Intel's calibration system. It identifies unique tracking systems, present calibration status, the individual support group and it serves as a visible indicator of unit serviceability. Some labels are valid only when sealed by a qualified calibration technician or supervisor with the appropriate site calibration stamp.

CALIBRATION STANDARDS

Uniform application of the calibration system at all Intel sites is a necessary part of the support effort. A rigid system of standards and procedures helps assure that a product will not have a "personality" based on its site of manufacture. The standards laboratories, located at major sites, report to the Director of Quality and Reliability through two channels: the site organizational structure and, more directly, the Intel Standards Labs Committee. The committee recommends the policies and practices to which all sites adhere. Compliance to requirements is monitored by the various Intel audit authorities. Figure 5-5 depicts the Intel Standards Labs.

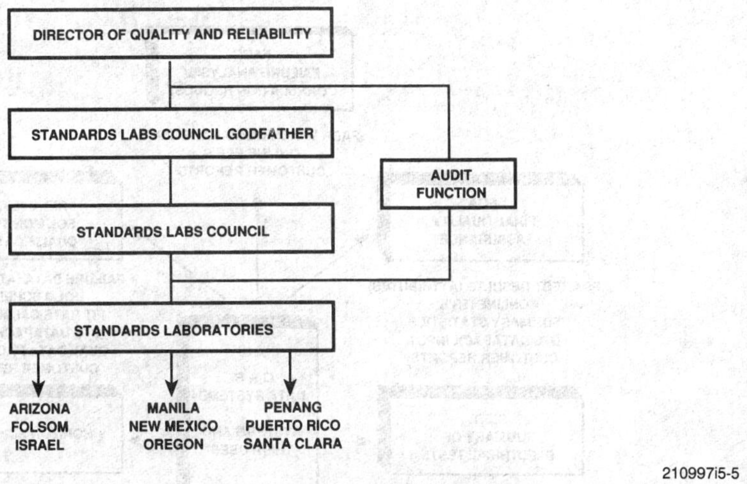

Figure 5-5. Intel Standards Labs

The Intel corporate calibration system supports all measurement and test equipment with calibrations, repairs and certifications. All calibrations are performed using MIL-STD-45662A as a guideline. By using the services of this system, drift or failure patterns can be recognized and corrected before inaccuracies affect products. If a parameter is important enough to measure, it must be accurately measured and documented.

DATA SYSTEMS

There are three major components to the data systems that support Q&R activities. All are maintained in an integrated mainframe computing environment with local access from all sites for data entry, statistical analysis and report generation. Figure 5-6 shows Q&R data systems and their uses.

Final Quality Assurance Database

The Final Quality Assurance Database (FQADB) includes reports from each final QA inspection performed. Each lot is tracked through the FQA area and logged into the database by lot number, product, inspection and many other variables (e.g., test temperatures, test tape revision) for control and reporting. Problem lots can be traced back into manufacturing using this database. Engineering evaluations for out-of-control lots are also archived on computer and linked to the FQA data by lot number. The FQADB system is used for direct customer support and as input to all regular Dock-to-Stock updates. Reports are also generated for management review and control at each test location, each Customer Support Center and at the business operation and corporate levels.

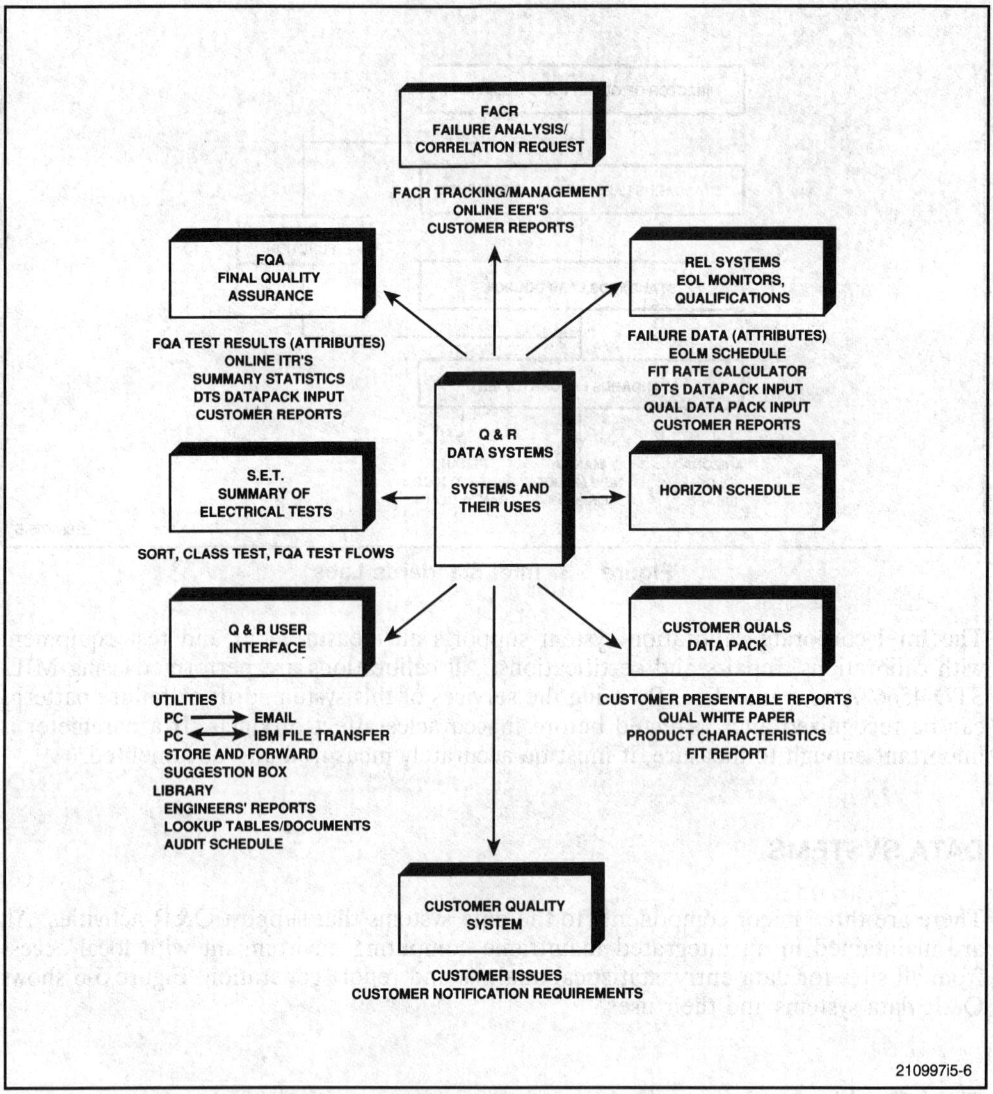

Figure 5-6. Q&R Data Systems

Reliability Engineering Database

The Reliability Engineering Database (REDB) contains all product monitor data and all process, package and product certification data. Units are pulled directly from production lines and subjected to accelerated stress testing. The results of intermediate and end-of-line readouts are entered into the REDB. Reports from this system represent an ongoing measure of the reliability of processes and plants. The information is available in summary form to Intel customers as part of the regular Dock-to-Stock updates. The monitor program is discussed in more detail in Chapter 4.

Failure Analysis/Correlation Request Database

This database allows Intel to track the customer failure analysis/correlation request (FA/CR) through the complex matrix of Intel locations to assure that the problem is properly addressed. This system is also used to report important customer service activities to Intel management and to identify product, process, or package trends.

These data systems provide Intel with the rapid feedback so vital in component manufacturing. They also provide important information to our customers, forming the basis of our Dock-to-Stock program.

Process Technology 6

CHAPTER 6 **Page**
PROCESS TECHNOLOGY

CHAPTER 6
PROCESS TECHNOLOGY

INTRODUCTION

Intel manufactures state-of-the-art semiconductor memory, microcomputer and microprocessor devices using scaled high-density n-channel MOS and CMOS VLSI technologies (HMOS and CHMOS respectively). These products are manufactured in several worldwide locations, as shown in Table 6-1. A limited number of process technologies are used for all device types, resulting in manufacturing efficiency and significant experience with a particular process in different device applications. This strategy accelerates Intel's progress on the learning curve and results in processes and products which are thoroughly characterized, inherently more reliable and of high quality.

Within each production area, processes meet a common set of key specifications and parameters, assuring product quality, reliability and uniformity, independent of the originating plant. As manufacturing changes are introduced to improve yields, quality or manufacturability, qualification procedures specific to the change are performed.

PROCESS TECHNOLOGY FAMILIES

There are two leading-edge VLSI MOS technology categories for specific device types in production at Intel: microcomputer (single poly) and EPROM (double poly). Figure 6-1a and 6-1b shows representative device cross sections typical of current production processes.

The most advanced microcomputer and EPROM technologies provide the obvious paths and significant learning curve experience for supporting the manufacture of state-of-the-art complex VLSI microprocessor and microcomputer devices. Each technology type is individually moving down the scaling path into higher yields, improved performance and better quality products at lower cost. SEM micrographs of transistor cross sections in

Table 6-1. Intel Wafer Fabrication Manufacturing Plants

Fab No.	Location
1	Santa Clara, CA
3	Livermore, CA
4	Aloha, OR
6	Chandler, AZ
7,9	Albuquerque, NM
8	Jerusalem, Israel

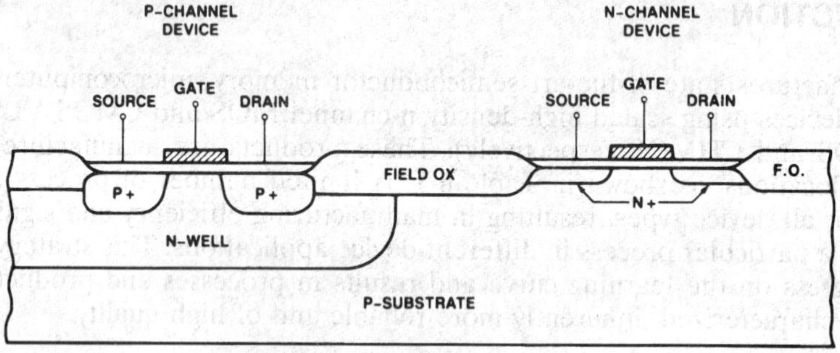

Figure 6-1a. CMOS Process Cross Sections

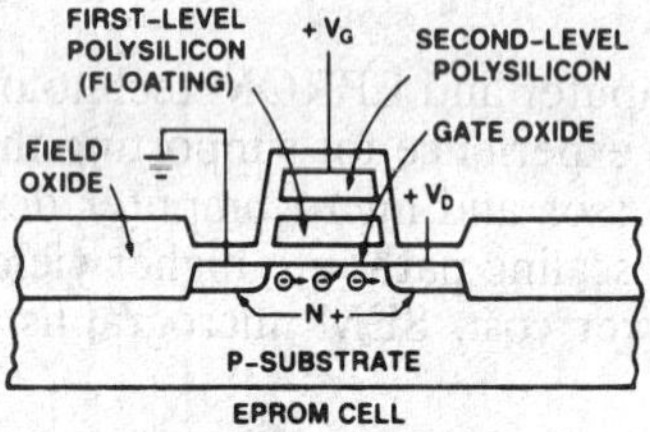

Figure 6-1b. EPROM Memory Cell Cross Sections

Figure 6-2 illustrate the magnitude of the scaling which has occurred in moving from HMOS I to CHMOS V technologies. Table 6-2 summarizes process technology evolution.

Microcomputer and EPROM technology evolution has occurred in this timeframe and scale. This has been accomplished by shrinking the feature size and introducing major process and device innovations into high-volume production. See Table 6-3 for a list of major device innovations.

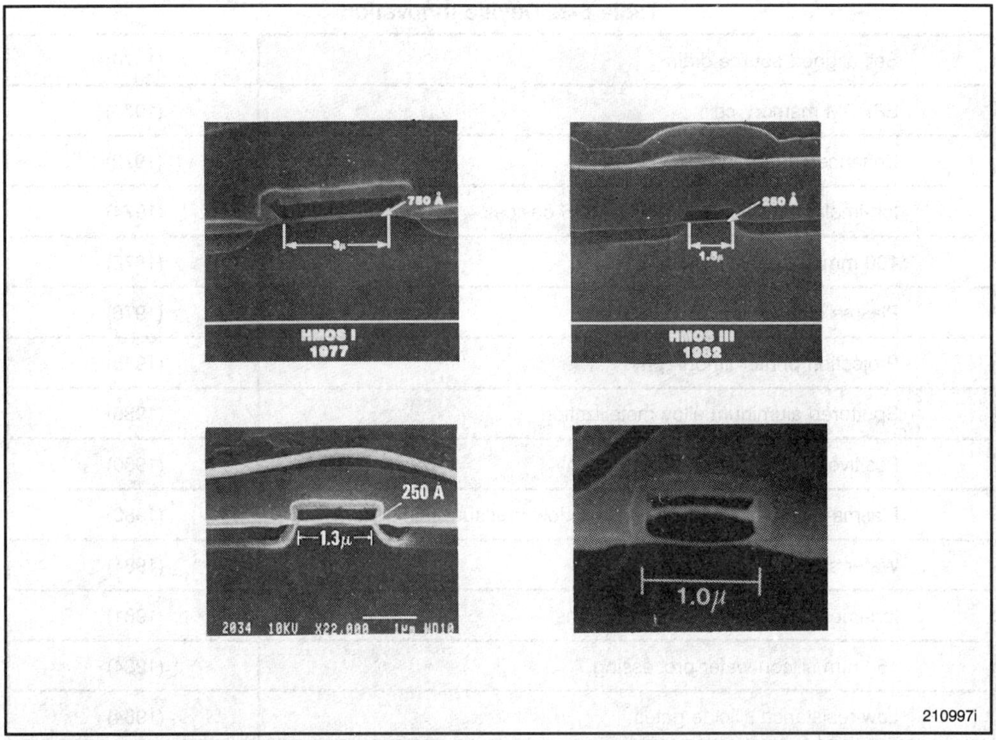

Figure 6-2. Typical Transistor Size, as Seen in Cross Section, HMOS I, HMOS III and CHMOS

Table 6-2. Process Technology Evolution

Technology Parameters	NMOS 1974	HMOS I 1977	HMOS II 1979	HMOS III 1982	CHMOS III 1985	CHMOS IV 1987	CHMOS V 1990
Layout density (gates/mm^2)	70	200	450	700	660	1650	4125
Area shrink factor	1	0.64	0.41	0.26	0.27	0.1	0.04
Speed power product (PJ)	4	1	0.6	0.25	0.04	0.03	0.02
Gate delay (ns)	3	1	0.5	0.2	0.2	0.14	0.1
Channel length (μ)	4	2.5	1.6	1.1	1.1	0.9	0.6
Gate oxide thickness (Å)	1000	700	400	250	250	200	150
Design rules (μ)	6	3.5	2.0	1.5	1.5	1	0.75

Table 6-3. Device Innovation

Self-aligned source-drain	(1970)
EPROM memory cell	(1971)
Enhancement mode n-MOS	(1972)
Ion-implanted depletion load n-MOS devices	(1974)
100 mm silicon wafer processing	(1976)
Plasma etch for thin film definition	(1976)
Projection printer lithography	(1975)
Sputtered aluminum alloy metallization	(1980)
Positive photoresist photolithography	(1980)
Plasma-deposited low temperature, low pressure thin films	(1980)
Wafer stepper lithography	(1981)
Ion-implanted source-drain diffusions	(1981)
150 mm silicon wafer processing	(1984)
Low-resistance silicide gates	(1984)
Dual layer metal CHMOS w/silicide gates	(1985)
Flash memory cell	(1988)
Silicide source drain	(1990)
Triple layer metal	(1990)
Contact plugs	(1990)

PROCESS FLOW

Individual fab runs are identified via a run card and each wafer within the run by a laser scribe in the wafer's flat area. Special identifiers are used for engineering priority lots to separate them from normal production. The flow for each process is documented by a master process flow spec that references individual module and inspection specifications.

Figure 6-3 shows a simplified flow for a typical single poly (single layer polysilicon conductor), single metal (single layer metal interconnect) CHMOS process. The following steps outline the single poly, single metal, CHMOS flow in more detail and discuss key on-line process control techniques.

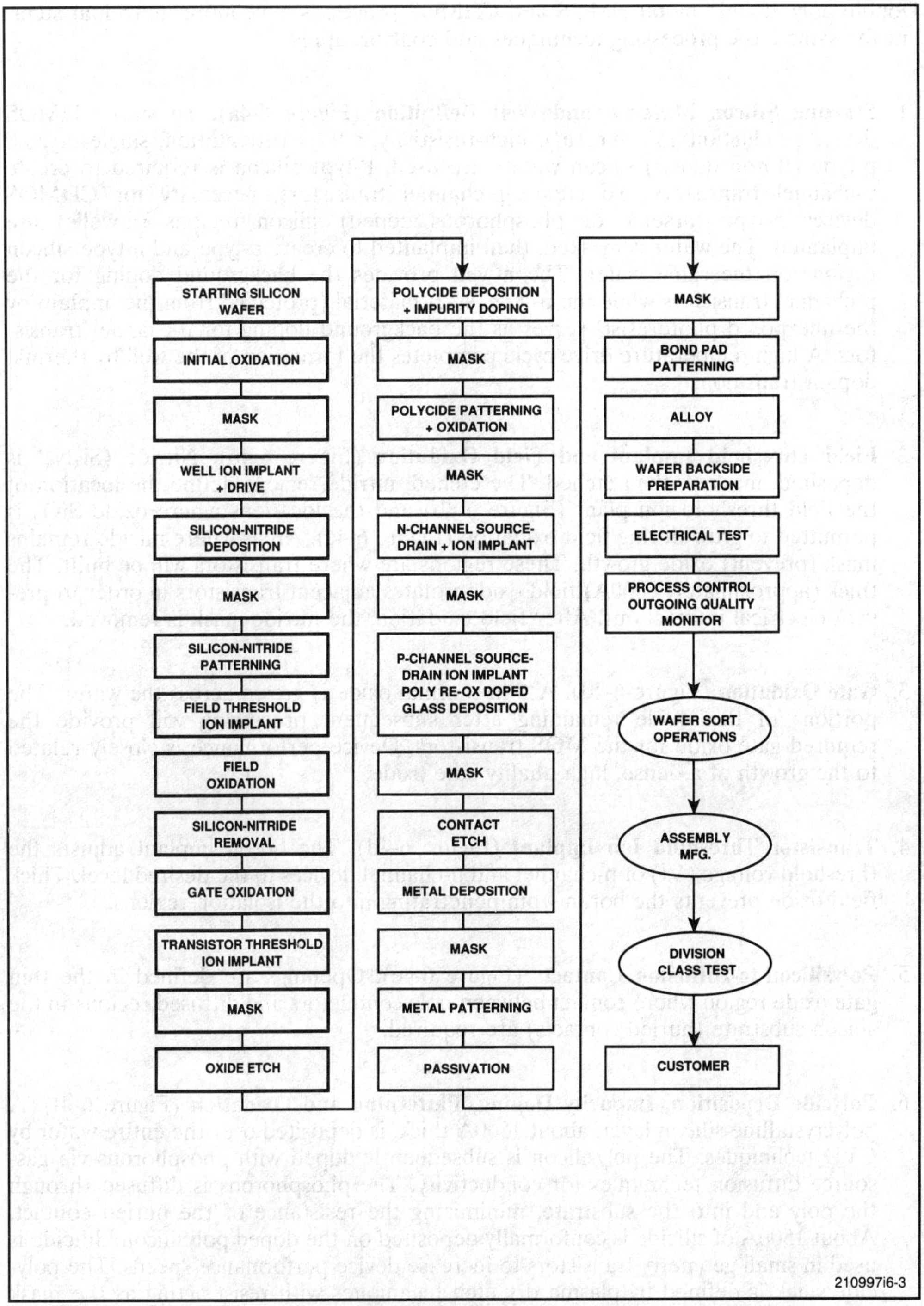

Figure 6-3. Schematic of Idealized Single Poly, Single Metal, CHMOS Process Flow

Double poly, double metal NMOS and CHMOS processes have more individual steps, but the same basic processing techniques and controls apply.

1. **Starting Silicon Material and Well Definition** (Figure 6-4a). To start CHMOS device production 150 mm (6″), high-resistivity, < 100 > orientation, single crystal, p-type (Boron doped) silicon waters are used. P-type silicon is required to create n-channel transistors. To create p-channel transistors, necessary for CHMOS devices n-type (arsenic or phosphorous doped) silicon regions (n-wells) are implanted. The wafer is masked, then implanted to create p-type and n-type silicon regions on the same wafer. The n-well provides the background doping for the p-channel transistors while the p-type, start material (protected from the implant by the unexposed photoresist) serves as the background doping for n-channel transistors. A high temperature drive cycle completes the formation of the well by thermal dopant transition.

2. **Field Threshold Implant and Field Oxidation** (Figure 6-4b). Nitride (Si_3N_4) is deposited, masked, then etched. The etched, nitride regions define the location of the field threshold ion plant (Figure 6-4b) and the locations where oxide SiO_2 is permitted to grow during field oxidation (Figure 6-4c). Areas where nitride remains mask (prevent) oxide growth. These regions are where transistors will be built. The thick (approximately 6000Å) field oxide isolates adjacent transistors in order to prevent electrical interactions. After field oxidation, the nitride mask is removed.

3. **Gate Oxidation** (Figure 6-4d). A thin thermal oxide is grown across the wafer. The portions of this oxide remaining after subsequent processing will provide the required gate oxide for the MOS transistors. Device performance is closely related to the growth of a dense, high quality gate oxide.

4. **Transistor Threshold Ion Implant** (Figure 6-4d). The boron implant adjusts the threshold voltage (Vt) of p-channel and n-channel devices to the desired level. Thick field oxide prevents the boron from penetrating into the isolation regions.

5. **Polysilicon-to-Diffusion Contacts** (Figure 6-4e). Openings are defined in the thin gate oxide region where contact between poly conductors and diffused regions in the silicon substrate (buried contacts) are required.

6. **Polycide Deposition, Impurity Doping, Patterning and Oxidation** (Figure 6-4f). A polycrystalline silicon layer, about 1500Å thick, is deposited over the entire wafer by CVD techniques. The polysilicon is subsequently doped with phosphorous via gas-source diffusion techniques for conductivity. The phosphorous is diffused through the poly and into the substrate, minimizing the resistance of the buried contact. About 1500Å of silicide is conformally deposited on the doped polysilicon. Silicide is used in small geometry transistors to increase device performance speeds. The polycide stack is defined by plasma dry etch techniques with resist acting as the mask (Figure 6-4g). The polycide stack is oxidized to protect the transistor gates.

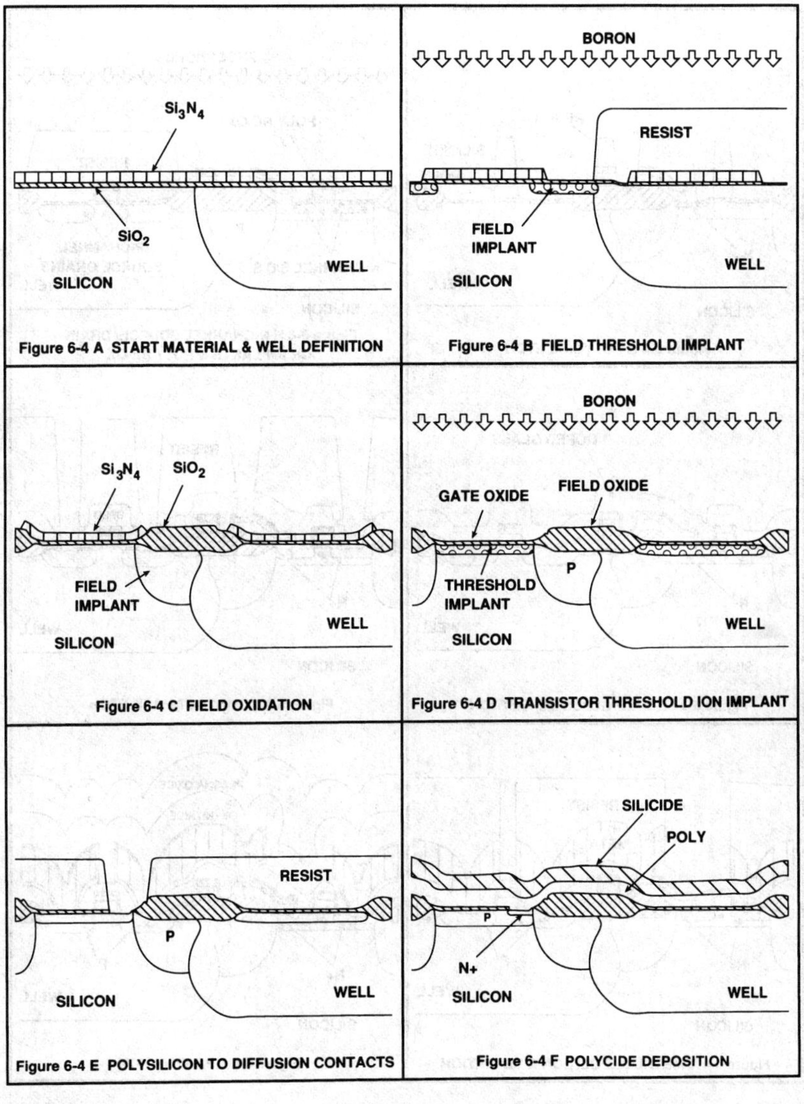

Figure 6-4a-f. Single Poly, Single Metal CHMOS Cross Sections

6

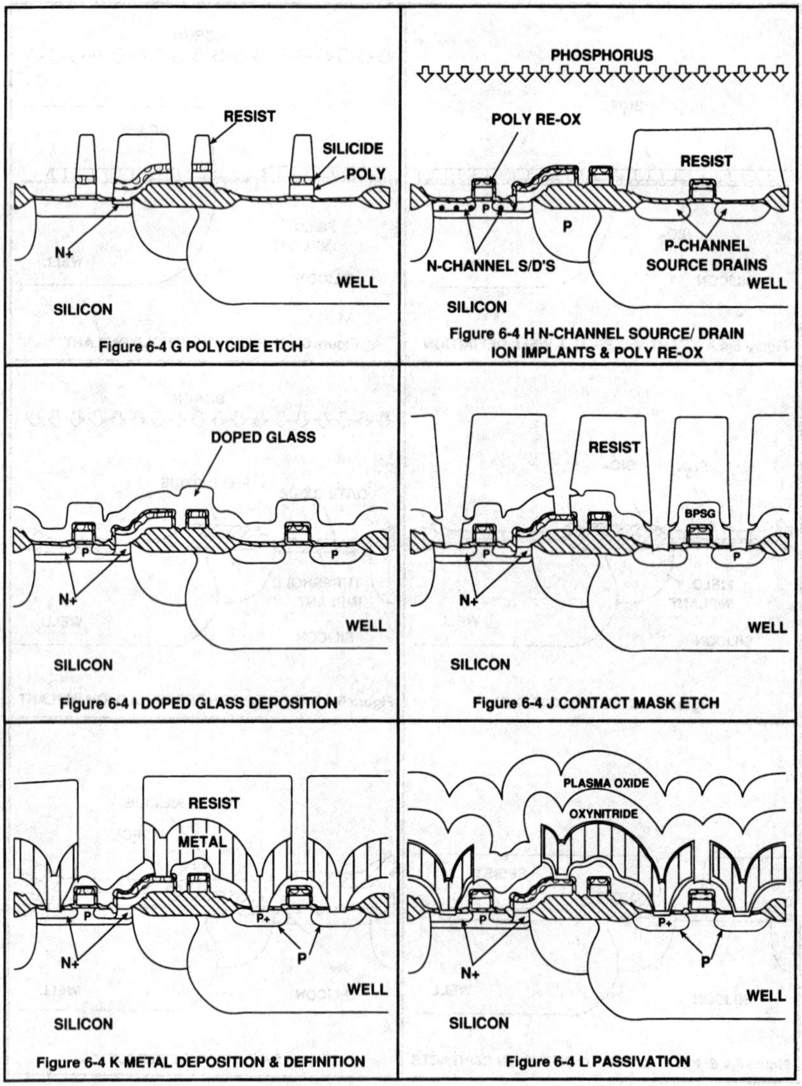

Figure 6-4g-l. Single Poly, Single Metal CHMOS Cross Sections (Contd.)

7. **Source and Drain Implant and Poly Re-Ox** (Figure 6-4h). The remaining polycide stack, thin oxide over the poly, field oxide and resist provide a mask for p-channel and n-channel source-drain implants which occurs at this point. (This technique is commonly known as a "self-aligned source/drain" process, since the source and drain are aligned directly to the gate, which defines their location relative to the channel area). All remaining poly oxide is the and the poly re-ox step performed. The re-ox step is a high-temperature thermal oxidation step which drives the source-drain implant into the silicon, provides a high-integrity dielectric on the polysilicon (essential in a double poly process) and grows an oxide on the exposed source-drain regions to prevent dopant out-diffusion during subsequent phosphosilicate glass deposition and processing.

8. **Doped Glass Deposition** (Figure 6-4i). A doped (boron, phosphorous or both) silicate glass layer, 5000Å to 10,000Å thick, is deposited via low-temperature CVD techniques to provide electrical isolation between the subsequent metal conductor lines and the underlying polycide gates and active device structures. The glass is then prepared for subsequent masking steps.

9. **Contact Mask and Etch** (Figure 6-4j). Windows in the resist are exposed and opened to define the location of metal-to-polycide and metal-to-silicon contact holes. Depending on the process, contact holes are wet, dry, or wet and dry etched. In a wet/dry combination, the wet etch gives a shallow slope near the top of the contact. This improves metal step coverage. The remaining doped silicon glass is then removed by an isotropic dry etch which leaves the contact sidewalls vertical.

10. **Metal Deposition and Definition** (Figure 6-4k). Metal conductor layer is sputter-deposited into the wafer and defined. The metal electrically connects the transistors to the outside world. The voltage applied by these metal lines turns the transistors "on" and "off."

11. **Passivation** (Figure 6-4l). Plasma enhanced CVD techniques are used to deposit a dual film passivation layer over the entire wafer surface. The dual layer consists of an oxynitride underneath a plasma oxide. The oxynitride provides long-term field reliability, by being designed to be a contamination and moisture barrier. The latter is particularly critical if the dice are to be assembled in plastic packages, plastic itself being a poor moisture barrier. The plasma oxide layer provides handling protection for the wafer and individual devices.

12. **Bond Pad Definition and Alloy** (Figure 6-4m). The passivation layer is photo-masked and etched to expose metal bond pads. Wire bonds will subsequently be placed in these regions for electrical connection of the device to the package. The actual opening in the passivation is typically formed by a plasma etch with end-point detection to avoid any residual passivation in the pads. A high temperature alloy step is performed to form a metallurgical junction between the metal and the poly and diffusion contacts. An H_2 ambient is used in this step to anneal surface state charge (Qss) in the gate oxide.

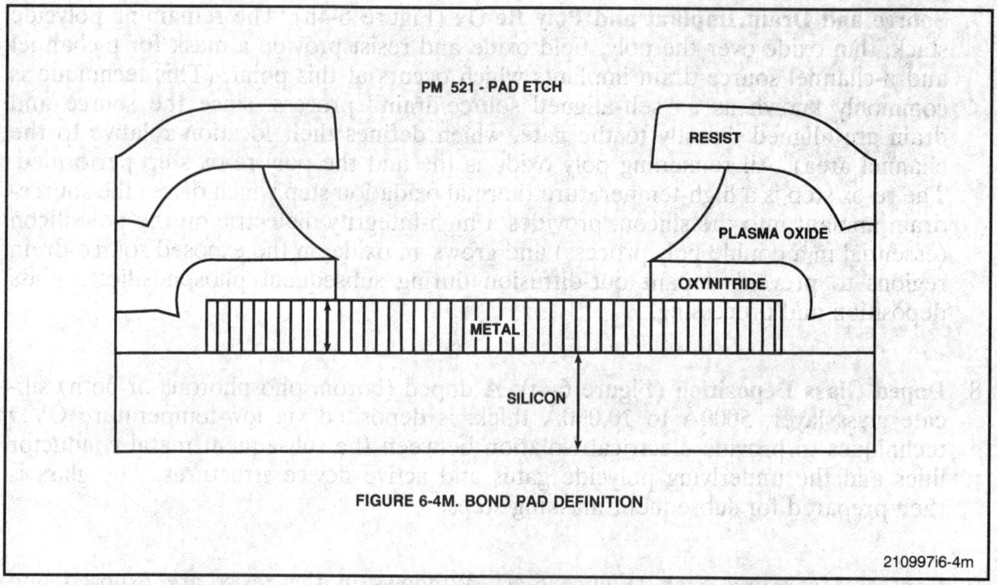

Figure 6-4m. Single Poly, Single Metal CHMOS Cross Sections (Contd.)

13. **Backside Preparation**. A protective layer is placed on the front side of the wafer and the backside is abrasively ground until the proper thickness is achieved for uniformity in assembly processing. A thin chromium layer is deposited, followed by a gold layer. Gold provides an excellent surface for the attachment of the sawed die into the package. The chromium provides uniform gold adhesion and a diffusion barrier so that silicon does not migrate to the surface prematurely, forming SiO_2, either during storage or during die attach. This step ensures that the surface will not cause dewet (voids) during die attachment.

14. **Electrical Test and Presort**. Sample wafers from each lot are subjected to electrical test. Built-in test structures on each wafer are probed to verify that device electrical characteristics are in control and meet specification. Measurements are made of transistor threshold voltages and current characteristics; poly and contact resistance; gate oxide and junction integrity; and specific parameters critical to the particular technology and device type. Wafer-to-wafer, across-the-wafer, run-to-run variation and conformance to spec limits are checked. Actual devices on wafers are presorted for yield and performance. Failures are analyzed for defect mode and wafer location.

15. **Outgoing**. Wafers are subjected to an outgoing quality inspection which includes both visual and physical quality. Visual inspection includes handling damage, particles, passivation defects, masking defects, bond pad corrosion and cleanliness. Backside gold adherence and final wafer thickness are checked and performance recorded. The wafers are subsequently packed and labeled by run number, process and device type and shipped to the Wafer Sort operations.

PROCESS DESIGN AND TRANSFER

Process Design

Increasingly complex and faster circuit designs have typically pushed the limits of available materials and equipment. However, today's circuits require technologies which touch some of the fundamental limits of physics. In such circumstances, reliability cannot be an afterthought; it must be an integral part of the process design and development.

To ensure that reliability is actually designed into the process, reliability characterization has become a fundamental part of process development at Intel. Each process module is investigated for wearout mechanisms and each process step characterized for repeatability and defects. The results are then incorporated back into the process design and used to establish process control limits and circuit design rules. Characterization and feedback are the responsibility of Reliability and Design personnel who are integrated into the Process Development Team.

The Development Team establishes reliability and process capabilities by processing test structures and memory devices. Specific test structures are stressed at accelerating temperatures and voltages to characterize reliability mechanisms. Memory devices are also given accelerating stresses with the fallout carefully analyzed to understand the root cause of the failures.

Once the reliability and process capabilities are established, designers are held to a rigid set of design rules. The design rules include protection from wear-out mechanisms (such as electromigration and hot electron injection) and infant mortality/early life mechanisms, such as electrostatic discharge (ESD) and CMOS latch-up. These rules also extend to cover identified process related defect mechanisms and package interactions.

6

Transfer

Process transfer from the development team to die production occurs after the process meets demanding yield and reliability goals. A process that meets such requirements achieves certification. (The certification process is coordinated by the Reliability group.) To ensure that we continue to meet yield and reliability goals in a manufacturing environment, it is essential that we duplicate the process in the manufacturing facility. Prior to process transfer, each process step and piece of equipment must be carefully characterized and the characterization extensively documented. The engineers establish control, disposition and scrap limits for each operation. The multi-disciplined process development team is responsible for defining all process controls and limits and for compiling a transfer document for each process step. The transfer documents include the characterization, process control and process limit information. A reliability transfer document is part of this procedure and includes the results of all the reliability evaluations, failure analysis, electrical test monitor requirements and life test data.

A die production team from the receiving manufacturing facility is responsible for ensuring that each process step is picked up exactly as it was run in the development facility. Key members of the die production team spend three to six months training with the development team before beginning the transfer. The Reliability Group again coordinates certification of the process in the receiving manufacturing facility.

THE MANUFACTURING ENVIRONMENT

The manufacturing environment has evolved dramatically in the last few years in response to new technologies. Major improvements have been made in the areas of particulate control, incoming quality control and training.

Low levels of particulate are key to producing a highly reliable product. With wearout and process control defect mechanisms minimized by careful process design and characterization, random defects due to particulate dominate the reliability failure paretos. Particulate must be controlled in the fab environment, in the equipment and in incoming materials.

Not long ago, Class 100 clean rooms were considered state of the art. New Intel facilities, however, are now very close to Class 1. Particle counts, which were once performed by operators on shifts, are now performed remotely, automatically and continuously throughout the fab area. The polyester bunnysuit has been replaced by a Gortex suit which includes a helmet with breathing apparatus to filter exhaled air. Equipment is arranged so that maintenance may be performed in Class 100 access corridors outside the Class 1 bays where processing takes place. Traffic is minimized in the process areas with such techniques such as piping chemicals to work stations, automated delivery systems and by severely restricting the number of people permitted entry. These techniques have been very effective in keeping particles and the resulting defects to a minimum. Figure 6-5 shows Intel's Fab Clean Room Environment.

Wafer Fab engineers have also done a great deal to control equipment particulate. It was extremely difficult to control particulate introduced by equipment during processing before the introduction of automated measurement tools such as the Surfscan. Equipment particulate are now routinely monitored at virtually every step in the process and the number and size of particles are now criteria for bringing up or shutting down equipment. As a result, engineers have dramatically reduced the particulate introduced by equipment and obtained large die yield increases with resulting product reliability improvements.

Incoming quality control has always been a significant issue in wafer manufacturing. Throughout the industry, processes have often been lost due to variations in incoming substrates, chemicals and materials. Consequently these are now rigorously specified and monitored. However, due to the ever shrinking geometries on newer processes, we are paying increasing attention to particulate levels in process gases, D.I. water and chemicals. Low particulate chemicals are used for critical steps in our newest facilities.

210997i

Figure 6-5. Intel Fab Clean Room Environment

The manufacturing environment also includes people, their attitudes and level of training. Intel strives to create an atmosphere in which people are motivated to perform with quality workmanship. Only certified operators are allowed to perform given manufacturing steps and certification must be renewed if the operator has not worked at an operation within a specified period. Technician and operator training programs cover all aspects of the manufacturing operation. Intel also has a large formal training group at each facility to provide training to all employees. Audits of each operational area within a fab, including operator knowledge and certification, are performed quarterly.

ON-LINE PROCESS CONTROL

The primary purpose of our on-line process control is to insure that our processes are producing reliable, high quality products. To accomplish this, we use a series of controls, including controls on input parameters, output parameters and end-of-module controls. The controls depend primarily on the maturity of the process. The fab quality and reliability group is responsible for ensuring that each of the processes have the controls necessary to produce reliable products.

When processes are developed, Intel takes a very conservative control approach. When a newly developed process is transferred into production, along with it are all of the controls necessary to ensure its reliability and manufacturability. Since the process development time is relatively short, many new processes are transferred with redundant controls. As the process matures, many of the original controls can be eliminated. The change control system (see Chapter 5) which is used in all of the manufacturing plants is the primary vehicle for ensuring that when controls are eliminated, the effect of elimination is well understood. Change control is also the vehicle for ensuring that customers are informed of changes if necessary. If Intel or a customer encounters a problem, the need for additional process controls is evaluated and appropriate action taken.

While our methodology is common throughout all of the Intel manufacturing plants, the implementation varies from plant to plant depending on the maturity of the processes in that plant and its organizational structure. Intel performs reliability stresses for all processes on finished product to ensure that in-line controls are producing the desired effects. The fabrication of integrated circuits consists of a series of modules, each of which may require several processing steps. Each module has specific output parameters and each of the steps that make up the module may have several input parameters. For instance, a gate oxidation will consist of the pattern where the oxide is to be grown, the cleaning of the wafer prior to oxide growth and the actual growth of the oxide. The input parameter would include the chemicals used in the cleaning, the duration of the clean, the temperature of the clean, the pressure of the gases during the oxidation, the temperature of the furnace, etc. The output parameter would be the oxide thickness and the electrical quality of the oxide at the end of the wafer fabrication. The proper controls may be on the input parameters, the output parameters or both depending on process capability and maturity.

The actual controls for each processing step are defined within the procedures for each of processing step. A sampling of the controls for one of our processes is shown in Table 6-4.

There are two primary results of continuous improvement in on-line control. First the process is fundamentally improved to the point where the monitors are no longer necessary. Second, the response to monitor signals improves. The first action is handled through our change control system. The second area is where much of the operator and technician improvement effort is directed. Intel has developed extensive troubleshooting guides and even artificial intelligence to assist operators and technicians in responding to control signals. Part of a 36 page troubleshooting guide is shown in Table 6-5.

ASSEMBLY

Intel offers three main package technology types for assembly processing: transfer-molded epoxy plastic, glass-sealed cerdip and metal-sealed multi-layer ceramic. Packages with a variety of lead counts and outlines (package families) are produced in each package technology. The packages are assembled in one of three Intel-owned assembly facilities or by an Intel-controlled subcontractor.

Package Families

Intel's package offerings are divided into two classes: insertion (through-hole) mount and surface mount. Insertion-mount packages include dual-in-line packages (DIPs) with pin counts ranging from 16 to 48 and pin-grid-arrays (PGAs) with pin counts ranging from 68 to 252 pins. Intel's current insertion-mount offerings are summarized in

Table 6-4. P645.XX Process Control Plan

Process Step	Control Parameter	Parameter Strength	Inspection Method	Inspection Strength	Target/ Historical Performance	Control Method	Sample Size/ Frequency
32 mask & wet/plasma ox etch, (resist strip) & anneal III	RC poly	Strong	E-test (Keithley)	Strong	80C51: 0.65 KOHMS	EOL monitor & control chart	8 product W/L; 3 S/W - every lot
	RCN+	Strong	E-test (Keithley)	Strong	80C51: 2.2 KOHMS	EOL monitor & control chart	8 product W/L; 3 S/W - every lot
	RCP+	Strong	E-test (Keithley)	Strong	80C51: 2.8 KOHMS	EOL monitor & trend chart	8 product W/L; 3 S/W - every lot
Ai/Si sputter	Etch rate at Ai/Si Sputter predip	Moderate	Nonspec	Strong	Etch rate: 2.25Å/sec	Mean control chart	Test run with 1 SiO_2 test wafer; 5 S/W - every shift and new acid
	Particles at Ai/Si Sputter predip	Moderate	Surfscan 4500	Strong	Pre-etch: <50 particles (0.08-5.12 μm) Delta-etch: 368 particles (0.08-0.05 μm)	Mean control chart	Test run with 5 bare test wafers — 3 times a week and new acid
	Ai/Si thickness	Strong	M-gage 300	Strong	12.5 KA	Mean control chart	1 Ai/Si test wafer —first load of each shift & every third load
	Particles at Ai/Si Sputter	Strong	Surfscan 4500	Strong	Pre-etch: <50 particles (0.08-5.12 μm) Delta-etch: 22 particles (1.0-5.12 μm)	Mean control chart	Test run with 2 bare test wafers — every shift
	Ai/Si reflectivity	Weak	AMT reflectometer (back up Leitz reflectometer)	Weak	>92%	Mean control chart	2 product wafers —first load of each shift & every third load

6

Table 6-4. P645.XX Process Control Plan (Contd.)

Process Step	Control Parameter	Parameter Strength	Inspection Method	Inspection Strength	Target/ Historical Performance	Control Method	Sample Size/ Frequency
Ai/Si sputter	Ai/Si sputter residual resistance (R2)	Moderate	R^2 measurement system	Strong	>8.2	Mean control chart	1 bare test wafer once per shift on a production load & 6 hrs. of equipment idle, pallet change, new target, chamber venting, or PM's
	Ai/Si sputter residual gas analysis (RGA)	Critical	Sputter system	Strong	N_2: <7.0E-8 torr O_2: <2.0E-9 torr N_2/O_2: >8.0	N_2: Mean control chart O_2 & N_2/O_2 Periodic in-line check	Once per shift on a production load & after 6 hrs. of equipment idle, pallet change, new target, chamber venting or PM's
	Ai/Si metal step coverage	Strong	SEM	Strong	<50% reduction in metal cross-sectional area	EOL monitor and trend chart	One product wafer a week; 3 S/W (thru diffusion contact)

Table 6-5. TMX Nitride Thickness Response Flow Checklist

Question U1

- Is the average thickness of this most recent test fire too LOW?

Response:

YES	Go to ACTION V
NO	Go to ACTION W

Question U2

- How many times have you adjusted the pressure and run a test since cleaning the ball joint, cold trap, and manifold?

Response:

1	Pressure has been adjusted ONCE before. Go to ACTION V
2	Pressure has been adjusted TWICE before. Stop Here. This tube is DOWN to Engineering.

Action V **Initial**

- Adjust the pressure (CLP) per spec.
- Run a test.
- Plot test run average and range measurements on control chart. Label it 'TEST.'

Data:	**Setpoint**		
Recipe Parameter	Current	Run #1	Run #2
CLP			
		Thickness	
		Run #1	**Run #2**
	Front		
	Center		
	Rear		
	Average		
	Range		

Question V

- Is the Average or the Range measurement for this test run outside the 2 sigma limits on page 1?

Response:

YES	Go to Question U2.
NO	Stop Here. The pressure needed to be adjusted. This tube is UP to production.

Table 6-6. Surface-mount packages include plastic-leaded chip carriers (PLCC) with pin-counts ranging from 20 to 84, leadless chip carriers (LCC) with pin counts from 18 to 68 and others defined in Table 6-7. Examples of typical Intel surface and insertion mount packages are shown in Figure 6-6. Full details of Intel's package offerings are available in the Intel publication, *Packaging Outlines and Dimensions*, Order No. 231369.

Package Technologies

Different package families have essentially the same assembly procedures when they use the same package technology. Consequently, it is possible to discuss assembly procedures for each of the three main package technologies independent of specific package families. However, it is convenient to discuss package technologies in terms of Dual Inline Packages (DIPs), since DIPs are produced in all three.

The assembly flow for each of the three package technologies is given in Table 6-8 and illustrated for DIPs in Figure 6-7. In the following sections, we describe each step in the assembly flow and differences between the package technologies.

Each assembly plants die preparation (die prep) operation is nearly identical, independent of package technology. Wafers are received from the wafer sort areas with electronically non-functional dice identified by ink dots. For plastic packages, die prep consists of the following steps: mount wafers on tape, saw wafer and perform die wash and die visual inspection. The tape-mounted sawed wafers are then delivered directly to the die attach operation. For hermetic packages, dice are removed from tape and placed in plastic die plates before delivery to the die attach operation.

Table 6-6. Insertion-Mount Package Offered by Intel

Lead Count	Cerdip	Plastic DIP	Ceramic* DIP	Ceramic PGA	Plastic Flatpack**
16	X	X	X		
18	X	X	X		
20	X	X			
22	X				
24	X	X	X		
28	X	X	X		
32	X	X	X		
40	X	X	X		
48		X	X		
68				X	X
88				X	
132				X	
224				X	
252				X	

*Ceramic DIP = Ceramic sidebrase LTD seal package
**The plastic flatpack is not a surface mount package

Table 6-7. Surface-Mount Packages Offered by Intel

Lead Count	PLCC	LCC	CF	SOJ	PQFP	CQFP	CERQUAD	TSOP	MM PQFP
18		X	X						
20		X		X					
28	X	X							
32	X	X						X	
44	X	X					X		
52	X						X		
68	X	X	X				X		
84	X				X				X
100					X				X
132					X				X
164					X	X			X
196					X	X			X

PLCC = Plastic Leaded Chip Carrier (J-Bend Leads)
LCC = Leadless Ceramic Chip Carrier
CF = Ceramic FlatPack (50 mil center leads)
SOJ = Small Outline J-Bend
PQFP = Plastic Quad FlatPack (25 mil center leads)
CQFP = Ceramic Quad FlatPack (25 mil center leads)
CERQUAD = Ceramic leaded chip carrier (j bend lead) (PLCC equivalent)
TSOP = Thin Small Outline Package
MMPQFP = Multilayer Molded PQFP (internal ground planes)

PLASTIC PACKAGE ASSEMBLY

6

Plastic packages consist of a metal lead frame encapsulated in a transfer-molded low stress epoxy novalac. They're generally the least expensive semiconductor package because they are assembled from only two major components: a lead frame and the molding plastic. A cross section of a typical plastic DIP is shown in Figure 6-8.

The metal lead frames used in the die attach operation are either Alloy 42 (42 percent nickel, 58 percent iron) or a high strength copper alloy with a silver spot-plate in the areas where the die and the wires are attached. In PDIP, a group of lead frames comprise a lead frame strip. Strips are handled as a unit until singulation. The lead frames are either etched or stamped from the rolls of raw material by the vendor. All are purchased from Intel-approved vendors.

The silicon dice supplied by the die prep area are attached to the metal lead frame by a silver-filled die attach adhesive.

All plastic encapsulated devices are thermosonically wire bonded using 1.3 mil diameter gold wire. Automatic bonders place a ball bond on the chip bond pad and either a crescent or stitch bond on the plated tip of the lead frame. Chip substrate bias is supplied by either direct bonding from a chip bond pad to the die attach pad, or from lead frame tip to the die attach pad. Alternatively, a bond tip may be tied directly to the die

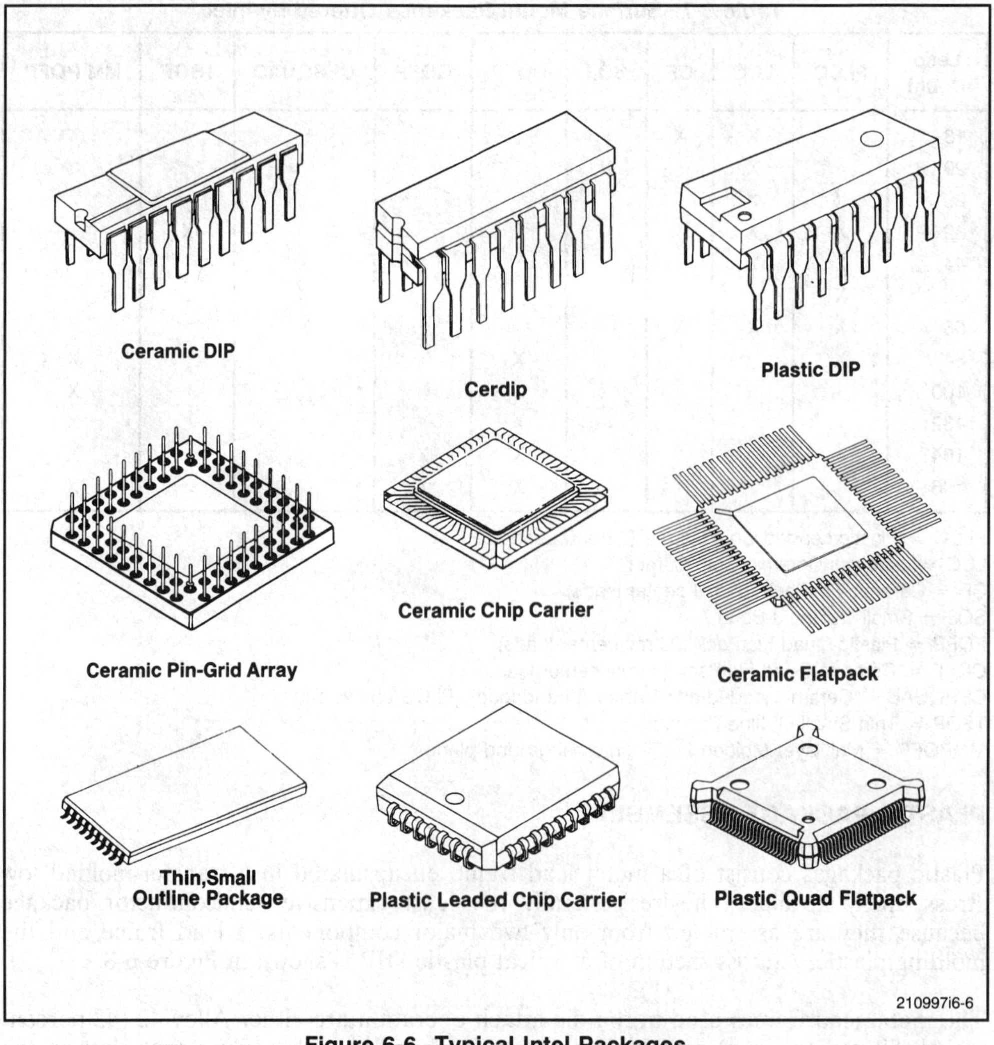

Figure 6-6. Typical Intel Packages

pad in the design of the lead frame, eliminating the need for a bond wire. The die attach pad is depressed below the plane defined by the lead tips. This reduces internal stresses on the silicon chip and package material and reduces the incidence of wire-shorting to the chip edge.

Strips of lead frames with die attached and wire bonded devices are encapsulated using conventional or automold technology. During the molding operation, hot thermosetting molding compound is transferred into the mold cavities where it completely surrounds the wire bonded die. After allowing the compound to set up, the molded strips are removed. Intel uses relatively few molding compounds. The typical characteristics are shown in Table 6-9.

Table 6-8. Typical Assembly Flows

Step	Cerdip	Ceramic	Plastic
Die prep	Saw	Saw	Saw
	DI wash	DI wash	DI wash
Inspection	Die visual gate	Die visual gate	Die visual gate
Die attach	Frame attach eutectic die attach	Eutectic die attach	Adhesive die attach
Bond	Aluminum wire (ultrasonic)	Aluminum wire (ultrasonic) or AU wire (thermosonic)	Gold wire (thermosonic)
Inspection	Internal visual gate	Internal visual gate	Internal visual gate
Encapsulation	Dry air atmosphere seal, 430°C for 11 min.	Neutral/reducing atmosphere seal, 320°C for 15 min.	Mold cure at 163°C to 175°C
Lead finish	Tin plate, gold plate or solder	As-received gold plate or solder (military only)	Deflash/trim and form (DTF)
	Trim	Trim	Solder/Tin Lead Plate
Inspection	External visual gate	External visual gate	External visual gate
Outgoing	Q.A. Tests Hermeticity Centrifuge Lead fatigue Die shear Bond pull Acoustic Solderability	Q.A. Tests Hermeticity Centrifuge Lead fatigue Die shear Bond pull Acoustic Solderability	Q.A. tests Lead fatigue Solderability X-ray

In an operation called deflash, excess plastic or resin bleed is removed from the lead-frame strips by a combination of chemical and mechanical means. Additional operations are then performed, such as backside mark and post mold-cure (PMC).

Plastic packages may have one of two types of lead finishes, depending on the application. The lead finish determines the remaining steps in the flow. The lead finish is a 200-1000 micro inch-thick tin/lead coating that facilitates board assembly.

Plastic surface mount (SMT) packages receive a tin/lead plate which is normally an 85% Tin/15% lead (85/15) coating. The leads are then trimmed and formed into their final configuration and separated from the lead frames (singulated) to form the final package.

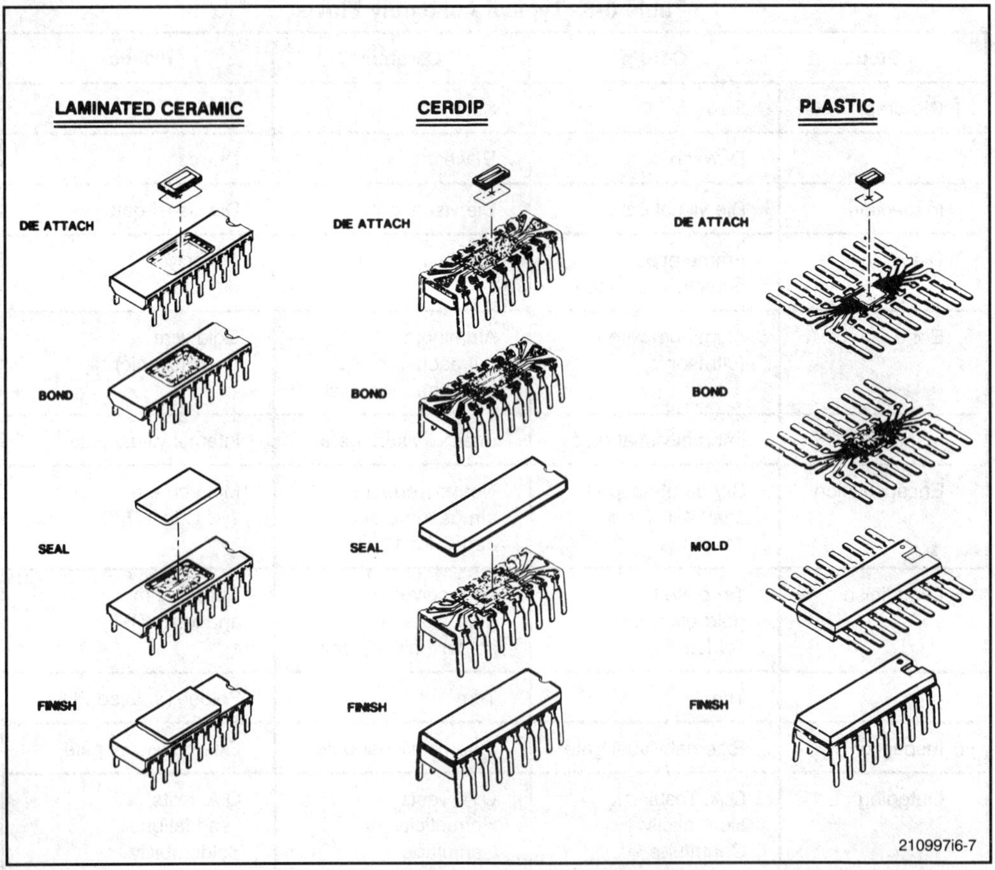

Figure 6-7. Steps in Plastic, Cerdip and Laminated Ceramic Package Assembly

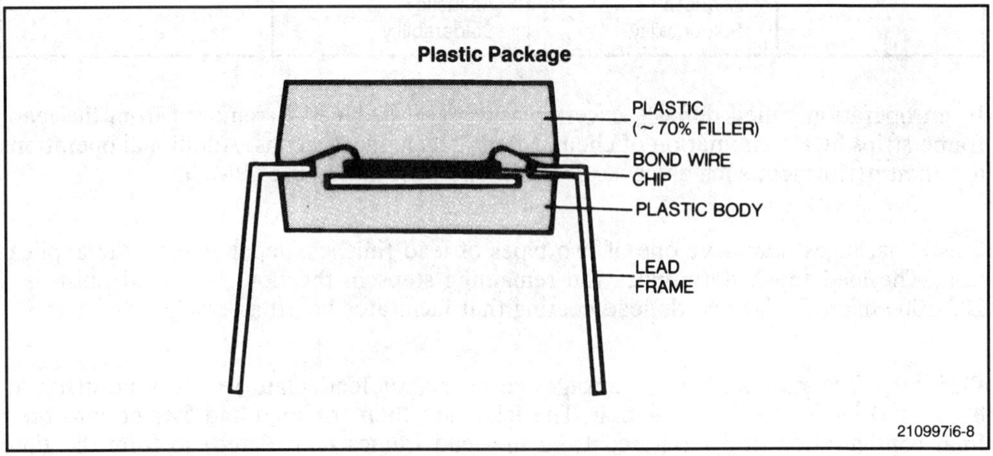

Figure 6-8. Cross Section of a Plastic DIP Package

Table 6-9. Typical Molding Compound Characteristics

Filler material	SiO_2
Filler content	68%-72%
Flame retardant	Yes
Mold temperature	163°C-175°C
Cure temperature	160°C-175°C
Hydrolyzable chloride	70 PPM maximum
Alpha count	0.05 count/cm^2 – hour maximum

Non-surface mount packages follow a different flow. After cure, the packages are processed through the trim and form operation, singulated and then wave-soldered using 60% Tin/40% lead (60/40) combination solder.

After singulation, the units are processed through an assembly final visual operation, packed and shipped to a test site for electrical testing.

CERDIP PACKAGE ASSEMBLY

Apart from the bond wire and preform, cerdip packages are made from three piece parts: a lid, a base and a lead frame. The cerdip package is simple in construction and uses a minimal amount of precious metals. It is the least expensive version of a hermetic package. The lid and the base are sealed together by a low-temperature sealing solder glass into which the lead frame is embedded (see Figure 6-9). EPROM packages requiring ultraviolet light penetration for device erasure utilize special vendor-supplied lids with a boro-silicate glass window.

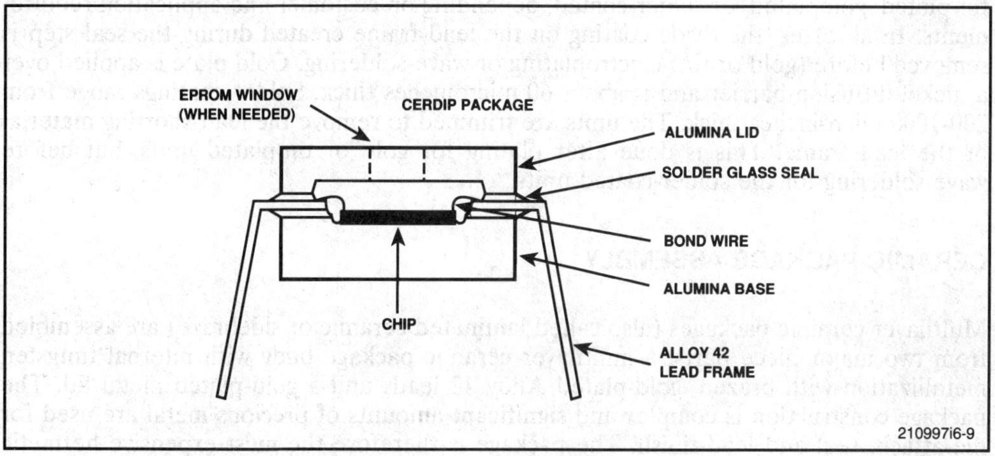

Figure 6-9. Cerdip Package

Cerdip packages come mostly in DIP configurations with 16 to 48 leads. However, there are square body J-leaded hermetic chip carriers called Cerquad which use the same glass seal technology.

The lead frame has aluminum-clad lead tips. The base is solder-glazed and has a plated frit silver or gold die-attach pad. The first step in cerdip assembly is to embed the Alloy 42 lead frame into the glazed base, which provides a frame-attached subassembly used for die-attach. This is done in a high-temperature belt furnace. Cerdip lead frames come individually, not in strips as do plastic lead frames.

Devices are attached to the ceramic base by forming a gold/silicon eutectic solder joint or by using a silver-filled epoxy. If a substrate bias is required, a "jumper chip" is used. A jumper chip is an iron/cobalt/nickel cube, about 0.5 mm on a side, coated on top with a 4-10 micron thick aluminum film and on the bottom with about 25 microns of gold. The gold side of the jumper chip is attached to the die-attach area of the cerdip base. The aluminum-coated side remains on top for a subsequent wire bond.

The next step is wire bonding. All cerdip packages use ultrasonically bonded aluminum wires 1.25 mils in diameter containing 1 percent silicon. Since the metal on the top of the jumper chip and on the lead tips is aluminum, this provides an all-aluminum metal system. This avoids the problem of gold-aluminum intermetallic formation that would occur in the subsequent seal step if gold wire were used.

Solder-glazed alumina lids are clipped onto the base/lead frame/die assembly and the unit is passed through a belt furnace at 430°C. The oxidizing atmosphere in the furnace prevents reduction to metallic lead of the lead oxide component of the solder glass, thereby preventing shorting of package leads. In the furnace, the seal glass melts and flows, making a seal around the package. Intel uses low alpha particle-emitting vitreous solder glass consisting of a mixture of PbO_2, ZnO, B_2O_3, fillers and coloring agents.

The final step in cerdip assembly is lead-finish and trim. The sealed packages are either tin-plated, goldplated, or solder-coated, depending on customer and application requirements. In all cases, the oxide coating on the lead frame created during the seal step is removed before (gold or tin) electroplating or wave-soldering. Gold plate is applied over a nickel diffusion barrier and is about 60 microinches thick. Solder coatings range from 200-1000 microinches thick. The units are trimmed to remove the lead-shorting material of the lead frame. This is done after plating for gold or tin-plated units, but before wave-soldering for the solder-coated units.

CERAMIC PACKAGE ASSEMBLY

Multilayer ceramic packages (also called laminated ceramic or sidebraze) are assembled from two major piece parts: a multilayer ceramic package body with internal tungsten metallization with brazed, gold-plated Alloy 42 leads and a gold-plated metal lid. The package construction is complex and significant amounts of precious metal are used for die-attach, seal and lead-finish. The package is therefore the most expensive hermetic package. However, because of the excellent thermal dissipation, superior electrical noise rejection properties, ease of assembly and wide package cavity, multilayer ceramic packages continue to play an important role at Intel. A schematic cross section of a typical multilayer ceramic DIP is shown in Figure 6-10.

The die is attached to the cavity of the package using gold-silicon eutectic. Substrate bias is provided by the internal metallized contacts or by a direct bond to the die attach surface. The seal temperature is low enough to prevent gold-aluminum intermetallic formation between gold wire and aluminum bond pads.

At wire-bond, either gold or aluminum wire may be used, because the subsequent seal temperatures are low enough to ensure reliability for gold wires. However, mixing of gold and aluminum wire within an assembly lot is not permitted.

Seal is performed at about 350°C in a neutral N_2 or reducing (N_2 plus H_2) atmosphere in a belt furnace. This prevents oxidation of the gold-tin seal preform. Lids are usually supplied by the vendor with seal preforms attached. The preform brazes the gold-plated package lid to the gold-plated ceramic body.

Since ceramic packages are supplied with gold-plated leads, no further lead-finish treatment is required for socketing applications. The units are only trimmed to remove the lead connection tie bars. For through-hole and surface mount applications, solder lead finish is provided.

Assembly Sites

Intel operates three assembly plants, in Penang, Malaysia (A1); Manila, Philippines (A2); and Chandler, Arizona (A4), USA. In addition, Intel utilizes subcontractor assembly plants located in the Far East. All assembly sites are full production plants. Not all sites assemble all package types; rather, each site specializes in one or more package families. They may, however, assemble comparatively small volumes of other package

6

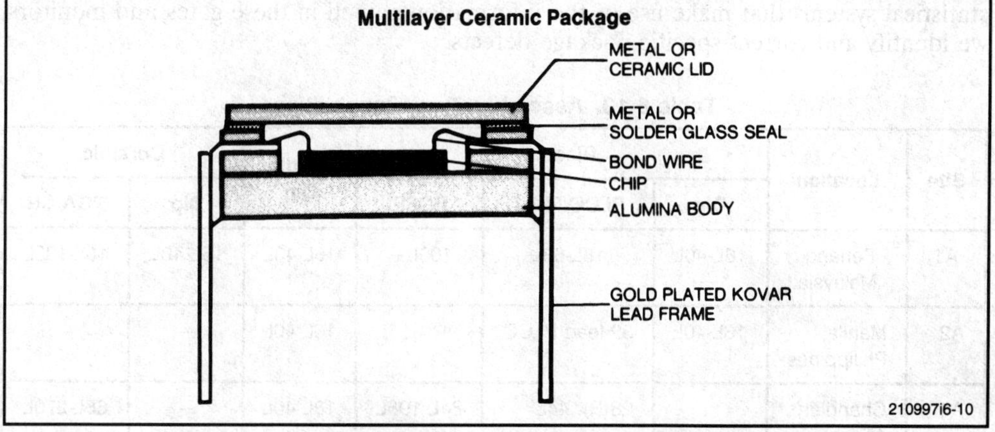

Figure 6-10. Cross Section of a Multilayer Ceramic Package

types. Table 6-10 shows assembly plant capabilities versus package family. This package mix is deliberately fluid; the actual mix fluctuates to better meet product demand.

All Intel-operated manufacturing facilities make extensive use of council systems, training courses, planning sessions, audits and individual technical meetings. These are necessary to maintain communication, standardization and cohesiveness between sites. Consequently, all assembly sites operate under identified guidelines even though they are geographically dispersed.

Process Control and Inspection

There are a variety of procedures used to control quality and consistency of Intel assembled product. These consist of equipment calibration and parameter control, specific process parameter control, product inspection, yield and gate points, package integrity testing as it leaves the assembly plant, package reliability monitors and general quality and technical audits. Some of these topics – calibration, reliability monitors and audits – are covered in other sections of this handbook. All activities described apply to both Intel-owned and subcontractor assembly sites.

PRODUCT VISUAL INSPECTION

There are three visual inspection gates inserted in the assembly process flow (see Table 6-8).

The assembly process control gates and typical frequency of the visual inspection steps are shown in Table 6-11. However, as quality continues to improve, inspection plans (single versus continuous) are subject to review and modification.

The line operators continuously perform a variety of visual inspection monitors of the quality of their assembly processes and products. Failing material is 100 percent rescreened. Visual inspection monitor issues are tracked by an inspection trouble report (ITR) system, which prescribes suitable corrective actions. Through the use of detailed statistical systems that make use of the information gained in these gates and monitors, we identify and correct specific package defects.

Table 6-10. Assembly Plant Capabilities

Site	Location	Plastic			Cerdip	Ceramic	
		Dip	PLCC/FLAT	PQFP	Dip	Dip	PGA/CR
A1	Penang, Malaysia	16L-40L	18L-68L	100L+	16L-48L	16L-40L	18L-132L
A2	Manila, Philippines	16L-40L	32 lead PLCC		16L-40L	–	–
A4	Chandler, Arizona		28(R), 44L	84L-196L	18L-40L	–	68L-270L

Table 6-11. Assembly Process Control Gates

Process	Real-Time Inspection	Manufacturing Inspection	QA Inspection
Incoming wafer	X		
Wafer/saw wash	X		
Frame attach visual	X		
Die visual (2nd opt)		X	X
Die shear test		X	X
Adhesive thickness		X	X
Die attach void		X	X
Bold line thickness		X	X
Die tilt		X	X
Bond pull		X	X
Pre seal stud pull		X	X
Internal visual (3rd opt)		X	X
Post mold visual	X		
Post mold X-ray		X	X
Post seal X-ray		X	X
DTF (leadform) visual	X		
Solder thickness		X	X
Plating thickness		X	X
Solderability		X	X
Lead trim visual	X		
Fine/gross leak test		X	X
Package visual (FVI)		X	X

6

PROCESS CONTROL

Each assembly process described previously has a set of equipment and process controls. In addition, Intel performs product inspections on a periodic basis. This section describes a cross section of these control activities. There are two specific areas of interest in process control: equipment-operating parameters, such as die attach heater block temperature and product measurement, such as bond pull strength. Many processes used in ceramic, plastic and cerdip assembly are generically similar, so even though there are specific equipment differences the process control activities will be described by generic rather than package family-specific process. Table 6-12 lists the majority of the process and equipment controls.

Table 6-12. Assembly Equipment Process Controls

Operation	Equipment Control	Process Control
Die prep Die attach	D.I. water resistivity Heater block temperature N_2 flow rate Adhesive thickness Adhesive viscosity	Continuous Die shear Visual Measurement Viscosity meter
Die attach cure	Time and temperature	Continuous charts
Bond	Heater block temperature Ultrasonic power Force	Temperature Bond pull – and bond shear Visual
Mold	Mold temperature	Spiral flow X-ray Visual
Post mold cure	Cure oven temperature	Continuous charts
Seal	Seal profile	Torque strength Package visual Centrifuge Thermal shock
Lead form	Tool cut	Visual
Lead finish (plating)	Bath composition Bath temperature Current density	Solderability Visual Thickness
Solder coat	Solder composition Solder height Solder thickness	Analysis Solderability Cross sections

Assembly Package Reliability Monitor

This program samples normal production material and then subjects it to stresses and tests to determine the reliability of the overall package. Table 6-13 represents the minimum level of monitors required by package. Customer and division monitor requirements are in addition to the listed monitors.

ASSEMBLY OPERATIONS

Die Prep

EQUIPMENT CONTROL

A possible source of die prep problems is signaled by a change in the deionized (DI) wash water resistivity. This resistivity is automatically measured in the DI water line and in the wash tanks.

DIE ATTACH EQUIPMENT CONTROL

Die attach temperature, coupled with inert gas flow and temperature, are the most important equipment parameters controlled. Other criteria such as bond line thickness, paste thickness and wet-out, are also monitored.

PRODUCT MEASUREMENT

Three product inspections for die attach are used: a visual examination of the die-attached die, a die adherence test and X-ray examination for eutectic coverage. The visual inspection analyzes preform fillet wetting, chip placement and visual defects. The X-ray radiography specifically analyzes the degree of eutectic coverage. Intel tests die adherence with shear test, where a measurable amount of shear force is applied to the

Table 6-13. Assembly Package Monitors

Inspection	Package		
	Plastic	Cerdip	Ceramic
Bond pull	X	X	X
Fine/gross leak		X	X
Centrifuge		X	X
Pin-D		X	X
Mark permanency	X	X	X
Body torque test		X	

edge of the die. Non-destructive testing (NDT) is occasionally used when maximum shear force is applied. This maximum stress is determined by the size/shear strength relationships and failure mode, according to military standard procedures.

Bond

EQUIPMENT CONTROL

There are a number of equipment controls in bonding, which is regarded as the single most complicated assembly process. Substrate temperature, bond force and ultrasonic power are considered the most important parameters.

PRODUCT MEASUREMENT

The single most widely used product control is bond pull, performed with an automatic bond puller. Bonds are pulled to destruction. A typical set of bond pull data is shown in Figure 6-11. Bond pull testing is performed for all package families, plastic, ceramic and cerdip packages. Bond shear is also tested.

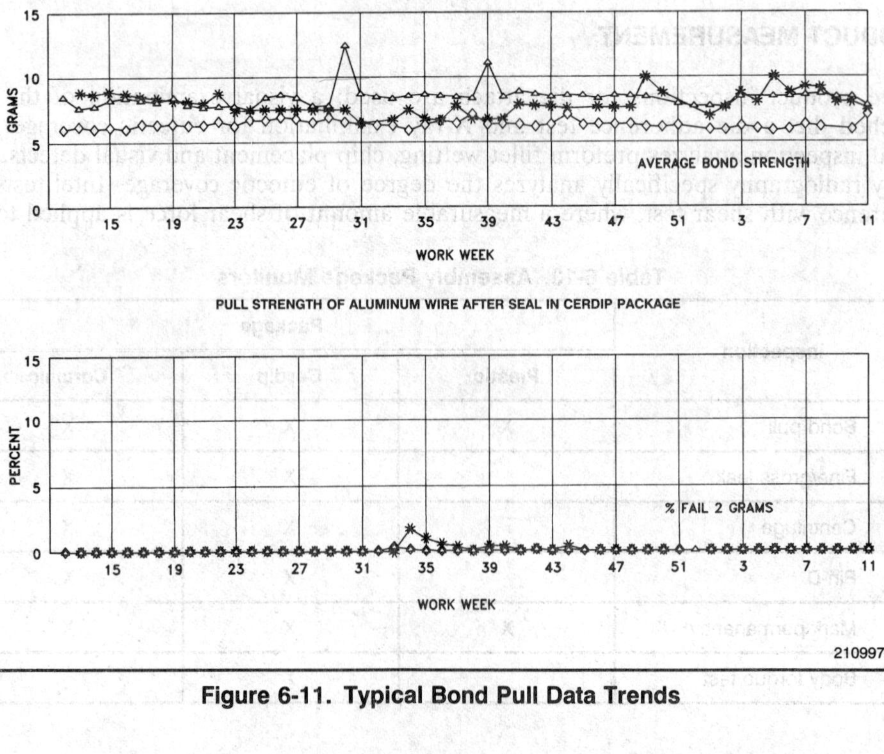

Figure 6-11. Typical Bond Pull Data Trends

Seal

EQUIPMENT CONTROL

The primary equipment parameter is the seal furnace profile. Of course, it depends on the specific furnace and package being sealed. The furnaces are profiled continuously with in-place thermocouples. In addition, dummy packages containing embedded thermocouples are periodically run through the furnace to verify profiles. A second control is on the furnace atmosphere, where the moisture content of the air in cerdip packages and the H_2/N_2 ratio of the forming gas in multi-layer ceramic packages seal atmospheres is continually sampled and analyzed.

PRODUCT MEASUREMENT

Because seal is so fundamental to providing high-quality, high-reliability hermetic packages, we pay a great deal of attention to measuring sealed package integrity. These measurements relate to such parameters as seal strength, cavity ambient composition, external appearance, die attach and bond integrity. All may be affected by uncontrolled seal processes. The moisture content in sealed cerdip packages is monitored daily for JAN product using specially designed moisture-sensitive test chips.

The fracture strength of the glass seal is measured using Intel-designed automatic torque testers and temperature cycling tests. Additional testing includes vibration and shock testing. Bond and die-attach integrity is tested using a centrifuge. In addition to thermal shock and temperature cycling, bond pull and die shear tests are used to verify product integrity.

Mold Equipment Control

Mold and post-mold cure temperatures are the equipment parameters most likely to affect molded package characteristics. On conventional molds, the temperatures are continually measured at each of 16 locations on top and bottom. Automolds are continually monitored by microprocessor-controlled heating systems. The post-mold cure is carried out in standard ovens controlled to ±2°C during the cure cycle.

PRODUCT MEASUREMENT

The mold process is monitored with a variety of techniques including spiral flow, X-ray radiography, visual inspection and steam testing. Spiral flow measurement ensures that the epoxy raw material retains its flow inside the mold. Visual inspection ensures that the molds are clean and well maintained. Pressure pot and steam testing methods detect corrosive contaminants that may contribute to reduced device lifetime.

Lead Finish

EQUIPMENT CONTROLS ELECTROPLATING

Lead finish electroplating controls are time, temperature, current density and bath composition. Careful control is required for plating because of the chemicals involved. Bath composition is maintained by a variety of techniques, such as titration, specific gravity, spectrometer analysis and other analytical methods.

A similar activity takes place for solder coating, where lead cleaning, solder coating and post-cleaning operations occur. Control of the lead finish operation is particularly important, because the package leads represent the major interface between the package and the outside world. Because the external lead of plastic packages is directly connected to the chip via the bond wire, it can provide a path for corrosive chemical ingress.

PRODUCT MEASUREMENT

Lead finish process controls consist of lead finish thickness, solderability, resistance to elevated temperature bakes and resistance to specific chemical immersion. Ultimately, reliability of finished product is dependent on the quality of the lead finish operation. Consequently, much attention is devoted to ensuring that lead finish operations are performed correctly.

TOPSIDE PACKAGING MARKING

Intel marks most ceramic packages and all plastic packages with a permanent topside laser mark that is etched into the package surface. A small group of large lead count ceramic packages are ink-marked with a bold Intel logo. Both are fully acceptable marking methods as outlined in Mil spec 883 and other industry committees.

This mark establishes traceability to the Fab lot number, the assembly plant, the date of manufacture and any ROM code or other customer shipment specific information.

ASSEMBLY OUTGOING TESTS

All shipments leaving an Intel assembly plant must pass rigid inspection criteria. All packages must pass at least a 3X visual inspection before being shipped to the test site, where they are electrically tested. These assembly inspections encompass all facets of the package body and leadfinish. A sampling: lead position, lead coplanarity, lead straightness, lead finish coverage, solderability, porosity, any chips, lead sweep and overall dimensions. (Exact inspected dimensions are listed in the *Intel Packaging Handbook*.) This information is used as immediate feedback to the production floor to control variances in product performance. A 100 percent rescreen is performed if any failures are detected.

The reliability monitor program that helps sample the outgoing quality is discussed in detail in Chapter 4. Briefly, this program is a sample basis program that continually watches the general lot integrity and quality.

All completed and inspected packages are then carefully boxed in special shipping boxes and shipped to test sites. There, the units are tested electrically, further inspected for package defects and boxed and shipped to either an interim warehouse or the final customer.

Reliability Measurements 7

CHAPTER 7 **Page**
RELIABILITY MEASUREMENTS

CHAPTER 7
RELIABILITY MEASUREMENTS

INTRODUCTION

Intel maintains a stringent and comprehensive reliability program that includes failure rate characterization and determination. Accelerated stress tests are performed on products, then these results are extrapolated to standard operating conditions. This section discusses the methods used to calculate and estimate a component's failure rate, as well as the assumptions used for the calculations.

ACCELERATED TEST EXTRAPOLATIONS

Since Intel uses accelerated stress tests in determining product failure rates, it is important to understand how the accelerated conditions are translated to standard operating conditions. Intel uses both temperature and voltage acceleration techniques and requires that the thermal activation energy (Ea) and voltage acceleration factor is determined, or assigned, for each failure mechanism. By using the appropriate Ea, data taken at an elevated temperature can then be translated to a lower standard operating temperature through the Arrhenius equation:

$$t1 = (t2)\ \exp\ [\ (Ea/K)\ (1/T1 - 1/T2)\ ]$$

where:

T1,T2	=	temperature in K
t1, t2	=	mean time to failure (MTTF) at T1 and T2 respectively
K	=	Boltzmann's Constant (8.62 x $1.0e6^{-5}$ ^{eV}/K)
Ea	=	thermal activation energy in eV

A graphic illustration of the temperature relationship, for several activation energies normalized to one hour at 250°C, is shown in Figure 7-1.

7

Voltage accelerated stress test results can also be translated to nominal voltage conditions, in a similar manner, by applying the appropriate voltage acceleration factor (VAF). In general Intel uses a voltage acceleration factor for time-dependent dielectric breakdown failure mechanisms only. This VAF is generally consistent throughout the industry and follows the equation:

$$VAF = \exp\ (C\ [V_s - V_o])$$

where:

VAF	=	the voltage acceleration factor
V_s	=	the applied stress voltage
V_o	=	the standard operating voltage
C	=	a constant that is a function of dielectric type

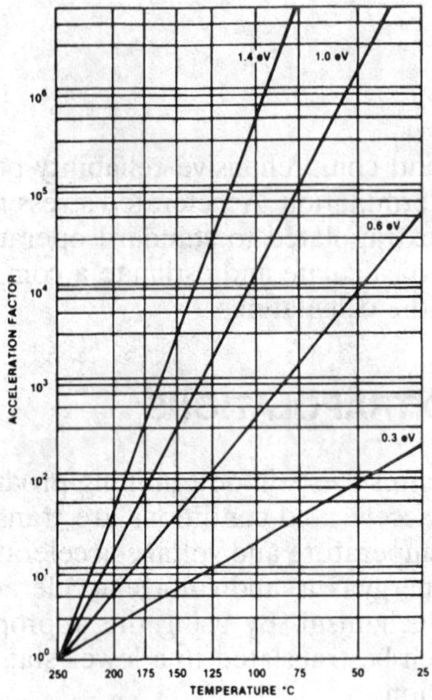

Figure 7-1. Graphic Illustration of the Arrhenius Temperature Relationship

Intel uses two different 'C' constant factors for dielectrics and range of constant factors or junction defects in its calculations that depend on the failure and dielectric type. For gate dielectrics 'C' is defined as being equal to the ratio of the gate oxide thickness (Tox) over 100 - Tox/100. The other dielectric 'C' factor used is applied to inter-level time-dependent dielectric breakdown failures associated with random particle defects. This and the 'C' factor or junction defects has been empirically derived from evaluations on memory test vehicles and varies somewhat as a function of the process technology and technology scaling. Or logic product technologies, used as the source of the reference data in this discussion, the 'C' factors are 1.8 or dielectrics and .41 for junction defects.

In using these acceleration factors it is important to quantify the voltage and temperature dependencies for the various failure mechanisms. In addition, analysis must be performed on accelerated stress test failures in order to identify the failure mechanism and properly apply the acceleration factors to the product failure rate extrapolations. Table 7-1 is a summary of the most common failure mechanisms found on the current generation technologies and their respective temperature activation energies and voltage acceleration factors.

At Intel, analysis is performed on all certification stress test failures, with the appropriate failure mechanism identified and acceleration factors assigned. Where failure analysis is unable to determine the exact mechanism, acceleration factors are assigned

Table 7-1. Common Failure Mechanisms

Mechanism	Temperature Activation Factor (eV)	Voltage Acceleration Factor ('C')
Gate Oxide Defect	0.3	Tox/100
Intermetallic Defect	0.3	1.5 - 3.0*
Poly to Metal Defect	0.3	1.5 - 3.0*
Silicon Junction Defect	0.8	0.0 - 0.5*
Masking (Poly, Diff., etc.) Defect	0.5	0.0**
Metallization Defect	0.5	0.0
Electromigration	0.5	0.0
Contamination (Surface and Bulk)	1.0	0.0
Charge Loss (EPROM's)	0.6	0.0
Assembly (Bond, Die Att., etc.)	0.5	0.0

* 'C' factors will vary with the processing technology and relative technology scaling. Factors are emperically derived during the technology development cycle.
** 'C' = 0.0 implies no voltage dependence and acceleration factor of 1.

according to the dominant failure mechanism observed on the product's process technology; that is, the undetermined product failure mechanism is assumed to be the same as the dominant technology failure mechanism. In the case where there is not a dominant mechanism, the most conservative acceleration factors identified for the technology are applied.

There are two commonly used failure rate calculation methods: instantaneous failure rate calculation and average failure rate calculation. The average failure rate method is meant to measure the assumed constant portion of the traditional "bathtub" curve. Early readouts, usually 48 hours or less, are considered to be infant mortality and are excluded from the long-term average failure rate calculation. The actual device-hours are calculated based on the remaining readouts. Appropriate junction temperature and voltage acceleration factors are applied for the failure mechanisms known to occur on the process technology to determine the equivalent device-hours. For each activation energy, a 60% upper confidence limit is calculated based on these equivalent device-hours and the number of failures assigned.

The 60% upper confidence limits for each activation energy are then summed to determine the total long-term average failure rate. This rate may be reported in percent failed per thousand hours, or more commonly FIT (Failures In Time) which is the number of failures per 10^9 device hours. When using this method, the infant mortality rate is commonly reported in DPM. This rate is simply the proportion of early readout failures to devices tested.

Intel has found that the traditional assumption of a constant failure rate is not accurate. A more accurate model is a declining failure rate until the onset of wearout. For this reason Intel is in the process of converting from the average failure rate calculation method to the instantaneous calculation method. An average failure rate can still be calculated with the new method, but it is averaged over an operating condition time period instead of a stress condition time period. This instantaneous calculation method will now be described in detail.

BASIC CALCULATION METHODOLOGY

Intel's standard procedure for reliability assessment and failure rate estimation is the instantaneous calculation method. The determination of an instantaneous failure rate is derived from a device's log normal distribution of cumulative percent fail versus time characteristics. That is, the instantaneous failure rate at any point in time (or time period) is the slope of the log normal cumulative percent fail curve at the specific point in time. In that there may be multiple failure mechanisms, each with different voltage-temperature dependencies, time-to-fail distributions (cumulative percent fail versus time) must be generated for each measurably contributing mechanism. The combined component time-to-fail characteristic is then the probability summation of the individual contributing mechanisms.

The example data shown in Table 7-2 can be used to illustrate the instantaneous failure rate calculation method. For simplicity, in this case there are two contributing mechanisms where, first, the voltage, temperature and net acceleration factors are determined for each mechanism relative to use conditions (5 Volts, 55°C junction temperature (Tj) in this case). The calculated cumulative percent failure points are then plotted versus equivalent time at use condition temperature. A line fit and line equation are determined for each mechanism using one of multiple statistically valid curve fitting techniques ("least square it" in this case) as shown in Figure 7-2. The total device cumulative percent failure versus time curve is then the probability summation of the curves for each mechanism, again shown in Figure 7-2.

If additional confidence is deemed necessary, upper confidence limits can be determined and failure estimates made. Confidence intervals can be determined using accepted statistical principles—as in this example of a 90% UCL determined using a standard confidence interval limits for log normal distributions. Curve fitting is done using the UCL data points as was described with the raw data. The combined 90% UCL time-to-fail characteristics is the probability summation of the 90% fit curves for each mechanism, as shown in Figure 7-3.

Table 7-2. Example 7V, 125°C Lifetest Data

	'C'	12 Hrs.	48 Hrs.	168 Hrs.	500 Hrs.	1000 Hrs.
Sample Size	–	20000	19970	5000	4994	4991
.3 eV Failures	1.8	20	10	4	2	1
.8 eV Failures	.41	10	5	2	1	0

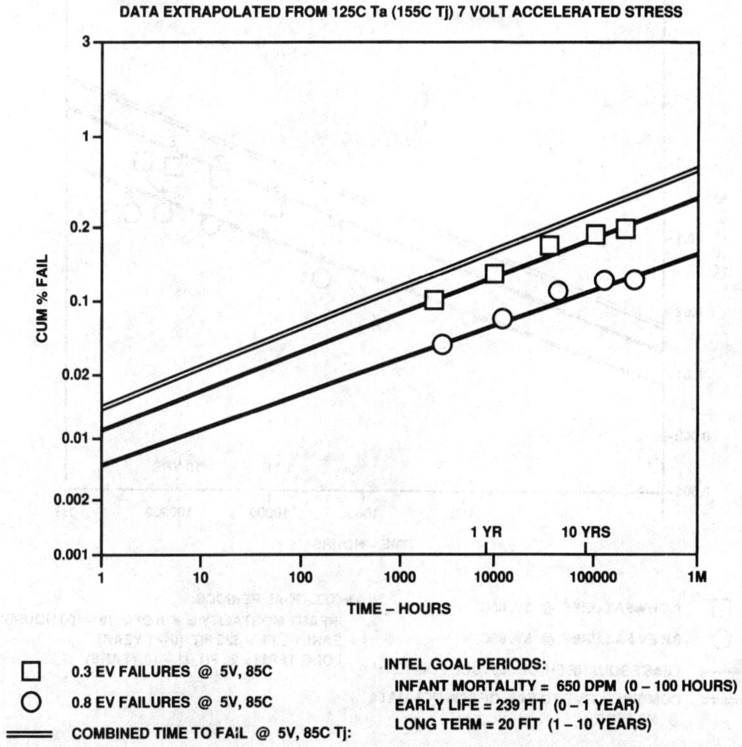

Figure 7-2. Cumulative Percent Fail Versus Time Failure Rate Calculation Method for Product with Two Contributing Failure Mechanisms

A component's instantaneous failure rate or average failure rate during any time period can then be estimated at any confidence level by determining the slope of the combined cumulative fail curve at or within the specified time. Additionally, this method directly yields systems removal rates. Using this method and example data failure rate estimates for multiple time periods and confidence levels can be calculated, as shown in Table 7-3.

Since a burn-in (high-voltage, high-temperature stress) is often used to improve reliability by screening, it is also necessary to account for the effect of burn-in in estimating failure rates. Since each failure mechanism may have different acceleration factors it is necessary to establish the effect of burn-in on each mechanism separately. If the curve

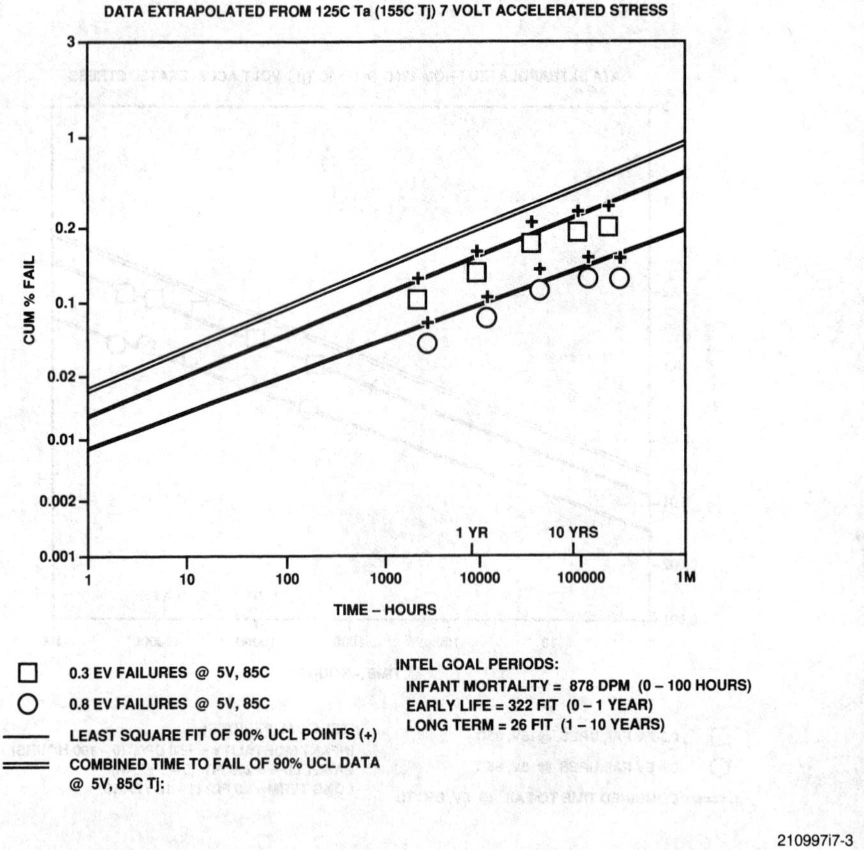

Figure 7-3. Cumulative Percent Versus Time Failure Rate Calculation Method Using 90% UCL

equation for a particular mechanism is “Cum Fail = f(x)” (where x = time) then the equation for the curve, taking into account burn-in, is as follows:

$$\text{Cum Fail} = f(x + \text{BIT}) - f(\text{BIT})$$

where:

x = time
BIT = equivalent burn-in time

By this method the time-to-fail characteristics of a given mechanism can be determined as a function of burn-in. This can be illustrated by using the .3 eV mechanism from the example data as shown in Figure 7-4. This same principle is applied to the curves for all mechanisms, with the component's resulting combined time-to-fail characteristics (with a

Table 7-3. Failure Rate Estimates Derived from Example Data in Table 7-2

Intel Goal Periods	85°C, 5V Failure Rate Estimates of Example Data		
	Best Estimate No Burn-In	90% UCL No Burn-In	Best Estimate 20 Hr., 7V BI
Infant mortality (0-100 hours)	650 DPM	878 DPM	11 DPM
Early life (0-1 year)	.21%/239 FIT	.28%/322 FIT	.06%/68 FIT
Long term (1-10 years)	20 FIT	26 FIT	18 FIT

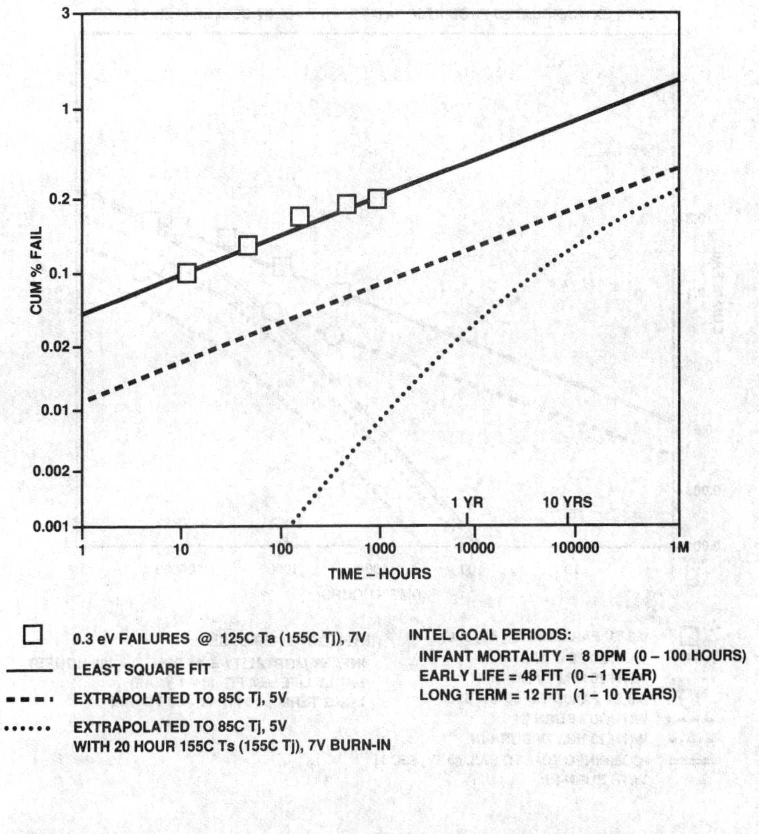

Figure 7-4. Illustration of the Effect of Burn-In on Cumulative Percent Fail Versus Time Curves for a .3 eV Failure Mechanism

given burn-in time) being the probability summation of the "burn-in curves" from each mechanism. This is shown in Figure 7-4, where the curves are derived from the example data in Table 7-3, using a best estimate curve fit, with a 10-hour, 7 volt, 125°C burn-in. The effect of this burn-in is summarized in Figure 7-5, with the calculated failure rates shown in Table 7-3.

A limitation in estimating a particular product's failure rate is the difficulty in performing failure analysis on random logic products and the relatively large volume of accelerated stress tests needed to generate sufficient failures for statistically valid interpretations. Recognizing this limitation, Intel has adopted a technology based method for estimating product failure rates. The assumptions in using this method are that a component's failure rate is limited by random manufacturing defects and that all products processed on the same technology will have the same defect distributions and time-to-fail characteristics, with magnitude varying proportionally with area.

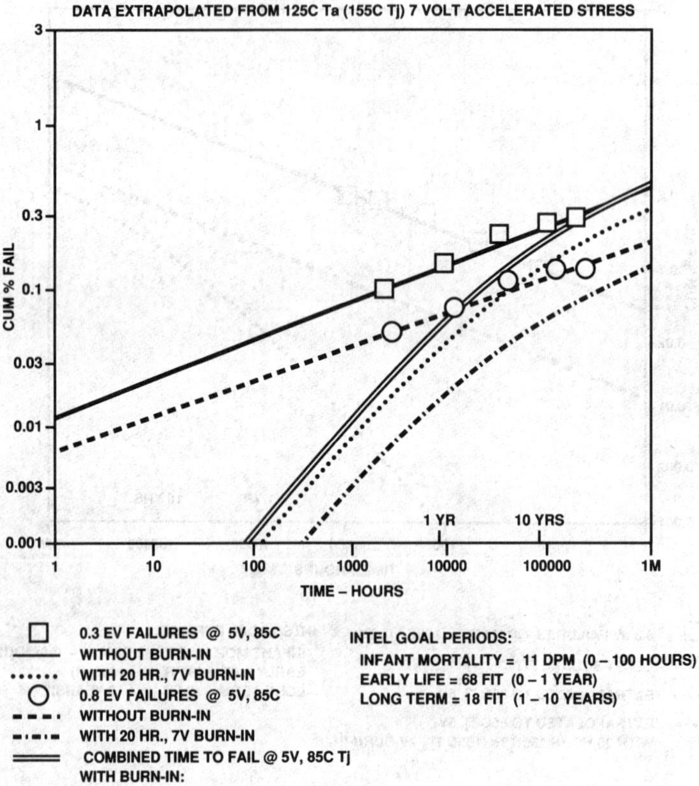

Figure 7-5. Failure Rate Calculation of a Product with the Multiple Contributing Failure Mechanisms and with a Burn-In

Verification of this assumption is an essential element of Intel's certification process. During a technology's development cycle, extensive reliability evaluations are performed to characterize and model technology failure mechanisms. This is to assure there are no intrinsic process-induced defects (reliability of technology-driven by random manufacturing defects). In doing so, a technology reliability defect density and time-to-fail distribution are established for each failure mechanism, as referenced in Table 7-4. Once this technology baseline is established, follow-on product reliability assessments and failure rate estimates can be made by verifying defect density equivalency and for additional confidence, defect distribution (slope) equivalency.

This is done by assuming that the distribution of failure mechanism types and time-to-fail characteristics are equivalent for all products manufactured on the same technology. Only the magnitude or level will vary, proportional to area. By using the technology baseline characterization a prediction of a product's time-to-fail characteristics at accelerated conditions can be made by an area proportional multiple of the baseline technology time-to-fail curve.

That is:

Cum Fail Product A: = (Area Product A/Baseline Product Area) × f(x)

where:

x = time
f(x) = equation for baseline technology curve

As shown in Figure 7-6, by using confidence level limits for the baseline technology data a prediction of a range of expected time-to-fail characteristics can be made. If a product's time-to-fail characteristics fall within the expected range, it is reasonable to assume that the distribution of failure mechanisms for the product is equivalent to the baseline technology. This is illustrated in Figure 7-7 for Intel's 486™ Microprocessor.

Time-to-fail characteristics of the product can then be estimated by fitting the technology curve characteristics to the specific product's accelerated test data. Then, a curve for each failure mechanism can be extrapolated to use operating conditions through the use of a fallout level proportionality multiplier and respective acceleration factors.

Table 7-4. Baseline Technology 7V 125°C Lifetest Certification Data

	Lifetest Results							
	'C'	3 Hrs.	11 Hrs.	33 Hrs.	168 Hrs.	500 Hrs.	1K Hrs.	2K Hrs.
Sample size	–	11955	11922	9872	5463	5436	5427	4918
.3 eV failures	1.8	13	1	4	2	3	1	1
.8 eV failures	.41	1	1	0	1	1	1	1

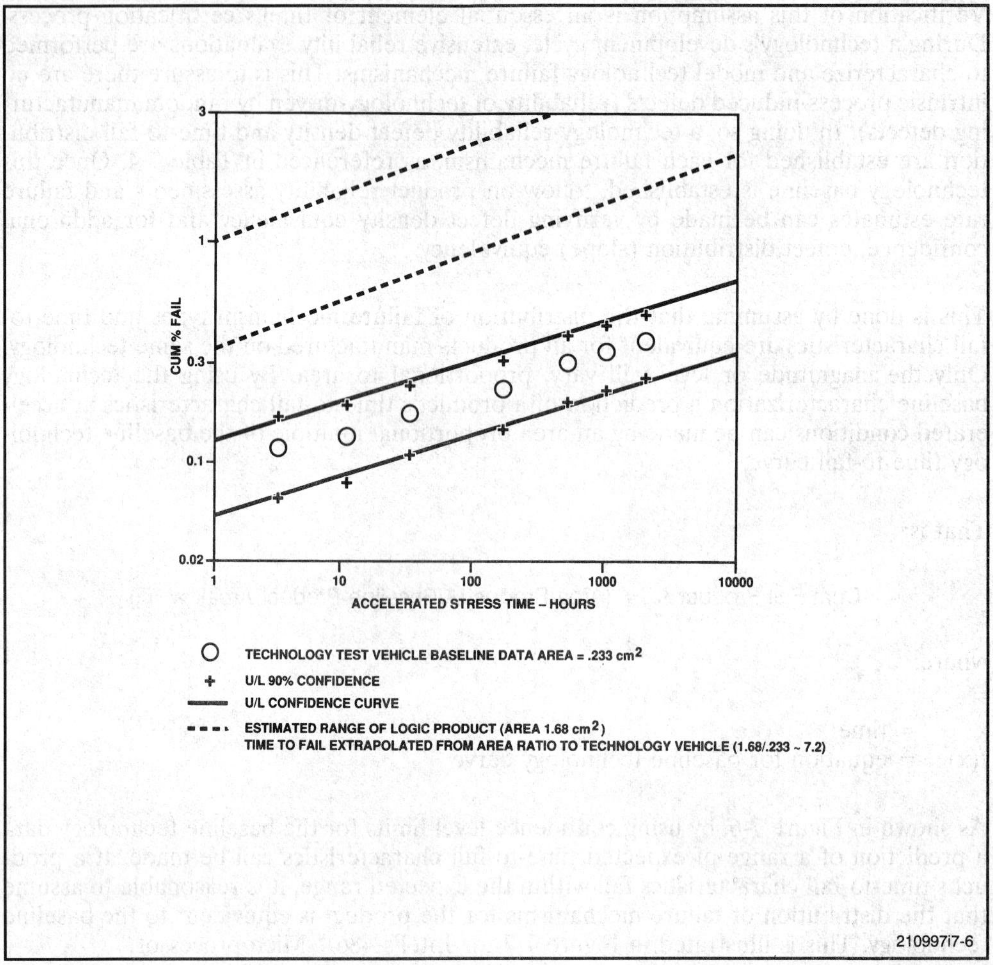

Figure 7-6. Predicted Range of Time to Fail Characteristics from Baseline Technology Data Based on Area Ratio

The product's time-to-fail characteristics of a specific mechanism is a multiple of the ratio of the accelerated test fallout curve to the baseline technology curve.

That is:

$$\text{Cum fail product A} = (\text{\% fail product A / \% fail baseline technology}) \times f(x)$$

where:

x = time
f(x) = equation for baseline technology curve.

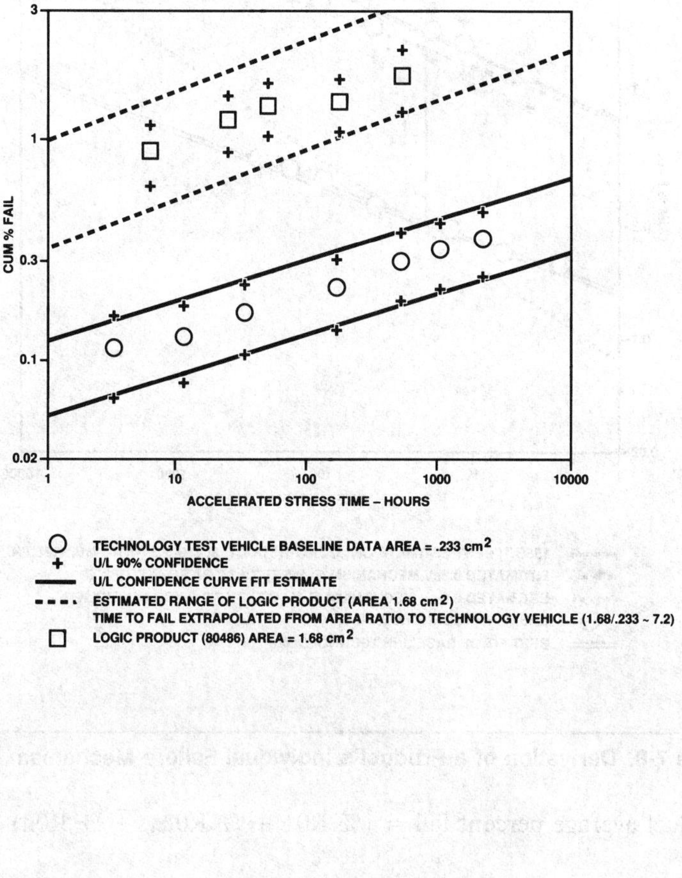

Figure 7-7. Illustration of Actual Results on Intel 486™ Microprocessor Relative to Predicted Range of Time to Fail Characteristics

The total product time-to-fail characteristics are then, as previously discussed, the probability summation of the time-to-fail curves for each contributing mechanism at use conditions. This method can be used for either single or multiple readout product data as shown in Figure 7-8, 7-9, and 7-10. In this case time-to-fail curves were generated from the example data in Table 7-4.

In Figure 7-8, multiple product readout data is compared to the baseline technology curve. The failure ratio is calculated based on the average percent fail of all product readouts at the average time of the readout.

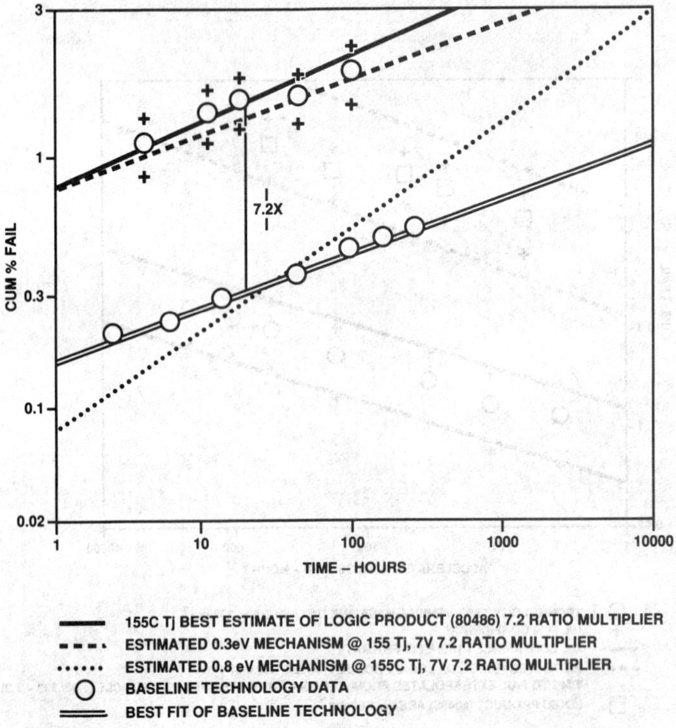

Figure 7-8. Derivation of a Product's Individual Failure Mechanism Curves

That is: Product average percent fail = (% R01 + % R02... + % R0n) / n

where:

% R0 is the cum percent fail at the interval readout

Average time = exp((log(t R01) + log(t R02) ... + log(t R0n)) / n)

where:

t R0 is the cumulative time at each readout interval.

The "Best Estimate" curve fit is a multiple of the baseline technology curve. The multiple is the ratio of the product's average percent fail to the baseline technology's percent fail at the average time. This multiplier is then applied to the baseline individual failure mechanism curves (.3 eV and .8 eV failure mechanisms in this case).

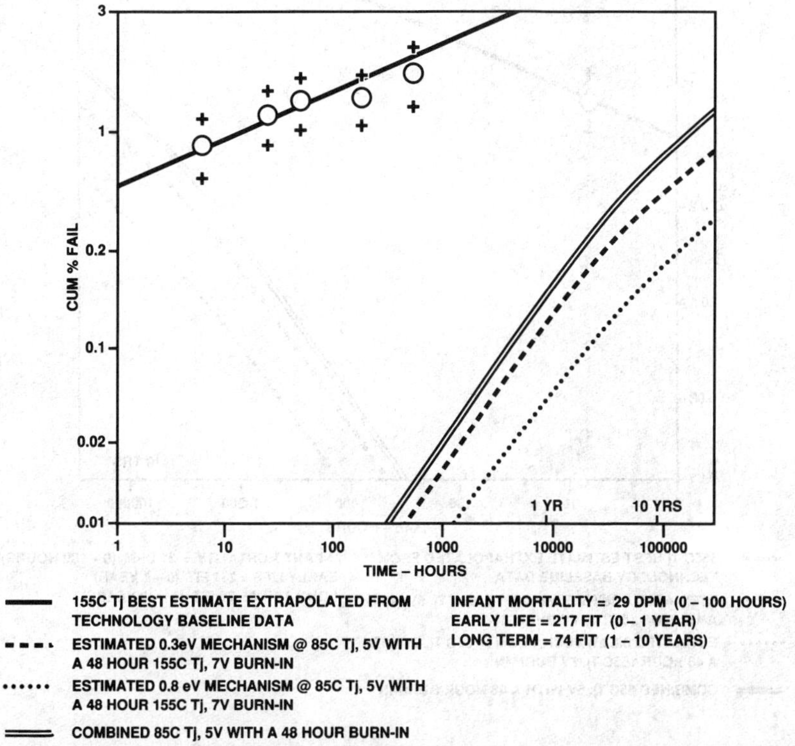

Figure 7-9. Failure Rate Estimate Using Derived Product Failure Mechanism Curves Extrapolated to 85°C Tj, 7V with a 48 Hour Burn-In

Once the curves for the individual product failure mechanism are determined failure estimates can then be made as has been previously discussed. In this case, as shown in Figure 7-9, failure rate estimates are made at 85°C Tj and 5 volts with a 48 hour 125°C Ta (155°C Tj), 7 volt burn-in, where Ta is ambient temperature.

The same methods can be used for single readout data with one exception. This is that the ratio multiplier is based on the percent fail at the single readout point. Again, as shown in Figure 7-10, failure rate estimates are made at 85°C Tj, and 5 volts with a 48 hour burn-in.

The first question anticipated is, "What is the accuracy or precision of the failure rate estimate?" First, one must recognize that extrapolations of failure rates, in the range of current industry standards, from accelerated testing and limited sample sizes is only an

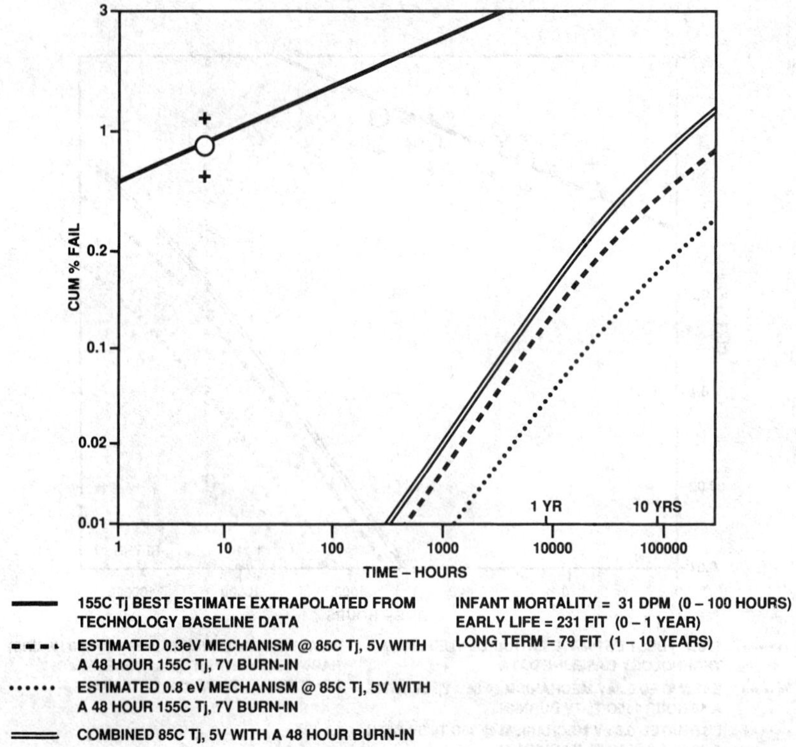

Figure 7-10. Single Readout Failure Rate Estimate Based Extrapolation from Baseline Technology

estimate. By using a range (best estimate – 90% UCL) for the failure rate estimate there can be a reasonable assurance that the real product failure rate will conservatively be within that range.

One must also recognize the difficulty in identifying the physical cause of failure (defect type/mechanism) on today's extremely complex random logic VLSI. This creates inaccuracies in identifying the specific failure mechanisms, failure rates, and estimates on complex VLSI that are somewhat questionable and difficult at best.

It also should be noted that the accuracy of the technology curve fit has minimal affect on a product's failure rate even considering a reasonable large variation in slopes. Even in a case where estimates are made from a single data point, variations in the slope of ± 25% will yield less variation in the extrapolated failure rate than the variation between the best estimate and 90% UCL.

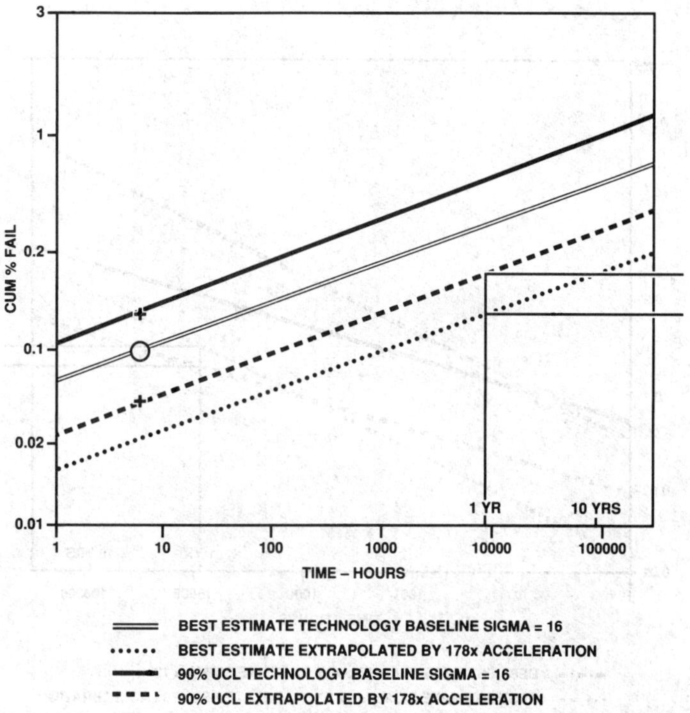

Figure 7-11a. Test Case of Failure Rate Estimates from Best Estimate and 90% UCL Curve Fits

This point can be illustrated (as shown in Figure 7-11a and 7-11b) by using an example baseline technology extrapolation through a relatively large 10/10,000 data point where the resulting slope of the time to fail characteristic has a sigma of 16.

By assuming a net acceleration factor of 178 for only 1 failure mechanism (for simplicity) the following failure rate estimates can be made:

	Fail – First Year	Avg. Fail Rate – First Year
Baseline Technology FIT		
- Best Estimate	.15%	175 FIT
- 90% CL	.24%	275 FIT
Best Estimate with Slope Variation		
– 25%	.18%	204 FIT
+ 25%	.14%	161 FIT

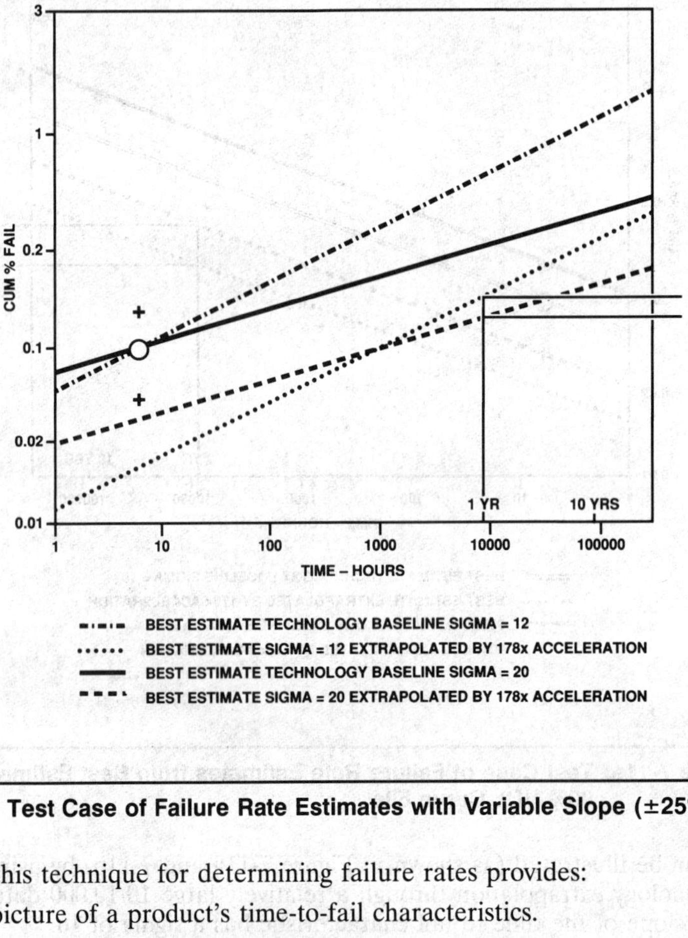

Figure 7-11b. Test Case of Failure Rate Estimates with Variable Slope (±25%) Curve Fits

In summary this technique for determining failure rates provides:

- Realistic picture of a product's time-to-fail characteristics.
- A meaningful interpretation of a specific failure mechanism's contribution to a product's failure rate at any point in time.
- A means to estimate failure rates on complex random logic VLSI without full reliance on failure analysis.
- A means to estimate failure rates from short-duration, high-volume evaluations that yield quick, real-time feedback.

Process Reliability/Failure Mechanisms

8

CHAPTER 8
PROCESS RELIABILITY/FAILURE MECHANISMS **Page**

CHAPTER 8
PROCESS RELIABILITY/FAILURE MECHANISMS

INTRODUCTION

The reliability of a product depends on fabrication process, the package process and the product design and product test. Strict design verification rules allow us to introduce new products without introducing new reliability problems. The process reliability groups focus on ensuring that new technologies provide a sound base for future products and for the continuous improvement of production processes.

Intel's product reliability system is based on three activities: certification of new process and package technologies, design and verification of products whose reliability is based on the base technology and the use of statistical process control to drive continuous process and reliability improvement.

This system results in highly reliable products whose performance is technology-dependent. Product reliability is therefore dependent on the level of integration and the amount of burn-in.

FABRICATION PROCESS RELIABILITY

In order to assure that products are reliable, it is necessary to build reliability into new process technologies. The process reliability group ensures that no intrinsic wearout mechanisms are built into the technology, that defect densities are reduced to sufficiently low levels to allow efficient and economical product manufacture and that layout and circuit design rules guarantee safe operation through the lifetime of the product.

Over the last two decades, MOS technology has been aggressively scaled to reduce die cost, increase chip performance and increase chip functionality. This aggressive scaling is expected to continue at the same rate in the future. Figure 8-1 shows the past and expected future trends of technology performance as measured by transistor density.

Faced with continually shrinking device feature sizes, the ability to increase levels of reliability performance requires a comprehensive and quantitative understanding of IC failure mechanisms, followed by statistical characterization and control of the key parameters that influence these mechanisms. The dimensional scaling that has been used to increase device density and performance has typically given rise to smaller signal strengths, larger current densities, higher chip temperatures and higher electric fields during device operation. The effect of device scaling through several generations of device shrinks has been to move device operating parameters closer to the limits at which fundamental reliability problems occur. Hence, the need for a more precise understanding of these limits and for an effective statistical process control system to avoid subsequent marginal device operation.

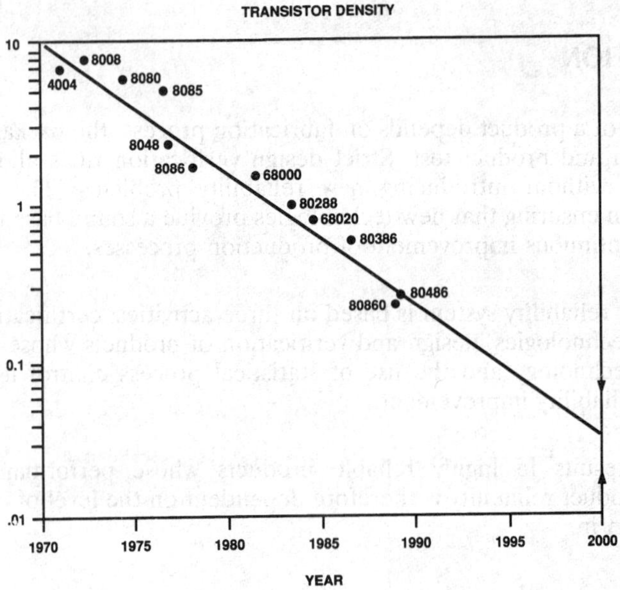

210997i8-1

Figure 8-1. Transistor Density

The main activities associated with process reliability are wearout prevention, detection and reduction of latent defects and contamination, determination of reliability-related layout design rules, reliability analysis of device structures and materials and fundamental studies of the physics of failure and prove out of new technologies on lead products. Each of these are discussed in the following sections.

ELECTROMIGRATION

Electromigration (EM) is the motion of the interconnect metallization due to momentum exchange from the electron current. A divergence of the metallic ion flux leads to void formation in the conductors and ultimately to open circuit failure, as shown in Figure 8-2. A convergence of the ion flux can lead to hillock formation or a buildup of metal in local regions. This can result in short circuits to adjacent or overlying conductors. Contacts of aluminum-silicon to silicon can fail by voiding the metal or spiking. Spiking is the diffusion of silicon into aluminum, followed by the diffusion of aluminum into the silicon void; this eventually shorts the underlying p-n junction. Figure 8-3 shows voiding in the "upstream" contact and Figure 8-4 shows Si nodules in the "downstream" contact. When Si from the Al-Si metallization is driven by EM to the contact area, silicon nodules result.

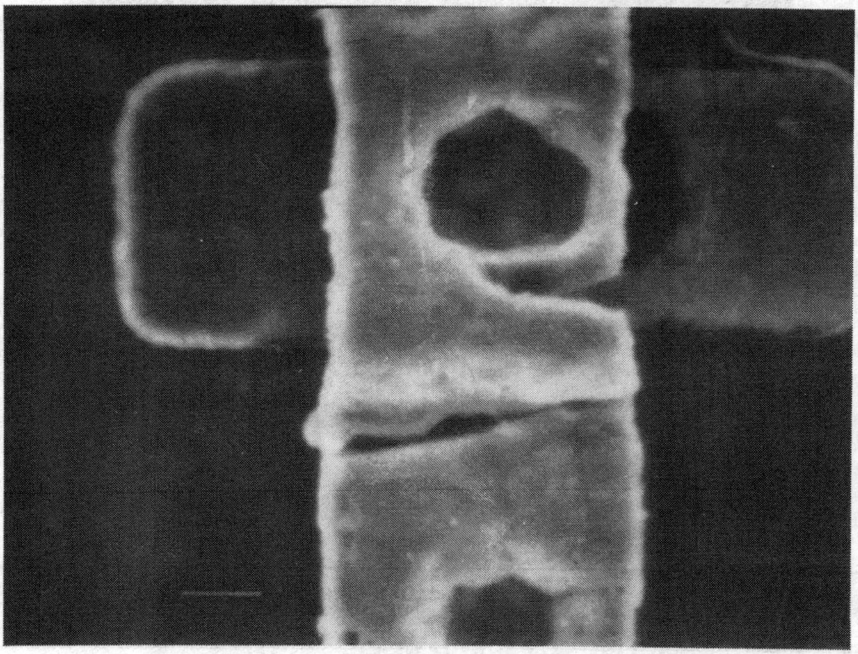

210997i

Figure 8-2. Electromigration Failure

Interconnect metallization occurs when specially designed test structures are subjected to elevated temperature and high current densities for the purpose of accelerating the EM process. The time-to-failure is measured at each stress condition and regression analysis used to best-fit a log normal distribution to the data. Each log normal distribution is characterized by a median time-to-failure (T50) and standard deviation (sigma) in units of logarithm base-e. Figure 8-5 shows typical failure distributions for aluminum alloy metallizations with and without a refractory metal layer. The figure shows that sandwich interconnects (aluminum alloy on top of a refractory metal) have both longer T50 and reduced standard deviation. This improved reliability is a result of the redundant current path provided by the parallel conductor, as shown in Figure 8-6.

The current and temperature acceleration factors are determined from the change in T50 with stress condition. Open and short circuit failure in aluminum-silicon alloy interconnects have a thermal activation of 0.5 eV, while aluminum-copper has a significantly higher activation energy (0.7 eV). Leakage in p-n junctions under silicon contacts is accelerated using a 0.8 eV activation energy, resistive contacts due to nodule growth have 0.7 eV activation energy and open contacts due to voiding of the metal sidewall have the same activation energy as metal line failures (either 0.5 or 0.7 eV).

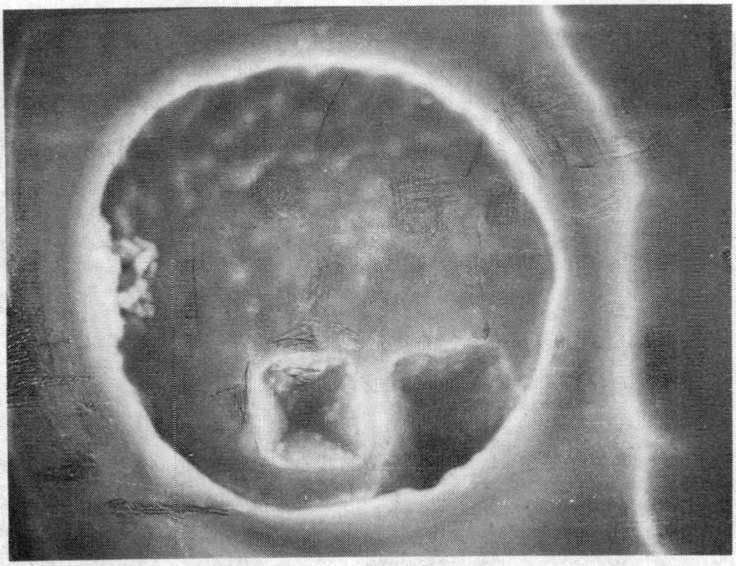

210997i

Figure 8-3. Fifth Contact in a Chain with Voiding

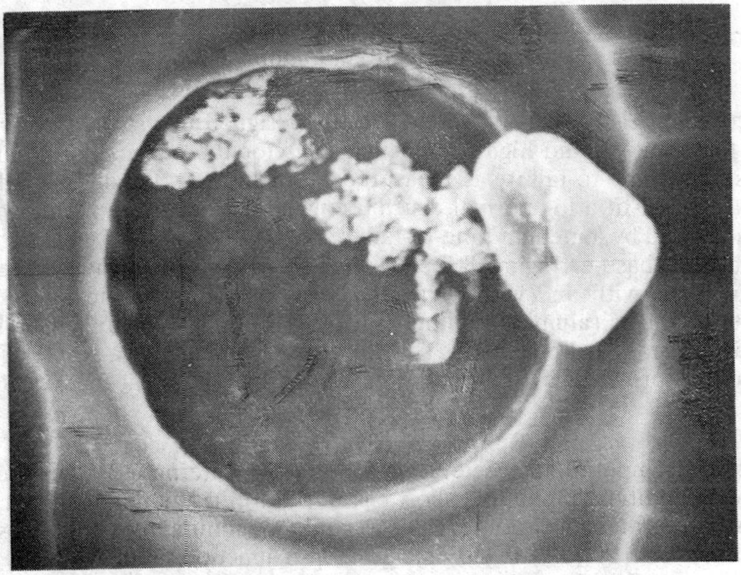

210997i

Figure 8-4. Sixth Contact in a Chain with Hillock Growth

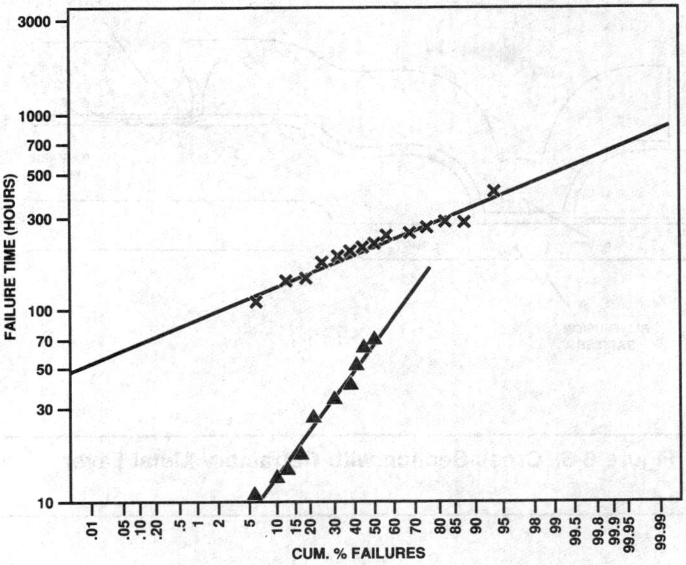

		MTTF HRS.	STD DEV	0.1% FT HRS.		
WITH REFRACTARY LAYER	×	224.13	.38	68.31	Ti / Al Si	ALL TESTS AT 175°C T_A NORMALIZED TO 60mA
WITHOUT REFRACTARY LAYER	▲	70	1.16	1.8	Al Si	

210997i8-5

Figure 8-5. Electromigration Time to Failure Distributions for Aluminum-Silicon with and without a Barrier Layer

After we characterize the temperature and current acceleration factors for a new metallization type or manufacturing process, we define appropriate design rules are defined to ensure that no more than 0.1% of products fail due to electromigration in 100K hours of operating life. The maximum current allowed for each line width is determined from measurements of test structures with various widths. During layout of each new product, we estimate the current carried in interconnect lines using computer simulation. The lines are sufficiently wide to reliably carry the current.

Interconnect reliability is routinely monitored as part of a continuous improvement of each manufacturing process. The process parameters which affect EM (such as deposition conditions and line width) are actively monitored using standard statistical process control (SPC) methods. We also run routine monitors for other parameters affect measured EM performance, including passivation integrity, metal resistivity ratio and metal step coverage. Scanning Electron Microscope (SEM) cross sections of metal lines with good and bad step coverage are shown in Figures 8-7 and 8-8, respectively. Figure 8-9

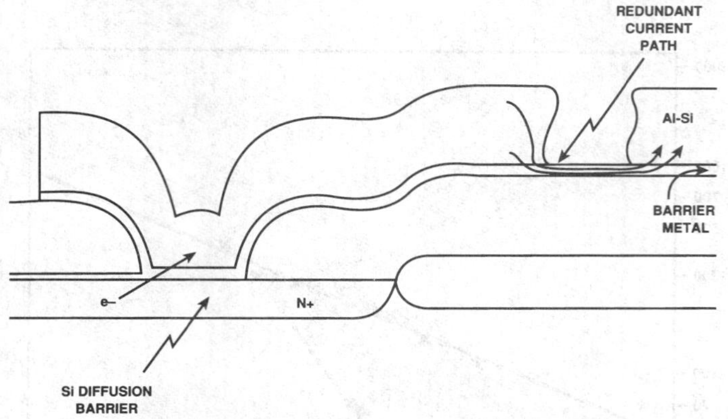

Figure 8-6. Cross Section with Refractory Metal Layer

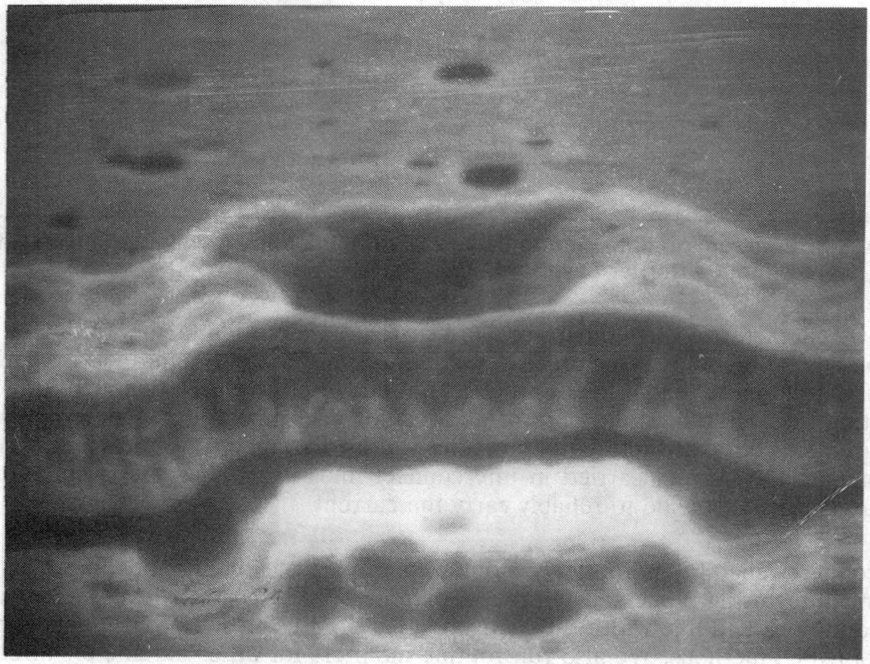

Figure 8-7. Metal Line with Good Step Coverage

210997i

Figure 8-8. Metal Line with Poor Step Coverage

shows a trend chart of the metal resistivity ratio for one sputterer. This parameter is sensitive to grain size and included contaminants. Finally, the EM performance itself is monitored and trended regularly using test structures included on product wafers.

HOT CARRIER INJECTION

Hot carrier conditions occur in most transistors when the lateral electric field in the drain depletion region or the channel becomes so large that the conducting electrons or holes gain energy from the electric field faster than they can lose it back to the silicon lattice via optical photon emission. These highly energetic carriers are termed hot carriers because they have a much greater distribution of energies than the silicon temperature would predict. As these carriers take on more energy from the electric field, they first gain enough energy (1.5 eV) to impact-ionize and create hole-electron pairs, which results in a measurable substrate current consisting of carriers created with opposite conductivity type to those in the channel. If the hot carriers further gain enough energy (3-4 eV) and through collisions obtain the proper momentum, they can surmount the Si-SiO_2 energy barrier and be injected into the overlying SiO_2. Hot carrier can also tunnel quantum mechanically directly into the oxide at lower energies.

Depending on the sign of the carrier's charge and the direction of the electric field in the oxide at the point of injection, the electron or hole is either drawn toward the gate or driven back toward the channel (see Figure 8-10). The direction of the oxide field above the channel is a function of both the gate and the drain voltage. While in the oxide, a

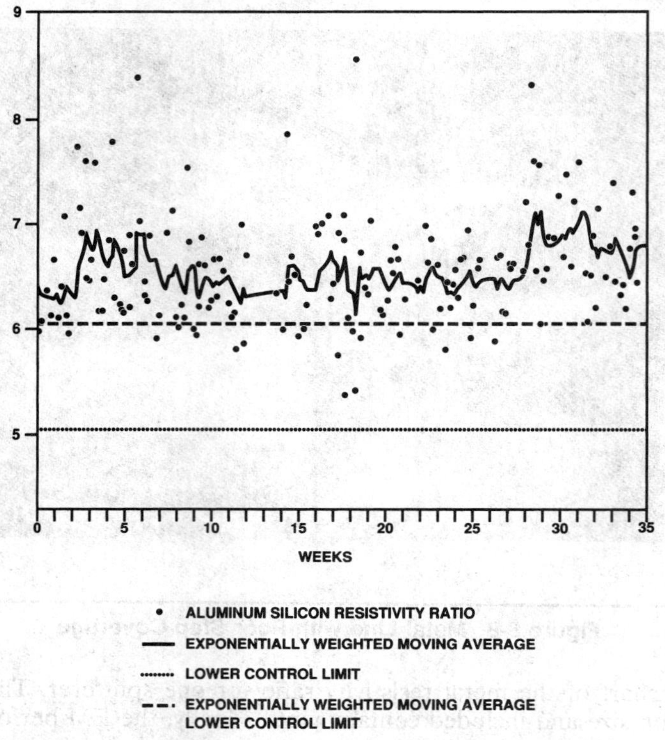

Figure 8-9. Trend Chart of the Metal Resistivity Ratio for One Sputterer

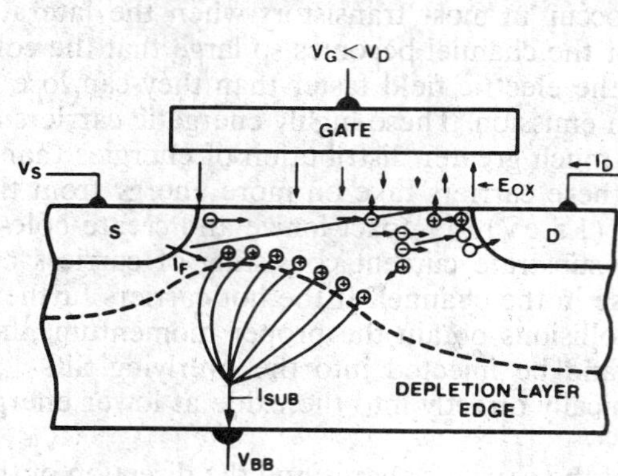

Figure 8-10. Impact Ionization and Hot Carrier Injection

percentage of the injected carriers will be trapped. These trapped charges can lead to transistor parameter shifts and subsequently to device malfunction. For example, electrons trapped above the channel of an n-type transistor can locally raise the threshold voltage and reduce the drain current. Holes trapped near the interface can lead to the formation of interface states which reduce the differential transconductance of a transistor. The reduced gain can subsequently lead to device failure.

Hot carrier degradation is a function of transistor geometry and bias voltages (which determine the electric fields) and of oxide quality (which affects the trapping characteristics). Transistors of each type and varying channel lengths are stressed at ambient temperatures with different combinations of gate and drain voltages and are characterized for threshold voltage shift, transconductance reduction and substrate current. Safe operating voltage conditions are determined for each device-type channel length using the characterized acceleration factors and the 60 meV negative activation energy.

For advanced technologies, we use hot carrier injection under AC (or dynamic) conditions. For example, as the input voltage increases for a typical CMOS inverter, a pulse of high substrate current occurs (see Figure 8-11). This substrate current (Isub) is associated with hot carrier injection. A quasi-static model, which assumes the effects of carrier injection behave similarly to DC degradation for small increments of time, can then be applied. Knowing the relationship between substrate current and hot carrier degradation, the total device degradation can be described (see Figure 8-12).

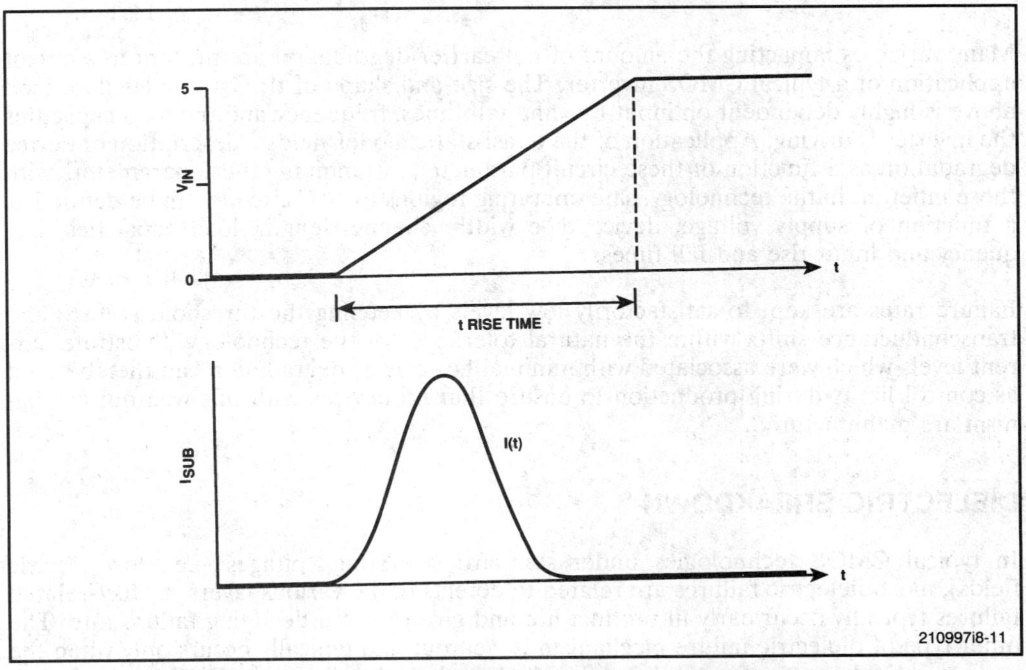

Figure 8-11. Substrate (Isub) Pulse from Inverter Circuit during Input Low-to-High Transition

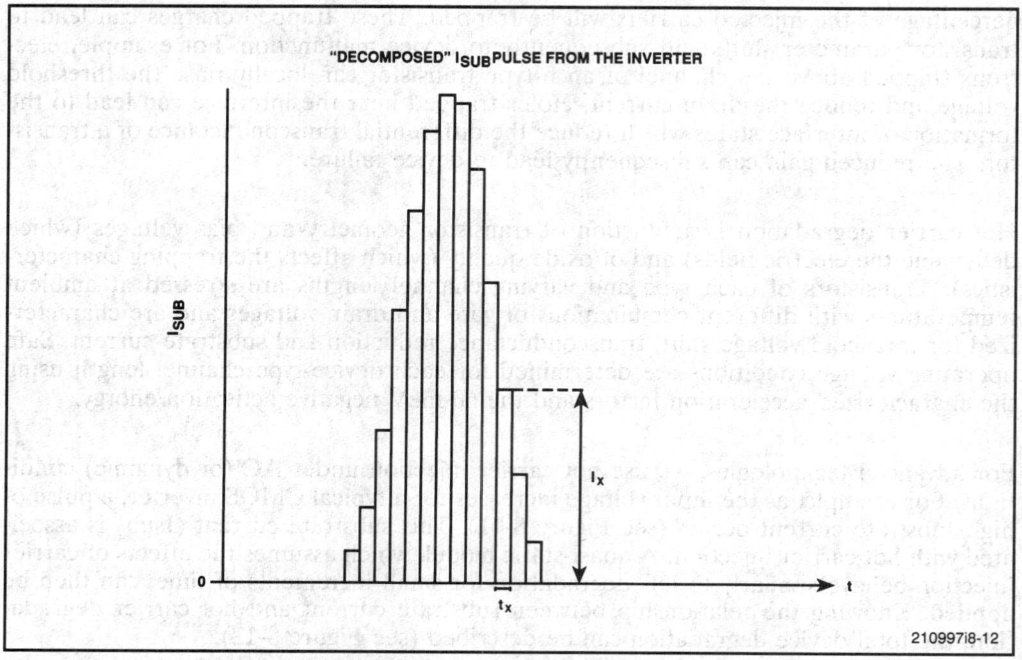

Figure 8-12. "Decomposed" Isub Pulse from the Inverter

Many variables impacting the amount of hot carrier degradation are present in a circuit application of a typical CMOS inverter. The size and shape of the Isub pulse described above is highly dependent on input rise and fall times, frequency and the load capacities the inverter is driving. Application of the quasi-static model yields a description of device degradation as a function of these circuit parameters. Combining these parameters with those inherent in the technology, safe operating regions for AC circuits can be defined as a function of supply voltage, device type width, channel length, load capacities, frequency and input rise and fall times.

Failure rates are kept to satisfactorily low levels by keeping the threshold voltage and transconductance shifts within the natural tolerances of the technology. Substrate current levels which were associated with minimal hot carrier degradation can then be used as control limits during production to ensure that no devices with this wearout mechanism are manufactured.

DIELECTRIC BREAKDOWN

In typical CMOS technologies under standard operating voltages (i.e., low electric fields), most dielectric failures are related to defects in the various layers. Defect-related failures typically occur early in product life and give rise to a declining failure rate. The other type of dielectric failure mechanism is wearout and typically occurs only when the operating field approaches the breakdown strength of the dielectric. Wearout is characterized by an increasing failure rate.

In both cases, the failure mechanisms for silicon dioxide are thought to be due to charge buildup near the silicon-silicon dioxide interface, enhancing the injection of charge carriers into the oxide. The charge buildup increases the electric field at the interface and since current is exponentially dependent upon the electric field (Fowler-Nordheim tunneling), a small buildup of charge dramatically increases the current flow. As the current increases, localized Joule heating can vaporize the silicon dioxide and silicon, causing a short between the substrate and gate electrode in gate oxides or polysilicon and metal in interlayer dielectrics.

Silicon Dioxide, the primary dielectric used in VLSI processes, can be characterized using a variety of techniques, including measuring the breakdown electric field distribution, charge-to-breakdown and time-to-breakdown under constant electric field stressing. The first two tests can be rapidly executed in a wafer level, allowing them to be used as in process monitors. The latter is very time consuming but allows easier derating to actual device operating characteristics.

A typical oxide breakdown distribution is shown in Figure 8-13. There is an intrinsic population centered around 10 MV/cm which is brought on through Fowler-Nordheim tunneling through defect-free oxide. A second distribution is sometimes found in the 0-2 MV/cm range and is typically screened out at sort; shows up as a yield failure.

Figure 8-13. Oxide Breakdown Distribution

Statistically monitoring die fallout for oxide failures is an effective methodology for flagging any major oxide excursion due to processing. The third distribution noted in Figure 8-13 is that which lies between the 2 MV/cm level and the intrinsic distribution at 10 MV/cm. These are often referred to as latent defects.

Although electrical prescreens are still used to reduce the level of latent defects, more emphasis is focused on reducing process-induced defects. This is especially important as oxides become thinner, to prevent stressing the oxide into the wearout region. Internally we qualify an oxidation and anneal process when both the defect and latent defect population are reduced below target levels and the appropriate monitors are in place. A second constraint an qualifying the process is to ensure that the dielectric will not fail due to wearout when subjected to production screens.

The prescreens, mentioned above, use high temperatures and accelerating electric fields. Both accelerate (reduce) the time to failure of a dielectric film. The effect of increasing electric field is shown in Figure 8-14. Higher electric fields result in much shorter failure time. There are several models in the literature for derating accelerated stressing to operating conditions (E-field vs 1/E field models), which can lead to very different results when derating. Intel uses the more conservative E-field model in order to provide

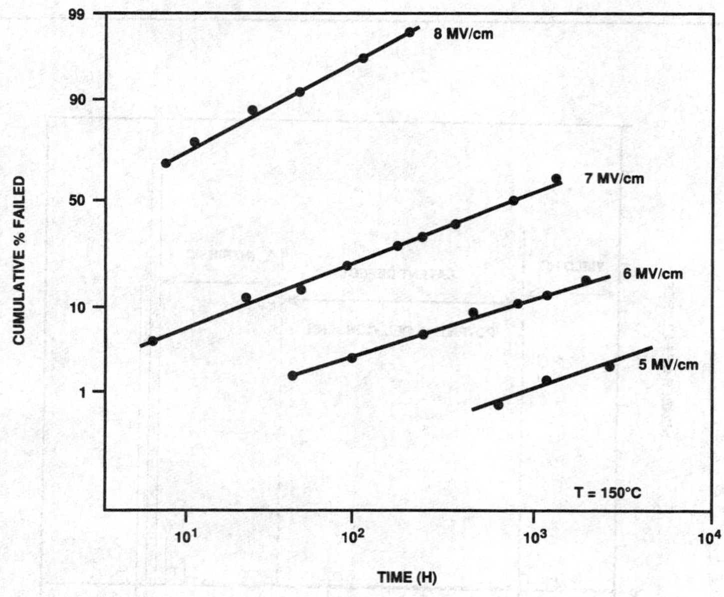

FIELD ACCELERATED WEAROUT IN 100-Å OXIDES. T=150° C

210997i8-14

Figure 8-14. Time Dependent Oxide Breakdown

customers with the necessary Quality assurance. This can give acceleration factors in the order of 10 MV/cm to > 1000 MV/cm, depending upon the exact stressing and oxide thickness. These factors are verified during our internal certification procedures. The result is that we are able to optimize our high-voltage test stresses in order to screen out virtually all devices with oxides defective enough to fail during the part's life.

NON-VOLATILE MEMORY RELIABILITY

EPROM and flash memory cells use a dual-layer polysilicon gate technology to permanently store charge. Floating gate technology is used to store charge that makes the memory cell conducting or non-conducting, thus implementing a logical 1 or 0. The floating polysilicon gate is surrounded by high-quality dielectric, giving these memory devices excellent data retention.

A floating gate NVM cell layout is shown in Figure 8-15a and a cross section is shown in Figure 8-15b. The memory cell uses a self-aligned floating gate to increase performance and density. When the EPROM cell is in the neutral state with no charge on the floating gate, it exhibits a threshold for conduction like a normal MOS transistor. The cell will

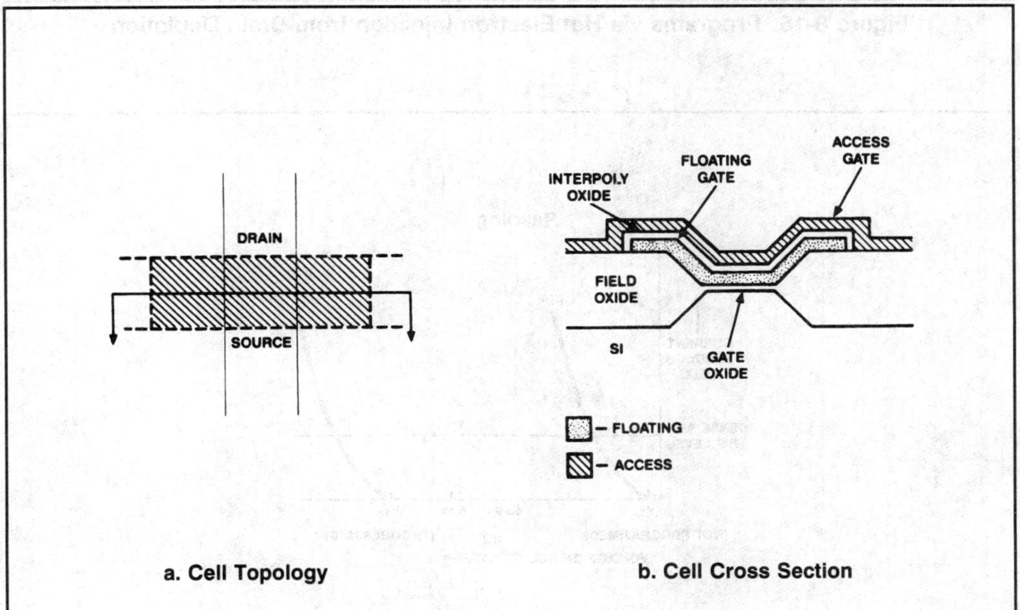

Figure 8-15. Floating Gate EPROM Cell Topology

conduct when the access gate is selected. The memory cell is programmed via hot electron injection from the drain depletion region, as shown in Figure 8-16. A programmed cell has enough electrons on the floating gate so the transistor does not conduct current. The sense amp reads a programmed bit as a logical 0, as shown in Figure 8-17.

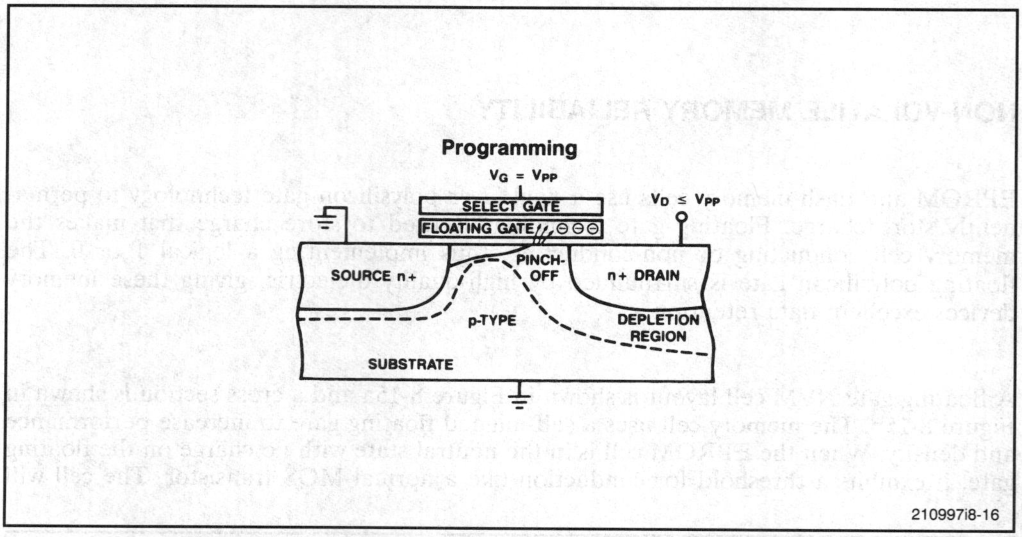

Figure 8-16. Programs via Hot Electron Injection from Drain Depletion

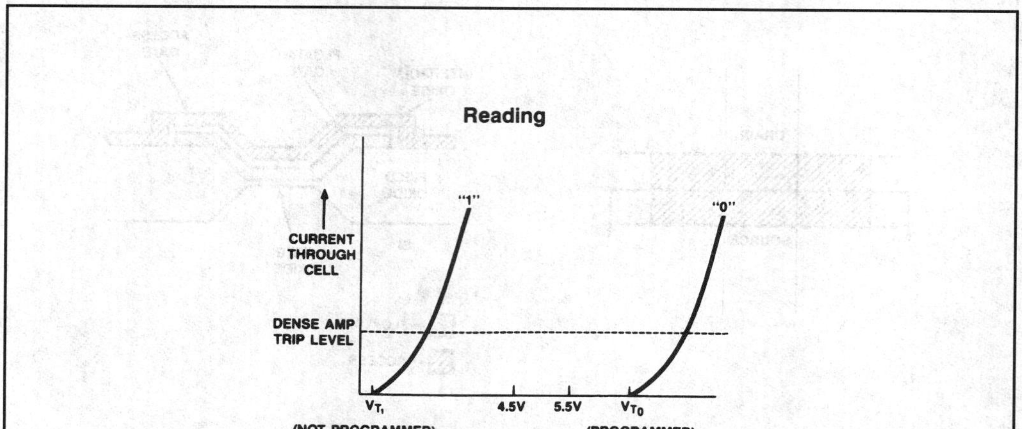

Figure 8-17. Reading

EPROM margin testing depends on the operating characteristics of the EPROM cell. An erased cell with no charge on the floating gate has a normal NMOS I-V characteristics, as shown in Figure 8-18, which results in an output of a 1 from the memory device. When the cell is programmed by injecting electrons onto the floating gate, the cell threshold shifts. This effect is shown in Figure 8-18 by parallel I-V shift so that a higher select-gate potential is required to cause the cell to conduct current. During normal operation a programmed cell does not conduct current and the sense amp reads a 0.

In order to margin-test an EPROM for program margin, the select-gate voltage is raised so that the cell begins to conduct and the sense amp reads 1. This voltage is then recorded as the program margin, as shown in Figure 8-18. If the device were to exhibit charge loss, the I-V characteristics would shift to the left and a lower program margin would be measured. Erase margin is measured in a similar fashion with the select-gate voltage to look for the point where the amp reads zero.

The primary motivation for using margin testing is to assure data retention. Data retention failure modes can easily be characterized using margin testing, which facilitates process improvements and screen development. Effective reliability screens require the use of margin testing in order to detect shifting units which might become a reliability hazard.

Charge Retention

A unique characteristic of the EPROM is the ability to store charge on the floating gate for an unlimited period of time. By surrounding the floating gate with high-quality, thermally-grown oxide-nitride-oxide, a 3.1 eV energy barrier traps electrons on the floating gate.

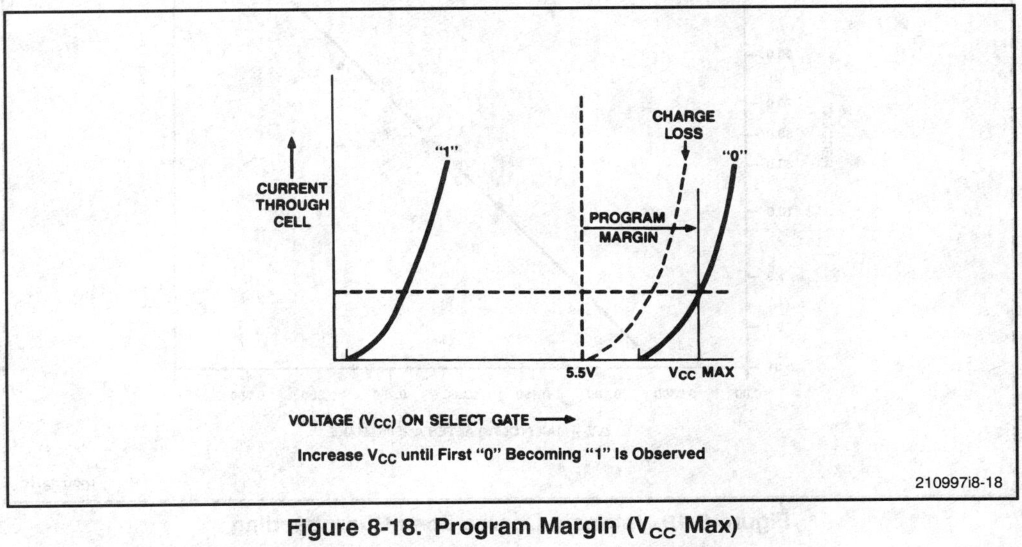

Figure 8-18. Program Margin (V_{CC} Max)

8

Typical EPROM cells have been shown to retain their charge forever. A leakage rate of one electron per second would cause an EPROM cell storing 100,000 electrons to lose data in a day. To analyze the charge loss of typical EPROM cells, margin testing is done before and after a 168-hour, 250°C bake. A distribution plot of typical charge loss on EPROM memories is shown in Figure 8-19. The figure shows that 99.7 percent of all devices evidence less than .35V margin shift. Analysis of this small amount of charge loss shows an activation energy of 1.4 eV. This charge loss is due to electrons trapped in the gate oxide during UV erase. By performing 168-hour, 250°C bake before programming, intrinsic charge loss does not occur in a subsequent bake if there has not been an intervening UV erase. Thus, a typical EPROM cell does not lose charge from the floating gate.

The failure rate of EPROMs is limited by dielectric defects, causing charge loss or gain. From the potential diagrams for a programmed EPROM cell (shown in Figures 8-20 and 8-21), you can see that a defect in either dielectric causes charge loss. However, during an erased stress where the select-gate is raised to V_{CC} or higher voltage, the defective dielectric can be detected. A gate oxide defect will cause electrons to flow from the channel to the floating gate, resulting in a 1 changing to a 0 from the charge gain, as shown in the potential diagrams of Figures 8-20 and 8-21. If the defect is in the poly dielectric, the floating gate will lose electrons until it becomes positively charged, causing the erase margin to increase. All Intel non-volatile memories receive 100 percent retention testing at sort to assure long-term reliability.

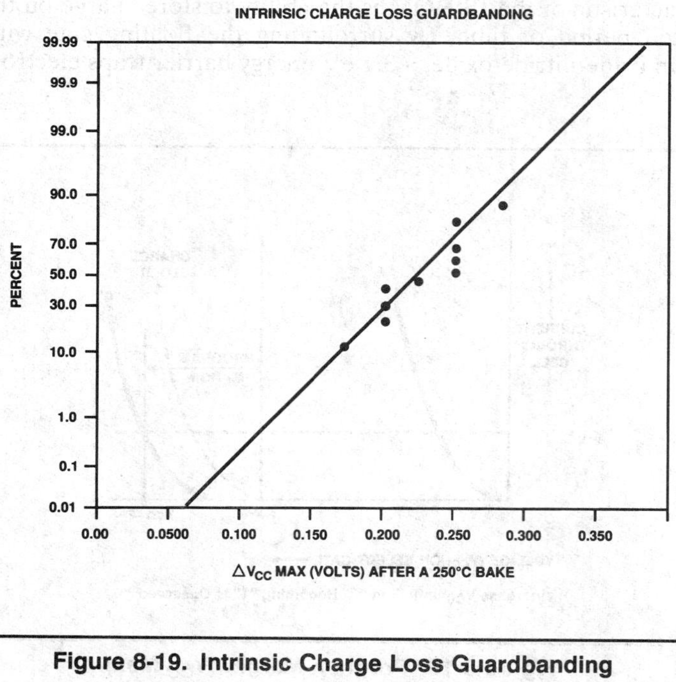

210997i8-19

Figure 8-19. Intrinsic Charge Loss Guardbanding

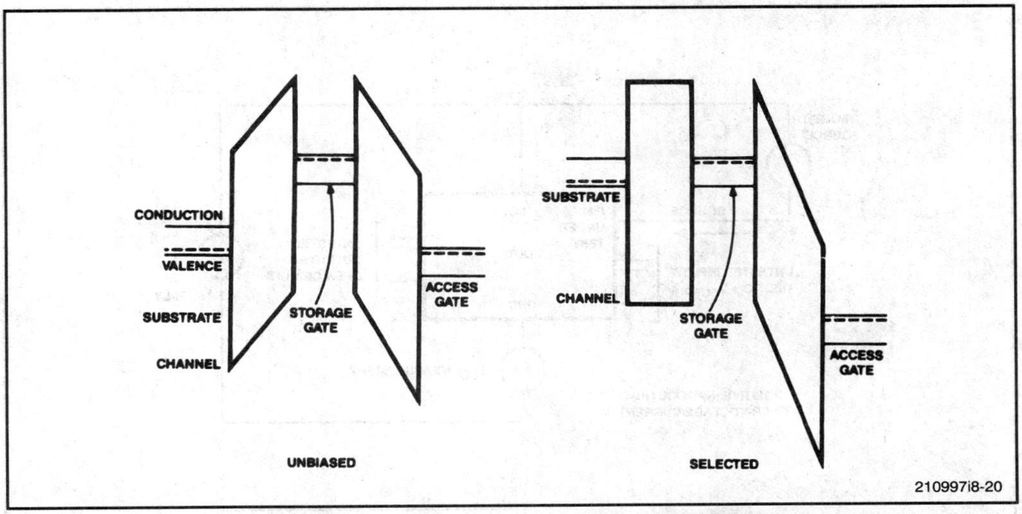

Figure 8-20. Potential Programmed EPROM Cell

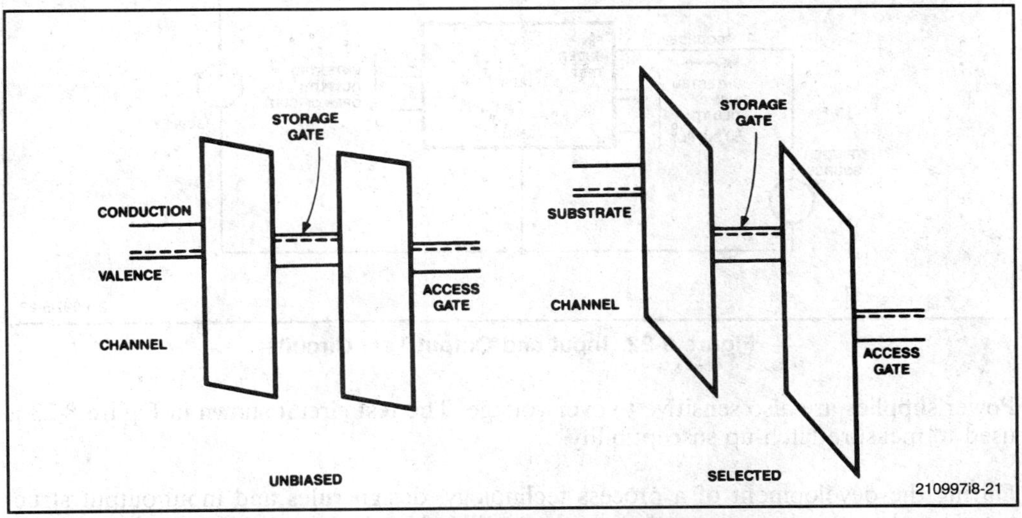

Figure 8-21. Potential Erased EPROM Cell

CMOS Latch-Up

CMOS products can be prone to over-voltages exceeding maximum device ratings, causing parasitic p-n-p-n SCRs to turn on. When the SCR turns on, it has a very low holding voltage, draws excessive currents and causes products to become non-functional or damaged by thermal runaway. Device Under Test (DUT), inputs and outputs are tested with the circuits (in Figure 8-22) for both positive and negative over-voltage.

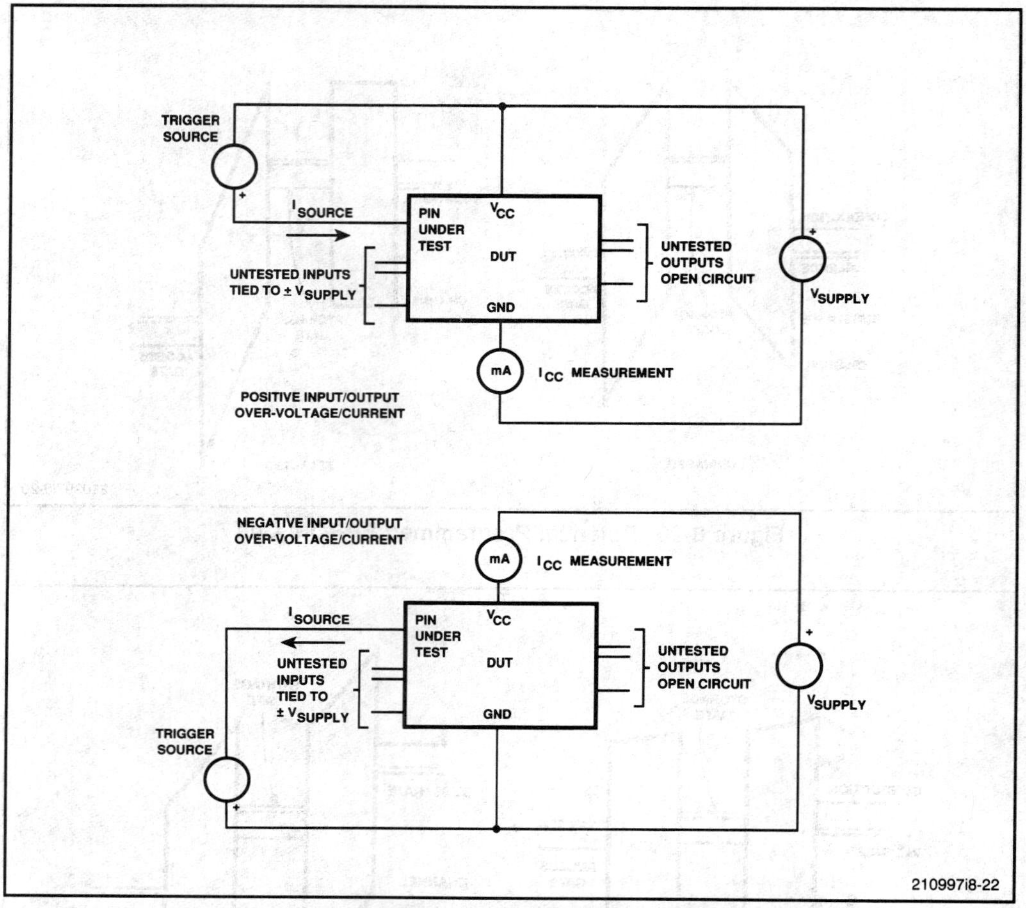

Figure 8-22. Input and Output Test Circuits

Power supplies are also sensitive to over-voltage. The test circuit shown in Figure 8-23 is used to measure latch-up susceptibility.

During the development of a process technology, design rules and input/output structures are developed to ensure that products will have adequate latch-up resistance.

Electrostatic Discharge

Electrostatic discharge into product input, output and power supplies is one of the leading causes of device failure in the user's manufacturing process. VLSI devices cannot be made resistant to ESD and are destroyed by excessive voltage. For example, a charge strong enough to produces a visible spark is equivalent to a 10 KV ESD event, more than VLSI devices can withstand. ESD protection devices protect internal thin oxide by converting high voltage to a high current in the protection device. The human body is used

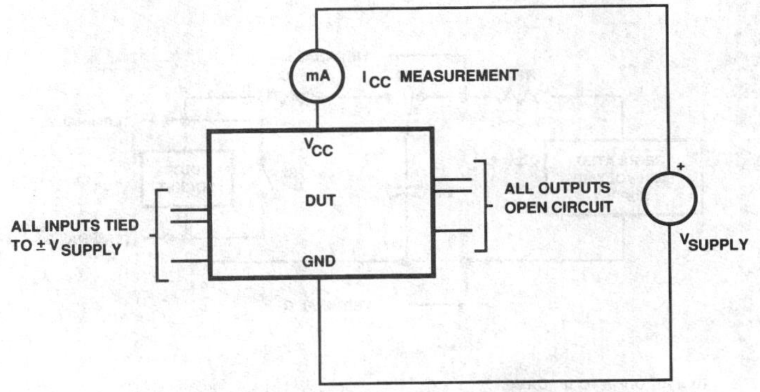

Figure 8-23. Power Supply Test Circuit

as a model to measure the ability of protection devices to absorb the energy of an ESD event. The charged device model, with its low series and resistance, measures the ability of the protective network to respond quickly to high voltages.

ESD resistance of all new products and technologies is tested to both the human body and charged device models. As part of the process technology development, standard cells and design rules are developed to ensure adequate ESD resistance. Human body model performance is tested to the MIL-STD-883c method 3015.7, whose circuit model is shown in Figure 8-24. Charged device performance is tested with the circuit in Figure 8-25. Inductance and resistance in the test circuit is minimized to simulate a device pin discharging to a ground plane.

RANDOM DEFECTS AND CONTAMINATION

Failure mechanisms resulting from random defects or contamination differ from wearout mechanisms in that they generally have a declining rather than an increasing failure rate with time. Because of their declining failure rate characteristics, they are manifested as infant mortality failures rather than long-term failures. These are easily eliminated from the production population through high-voltage and/or high-temperature stress test or burn-in. Nevertheless, in order to ensure that new technologies are acceptable from a manufacturing standpoint, the level of random defect or contamination must be measured and controlled as part of the technology development cycle.

Random Defects

Failure mechanisms resulting from random defects, typically particles from the process flow/process equipment, are characterized by a rapidly declining failure rate over time. Unlike wearout mechanisms, there is a finite number of devices potentially affected by a

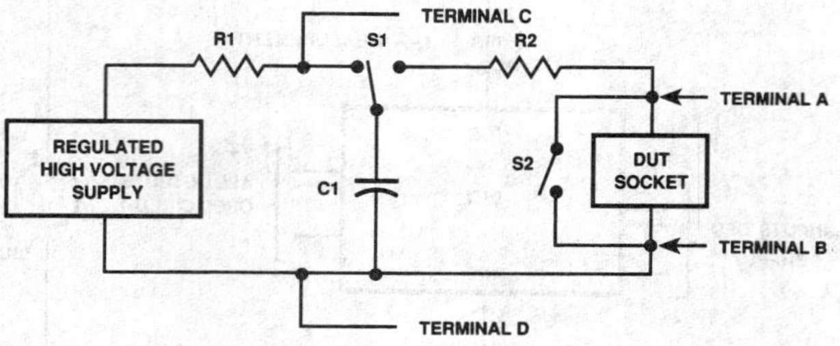

R1 = 10^6 OHMS TO 10^7 OHMS
C1 = 100 PICOFARADS ± 10 PERCENT (INSULATION RESISTANCE 10^{12} OHMS MINIMUM)

R2 = 1500 OHMS ± 1 PERCENT
S1 = HIGH VOLTAGE RELAY (BOUNCELESS, MERCURY WETTED, OR EQUIVALENT)

S2 = NORMALLY CLOSED SWITCH (OPEN DURING DISCHARGE PULSE AND CAPACITANCE MEASUREMENTS)

210997i8-24

Figure 8-24. ESD Test Circuit

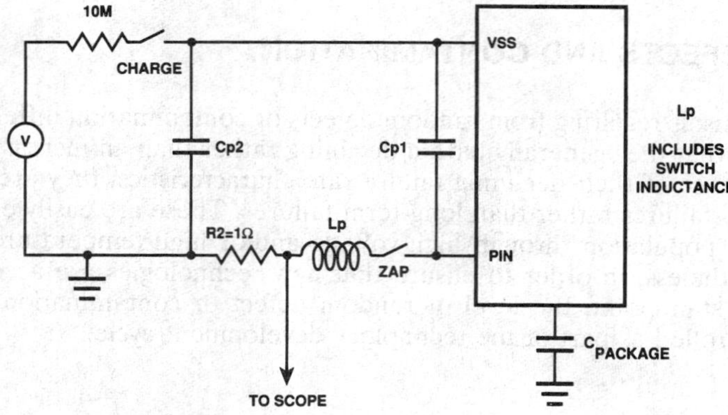

210997i8-25

Figure 8-25. Charged Device Test Circuit

random defect. As the defects are removed from the population, the percentage of devices with defects decreases, as does the failure rate. The time dependency associated with these random defects is actually a function of the physical mechanism resulting from the type or form of the defect.

A common type of random defect is the conductive particle which causes a short or leakage path between interconnects (at any layer or between layers). Defects that are not detected in the time-zero electrical test have a thin insulating layer (dielectric) between the particle and the interconnect conductors. The physical mechanism of failure and corresponding time dependency take the same characteristics as gate dielectric failures. Other forms of these defects include localized contamination sites; particles in photo-resist layers creating a notch or voiding resulting in a blown or electronic rated line; and particles in contacts creating "pinholes" in barrier metals, resulting in localized junction spiking sites. As with the dielectric particle failure, the time-dependence characteristics and acceleration factors of these defect types is the same as the physical mechanism of failure.

Even though a new technology has been characterized and designed to ensure acceptable reliability margins from a fundamental or intrinsic standpoint, random defects introduced during the manufacturing process can result in yield loss and reliability failures. Continuous reduction of these random defects is an integral part of new technology development. We design special test patterns to characterize and monitor defect densities at each thin-film conductor layer and use automated particle-count techniques at each layer. Each of these methods is an essential element in continuously improving defect reduction. Through the certification a technology is not introduced until it meets target objectives for both yield and reliability. Beyond certification, both yield and reliability continue to improve through in-process defect reduction efforts.

Early in a technology's life (and because of the characteristics rapidly declining failure rate), we achieve further reliability defect reduction through screening. Though long-term, the preferred and more effective improvement method is in-process control-defect reduction, a high-voltage, high-temperature burn-in that is an effective means to reduce early failures resulting from random defects. This accelerated stress burn-in, or lifetest, is also used to monitor the outgoing reliability impact of random defects. By knowing the physical mechanism of these defects, accelerated stress test data can be extrapolated to nominal use conditions.

Ionic Contamination

There are two distinct forms of contamination failures: one intrinsic and localized. In both cases the physical cause of failure is the same; that is, mobile ion (Na, K, Cl, etc.) movement into critical areas, causing device or field threshold shifts. Intrinsic contamination is associated with substantial ionic contaminates and/or a basic design-layout marginality. In this case contamination is a wearout mechanism where all product is subject to failure and there is characteristically a geometrical or layout pattern associated with the failure signature. Intrinsic contamination sensitivity is well characterized during the technology development. Certification cycle and sensitivities within process control limits are designed out.

Process monitoring of intrinsic contamination is performed by measuring flat band shifts after a biased high-temperature stress on test wafers with a simple capacitor structure at various steps in the process. The more commonly observed localized contamination, is the result of random manufacturing defects in the form of an ionic contaminated particulate or other manufacturing defect (particle, masking, etc.). These create a localized collection or gathering site for the small levels of contamination inherent in the process flow. As in the case of Random Defects described in the previous section, localized contamination creates a finite number of randomly distributed failures characterized by a rapidly declining failure rate. Methods for defect identification and reduction are, generally identical to those described for random defects.

In that ionic movement is the physical cause of failure in each form of contamination, the thermal activation energy is the same -1.0 to 1.4 eV. Conservatively, a 1.0 eV activation energy is used for reliability assessment and failure rate estimates. Figure 8-26 shows the effect of mobile ion contamination.

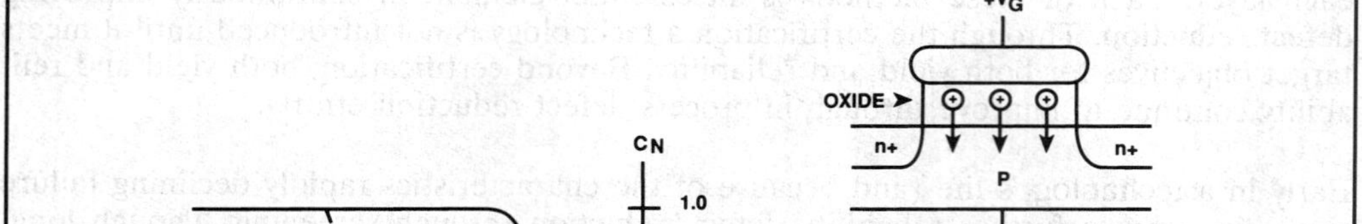

Figure 8-26. Effect of Mobile Ion Contamination

RELIABILITY-RELATED LAYOUT DESIGN RULES

To ensure that all circuit designs on a new technology have a reliability performance equivalent to the built-in reliability of the process, the Process Reliability Department develops a set of circuit layout design rules. The most important reliability-related layout rules are:

1. Those that impact metal and contact electromigration.
2. Those that impact the hot carrier-associated problems of threshold instability avalanche breakdown and bipolar latch-up.
3. The combinations of design rules that control CMOS latch-up.
4. The isolation spacings and channel lengths which limit chip voltages due to punch-through.
5. Those for the input and output structures that determine ESD susceptibility.
6. Those for guard ring and scribe line structures needed for contamination and moisture protection.

These design rules are based on the results of a series of reliability evaluations. The validity of each of these sets of rules is verified under the combination of worst-case conditions for both critical dimensions and alignment.

FUNDAMENTAL RELIABILITY STUDIES

The Process Reliability Department undertakes fundamental reliability studies when the details of a failure mechanism are not well understood. Some examples of fundamental reliability studies include:

- Sequence of events, mechanisms and structural dependence of electrostatic breakdown and failure on CMOS inputs.
- Mechanisms of CMOS latch-up spreading and methods for determining the originating site.
- Layout and structural dependencies of CMOS latch-up susceptibility.
- Layout and structural dependencies of charge collection on critical nodes of alpha-particle-generated minority carriers.
- The impact of AC or pulsed DC operation on electromigration design rules.
- Contact aspect ratio and other geometrical influences on contact electromigration behavior.

The purpose of these fundamental studies is to understand in detail the physics of the failure mechanisms; understand circuit configuration, layout and operation dependencies; forecast both environmental and electrical accelerating and decelerating factors; develop failure rate models of each mechanism; and identify the key physical and/or electrical parameters and their safe limits for process control. Based on the understanding derived from these studies, we develop methodologies to deal with these issues.

PACKAGE FAILURE MECHANISMS

Introduction

Failure mechanisms in which an interaction with the package or assembly process is an essential part of the mechanism are termed package failure mechanisms. Not all failure mechanisms are package-related. Examples of non-package related failures include hot electron effects, gate oxide defects and electromigration. Figure 8-27 illustrates the possible root causes of package failure mechanisms.

It is obvious that errors in package design and assembly processing can lead to package-related failures. More subtle is the fact that not all package-related mechanisms have their root cause in the package. It is possible that error in the wafer process or die design interacts with the package and leads to failure. Package dice are components which Intel's customers assemble into their systems. Customer board assembly processes can stress the package and lead to subsequent failure. This is a difficult area to control because of the large number of customers and variations among board assembly processes.

The failure mechanism is also determined by the environment. Environmental stresses include temperature, humidity, mechanical stress, electrical stress or any combination of these. Traditionally, the environmental stresses indicated in Figure 8-27 are the stresses

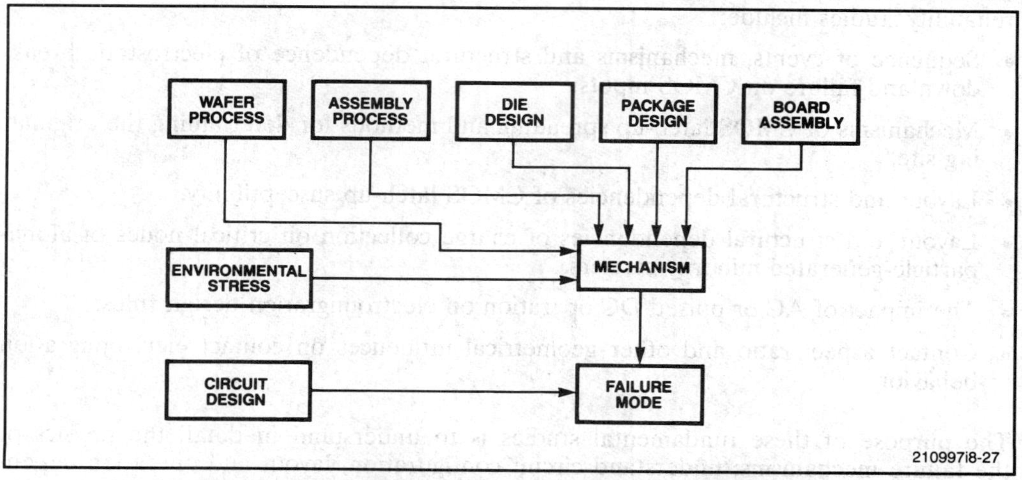

Figure 8-27. Block Diagram of Root Causes of Failures

a device undergoes in its service life or a controlled accelerated simulation of that stress. In recent years, customers' assembly processes, particularly surface-mount processes, have been found to contribute to package failures.

Finally, the interaction of the physical failure mechanism with the circuit on the die leads to a specific electrical manifestation: the failure mode. It often requires detailed knowledge of the circuit to interpret the failure mode in terms of a failure mechanism.

Package Testing

It is always more cost-effective to ensure the reliability of a system by using reliability-assured components than it is to do reliability testing only at the system level. This strategy only works, however, if the system assembly process itself does not introduce failures in the components. This demands that accelerated reliability stressing realistically simulate the customer's board assembly process and the subsequent service life. Thus, the stressing for package reliability characterizations should be accelerated simulations of both the Board Assembly and the environmental stress boxes shown in Figure 8-27. Some packages, particularly plastic surface mount types, require tests that simulate shipping storage, attachment to the board and rework, in addition to the service environment.

Package integrity tests serve three function qualification of new packages, assembly plants, wafer or assembly process changes piece part changes, or new processing equipment; to serve as a routine production monitor from all assembly plants to detect any long-term shifts in package performance; and to act as process controls.

The stress used to qualify a new package or plant depends on the particular package technology and the specific failure mechanism of interest. There are four main package technologies: laminated ceramic (C), pressed ceramic (D), molded plastic (P), and controlled-collapse chip connection (C4). The first two are hermetic, while molded plastic and C4 are non-hermetic. Each of the four technologies has certain likely failure mechanisms. Table 8-1 shows which stresses are appropriate for each package technology. Not all of the tests in Table 8-1 are necessary for all new package or assembly process change. It is only necessary to focus on weakness likely to be introduced by the change. Table 8-2 summarizes the tests required for various types of changes.

Thermomechanical Failure Mechanisms

8

Thermal coefficient of expansion (TCE) and elastic modules mismatch among the materials of a package, including the silicon die, drive a number of failure mechanisms in each of the three package technologies. Table 8-3 shows some of the TCEs and elastic module used in packaging materials. The stresses used to accelerate these mechanisms are usually temperature cycling or thermal shock. Failure rates for thermomechanical failure mechanisms are typically measured by the number of cumulative distribution of temperature or stress cycles to failure.

Table 8-1. Typical Package Qualification and Inspection Test Conditions

Test	Mil. Std.	Test Conditions	Test Duration	End Point
High T Storage	1008 1008C 1008C	280°C (D) 200°C (P) 200°C (P)	168 Hrs. 48 Hrs. 48 Hrs.	E E Wire Pull
Temperature Cycle	1010B 1010C	−55°C to + 125°C (P) −65°C to + 150°C (C,D)	500 Cycles	EVH
Thermal Shock	1011B	−55°C to + 125°C (C, D, P)	200 Cycles	EVH
Steam	—	121°C, 2A (P, C, D)	96 Hrs.	EV
Humidity	—	85°C, 85% RH (C, D, P)	1000 Hrs.	EV
Salt ATM	1009A 2004B	35°C (C, D, P)	24 Hrs.	V, Lead Fatigue
Solvents	2515C	Chemical (C, D, P)	1 Hr.	V
Mechanical Shock	2002B	1.5 KG Peak (C, D)	6 Orient.	H, E
Vibration	2007	20 g Peak (C, D)	3 Orient.	H, E
Centrifuge	2001D	20/30KG (C, D)	Z Orient.	H, E
Acoustic/PIND	2020A	250 Hz (C, D)		H, E
Mechanical Sequence	2002B 2007		Z Orient.	H, E
Die Adherence	2019	Die Shear (P, C, D)		To Destruction Adherence
Wire Bond	2011	Pull Wires (P, C, D)		To Destruction
Cavity Moisture	1018	100°C Bake (C, D)	1 Cycle	ppm H_2O
Seal Integrity	2024	Torque (D)		Strength
Lead Strength	2004	Bend/Fatigue (C, D, P)		To Destruction
Solderability	2025 2003 —	Bend (C, D, P) 100°C Steam (P, C, D) 200°C (P, C, D)	8 Hours	To Destruction Visual Visual

P = Plastic
C = Ceramic
C = Cerdip
E = Electrical Test
V = Visual Inspection
H = Hermeticity Test

Table 8-2. Package Qualification Tests Required for Assembly Module Changes

Assembly Modules Tests	Die Preparation C, D, P	Frame Attach D	Die Attach C, D, P	Wire Bond C, D, P	Seal Mold C/D	Mold Cure P	Lead Finish C, D, P	
1. A Operating Lifetest	X				X	X		
1. B High-Temp Storage				X	X	X	X	X
2. A Temp Cycle	X		X	X	X	X		
2. B Thermal Shock	X	X	X	X	X			
3. A Steam		X			X	X	X	X
3. B THB	X				X	X		X
3. C Salt Atmosphere	X				X		X	X
3. D Solvents					X	X		
4. A Mech. Shock			X	X				
4. B Vibration			X	X				
4. C Centrifuge	X		X	X				
4. D Acoustic (PIND)			X	X				
4. E Mech. Sequence	X	X	X	X	X			
5. A Die Adherence	X	X			X			
5. B Wire Bond Pull	X	X	X	X	X	X		
5. C Cavity Moisture		X			X			
5. D Glass Seal Integrity					X		X	
5. E Lead Integrity							X	X
5. F Lead Solderability							X	X

D = Pressed ceramic
C = Laminated ceramic
P = Molded plastic
C4 = Controlled-collapse chip connection

Table 8-3. Thermal Coefficients of Expansion and Elastic Moduli for Materials Used in Packages

Material	TCE (ppm/°C)	Young's Modulus (GPa)
Copper	17	119
Alloy 42	4.7	145
Silicon	3	131
Molding Compound	21	18
Alumina	6	225

DIE CRACKING IN CERAMIC PACKAGES

In laminating ceramic packages, the silicon die is brazed to the cavity of a ceramic package at about 360°C using a goldsilicon eutectic. When cooled to room temperature the TCE mismatch causes the bottom of the silicon die to be in compression, while the top is in tension. If there are voids in the goldsilicon eutectic brazing material, as shown in Figure 8-28, there is a tendency for stresses in the silicon near the silicon/eutectic interface to become less compressive near the voids. If the void is near the center of the die, the stresses remain comprehensive but less so locally. (See the dotted line in Figure 8-29.)

In Figure 8-29, positive stresses are tensile. If the void is near the edge of the die, however, local regions of tensile stress can occur. This is shown as the solid line in Figure 8-29.

Tensile stress is a necessary condition for the initiation and propagation of a crack on the back of the wafer. When tensile stress is present, the nature of the finish of the back of the die determines whether a crack is initiated. Once a crack has started, it will propagate to the front of the die as in Figure 8-28, where it will cause functional failure. The condition of the back of the die (roughness, degree of oxidation, etc.), the temperature and ambient gas is controlled to optimize the wetting characteristics of the gold eutectic braze. Mencinger et al. have developed a die backside wetability measurement

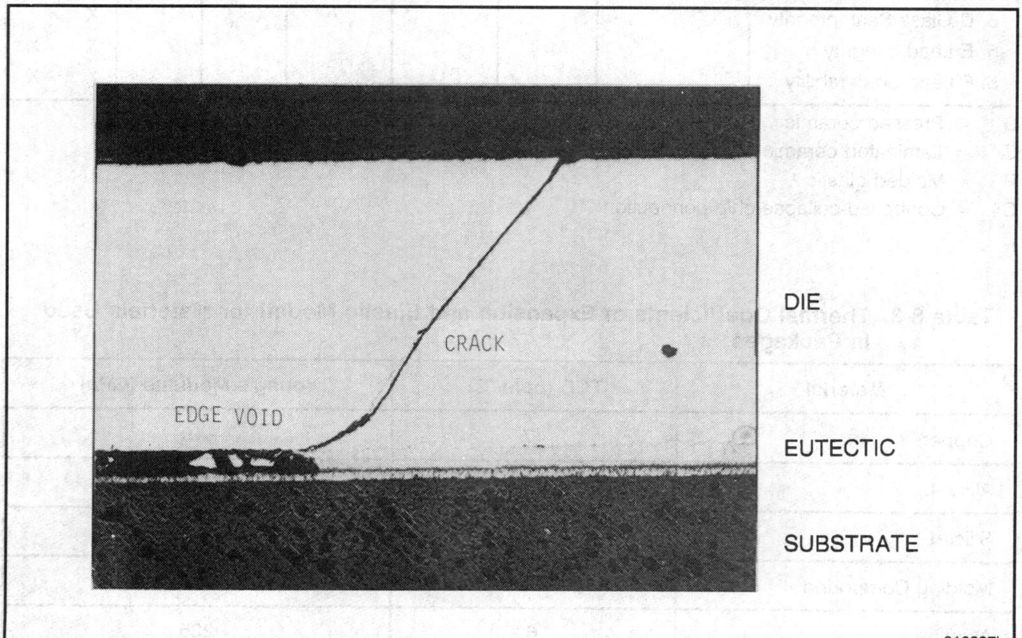

Figure 8-28. Die Crack Nucleated and Propagated from Edge Void

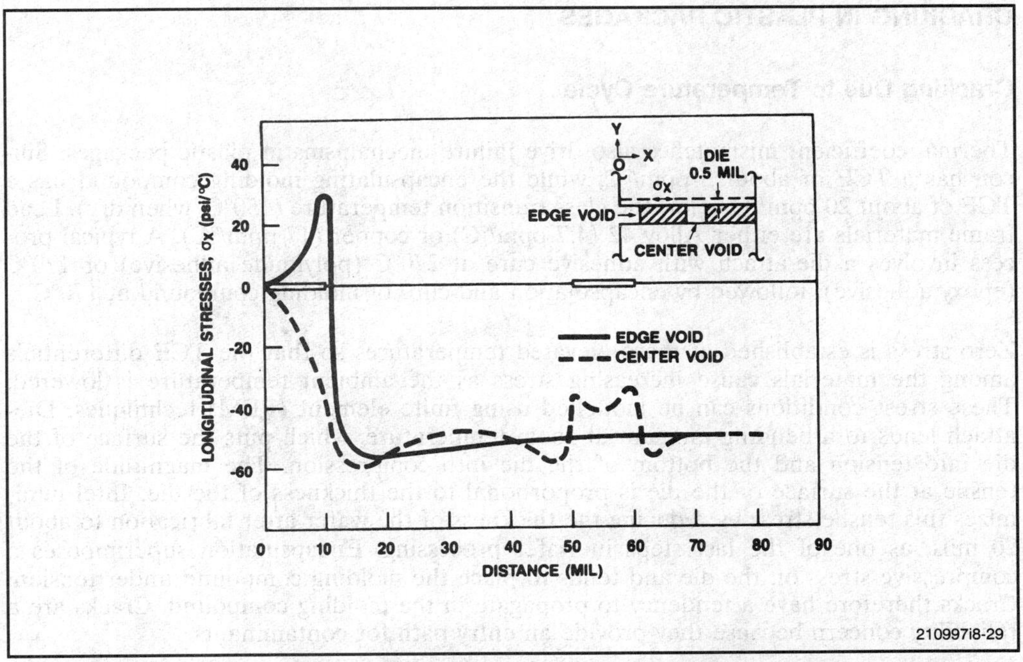

Figure 8-29. Longitudinal Stress as a Function of Distance from Chip Edge

technique to study the suitability of die backsides for gold-eutectic die attach and have determined optimum roughness and Cr/Au coating parameters for assuring a good shelf-life for the wetting characteristics of back-side prepared wafers.

A similar mechanism in which cracks nucleate from die-edge damage due to partial saw and break die separation has been observed in silver-filled glass-attached pressed ceramic packages. Intel uses 100 percent saw-through for die separation.

Tests used to monitor or study these phenomena include:

1. Stud pull, in which the force and fracture mode is recorded when the die is pulled from the cavity on test units in uniaxial tension.

2. Temperature cycling of fully assembled packages.

3. Centrifuge testing.

4. Visual inspection of the fillet around the die to ensure optimal wetting.

5. X-ray examination.

CRACKING IN PLASTIC PACKAGES

Cracking Due to Temperature Cycle

Thermal coefficient mismatches also drive failure mechanisms in plastic packages. Silicon has a TCE of about 3 ppm/°C, while the encapsulating molding compound has a TCE of about 20 ppm/°C below the glass transition temperature (150°C, when dry). Lead frame materials are either Alloy 42 (4.7 ppm/°C) or copper (17 ppm/°C). A typical process involves a die-attach with adhesive cure at 270°C (polyimide adhesive) or 170°C (epoxy adhesive), followed by encapsulation and cure of molding compound at 170°C.

Zero stress is established at these elevated temperatures so that the TCE differentials among the materials cause increasing stress as the ambient temperature is lowered. These stress conditions can be modelled using finite element (FEM) techniques. Die-attach leads to a bending moment at room temperature, which puts the surface of the die into tension and the bottom of the die into compression. The magnitude of the tensile at the surface of the die is proportional to the thickness of the die. Intel minimizes this tensile stress by reducing the thickness of the wafer after fabrication to about 20 mils, as one of the last steps in wafer processing. Encapsulation superimposes a compressive stress on the die and tends to place the molding compound under tension. Cracks therefore have a tendency to propagate in the molding compound. Cracks are a reliability concern because they provide an entry path for contaminants.

Cracks will initiate at stress concentrations at the top edge of the die or at the bottom edge of the lead frame. An example of this is seen in Figure 8-30. Cracks can also be initiated by stress concentrations at voids that become incorporated into the molding compound. Figure 8-31 shows a void-induced degradation in package strength.

Once cracks in the molding compound are initiated they will become longer as the number of temperature cycles increases. The mechanism is fatigue crack propagation. Nishimura et al. have studied the rate of crack growth in notched samples and find that the rate of crack propagation is given by

$$da/dN = C(\text{deltaK})^m$$

where:

a	is the crack length
N	is the number of cycles
deltaK	is the stress intensity factor range
C and m	are constants

They find that m is about 20, much higher than for fatigue crack propagation in metals (typically from 2 to 8). In packages molded from the same compound they find that crack propagation is governed mainly by the lowest temperature reached during temperature cycling, not by the range of temperatures. In packages, deltaK depends on the difference between the molding/curing temperature and the low-temperature extreme. In addition to crack propagation, delamination between the die and the molding compound and

Figure 8-30. Cross Section of Temperature-Cycled Epoxy Package Through Cracks Nucleated at the Top Edge of the Die and the Bottom Edge of the Leadframe

between the lead frame will propagate during temperature cycling. Edwards et al. have used a bare metal smear test structure to measure the progress of delamination at the die/molding compound interface.

Package cracking is controlled in several ways:

- The die pad is "down-set" below the plane of the leads so that there is roughly an equal thickness of molding compound above the die and below the die pad.
- Modifications to the molding compound to control the crack propagation characteristics include filler coatings to reduce delamination at the epoxy/filler interface and control of filler size distribution.
- Monitors and process controls to minimize the occurrence of voids.

8

Cracking of Plastic Surface-Mount Devices in Board Assembly

In recent years, package cracking has become an even greater industry-wide concern as plastic surface-mount components (PSMC) become more widely used. PSMCs are subjected to higher temperatures and are exposed more directly to corrosive chemicals than through-hole mounted components such as DIPs. The heat and chemical fluxes required to solder PSMCs to a board are applied on the same side of the board as the component,

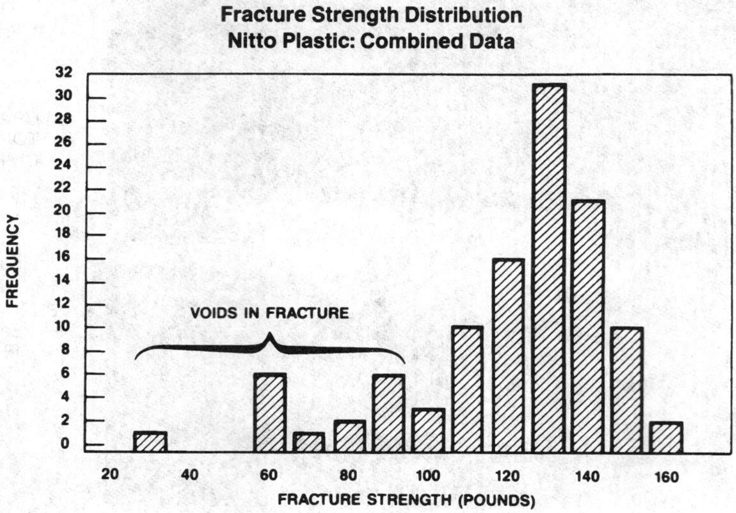

Figure 8-31. Distributions of Fracture Loads for 18-Lead PDIP in 3-Point Binding

whereas for through-hole-mounted devices they are applied on the opposite side of the board. During board assembly, PSMCs are subjected to temperatures in the range of 215-260°C and heating rates as high as 25°C/sec.

In addition to the TCE-driven stresses, there are two additional components of internal package stress. First, if heating or cooling rates 10°C/sec, thermal stresses associated with internal temperature gradients can be appreciable. Second, moisture absorbed by the molding compound will vaporize in cavities (particularly the small gap under the lead frame paddle) and create an internal pressure which causes cracking. This popcorn mechanism is illustrated in Figure 8-32. It is possible for PSMCs to absorb enough water vapor during storage in normal ambients for the vapor-driven stresses to dominate the mechanics of the package. This mechanism has been discussed by several workers; the main factors influencing the propensity to crack have been found to be:

- Peak temperature reached during soldering.
- Moisture (percentage weight gain) content of molding compound.
- Dimensions of die paddle.
- Thickness of molding compound under paddle.
- Adhesion of molding compound to die and/or lead frame.

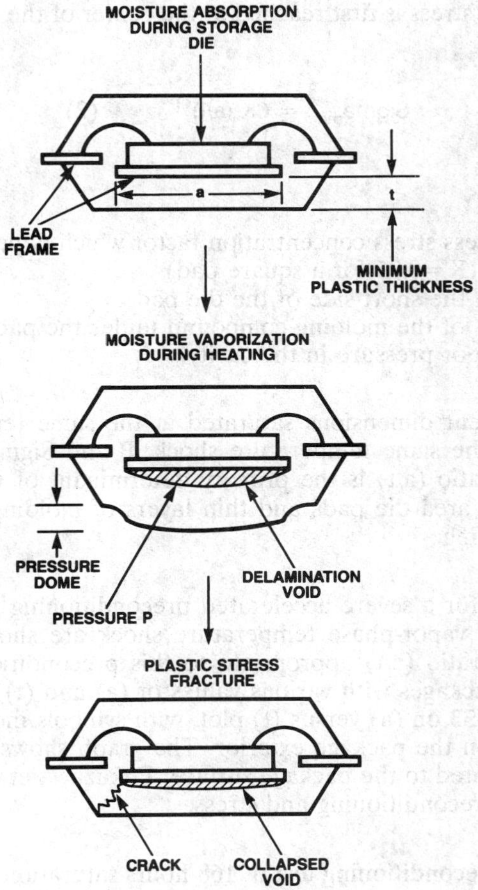

Figure 8-32. Plastic Surface-Mount Cracking During Solder Caused by Previously Absorbed Moisture

These factors have been tied together in a simple model by Fukuzawa et al. The steam vapor pressure in the gap under the die pad, Figure 8-32, causes the molding compound to delaminate from the pad, expand and form a dome. A crack occurs where the maximum bending stress, $Sigma_{max}$, exceeds a fracture stress characteristic of the molding compound at the elevated temperature (T_{vps}),

$$Sigma_{max} > Sigma_{crit}(T_{vps}) \qquad (1)$$

The maximum bending stress is first reached at the center of the long side of the die pad and is given by

$$Sigma_{max} = 6K\,(a/t)^{2P} \qquad (2)$$

where:

K — is a dimensionless stress concentration factor which depends on the aspect ratio of the die pad (K=0.05 for a square pad)
(a) — is the length of the short side of the die pad
(t) — is the thickness of the molding compound under the pad
(P) — is the water vapor pressure in the cavity.

For packages of different dimensions saturated at the same temperature and relative humidity followed by the same temperature shock, P and $Sigma_{crit}$ are the same. For these conditions, the ratio (a/t) is the primary determinant of whether a package will crack. Generally, large area die pads and thin layers of molding compound under the pad lead to more cracking.

Package cracking data for a severe accelerated preconditioning test of 85°C/85 percent RH followed by 215°C vapor-phase temperature shock are shown in Figure 8-33. To determine the critical ratio (a/t) appropriate to this preconditioning and vapor-phase shock, a selection of packages with various values of (a) and (t) was tested. The values are plotted in Figure 8-33 on (a) versus (t) plot, with symbols indicating whether or not cracks were observed on the package exterior. The graph shows that if (a/t) equals 4.5 then cracks are propagated to the package surface. Fukuzawa et al. found a critical (a/t) value of 5 for similar preconditioning and stress.

Intel uses a standard preconditioning test of 168 hours saturation at 85°C/30 percent RH followed by a 215°C vapor-phase shock and a criterion of visible internal crack length to determine whether a package should be considered crack-sensitive.

To predict the cracking sensitivity as a function of the moisture saturation or dry-out history, a model for P in Equation (2) is needed. Kitano et al. measured the water vapor absorption and water diffusivity of molding compound. They also deduced the internal vapor pressure as a function of temperature from deflection measurements of the pressure dome. During a solder temperature shock there is not enough water vapor in the gap under the die pad to account for this pressure. However, the molding compound is

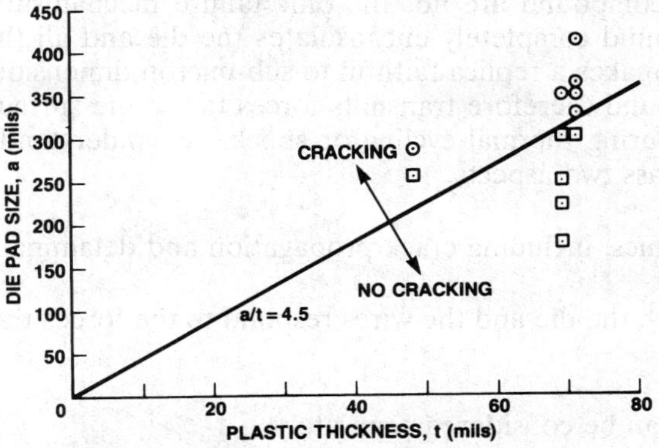

Figure 8-33. Crack Sensitivity in 85/85 Followed by Vapor-Phase Shock Test as a Function of Pad Size and Molding Compound Thickness

hygroscopic, so a much larger amount of water is available to generate steam pressure within a (moisture) diffusion length (1 or 2 mils) of the cavity over the duration of the temperature shock. This leads to the following expression for (P) in Equation (2):

$$P = H\, P_{sat}\,(T_{vps}) \qquad (3)$$

where:

H is the relative humidity of the saturation ambient prior to the temperature shock

T_{vps} is the peak temperature of the temperature shock.

Equation (3) agrees well with the empirical results of Kitano et al. It is interesting that Equation (3) is independent of the temperature of the saturation ambient. The derivation of Equation (3) assumed that the package has reached moisture saturation before the vapor phase shock. Equations (1), (2) and (3) give a complete model for prediction of package cracking sensitivity as a function of all the factors mentioned above.

Our understanding of the popcorn fracture mechanism has led to test, packaging and application procedures that ensure that Intel's product is reliable in the customer's application. For example, product determined to be crack-sensitive is baked in forced-air convection ovens at 125°C for 24 hours, then packed in heat-sealed moisture-barrier bags with desiccant. Units should be used within 48 hours of opening the bag or re-baked. The units should be re-baked only once, because each bake cycle causes the growth of Cu_6Sn_5 at the interface between the solder on the lead frames and the copper lead frame. Excessive growth of this intermetallic phase can lead to poor solder wetting during the solder reflow cycle. Full details of the application procedures are available from Intel.

Wire Damage and Thin-Film Cracking in Plastic Packages

Cracks in molding compound are not the only failure mechanism in plastic packages. The molding compound completely encapsulates the die and all the wires. In fact, the molding compound makes a replica faithful to sub-micron dimensions of the die surface. The molding compound therefore transmits forces to the die surface and the wires that may cause failure during thermal cycling or shock. An understanding of these mechanisms must encompass two aspects:

1. Package mechanics, including crack propagation and delamination.

2. The way in which the die and the wires respond to the forces transmitted to them by the package.

These two aspects can be considered separately.

Consider the forces acting on the surface of a die shown in Figure 8-34. This is drawn for a temperature less than the neutral stress temperature of the package (about 170°C) as might occur at the minimum temperature of a temperature cycle test. There are two components: a shear force directed towards the die center and vanishing at the die center and a comprehensive normal force roughly constant everywhere on the die surface and compressive. If a crack starts to propagate from the top edge of the die, it

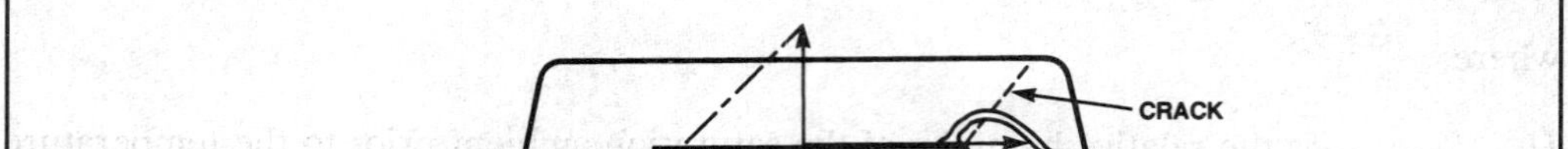

Figure 8-34. Shear and Normal Forces Acting on the Die Surface in a Plastic Package

redistributes forces acting on the die surface. The crack will increase the shear stress acting near the edge of the die and change the normal stress from compressive to tensile. The situation is different during a solder temperature shock because the shear forces are outwardly directed along the die radius. In any case, these forces drive important failure mechanisms.

The molding compounds used for plastic packages are thermosetting, meaning they flow into the mold cavity with a low viscosity and then begin to set. Studies using multi-colored molding compounds show that there is a complicated yet well-defined solidification sequence. These internal polymerization gradients cause built-in stresses on the die and the wires which depend on where the wires are relative to the inlet gate for the individual package mold cavity. Koch et al. and Shirley and Blish have observed that the largest incidence of sheared ball bonds in temperature cycling experiments occurs opposite the inlet gate.

Wire and Wire Bond Damage

Figure 8-35 shows a magnified view of a wire bond near the top right edge of the die shown in Figure 8-34. The crack which has been propagated by temperature cycling has intersected a wire and sheared it. An example of this kind of damage is shown in Figure 8-36. The normal and shear stresses on the ball bond are enhanced by delamination between the molding compound and the die surface. The bonds may or may not shear. Figure 8-37 shows a sheared and unsheared bond. If the bond does not shear, a separation between the molding compound and the bond occurs (Figure 8-37, bottom).

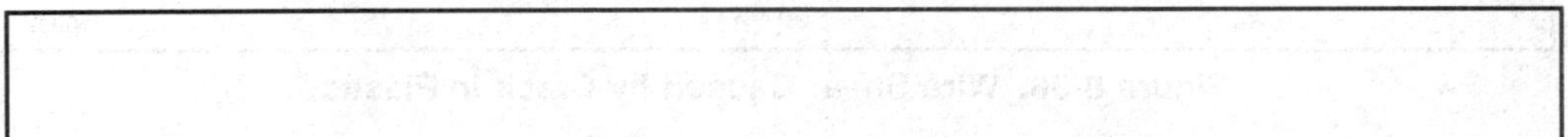

Figure 8-35. Wire and Wire Bond Damage

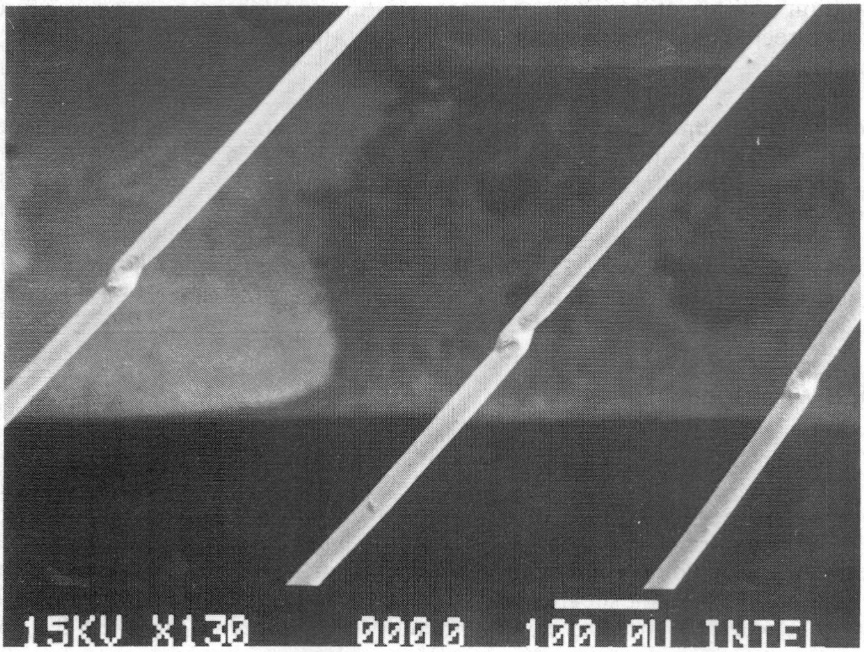

210997i

Figure 8-36. Wire Shear Caused by Crack in Plastic

Also, if the bond does not shear the displacement of the molding compound, normal to the die can place a severe stress on the wire at the neck of the ball. This is because the wire tends to move with the molding compound whereas the ball bond remains fixed relative to the chip (if it does not shear). The wire at the neck of the ball is particularly susceptible to deformation because it has been annealed during ball formation. An example of necking damage is shown in Figure 8-38.

If the bonding process introduces substrate damage, such as cracks in the silicon under a bond pad, then shear forces can propagate the crack. The bond then breaks loose with a piece of the silicon substrate attached. This type of failure is termed cratering. Koch et al. have shown that bonding causes more damage for softer glass films under bond pads (such as high-phosphorous glass) and when silicon precipitates nucleate on the Al/glass interface from Al/Si metallization on the bond pad.

When temperature cycling propagates silicon cracks under the bond pad, another type of cratering (shown in Figure 8-39) occurs. Shear forces are directed towards or away from the center of the die, so the morphology of the fracture surfaces in Figure 8-39 has a definite orientation relative to the die radius. This occurs mostly in the corners of the die and especially opposite the mold cavity gate. Bonding parameters (force, ultrasonic

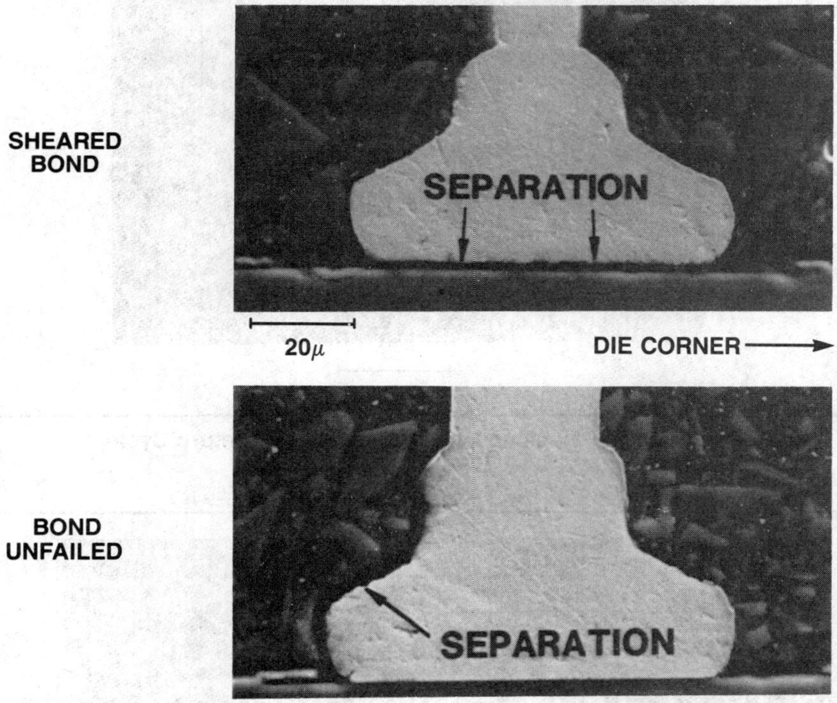

Figure 8-37. Ball Bonds in Plastic Package after Temperature Cycle

power, velocity, temperature, etc.) and thin films under bonding pads can be optimized to minimize bonding damage, which leads to crater failures such as those shown in Figure 8-39. A thin film of titanium under the aluminum metallization effectively provides resistance to cratering.

Thin-Film Cracking

The shearing forces exerted by the package on the die can damage thin-film structures, particularly near the corners of dice encapsulated in PLCC packages. Temperature cycling or thermal shock accelerate the mechanism. Some typical thin-film cracking damage is shown in Figure 8-40. Displacements are several microns. A schematic plan view of a corner of a die is shown in the upper part of Figure 8-41. Shear forces tend to displace the wide aluminum bus inward towards the center of the die, producing visible cracks in the passivation over the aluminum.

Figure 8-38. Necking Damage after Temperature Cycle

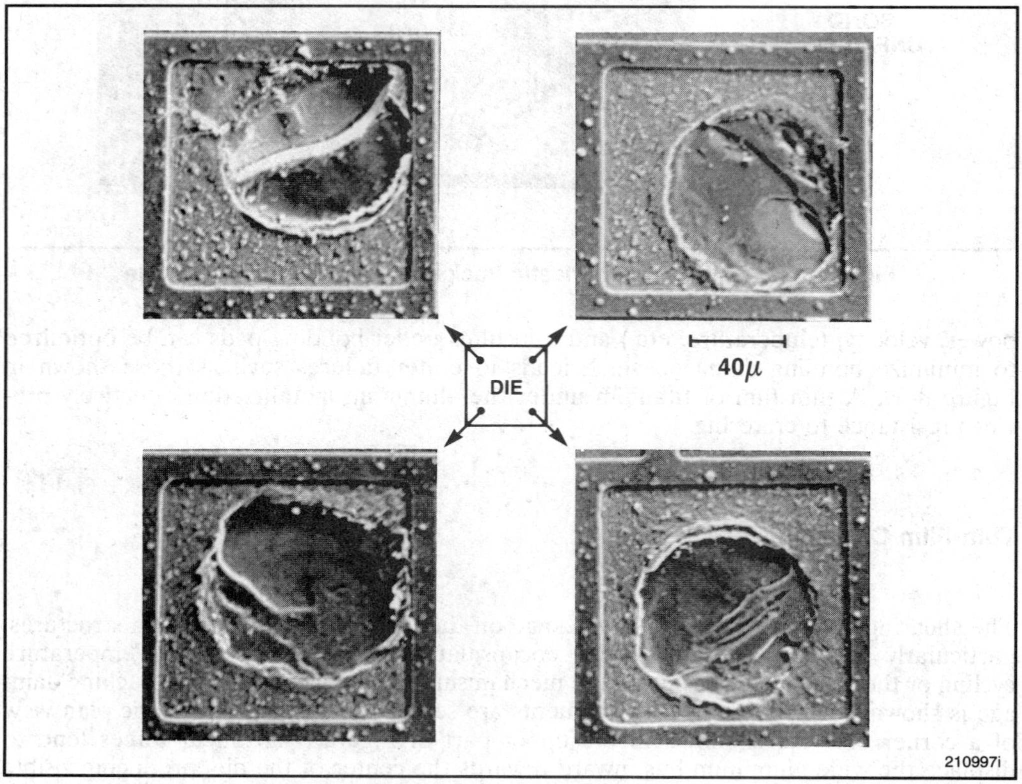

Figure 8-39. Bond Shear (Cratering) at Die Corners after Temperature Cycle

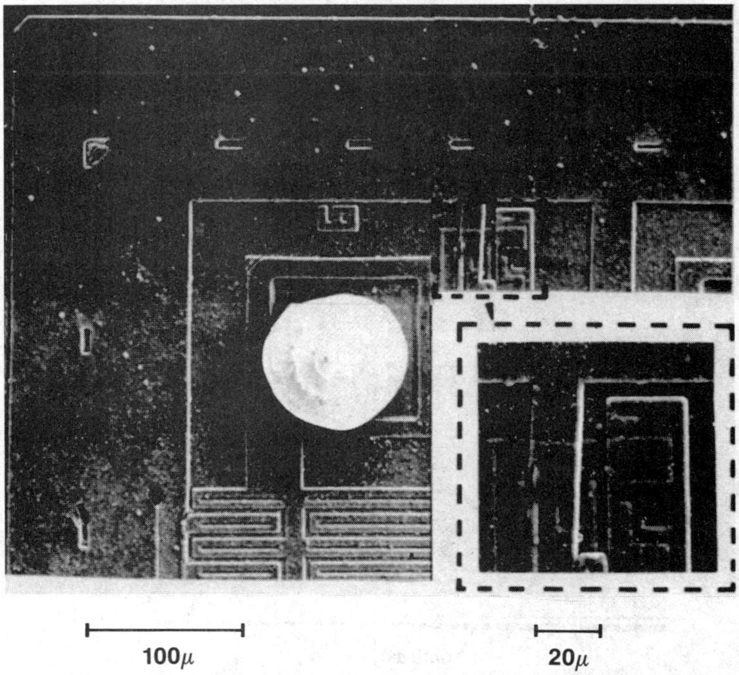

Figure 8-40. Thin-Film Cracking Near Die Corner after Temperature Cycle

In the lower part of Figure 8-41 a cross section (AB) through part of the structure shows cracks at the edges of the displaced aluminum bus running downward into the underlying thin films. These cracks may expose phosphorous-doped glass, which might lead to later corrosion failure, or they may cause immediate functional failure if they intersect active circuitry. In Figure 8-41, one of the cracks (left) is shown intersecting a polysilicon gate in, say, an output driver. This will prevent the transistor from being turned fully off or on and be manifested as a functional or parametric failure. Input/output circuitry is particularly susceptible to thin-film cracking damage because of its typical location on the die periphery.

The main factors affecting thin-film cracking are:

- Die size
- Molding compound selection
- Aluminum bus width
- Die coat versus none
- Amplitude of thermal cycle or shock

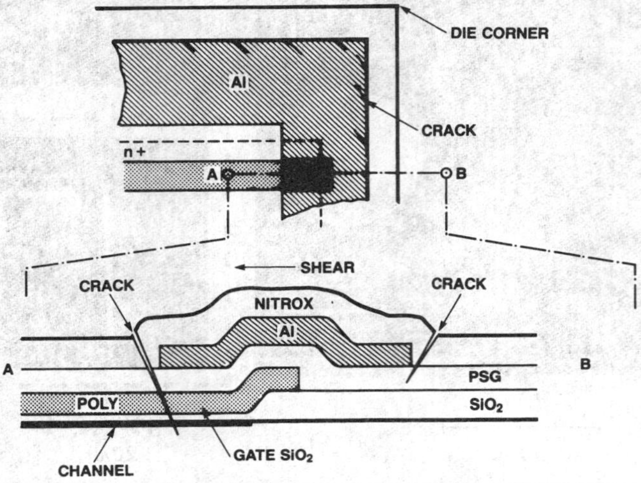

Figure 8-41. Plan and Cross Section Schematic of Thin-Film Cracking Mechanism

Thomas, Isagawa et al. and Edwards et al. used metal deformation to study the effect of molding compound and die-coats on thin-film cracking. They found that post-wire bond die coats reduce thin-film cracking but cause high wire damage failure rates due to high stress where the coating wicks up the wire bond. An electrical technique based on the mechanism described in Figure 8-41 was used by Shirley and Blish to study the effect of the layout of the circuitry. A polysilicon resistor meandered back and forth under the inner edge of an aluminum bus at the corner of a test chip. Comparisons of failure rates (open polysilicon resistors) were made among eight different combinations of slotted/unslotted aluminum buses, with or without contacts to the substrate as a function of number of condition C temperature cycles. (See Figure 8-42.) Cumulative failures for variant number 3 and all others combined are plotted in Figure 8-43.

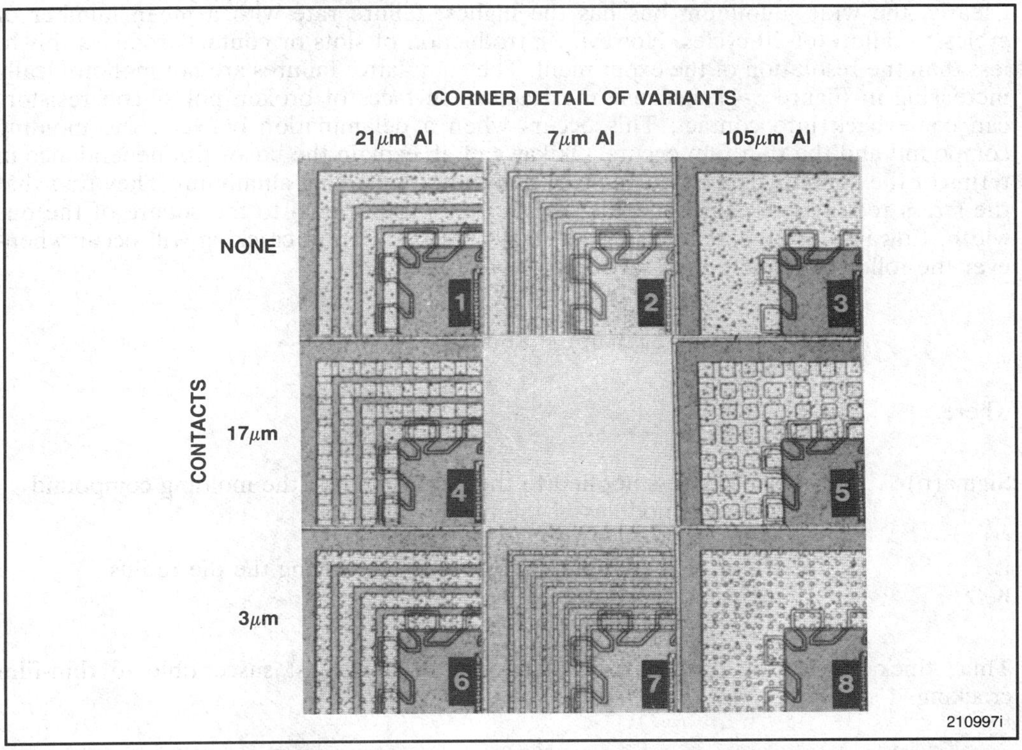

Figure 8-42. Eight Variations of Bus Layout Compared for Thin-Film Cracking. Notice Polysilicon Meander Used for Electrical Detection of Cracking

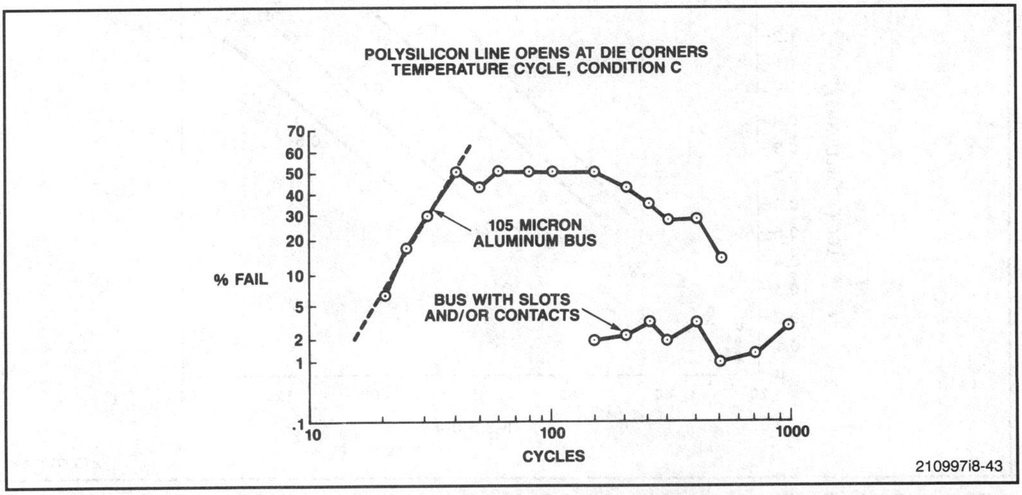

Figure 8-43. Cumulative Opens of Polysilicon Meanders Used as Thin-Film Cracking Detectors. Variant 3, Figure 8-41, has the Highest Failure Rate.

Clearly, the wide aluminum bus has the highest failure rate with a mean number of cycles to failure of 20 cycles. However, introduction of slots or contacts reduces this to less than the resolution of the experiment. The cumulative failures are not monotonically increasing in Figure 8-44, because the fracture surfaces of broken polysilicon resistors can come back into contact. This occurs when a delamination between the molding compound and the thin film occurs. Okikawa et al. explain the bus-width dependence in terms of the stability against buckling of passivation overlying aluminum. They find that the stress required to cause buckling is inversely proportional to the square of the bus width. Edwards et al. extended this to show that passivation cracking will occur whenever the following condition is satisfied:

$$\text{Sigma(p)} = KE(t/L)^2 \qquad (4)$$

where:

Sigma(p)	is the shear stress applied to the passivation by the molding compound
E	is the Young's modules of the passivation
(t)	is its thickness
L	is the width of the aluminum bus measured along the die radius
K	is a dimensionless constant.

Thus, thick passivation over narrow aluminum lines is least susceptible to thin-film cracking.

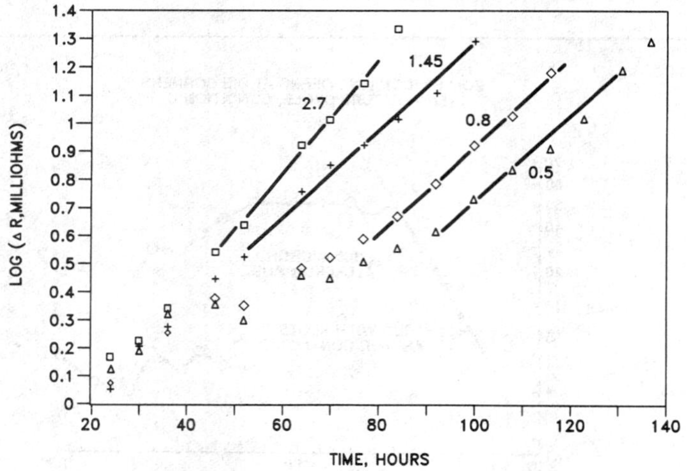

Figure 8-44. Resistance Increases of Gold-Aluminum Bonds Due to 200°C Bake as a Function of Time for Molding Compounds with Various Levels of Br Flame Retardant. Curves are Labeled with Weight Percent of Br.

Occasionally the normal force on the die surface can be concentrated at a point by a large filler particle and crack the passivation. Matsumoto et al. have shown that this can be controlled by limiting the filler particle size to less than 5 microns or applying a die coat.

Intel minimizes thin-film cracking by carefully choosing molding compounds and optimizing the circuit layout.

Thermal/Moisture-Related Failure Mechanisms

Thermochemical package failure mechanisms are either non-moisture-related or moisture-related. The non-moisture-related mechanisms usually involve intermetallic diffusion in either the wire bonding metallurgy or the external lead finish and are well described by Arrhenius relationships. Moisture-related mechanisms are either external or internal to the package. External moisture-related mechanisms usually involve external lead corrosion, galvanic effects or dendrite growth. Internal moisture-related mechanisms are only relevant for non-hermetic (plastic) packages and usually involve corrosion of the aluminum metallization of the die or subtle electrical leakage currents which disrupt the electrical function of the circuit. Tests used to accelerate these mechanisms include bakes, steam, temperature/humidity/bias (85/85 or HAST) and salt atmosphere.

THERMAL DEGRADATION OF GOLD WIRE BONDS

Gold and aluminum are known to interdiffuse readily to form intermetallic phases such as the so-called "purple plague" ($AuAl_2$). Imbalance in the atomic fluxes of Au and Al is balanced by a vacancy flux. The vacancies coalesce to form Kirkendall voids. These voids lead to a mechanical weakening of the bonds as measured by bond shear testing or traditional bond-pull testing. This effect can be seen in Figure 8-45. The figure shows an Arrhenius plot of the time to 10 percent failure by a combination of cratering (fracture involving the silicon substrate) and fracture through the brittle intermetallic phase. The plot shows that a single mechanism with an activation energy of 1.26 eV is active over the entire range 160°C to 350°C.

The Kirkendall voids which weaken bonds also change their resistance. Blish and Parobeck used Kelvin measurements of resistance to demonstrate the correlation between low pull force and resistance increase. This provided a convenient electrical technique to extend earlier work on the kinetics of bond degradation due to bromine-containing flame retardants in the molding compound. The life-shortening effect of Br-containing flame retardant is clearly shown in Figure 8-44. For chip temperatures of 160°C and above there is a substantial acceleration (20-fold) of failure rates for flame-retardant relative to the non-flame retardant epoxy. However, for chip temperatures of 140°C and below, flame-retardant decomposition has negligible effect. Accordingly, Intel specifies a maximum chip service junction temperature of 140°C and uses a bromine content consistent with product safety (flammability per UL 94 VO, 1/8″ rating).

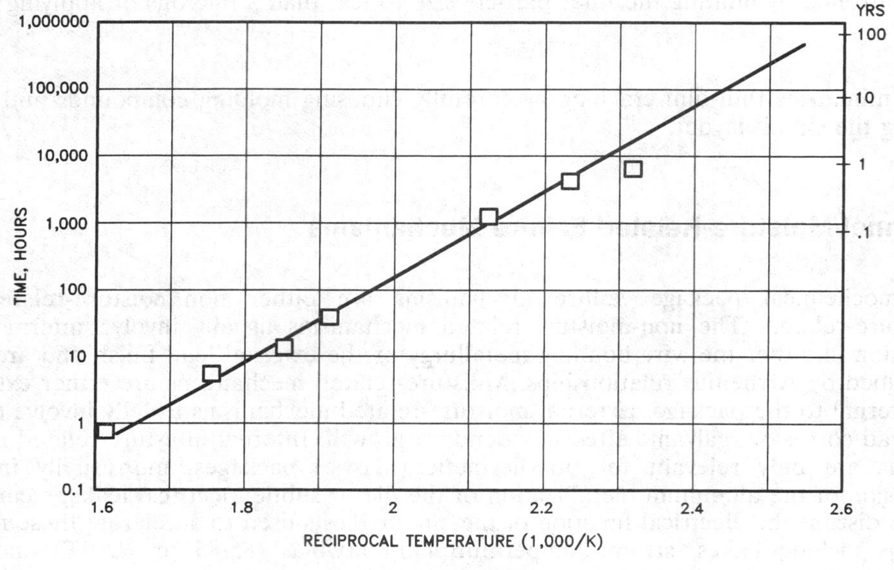

Figure 8-45. Arrhenius Plot of Time to 10% Bond Pull Failure for Gold Bonds to Aluminum

Contaminants on bond pads can affect bond reliability. Silicon dust from inadequate wash after saw can accelerate gold-aluminum interdiffusion. Residual passivation from under etched bond pads can inhibit intimate contact of gold and aluminum. Figure 8-46 shows a cross section of a bond that was deliberately produced with residual passivation and then baked for 200 hours at 160°C. Brittle $AuAl_2$ phases, areas of no reaction and passivation fragments are visible in Figure 8-46.

Today, thermal degradation of wire bonds is not a major issue because processing temperatures are much lower. A major factor has been the advent of thermosonic bonding in which application of ultrasonic energy has permitted much lower bonding temperatures (270°C) than was possible with thermocompression bonding (360°C). Programs to further reduce bonding and other processing temperatures are active at Intel.

THERMAL DEGRADATION OF LEAD FINISH

High-temperature bakes, such as burn-in, can degrade the solder wetting characteristics of lead finishes because of oxidation or intermetallic growth. This can lead to board assembly problems or board-level reliability problems because of tenuous solder contact caused by incomplete wetting. Intermetallic growth is not an issue for Alloy 42 lead frames, but it is important for solder-coated or tin-plated copper lead frames, which are becoming more common. This is because of the relatively rapid growth kinetics of the

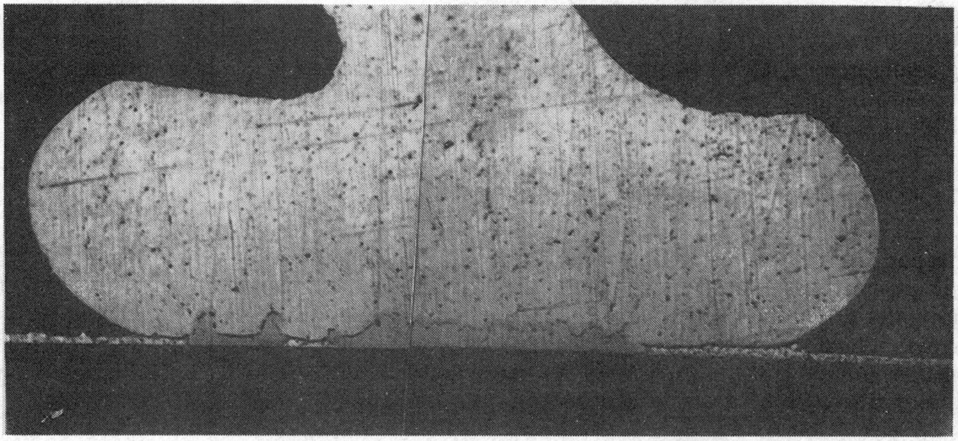

210997i

Figure 8-46. Cross Section of a Gold Ball Bond with Passivation Fragments at the Au/Al Interface, After Bake for 200 Hours at 160°C

Cu_3Sn and Cu_6Sn_5 intermetallic phases. These phases grow at the solder/copper (or tin/copper) interface with a square-root time dependence and with a diffusion activation energy of 0.74 eV. If this phase grows to the surface of the solder, then the lead will not wet at this location. Intel has solder thickness and uniformity standards and monitors which prevent this from becoming a problem. It must be recognized that this mechanism limits the burn-in and dry-out bake (to prevent popcorn fracture) options for surface-mount devices.

EXTERNAL MOISTURE-RELATED MECHANISMS

Moisture can accelerate galvanic and metal migration failure mechanisms, which affect the external lead finish of packages. For example, incompatibility between the package lead finish and the socket can lead to substantial difference in electrochemical potential and consequent galvanic action. Intel therefore recommends that gold-finished sockets be used with gold-finished hermetic packages. Similarly, tin-finished sockets should be used with devices which have tin or solder-lead finishes.

A similar galvanic failure mechanism can occur on gold-finished hermetic packages independent of the socket. If a pinhole or scratch in the gold exposes ferrous base metal or silver/copper eutectic brazing material, a strong electrochemical corrosion cell can be activated. All of Intel's gold-finished hermetic packages uses have a passive nickel barrier layer beneath the gold. Intel periodically inspects incoming gold-finished piece parts for exposed base metal.

Tin, solder and especially silver are capable of migrating under the influence of humidity and electric fields. Side-braze packages are plated with nickel and gold to prevent exposed silver from the silver/copper eutectic brazing material. On cerdip packages, an out-of-control electroplating process can cause lead shorting due to tin migration. Tin migration is also a possibility in saturated steam exposure. These problems are only infrequently observed; still, there is a trend towards ever finer lead pitches so the potential for this failure remains.

INTERNAL MOISTURE-RELATED MECHANISMS

Fine and gross leak test monitors and careful control of cavity moisture ensures that internal moisture-related mechanisms are not an issue in hermetic packages. Unfortunately, the seal in hermetic packages can be broken by improper handling after the final hermeticity check. The device then presents a reliability jeopardy due to internal moisture-related mechanisms. This is a manufacturing issue and is controlled by proper shipping procedures characterization and board assembly.

There are four prerequisites for internal moisture-related mechanisms in plastic packages: path, contaminant, moisture and voltage. All are always present in plastic packages. The idea is to control them to minimize the failure rate.

The issue of whether or not there is a path to the die is more important for impurities than for moisture because the plastic package is relatively transparent to moisture, especially for accelerated temperature/humidity test conditions. There is always a path to the die for moisture. The path to the die for impurities may be along interfaces inherent to the construction of the package or along unintentionally introduced cracks. Figure 8-47 shows that interfaces between lead frame and epoxy and between wire and epoxy,

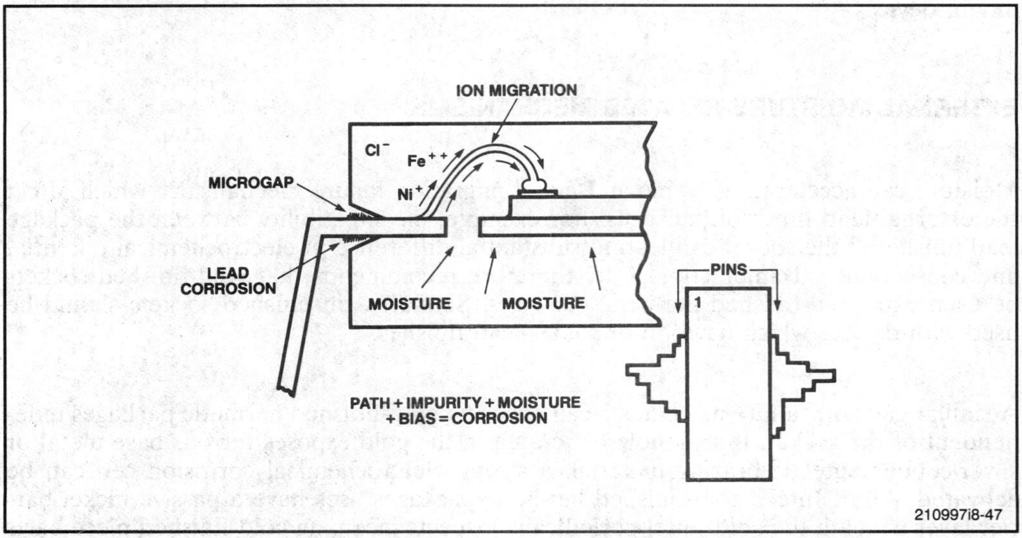

Figure 8-47. Path + Impurity + Moisture + Bias = Corrosion

provide paths to the die. The diagram at the lower right of Figure 8-47 is a top view of a PDIP on the sides of which histograms of the failure-causing pins have been superimposed. It is clear that the pins that failed had the shortest path along the lead finger to the die. This is evidence that impurities diffuse along the interfaces between the epoxy and the lead frame. Paths to the die can also be provided by cracks which can occur

- During mold ejection.
- During DTF (deflash, trip, form) due to dull or misaligned tooling.
- During solder dip or vapor-phase reflow during board insertion.
- Due to temperature cycle or thermal shock.

Once the moisture and/or impurities have reached the die, the path to active circuitry is provided by

- Pinholes in passivation.
- Passivation cracks due to thermomechanical stressing of the package (thin-film cracking).
- Cracks at poor step coverage by passivation.

Contaminants may reach these die by one of the paths or they may be introduced with the die or epoxy. When accelerated by temperature, humidity and bias, two main types of failure may occur: aluminum metallization corrosion or a more subtle circuit malfunction.

Aluminum metallization corrosion is well understood and can occur in two ways:

- Moisture combines with phosphorous from phosphosilicate glass (PSG) to form phosphoric acid. This can cause corrosion with or without bias. Under bias, cathodic corrosion of aluminum occurs. PSG can be exposed to moisture by misaligned passivation openings or cracked passivation.
- Ionic chlorine is an efficient catalyst for anodic corrosion of aluminum. Typical sources of chlorine are chemical deflash (in a now obsolete process), old generation molding compound, oxide stripper (for cleaning leads after burn in) and handling.

Metallization corrosion is no longer an important failure mechanism in plastic packages. The phosphorous content of glass exposed to moisture is carefully controlled and chlorine and other ionics have been greatly reduced in new-generation molding compounds and processing. Monitors and qualification procedures incorporating steam and 85/85 stressing are put in place to catch any problems before customer ship.

Now that aluminum metallization corrosion has been controlled, plastic-encapsulated devices last much longer in moisture stress and fail by subtle circuit malfunctions such as ionic migration through passivation defects leading to discharge of an internal circuit node. For example, in the 1970s typical mean times to failure were 500 to 1000 hours in biased 85/85 with pad corrosion. Today, mean times to failure of greater than 5000 hours in this stress are common and transistor degradation is the usual failure mechanism.

The remarkable improvement in the internal moisture reliability of plastic packages has made the traditional biased 85/85 stress inconvenient because of the long testing times and large sample sizes required. This has motivated the development of a higher temperature unsaturated biased moisture stress called HAST (Highly Accelerated Temperature and Humidity Stress Test). HAST applies high temperatures (100°C to 150°C) and high humidity (but less than 100 percent) to biased devices. High temperature and high humidity require the use of pressurized test chambers.

Industry standards for HAST have been established by Joint Electron Device Engineering Council (JEDEC) and other industry groups. The JEDEC standards have been published as JEDEC Standard No. 22-A110, "Test Method A110, Highly Accelerated Temperature and Humidity Stress Test (HAST)." This test method establishes the standard test conditions shown in Table 8-4.

The most popular industry standard test condition is 130/85, however, for internal process development applications, Intel uses even higher stresses, up to the limit of the pressure vessel. Typical vessels are rated to 5 atmospheres (gauge), so that 159/85 is accessible. Intel uses 159/85 for internal process development to compare, for example, various passivation options in as few as 200 hours of stress time.

Accelerations attainable are illustrated in Figures 8-48, 8-49 and 8-50. Figure 8-48 shows early 64K DRAM data which shows that 134/95 provides an acceleration of about 20 relative to 85/85. Subsequent more detailed work by Danielson, et. al on 256K DRAMs and EPROMs showed that determinations of acceleration factors are complicated by two factors:

1. Failure distributions in time usually show two distinct populations: An early failure distribution due to defects, and a later, tighter distribution due to the intrinsic moisture penetration properties of the passivation.

2. If precautions are not taken to avoid introducing ionic contamination into the test chamber, then failure distributions are considerably broadened in time.

In HAST testing, considerable care is taken in handling units for test, whereas the usual procedures for 85/85 testing introduce appreciable levels of ionic contamination. The result of this can be seen in Figures 8-49 and 8-50 where the 85/85 data shows a greater "spread" in time than HAST data. Figures 8-49 and 8-50 also shows the two distinct "defective" and "intrinsic" populations. It should be noted that all the failures in

Table 8-4. Standard Test Conditions

Code	Temperature	RH (%)	Press (atm, gauge)
A	110	85	0.41
B	120	85	0.95
C	130	85	1.66
D	140	85	2.57

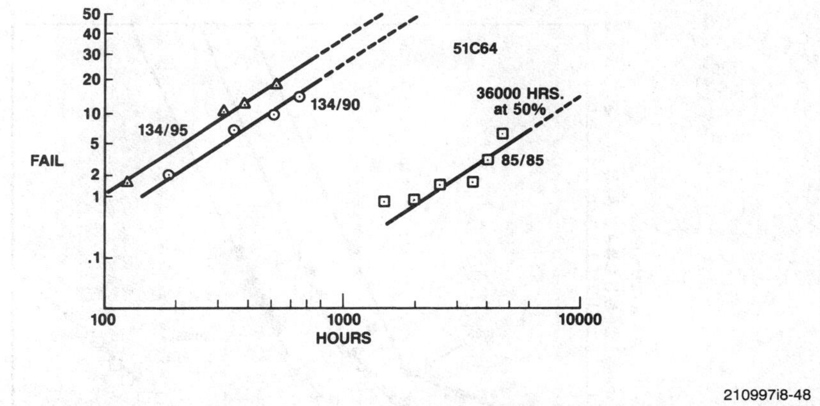

Figure 8-48. Cumulative Single Bit 64K DRAM Failures in Biased 85/85 and Biased HAST Stress Showing an Acceleration of About 20. Peck Model Prediction is 25 for 134/90 and 29 for 134/95.

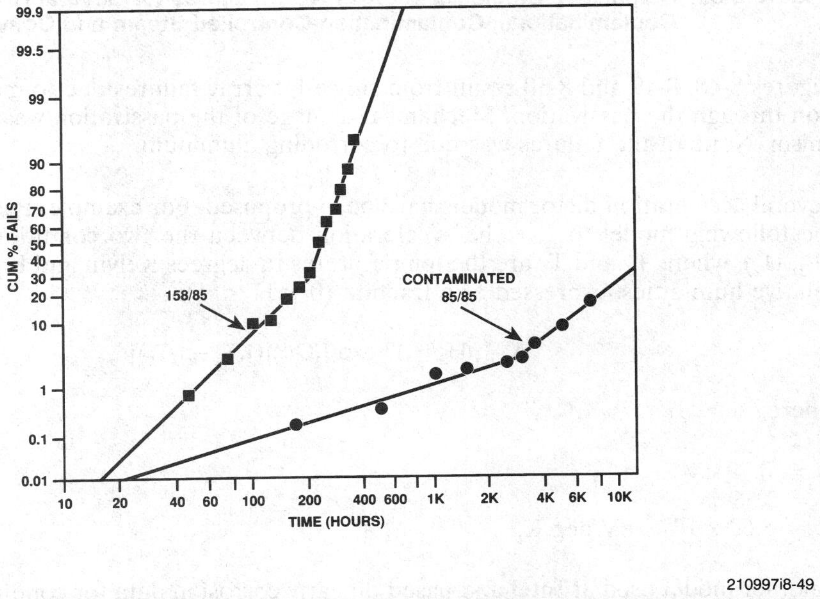

Figure 8-49. Cumulative Single Bit 256K DRAM Failures in 158/85 HAST and Conventional 85/85. Note the Wide Spread of Failure Times in 85/85 Due to Lack of Contamination Control.

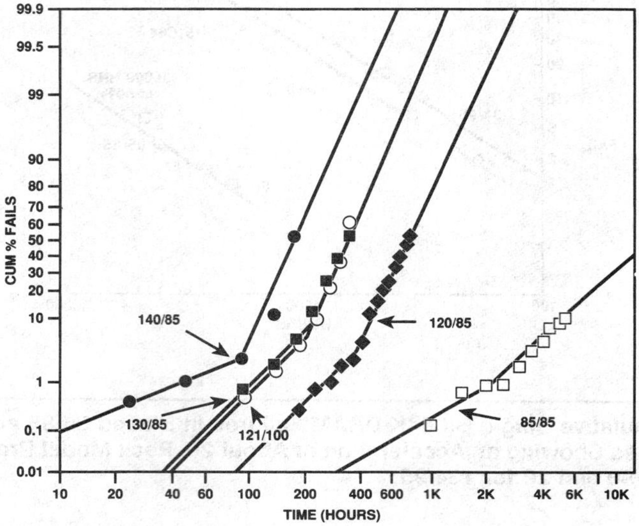

210997i8-50

Figure 8-50. Cumulative Single Bit 256K EPROM Failures for Several HAST Conditions, Contaminations, Contamination-Controlled Steam and Conventional 85/85.

Figures 8-48, 8-49 and 8-50 result from single-bit array failures due to moisture penetration through the passivation. Mechanical damage of the passivation was a typical mechanism. None of the failures was due to corroding aluminum.

Several acceleration factor models have been proposed. For example, Peck has proposed the following model to give the acceleration between the two conditions (T_1, H_1) and (T_2, H_2), where T_1 and T_2 are the temperatures in degrees Kelvin and H_1 and H_2 are the relative humidities, expressed as a fraction ($0 < H < 1$):

$$A = (H_2/H_1)^n \exp[(Q/K)(1/T_1 - 1/T_2)]$$

where:

$Q = 0.79$ eV
$n = 2.66$
$K = 8.62 \times 10^{-5}$ eV/deg K.

Another model used at Intel and based on early corrosion data for conditions less severe than 85/85 is a so-called "Eyring" model in which A is given by:

$$A = \exp[(Q/K)(1/T_1 - 1/T_2) + B(H_2 - H_1)$$

where:

Q = 0.53 eV
B = 11.5
K = 8.62×10^{-5} eV/degK

Predictions of the models in relation to common service and test ambients are conveniently displayed on a temperature versus relative humidity plot, such as in Figure 8-51. Common test ambients are indicated, along with their accelerations relative to 25/65 as predicted by the Peck model. The predictions of the Peck model are shown as iso-acceleration contours in Figure 8-51. The same could have been done for the Eyring model. Interestingly, there is a locus on the T versus RH plot along which the predictions of the two models agree and this is shown in Figure 8-51. It can be seen that over the span of common operating ambients (25/65) and traditional test ambients (85/85 and 121/100), the two models agree. Data for HAST test ambients of 130/85, 140/85 and 159/85 will resolve which model is better. Agreement between 130/85 and 121/100 test

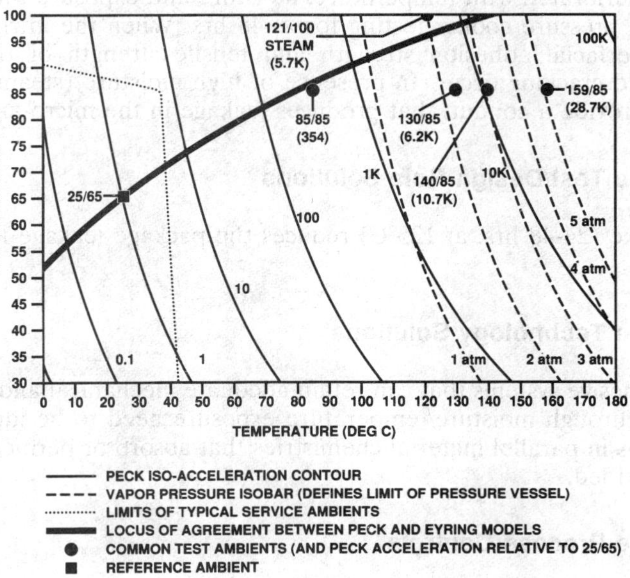

Figure 8-51. Peck Model Accelerations Relative to 25/65. Range of Service Ambients and Pressure Vessel Limits are Shown. Typical Stress Conditions and Predicted Peck Accelerations are also Shown.

data for EPROMs seen in Figure 8-50 would indicate that the Peck model is to be preferred, since both of these conditions lie on the same Peck iso-acceleration contour. The Eyring model predicts that 121/100 is a factor of 3.9 more accelerated than 130/85, contradicting the data.

There are limitations on the acceleration factors accessible with HAST stressing. Figure 8-51 shows isobars indicating the water vapor pressure. To the left of the 1 atmosphere isobar, a pressurized chamber is not needed. Thus, the Peck model would predict that accelerations of much more than 1K (relative to 25/65) are not possible unless the chamber is pressurized. For a chamber rated to 5 atmospheres (gauge), Peck predicts accelerations of about 30K, relative to 25/65. Other limitations may reduce the accelerations possible. For example, if failure mechanisms are induced by a glass transition in the epoxy molding compound at temperatures above 130°C, then accelerations would be limited to about 10K. Detailed failure analysis will resolve whether or not this is a limitation in any particular case.

Plastic Package Failure Mechanism Definition

There is an intrinsic tensile stress in the tape/adhesive system of some plastic packages due to the mismatch of thermal co-efficients of expansion between the copper and tape system. The mechanical properties of the tape/adhesive system and the adhesive interfacial strength deteriorated with temperature, moisture and exposure time, most predominantly in steam pressure cooker testing for $\geq$ 48 hrs. When the intrinsic tensile stress exceeds the interfacial adhesion strength and tensile strength of the tape/adhesive, delamination and cracking occur. In presence of high moisture (steam), the cracks and delaminations provide a conduit that produces leakage in the micro-amp range.

Plastic Package Test/Design Rule Solutions

Appropriate bake (24-48 hrs. at 125°C) reduces the package leakage levels to the nano amp range.

Plastic Package Technology Solutions

Tape carrier/adhesive systems that can retain adequate mechanical and interfacial adhesive properties through moisture/temperature exposure need to be identified. Alternatively, or perhaps in parallel material chemistries that absorb or permeate less moisture, need to be identified.

Plastic Package Process Controls

Process controls for this failure mechanism remain to be identified.

Future Trends

Most of the future activity in package failure mechanisms in the future will be in connection with plastic packages, focusing on moisture and thermomechanical mechanisms.

Moisture performance has improved greatly over the past five years due to improved molding compounds. Future internal moisture performance improvements will come with improved die hermeticity. Passivations with fewer defects and less cracking tendencies will help, but the Achilles heel of the wire-bonded molded plastic technology is still bond pads, which are necessarily exposed. Tape-automated bonding (TAB), in which bond pads are completely covered with bumps, might be the solution. As lead pitches become finer, we expect to see more frame/lead problems in moisture testing, such as pin-to-pin leakage currents, metal migration, etc. HAST will become an industry-standard stress.

Thermomechanical mechanisms in plastic packages will continue to demand attention. Plastic surface-mount technology is permitting large dice to be placed in small packages. There is pressure to put high performance chips into plastic packages, so package designers want to use extra metal planes to improve electrical (ground planes) and thermal (heat spreaders) performance. Moreover, surface-mount packages suffer very large temperature shocks during board assembly processes. All of these trends increase the likelihood that failure due to fracture, delamination, wire damage, etc., can occur. Solutions may come in the form of compliant planarized passivations, TAB (more robust interconnects), etc.

Intel has active programs to ensure that new advanced packages will meet the reliability standards the industry demands.

Failure Analysis/Analytical Techniques

9

CHAPTER 9
FAILURE ANALYSIS/ANALYTICAL TECHNIQUES

Page

CHAPTER 9
FAILURE ANALYSIS/ANALYTICAL TECHNIQUES

INTRODUCTION

The primary purposes of our failure and materials analysis efforts are:

- Failure analysis closes the loop between the customer and the factory for customer-returned parts. Since Intel's Dock-to-Stock program has eliminated most customers' incoming inspection, the failures which need to be analyzed usually occur on the manufacturing floor or in the field. Failure analysis tells both the customer and Intel what caused the failure so appropriate action can be taken.

- Failure analysis of Intel's stress monitors (burn-in, steam, electromigration, etc.) provides data for continuous improvement in the reliability of Intel products and technologies.

- Failure analysis constitutes part of the fundamental studies of a technology or product that lead to improved product reliability. Examples include electrostatic discharge (ESD) research leading to new ESD design rules; soft-error research leading to improved packaging, device designs and chip layouts; and dielectric composition studies, which brought about improved moisture (steam and 85/85) performance.

- New tool development for failure analysis allows us to keep up with the increased complexity of our products. Recent examples include dynamic fault imaging (DFI) for VLSI logic circuits, the use of focused ion beam tools for microsurgery on circuits for diagnostic purposes, the emission microscope that locates the source of current leakage in a device and the reactive ion etcher that removes passivation without degrading circuit functionality.

- Materials and failure analysis forms an important part of Intel's new technology package and product certification. A significant amount of process characterization and materials analysis is required in order to develop reliable, leading-edge technologies. The synergy between technology development and reliability engineering helps us to refine and improve our materials and failure analysis skills.

In this chapter, we first describe the electrical test methods used to verify failures and characterize them quantitatively (e.g., measure the leakage, determine the current versus voltage (IV) curve or isolate the failed instruction). Then we summarize the flow of analytical procedures used for locating the failure on the chip, making use of bit-mapping, the emission microscope, microsimulation, internal probing (picoprobe or electron beam) and other tools and techniques.

Finally, we discuss the analytical techniques applied to process characterization and to find the root cause of failure, for example, RIE, SEM, TEM, AES, SIMS, EDX, FTIR, C-SAM etc. – and give examples of how these tools have been used successfully in failure analysis.

ELECTRICAL TESTING

The flow chart for device failure analysis is shown in Figure 9-1. The first step in analyzing a failed device is to electrically confirm the failure using production tests and test equipment. For all products, these include tests for shorts, opens, leakage, basic function and parametrics. The datalog generated by the production tester provides information on where in the test program the part failed (e.g., which vector and how far into the vector the failure was detected) and what pins failed.

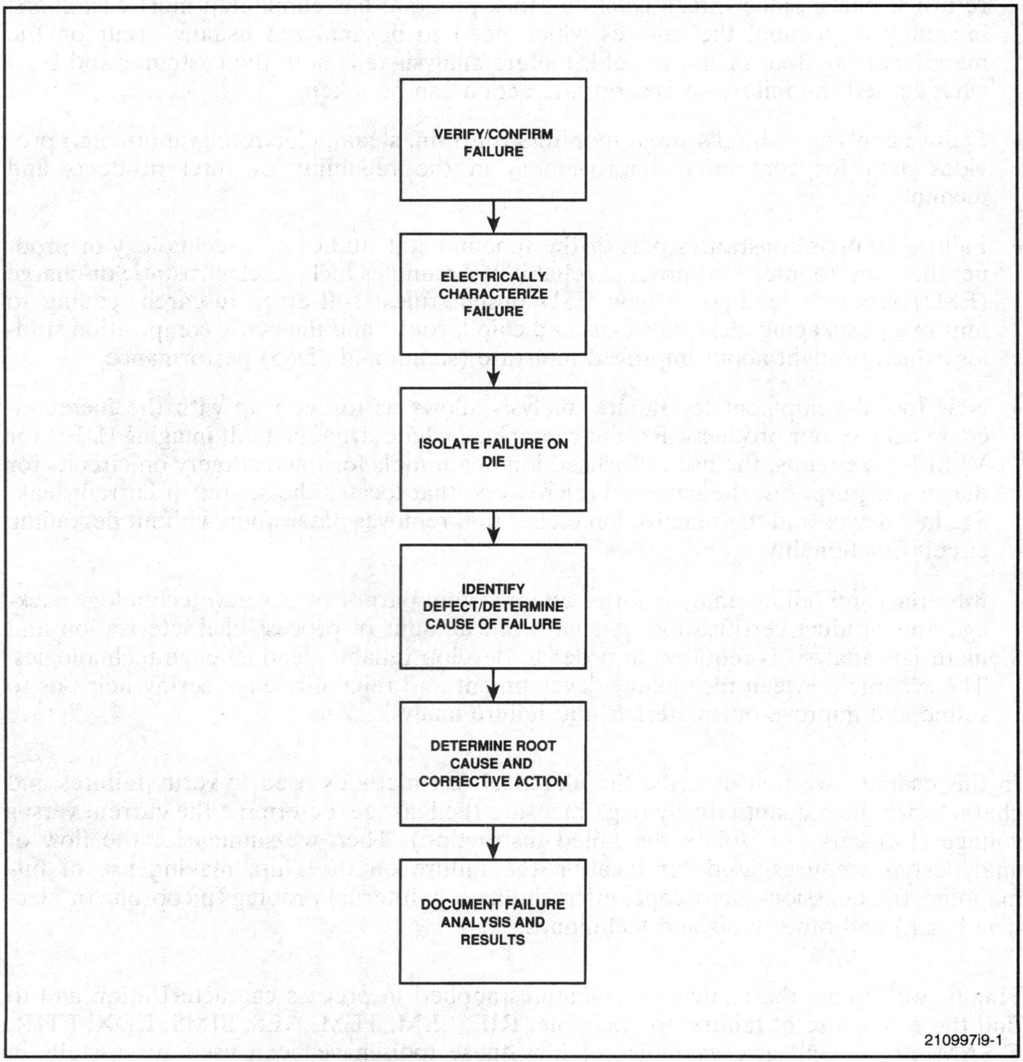

Figure 9-1. Generalized Failure Analysis Flow

Failure Classification

If the part fails for opens/shorts or leakage, the pins are analyzed on a curve tracer. For all other types of failure, the next step is to analyze the part on a general purpose functional tester (gpft) or a special engineering test system (test bed). For memory products, an array failure can be characterized by using an engineering test system to bit-map the array, providing the X-Y coordinates of each failed bit. Furthermore, EPROMs incorporate many built-in self-test modes, which enable external characterization at the memory cell level. For logic products, a general-purpose functional tester or product test bed is loaded with either part or all of the failing test patterns and the failure is verified. Initially, a variety of tests and programs related to the failing pattern are used to characterize the failure as much as possible before any destructive analysis is carried out.

FAULT ISOLATION

The next step in failure analysis is to locate where the failure occurred on the die. This is called fault isolation or fault location. For memory products, this is usually straightforward, requiring relatively simple equipment and software algorithms that raster the memory array. For logic products, such as microprocessors, fault isolation can pose a significant challenge. A number of special techniques and methods have been developed to perform fault isolation on logic chips. Those are described later in this section.

Delidding the Package

Since further analysis typically requires visual examination of the chip itself, the package must now be opened without damaging the functionality of the circuit or changing the failure mode of the device. The package is opened using a variety of techniques. For plastic packages, jet etchers are primarily used to remove the plastic over the die. These work by focusing a continuous jet of acid to etch the plastic away from the surface of the die. Alternatively, a manual method can be used. In this case, a cavity slightly larger than the die is milled out of the plastic in the die area, followed by etching with red fuming nitric acid. Once the die is exposed (for both cases), the die and package are rinsed with acetone.

A "dry removal process can be used where functionality of the die is not required and it is desirable to avoid artifacts and etching caused by the "wet" plastic removal process. In this case, the plastic package is abraded away on a coarse grinder until the die paddle is exposed. The die paddle with attached die is then "plucked" from the package with needlenose pliers.

In the case of cerdip packages, the two pieces of ceramic material sealed together with glass need to be separated. This can be accomplished either by cracking the glass seal between specially shaped vise blades or sawing through the seal with a diamond saw.

If the package is sidebrazed or laminated ceramic, the die can be exposed by removing the gold-plated lid hermetically sealed to the body of the package. The lid can be removed by heating the package to about 400°C to melt the seal which holds the lid in place, or by using a sharp blade to pry the lid apart from the package.

Identifying Gross Electrical Leakage

With the package delidded, various tools can be used to identify leakage spots. Generally, gross leakage measured on the external package pins can arise due to electrostatic discharge, electrical overstress, or various types of contamination which damage the IC performance. The leakage can amount to tens of microamperes. Leakage failures are initially identified with a curve tracer. To locate the physical leakage site on the chip, liquid crystal or emission microscopy can be used. When the leakage is large enough to cause local heating, liquid crystal techniques can be used to locate the leakage site. In the case of leakage mechanisms that do not give rise to hot spots, the emission microscope is more effective. The emission microscope and liquid crystal techniques are described in a later section.

Failure Location Techniques

For memory products, information from the bit-map of the array isolates the failing row, column or bit. Further failure location, if needed, is generally done with liquid crystal, emission microscope and visual techniques. Physical defect identification is normally straightforward at this point.

For logic products, finding the precise failure location on the die is more difficult. A tester, a prober and some kind of device reference are used interactively to electrically isolate the failure. As previously mentioned, a general-purpose functional tester (gpft) or a product test bed is used to stimulate and test the device. To probe the device, mechanical and electron-beam probing techniques are used. Electron beam (E-beam) probing techniques are described in more detail in a later section. For device reference, schematics and composite plots are needed. Design manuals, logic simulators and functionally good units ("golden" units) are used to compare proper operation of the device to the failure. For Intel's most advanced logic products, a gpft, an E-beam prober and a logic simulator are used interactively and extensively to isolate the failure.

Functional Characterization

To facilitate E-beam probing, it is necessary to generate a special test program which repetitively executes the failing pattern in an infinite loop. Sometimes the code for this can be extracted from the existing test program; on other occasions a program has to be specially written. The test program in essence controls the state of internal faulty nodes and enables continuous probing of internal nodes. To minimize the sampling time, the test program length should be as short as possible.

In parallel with the test program activity, a logic simulator is used to simulate the digital activity of internal signal nodes for the failing test pattern. The output of the simulator is useful for several reasons. First, the logic levels of strategic internal nodes are now known. These nodes can be subsequently probed in the real chip and the results compared with simulated values to trace the failure systematically. Second, a view into the internal logic activity of the suspected circuit unit or block gives insight into the possible causes of the failure, thereby eliminating unnecessary physical probing.

The combination of identifying the failing instruction and the results of the logic simulator can generally narrow the failure down to specific cells or, in some cases, to individual gates. In this way the amount of physical probing can be reduced to a small number of nodes. If access to a logic simulator is not possible for a specific product, the analysis can proceed with a comparison of a good versus a failing device to highlight differences in the logical activity of the failing chip.

Sample Preparation

To physically probe the chip, especially for functional fails, it is necessary to remove the passivation layers protecting the chip. Removal of the passivation has to be carried out carefully to minimize device damage and possible change of functionality. Dry etching techniques can be used to accomplish this, for example reactive ion etching (RIE), as described later in this chapter.

The capacitive coupling mode of voltage contrast operation (described in a later section) does enable data to be measured from nodes that are buried under passivation or interlayer dielectric glass. The glass must first be thinned to several thousand angstroms to minimize charging effects. Absence of the glass is the best scenario and the preferred mode of operation.

E-Beam Probing of the Chip

At Intel, E-Beam probing is the preferred method of physically probing our most complex logic products. Initially, logic state maps (LSMs) or waveforms are taken from major internal signals to provide a starting point for analysis. This usually verifies the internal operation of the suspected failures at suspected node sites. LSMs/waveforms are compared to the data from the logic simulator or from a good device. The process of taking LSMs/waveforms and comparing them to reference data is methodically repeated until the failure is traced back to the fault. The electrical failure should now be isolated to a cell or gate and perhaps even a transistor, depending on node accessibility. Other analytical tools are then used to carry the analysis further for defect identification and root-cause determination.

Generally, if access to a logic simulator is not possible, data taken from the good device is the only reference data for device operation. When the chip is analyzed with reference to a good device, the techniques used are known as dynamic fault imaging (DFI).

In the case of functional failures for which there is minimal activity in the internal logic, such as failures that do not come out of reset, certain internal circuits are probed first. These include clock, reset circuitry and the inputs and outputs to the microcode ROM. This usually leads to a starting point from which the analysis can proceed.

LSMs/waveforms are extremely useful for localizing a failure down to the gate level in digital logic. Analysis may be hampered in getting to the gate level because the relevant circuitry may be in lower metal or polysilicon. If the circuitry is buried under the top metal, this metal has to be removed using a localized etching technique, such as focused ion beam milling. These techniques are discussed in greater detail later in this chapter.

DIAGNOSTIC TOOLS

A number of specialized tools for fault isolation have been mentioned in the preceding sections. This section describes the operation of those tools in more detail.

Voltage Contrast (E-Beam Probing)

Voltage contrast is a contrast mechanism that arises in a Scanning Electron Microscope (SEM) used as a microprobe instrument. When an electron beam impinges on an operating integrated circuit on which microfields are present, the yield and energy distribution of the secondary electrons generated is modulated by voltages on the chip. Depending on the type of electron detector employed, this energy modulation can manifest itself as various forms of voltage contrast.

Qualitative Voltage Contrast

The natural energy filter that exists above the chip surface will change the energy modulation into a modulation of the secondary electron yield as a function of the surface voltage. This conversion leads to classical voltage contrast in which positively biased lines appear dark (low electron yield) and grounded or negatively biased lines appear bright. This mechanism is useful for analyzing digital logic. The relationship between surface potential and secondary electron yield is not linear, but the voltage can be determined to an accuracy of about 1 Volt. A voltage contrast image showing qualitative contrast is illustrated in Figure 9-2a.

Quantitative Voltage Contrast

The energy modulation that the secondary electrons undergo is tracked to determine the true voltage at the emission point at the chip. This requires the use of a special detector known as an energy analyzer, which converts the energy fluctuations of the secondary electrons into an output voltage. The quantitative contrast is useful for determining actual voltage levels on operating chips.

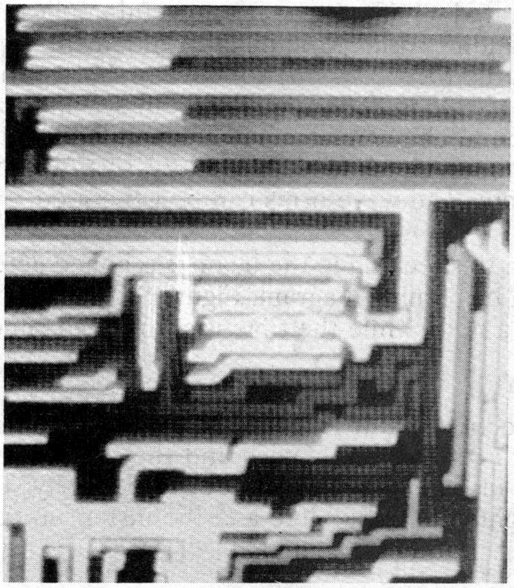

a) A Voltage Contrast Image Bright is Logic Low and Dark is Logic High

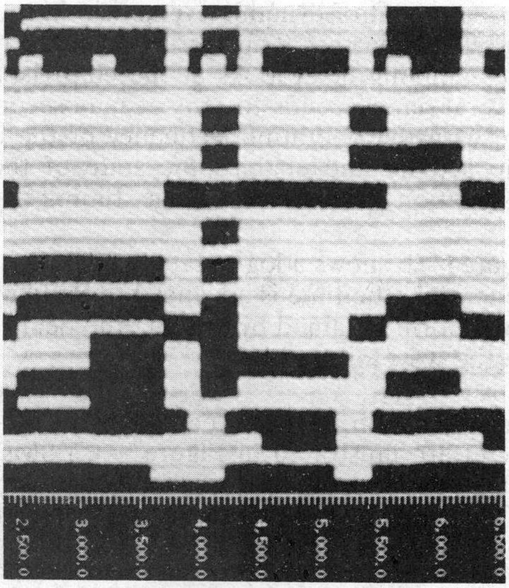

b) A Logic State Map of an Internal Bus. Time in ns Along the Horizontal Axis

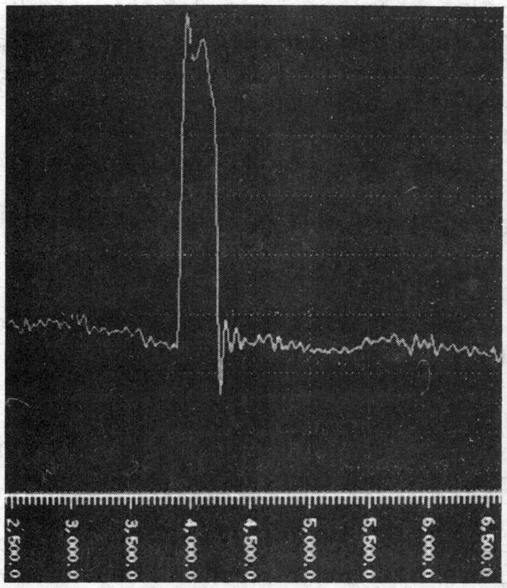

c) A Quantitative Waveform with Time in ns Along the Horizontal Axis and Volts in the Vertical Axis

210997i

Figure 9-2. Voltage Contrast Examples

Stroboscopic Voltage Contrast

Measurement of dynamic events within integrated circuits is the most useful application of voltage contrast. This can be achieved by adding a sampling head to the microscope. The sampling head looks at the chip (i.e., turns the beam on) for a very short period (several nanoseconds to tens of nanoseconds). This is done repetitively in synchronization with the operating frequency of the circuit. This stroboscopic method freezes the chip activity and enables the state of the nodes to be determined. By scanning the observation strobe over a range, timing diagrams and waveforms can be generated.

Figure 9-2b shows a logic state map (LSM). In this technique the beam is scanned across a bus while the time is advanced to build up a bus timing diagram. Figure 9-2c illustrates a waveform obtained by parking the beam at a node while the time is scanned to generate the waveform.

An application of these techniques to the electrical fault isolation of a microprocessor circuit are illustrated in Figure 9-3. LSMs of a functioning device and the same device failing due to a voltage marginality are shown in Figures 9-3a and 9-3b, respectively. The difference image shown in Figure 9-3c highlights the failing line and the instant in time when the failure occurs.

Interface to a CAD Database

A significant aid in locating nodes on a complex chip is a link between the E-beam prober and the chip design database. This is accomplished by extracting design coordinates from the layout database and directing the E-beam to the appropriate coordinate location on the die. Having the additional capability of mapping between schematics and layouts is also useful for improved productivity.

Emission Microscopy and Liquid Crystal

The emission microscope and liquid crystal are two tools commonly used to isolate the failure region. They are capable of detecting localized conduction phenomenon in complex circuits. The former detects light emission from the conduction spot, while the latter senses the temperature difference between the conduction spot and its background.

The emission microscope is an Intel-designed tool based on state-of-the-art night vision technology. It consists of a standard wafer probe station, an intensifying camera and a video image processor. By detecting the extremely low level of light emission from a malfunctioning chip, the emission microscope can provide vital clues to the root cause of the failure. To date, several emission mechanisms that involve the recombination of electrons and holes in the silicon have been identified. These are 1) p-n junctions in either forward bias or reverse bias near avalanche breakdown, 2) saturated MOS transistors and 3) current conduction through dielectric films via quantum mechanical tunneling. Common circuit failures such as junction damage, oxide damage and contact spiking may induce one or more of the above mechanisms. With a circuit layout diagram and appropriate circuit knowledge, it is possible to determine the root cause of failure.

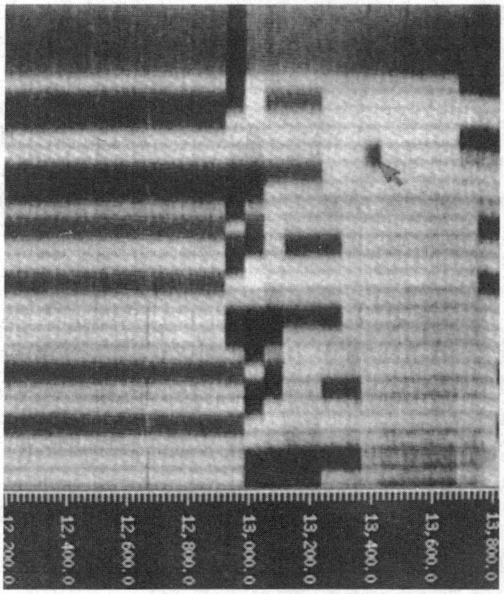

a) Shows the LSM of a Functional Device

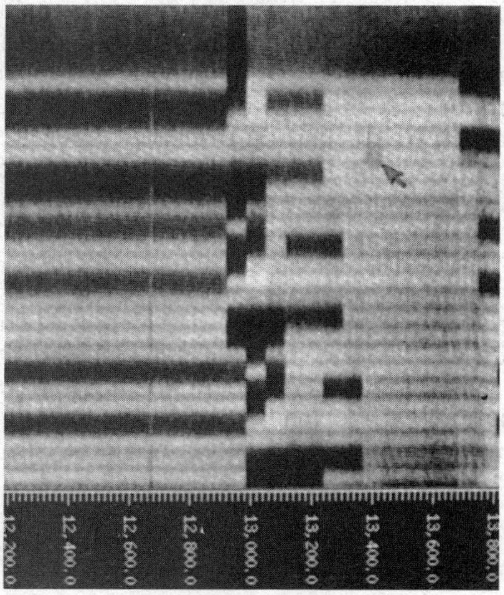

b) For a Device Failing Due to a Voltage Marginality

c) Shows the Difference Image

210997i

Figure 9-3. An Example of LSMs Applied to Electrical Fault Isolation

Figure 9-4 shows an example of a repeating oxide damage problem solved with the aid of this microscope. The figure is an emission microscope image which shows the failure location at the intercept of the gate edge, diffusion edge and field oxide edge, where the highest electric field is present across the oxide. After locating the failure site, it can be seen that the polysilicon gate over the oxide area of the transistor is connected to a long polysilicon interconnection. This pointed out that the root cause was likely to be the ion implantation step during device fabrication. The charge collected by this polysilicon "antenna" during this process step was likely to have been discharged through the gate oxide. Beyond a certain threshold, the gate oxide cannot handle the level of current flow required and this eventually leads to breakdown. The knowledge obtained from this emission microscope study was given to the process engineers and methods were found for preventing the excess charging.

The emission microscope can detect leakage currents as low as 0.1 μA in the case of oxide defects and junction defects. The spatial resolution is better than 1 micrometers (1 μm). However, since light emission requires excess electron-hole pairs, there are situations where leakage may be excessive but without light emission. For example, a metal-to-metal or poly-to-poly short will not emit. An MOS transistor biased in the linear region would not emit, because the channel is resistive. In these cases, which are normally high-current events, a liquid crystal with proper phase transition temperature

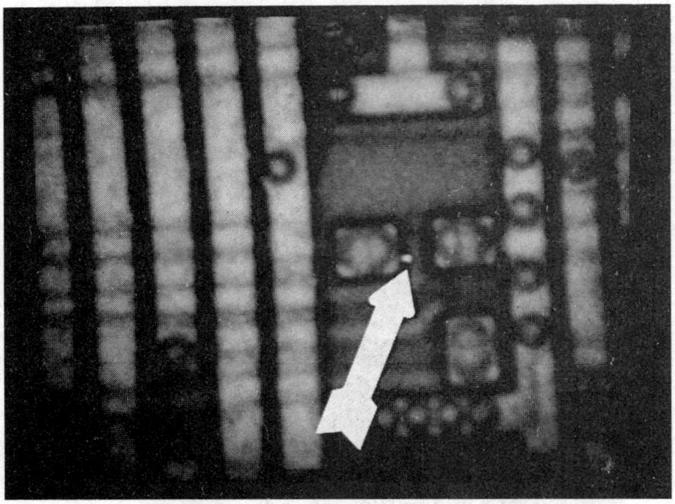

210997i

Figure 9-4. Emission Microscope Image of Oxide Damage Caused by So-Called "Antenna Effect"

can be used to sense the Joule heating produced by the current flow. The liquid crystal is ideal for detecting gross leakage problems, but its sensitivity and spatial resolution are much poorer than the emission microscope.

SAMPLE PREPARATION AND MODIFICATION

In order to effectively apply the failure analysis methods discussed in this section and to identify the root cause failure mechanism, it is frequently necessary to expose the region of interest by selectively removing overlying layers, or by precisely sectioning the device. Conventionally, this preparation is achieved through a combination of metallographic sample preparation and chemical stripback techniques. It is also desirable to modify circuits on a microscale as an aid to failure analysis or even to verify that a design modification may fix a given failure mode. In the past, conductors have been exposed by stripback techniques and lines broken by scribing with a needlepoint probe or a laser cutter. In this section, we describe a number of more advanced approaches to sample stripback, cross section and circuit modification. These methods are finding everyday application on advanced technologies and in fact, lend themselves to attacking problems in new ways.

Reactive Ion Etch

A critical step in physically probing the internal nodes of a chip, as mentioned previously, is the removal of the passivation layers protecting the metal interconnections. This must be done without damaging functional circuitry and with as little disturbance as possible to any evidence which might lead to understanding of the root cause for failure. Reactive ion etching (RIE) is now the preferred technique for passivation layer removal versus wet etching, or conventional barrel-type and parallel-plate plasma etching.

RIE makes use of an RF plasma discharge with a low-pressure gas mixture of, for example, carbon tetrafluoride and oxygen. RIE differs from conventional plasma etching in that the pressure is lower (typically 20-80 millitorr, compared to 150-400 millitorr). Also the lower electrode, on which the sample is placed, is connected to the RF supply, whereas the lower electrode is grounded normal in plasma etching.

Intel has developed special proprietary RIE techniques and processes to accomplish passivation stripback in keeping with these requirements. In particular, we have been able to remove chemically vapor-deposited (CVD) and plasma CVD oxides, nitrides and oxynitrides over metal layers without circuit damage. Figure 9-5 presents a case where two metal layers have been exposed in a complex logic chip without loss of functionality.

In order to maintain functionality, RIE methods have been developed which prevent:

1. Charging damage to thin-gate dielectrics
2. Sputtering of metals or other non-volatile materials from the package or electrodes
3. Polymerization of the fluorocarbon gas mixtures used for etching

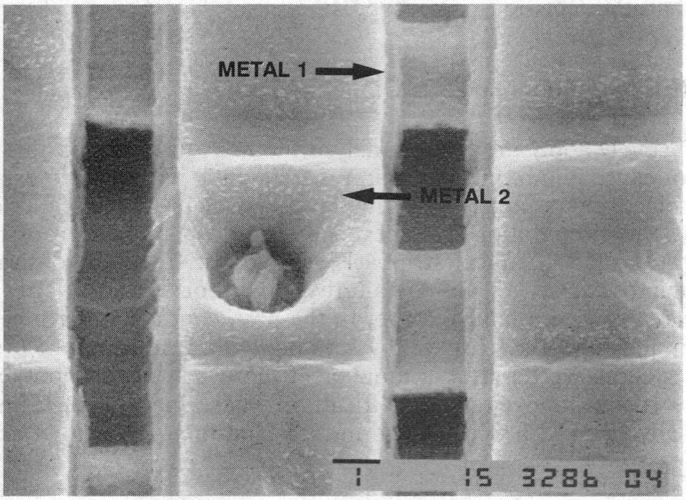

Figure 9-5. SEM Showing Metal Lines (Metal 1 and Metal 2) Crossing at 90°. Passivation has Been Removed Using RIE. Circuit is Still Functional.

Also, etching parameters have been developed which allow the selective removal of passivation or interlayer dielectrics without damage to other dielectric or silicon layers under the metal and metal lift off.

In addition to preparing samples for physical probing, RIE has also been found useful in conjunction with the scanning electron microscope for the study of various metal defects (hillocks, voids, silicon precipitates), and for uncovering particles and other defects for visual and energy dispersive X-ray (EDX) analysis. RIE can be used to etch and delineate aluminum grain boundaries and in the analysis of failures from electromigration stressing. Examples are shown in Figures 9-6 and 9-7.

In failure and low-yield analysis, RIE has been used as the first step in the layer-by-layer strip back search for defects. This is particularly useful after a precise location for the failure has been determined, for example, by bit-mapping or by one of the other methods described. The exact cause of failures associated with individual defects such as particles and oxide breakdowns have been identified using these techniques.

Focused Ion Beam Mill

The use of a focused ion beam mill (FIB) is now emerging as a powerful technique for both circuit modification and failure analysis. The FIB utilizes a finely focused beam of 20-30 KeV Ga ions to selectively remove sections of the device. The use of liquid metal ion source (LMIS) technology, in conjunction with appropriate ion optics, enables the

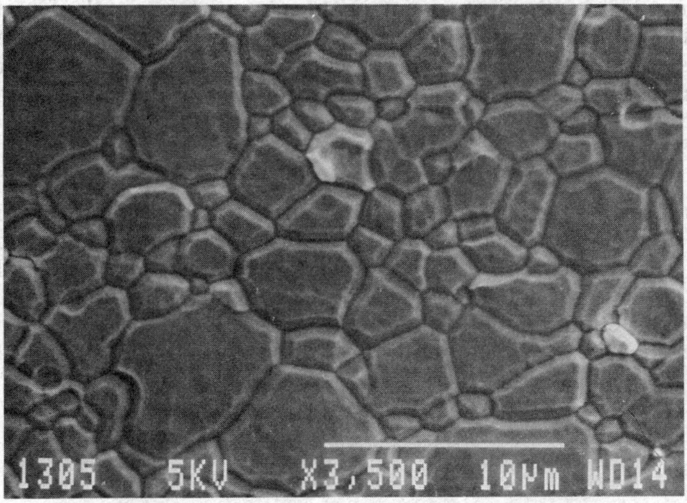

210997i

Figure 9-6. SEM Showing Aluminum Grain Size. Specimen has been Etched Using RIE to Delineate Grain Boundaries.

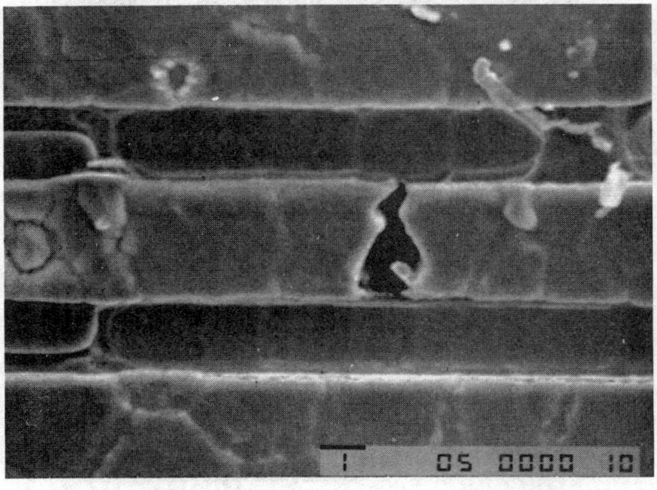

210997i

Figure 9-7. SEM of Electromigration Failure Showing Aluminum-Silicon/Titanium Metal Line

generation of beam sizes in the order of 300Å, while maintaining sufficient current flux to achieve an adequate rate of material removal (a few cubic microns/minute). In the case of failure analysis, the instrument enables precise removal of material in failed regions, exposing underlying areas. The FIB tool has enabled major breakthroughs in the ability to cross section through sub-micron contacts, removing material around particles for more accurate analysis and the precision sectioning of defect locations. These functions are greatly enhanced by automated beam control.

Figure 9-8a is a SEM image of a resist defect that was observed following a bond pad opening etch. A FIB cross section at this defect location (Figure 9-8b) shows resist thinning over Metal 2 has resulted in passivation damage during etch. The use of the FIB provided a cross section which would be difficult if not impossible to obtain by mechanical cross-sectioning due to the small size and low density of the defects and the fragility of the photoresist, which breaks up during normal polishing.

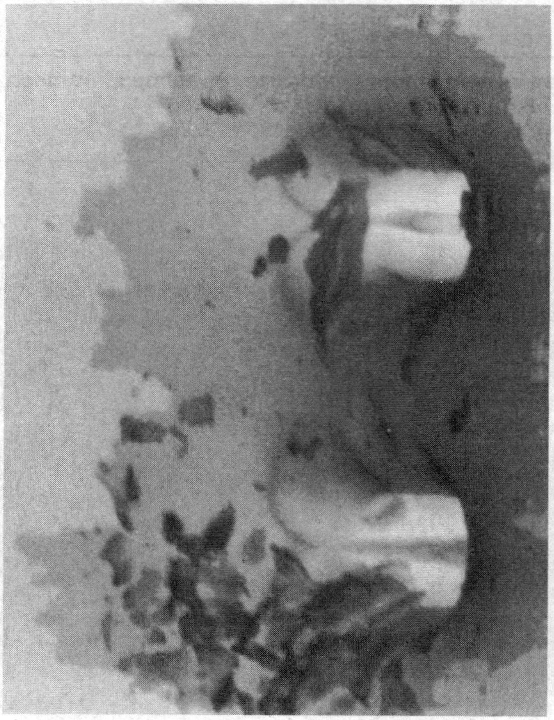

210997i

Figure 9-8a. Top View of Resist Top Surface Showing Morphology of Defect to be Cross Sectioned

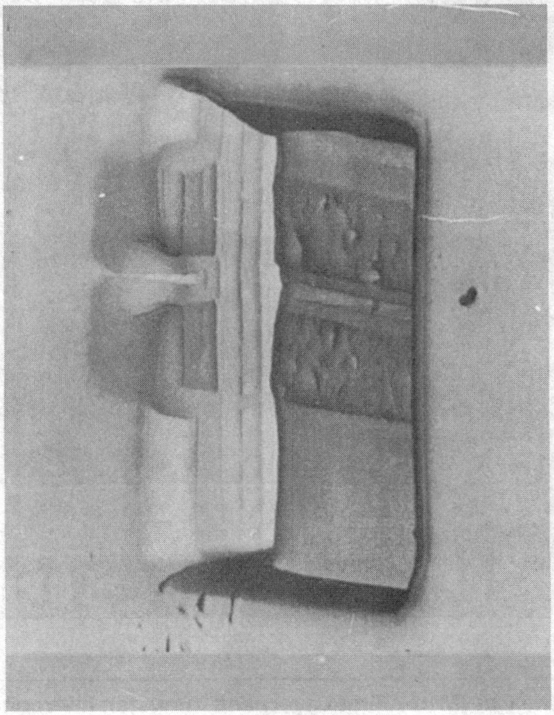

210997i

Figure 9-8b. Ion Mill Cross Section Showing Resist Thinning Over Metal 2 Resulting in Passivation Damage during Bond Pad Etch

By using the ion mill to cut through interconnects, it is possible to isolate failures and electrically characterize specific structures. In addition, provision of a $W(CO)_6$ source makes possible the ion beam-assisted deposition of tungsten interconnect lines in a very well controlled fashion. By opening vias through passivation and interlayer dielectric, underlying conductors can be exposed and connected by these precisely deposited lines. Underlying conductor nodes can also be exposed by ion milling enabling accurate e-beam probing or probing in regions not normally possible. Pads for needlepoint electrical probing can also be added.

Figure 9-9a and 9-9b are SEM micrographs of a microprocessor device which has been modified using these techniques. During the characterization of complex logic circuitry, the FIB provides a means of implementing circuit fixes on existing devices. This enables further electrical device testing and fault isolation to be performed without generation of a modified mask set.

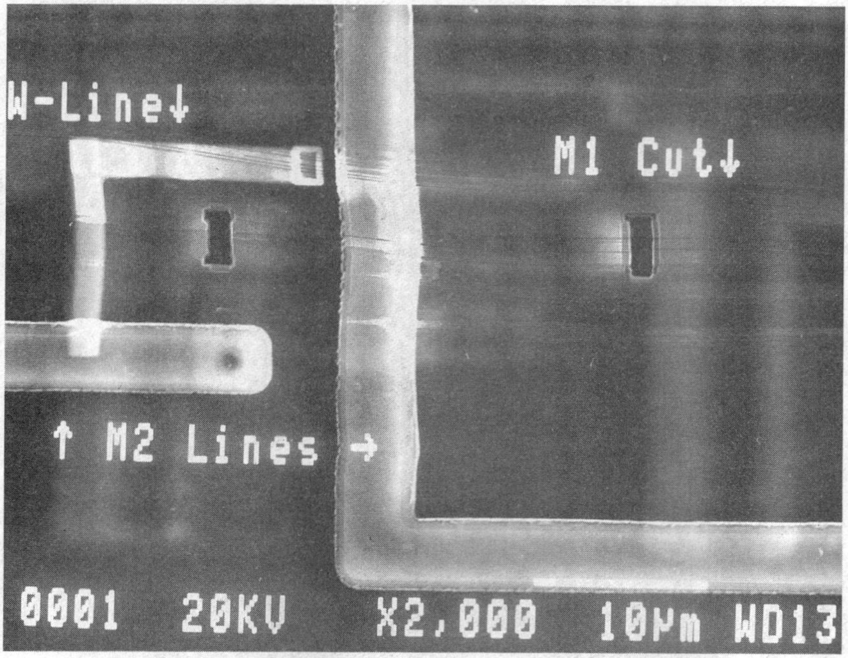

210997i

Figure 9-9a. Metal Line Cut (M1 or First Layer) and Tungsten Interconnect Added Between Two Second Layer Metal Lines (M2)

Microexposure

Microexposure is a lithographic, low-cost alternative to the micro ion mill that can be used for locally removing materials from the surface of a chip in areas one micron or larger in diameter. The tools required are a microscope with equipped apertures, a photoresist spinner and an oven. The sample is coated with photoresist (for example one of the AZ 1300 series of positive resists) using the spinner, softbaked and exposed using a Halogen light source with a 200 μm aperture and 40X objective lens. This can produce an exposed region in the photoresist as small as 5 μm, which can be precisely placed. Red cellophane inserted into the microscope illumination source to absorb the short wavelengths enables location of the desired area without causing resist exposure.

After developing the resist the sample is hardbaked. The resist is then developed and sample etched. This technique can be used with the RIE as a method to remove passivation or dielectrics locally, without disturbing other areas. A phosphoric acid etch can be used to locally remove a portion of metal line, to isolate a portion of circuitry or to make underlying circuitry visible.

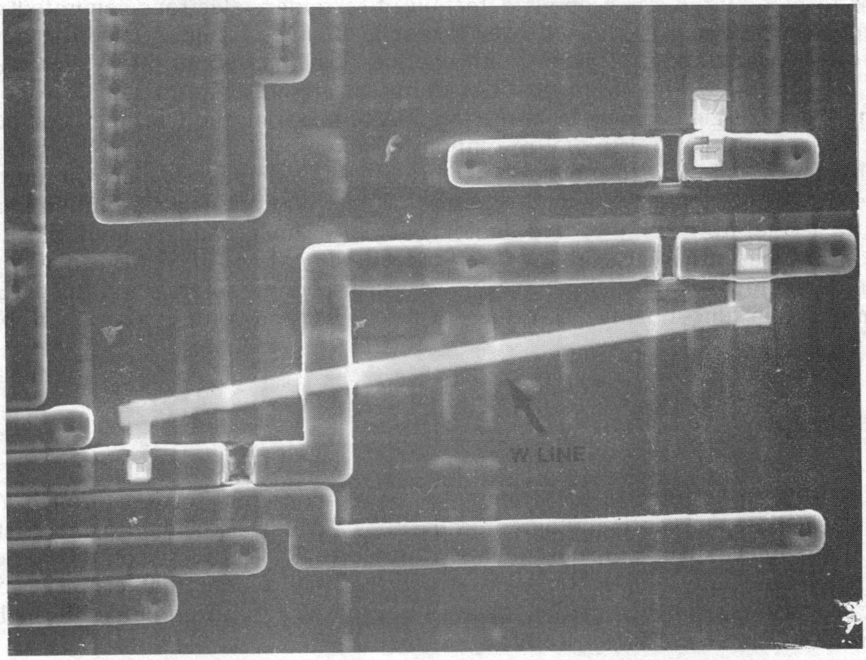

Figure 9-9b. FIB Circuit Modifications of Microprocessor Device. Vias Have Been Cut to M2 for W Metal Line Interconnect in Both Cases.

Finally, the resist is removed with acetone and the sample is ready for further analysis. This technique can be used to remove metal layers blocking the source of light for emission microscopy, provided circuit functionality is not impaired.

PHYSICAL ANALYSIS METHODS

To perform process characterization, to find defects and determine failure root cause, it is often necessary to do physical analysis, sometimes called destructive analysis (or Destructive Physical Analysis, DPA). A number of physical methods are frequently used and described more completely in the following sections.

Scanning Electron Microscopy

The high-resolution imaging capabilities of the scanning electron microscope (SEM) continue to be crucial to VLSI device development and fabrication. The image in the SEM is formed by the synchronous detection of secondary electrons generated while a focused electron beam is scanned over a sample. In the secondary electron detection mode of SEM operation, electrons with energies less than about 50 eV dominate the image. This mode of operation provides the greatest sensitivity to sample topography with most of the signal coming from the top 50Å of material, the typical escape depth of <50 eV electrons. Lateral spatial resolutions of about 50Å are achievable using a conventional thermionic electron source. High brightness field emission electron sources can increase resolution to better than 20Å and providing relatively high resolution images at very low accelerating voltages and avoiding circuit damage and without the need to conductively coat insolating samples. The field emission SEM (FESEM) is now routinely used in our failure analysis labs to permit device inspection before and after RIE stripback, and retain functionality for further electrical test and voltage contrast probing.

Metallography

Figure 9-10 is an example of SEM image of a precision cross section through a failed contact. The sample was metallographically polished perpendicular to the first layer metal interconnect (M1) and subsequently exposed to a selective silicon dioxide etch in order to clearly differentiate the layer structure. It is evident that extensive contact spiking has occurred in the failed contact, as a result of a localized defect in the barrier metallization.

The pair of micrographs in Figure 9-11 shows how different wet-etch techniques can be used to emphasize certain features during SEM observation. In this example, a cross-section was polished parallel to the metal bit lines (columns) of an EPROM array, which are perpendicular to the polysilicon wordlines (rows). In Figure 9-11a, a silicon etch (hydrofluoric/ acetic/nitric acid mixture) was used to decorate the section. This etch attacks the poly in both the floating gate and wordline. Also visible are the arsenic-doped source and drain junctions. The oxide under the floating gate appears thick, because the cross section was taken along one edge of the transistor, where the poly line goes up over the field oxide. In Figure 9-11b, an oxide etch (hydrofluoric acid/ ammonium fluoride) was used to etch back the glass layer over the "poly stack," as well as the thin nitride layer between the two poly silicon layers, which forms part of the oxide/nitride/oxide (ONO) poly-poly dielectric. Now different structural features can be seen.

The large depth of field of the SEM makes it an invaluable tool in examining wire bonds, bond tools and die attach wetout at low magnification. Figure 9-12 shows an example where the initiation of wire necking above a ballbond attached to a device can be clearly seen where in normal optical microscopy this defect would be harder if not impossible to see.

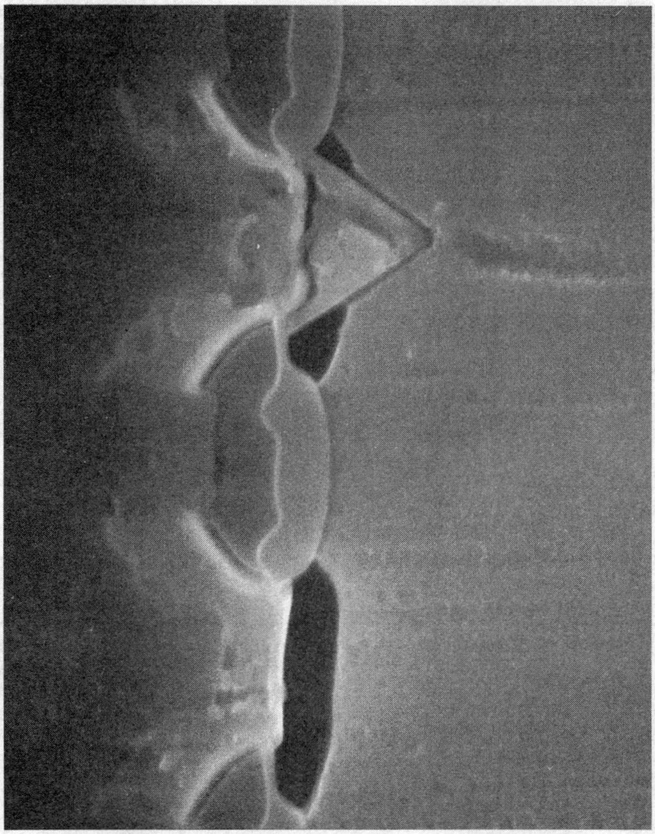

210997i

Figure 9-10. SEM Cross Section Through a Failed Contact Region

An alternative mode of SEM operation involves the detection of higher energy backscattered electrons for image formation. The backscattered electrons, which are generated by scattering of the primary electrons by the atomic cores, originate much more deeply within the sample than the secondary electrons. (This is due to their high energy and associated larger escape depth.) The back scattering yield is sensitive to the average atomic number of the region being probed and therefore can be used to distinguish regions of differing elemental composition. The backscattered electrons yield is also sensitive to the presence of subsurface voids. Figure 9-13 shows an application of backscatter SEM imaging for the examination of subsurface voids generated in a passivated aluminum line as a result of thermal cycling.

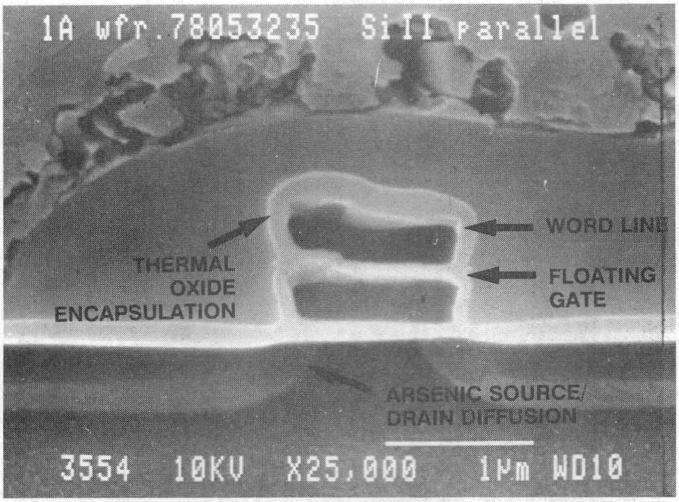

Figure 9-11a. SEM Micrograph Showing X-Section Perpendicular to Polysilicon Word Lines. Polysilicon has been Etched. Clearly Visible is Thermal Oxide Encapsulation, Word Lines, Floating Gate and Arsenic Diffusions.

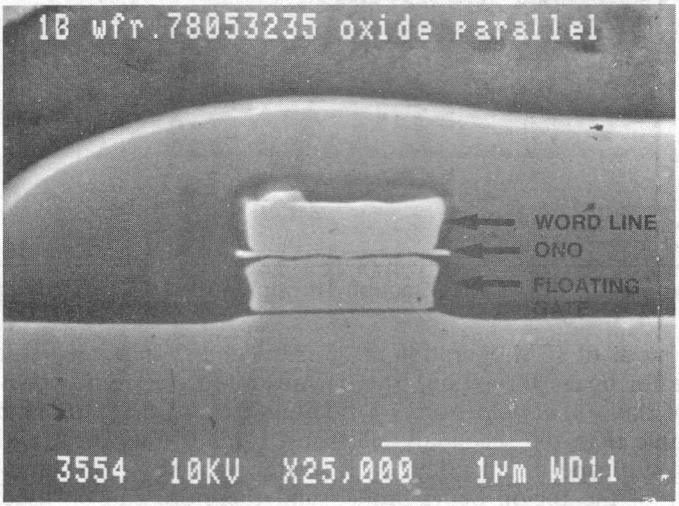

Figure 9-11b. SEM Micrographs Showing Polysilicon Stack with Thermal Encapsulating Oxide Removed

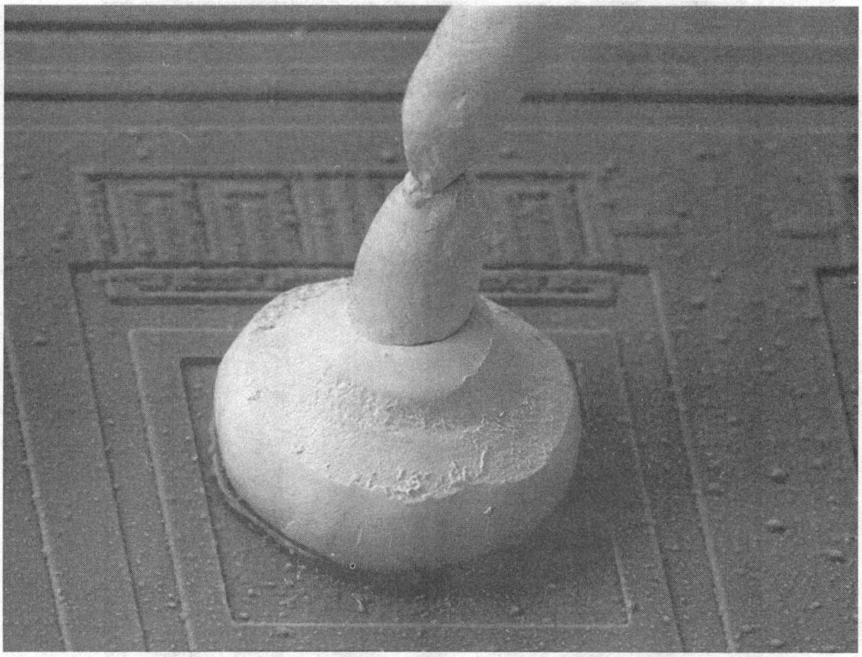

210997i

Figure 9-12. SEM Image of Gold Wire Bond Showing the Large Depth of Field in the SEM Which is Very Useful in Detecting Initiation of a Wire Necking Failure

X-Ray Microprobe Spectroscopy (EDX, EDS, WDX)

In addition to providing morphological information, many scanning electron microscopes are equipped with energy- or wavelength-dispersive X-ray (EDX or WDX) detectors which provide the capability for chemical microanalysis of specimens by X-ray spectroscopy. X-ray spectroscopy is performed in conjunction with SEM examination and qualitative analysis is possible in a few minutes. This is often the first analytical tool used for the identification of unknown and contaminant species present in a microelectronic device.

The X-ray microprobe method relies on the fact that irradiation of the sample by the primary electron beam induces core-level ionization of the near surface atoms (to a depth of up to 2 μm depending on excitation voltage). The core holes created in the excited ions are subsequently filled by the decay of electrons from higher level orbitals, a process that is accompanied by the emission of a characteristic X-ray. Due to the penetration and scattering of the incoming primary beam the analysis volume of X-Ray spectroscopy is typically in the order of 1 cubic micrometer. In principle all elements, with the exception of hydrogen, can be detected by X-ray spectroscopy. However, sensitivity

9

210997i

Figure 9-13. Backscattered Electron Image Showing Voiding in Aluminum Lines Under Passivation (25 KeV Excitation Voltage)

for low Z-elements is limited both by low excitation cross sections (preference for Auger versus X-ray emissions) and by the less efficient detection of soft X-rays. Figure 9-14 is an EDX spectrum of a silicon oxynitride passivation film obtained using an ultrathin window detector permitting the analysis of low energy X-rays emitted by light elements. The characteristic X-rays from oxygen, nitrogen and silicon are seen superimposed on a background of bremstrahlung radiation.

Quantification of X-Ray spectra can be achieved by comparing peak intensities obtained from the unknown with those generated from a set of standards of known composition. This approach is often used in monitoring the composition of thin films, for example, the phosphorus content of doped glasses; or the thickness of thin-film layers, for example <1000Å Ti or Cr layers commonly used in IC processing.

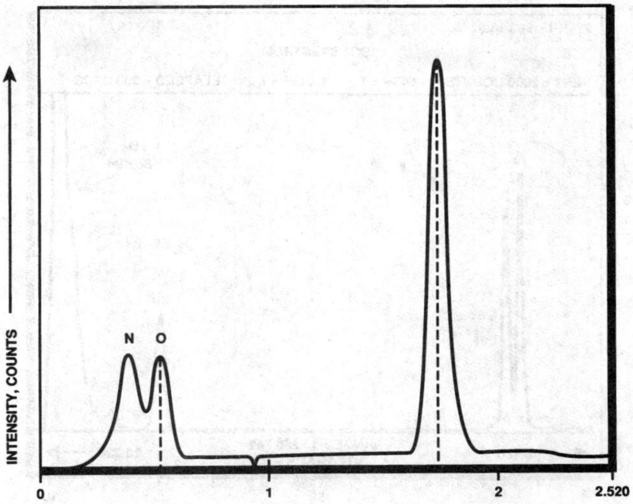

SPECTRUM OF A SILICON OXYNITRIDE PASSIVATION FILM. THE SPECTRUM WAS OBTAINED WITH AN ULTRATHIN WINDOW DETECTOR, ENABLING DETECTION OF THE CHARACTERISTIC X-RAYS GENERATED FROM OXYGEN, NITROGEN, AND SILICON. RANGE = 10.23 keV.

210997i9-14

Figure 9-14. EDX Spectrum of a Silicon Oxynitride Passivation Film

X-Ray Fluorescence Spectroscopy (XRF)

X-Ray fluorescence spectroscopy (XRF) is analogous to X-ray microprobe spectroscopy, except that X-rays, instead of electrons, are used as the primary excitation source. X-ray fluorescence spectra have the advantage that they do not have a bremstrahlung background and the improved peak-to-background ratio results in sensitivities of up to a few hundred parts per million. Because no charged particles are involved, insulating samples can be analyzed without a conductive coating as required in normal SEM inspection. In addition, less stringent vacuum requirements and the lack of focusing optics make the XRF spectrometer a much simpler instrument to incorporate into an IC manufacturing environment and units capable of handling full wafers are readily available.

The primary disadvantage of the XRF instrument is the relatively large depth of penetration for thin-film analysis and the fact that it is a relatively large area analytical technique $\geq$80 μm, which limits its application to the monitoring of relatively large areas or of unpatterned thin films. XRF spectrometers are widely used as in-line monitors for both composition and thickness measurement applications. Figure 9-15 shows an example of an XRF spectrum obtained from an Al-1% Cu film. In this case X-ray radiation from a secondary rhodium target was used to maximize the Cu yield.

9

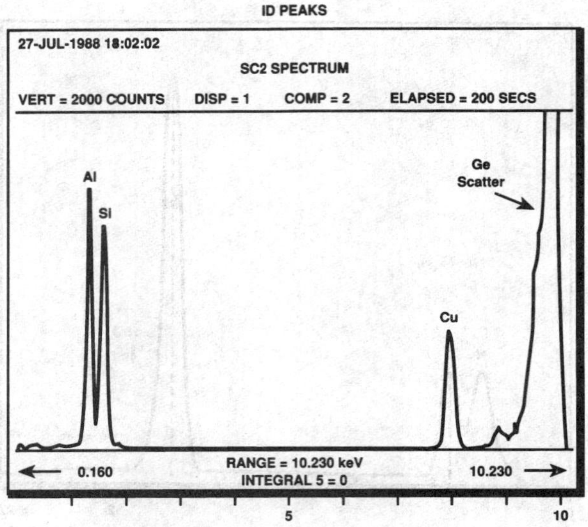

210997i9-15

Figure 9-15. XRF Spectrum of 1 μm Al-Cu Film Excited by Rhodium Radiation

XRF is also used in assembly manufacturing to measure solder plating thickness on the external leads of IC packages. Thickness control is important to avoid exposed copper-tin intermetallic compounds and dewet during the customer board mount operation.

Transmission Electron Microscopy (TEM or STEM)

Transmission Electron Microscopy (TEM) provides the capability to achieve atomic resolution imaging of semiconductor structures. The TEM utilizes the information contained in high-voltage (100 to 1000 KeV) electrons after transmission through the specimen of interest. The TEM technique requires that specimens be thinned to electron transparency, typically in the range of 100 to 1000Å depending on the material and the acceleration voltage possible with the available instrument.

As the electrons penetrate the sample, both attenuation (absorption) and diffraction processes occur and are responsible for final image contrast. The degree of attenuation of the electron beam is a function of both the thickness and atomic number of the materials present in the sample. The analysis of electron diffraction patterns obtained can be used to identify crystalline phases present in the sample.

The creation of electron-transparent TEM specimens from semiconductor materials involves the careful application of mechanical grinding, ion milling and/or chemical etching to achieve the required degree of thinning. Through the application of appropriate techniques, it is possible to produce both planar and cross-sectional views of semiconductor specimens.

The TEM is extensively used in process development and manufacturing support applications. Specifically, TEM can be used to characterize the internal microstructure of thin-film materials and for determining the morphology of device structures. For example, the grain sizes in metal lines, as shown in Figure 9-16. In this example more detailed information about grain structure, the location of silicon or copper precipitates, etc. is available from TEM than in any other method.

TEM also provides the ultimate resolution for examination of device cross sections. Cross sections are made in a plane perpendicular to the wafer surface and can be used to measure critical parameters such as film thickness variation, interfacial reactions between layers or substrate ion implant damage. Because the electrons are transmitted much differently in amorphous and crystalline materials, we can obtain high-contrast images of device cross sections without the selective etching techniques used for SEM preparation. For example, double-poly EPROM structures can be studied in the as-thinned V condition with very high edge definition and resolution, as shown in Figure 9-17. This example clearly illustrates the ability to resolve an ONO layer which exists between the polysilicon gate and the word line.

210997i

Figure 9-16. Planar TEM Micrograph Showing the Microstructure of an Aluminum Film. TEM is the Method of Choice for Measurement of Grain Size and Grain Size Distribution. Electromigration Performance is Strongly Influenced by these Microstructural Parameters.

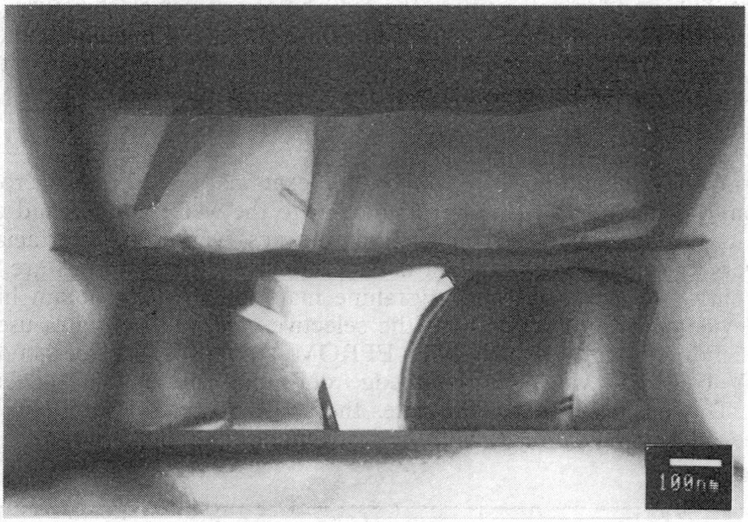

Figure 9-17. TEM Cross Section of an EPROM Polysilicon Stack Structure. Please Note the Detailed Information Given in this Micrograph: Gate Oxide Thickness, Polysilicon Grain Size and Shape and Corner Morphology, Inner-Poly Dielectric Thickness and Roughness. The Thin Layer Between the Polysilicon is Nitride Which is Part of the ONO Dielectric.

X-ray compositional analysis in the TEM has increased sensitivity and spatial resolution compared to the SEM/EDX. This is due to the thin specimen, which eliminates most of the spectral background, reduces fluorescence and absorption effects and results in minimal beam broadening that occurs during transit through the specimen.

The power of EDX and the electron diffraction techniques available during TEM examination are shown in the example shown in Figure 9-18, 9-19, and 9-20. The presence of sub-micron BPO_4 crystallites in this boron-doped phosphosilicate glass (BPSG) film are conclusively proven by the image, electron diffraction pattern and EDX results. The TEM image in Figure 9-18, shows the size, shape and distribution of the BPO_4 crystallites. Figure 9-19, which is an EDX spectrum from the particle, shows the presence of a high level of phosphorous and the electron diffraction pattern, Figure 9-20, was indexed exactly to the BPO_4 compound.

An example of the ultra high spatial resolution EDX analysis capability provided by the TEM is shown in Figure 9-21. In this example EDX spectra were obtained from 70Å diameter regions of a TEM cross section, enabling clear elemental characterization of individual layers of a multilayer structure.

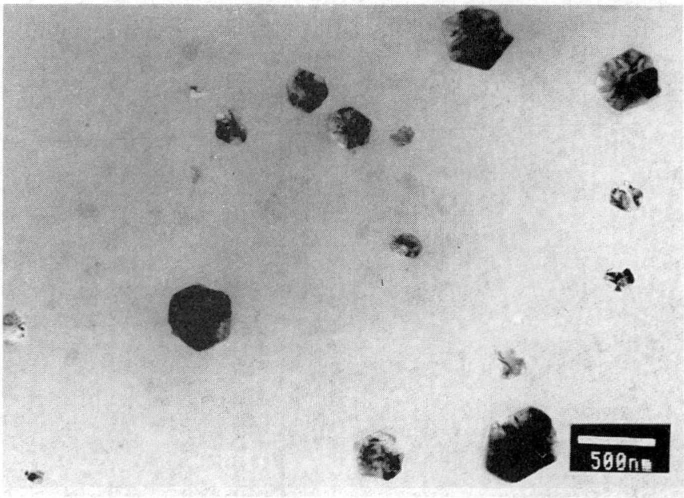

210997i

Figure 9-18. TEM Showing Size, Shape and Distribution of BPO_4 Crystallites

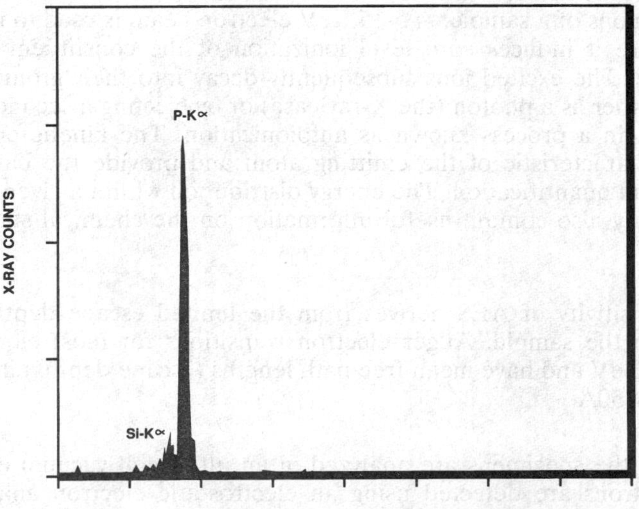

210997i9-19

Figure 9-19. BPO_4 Crystallite

210997i

Figure 9-20. TEM Showing Electron Diffraction Pattern of BPO_4

Auger Electron Spectroscopy (AES)

Auger electron spectroscopy (AES) is used to provide chemical information from the near-surface regions of a sample. A 5-15 KeV electron beam is used to irradiate the area of interest where it induces core level ionization of the constituent atoms as in the SEM/EDX case. The excited ions subsequently decay into their ground state, emitting excess energy either as a photon (the X-ray case) or by ejecting a secondary electron, the Auger electron, in a process known as autoionization. The kinetic energies of Auger electrons are characteristic of the emitting atom and provide the basis for elemental identification and quantification. The energy distribution within a given Auger transition (peak shape) may also contain useful information on the chemical state of the species under analysis.

The surface sensitivity of AES derives from the limited escape depth of the emitted electrons within the sample. Auger electron transitions for most elements fall in the range of 50-2000 eV and have mean free path lengths (escape depths) in the corresponding range of 10-150Å.

Experimentally, the specimens are analyzed in an ultra-high vacuum environment, and the Auger electrons are detected using an electrostatic electron analyzer. Elemental detection limits of 0.05-0.1 atomic percent can be obtained. Laterally resolved chemical information can be obtained by scanning the area of interest with a finely focused electron beam. In modern Auger instruments, analysis areas as small as 1000Å are achievable. Most Auger spectrometers are equipped with an auxiliary ion gun which is used for

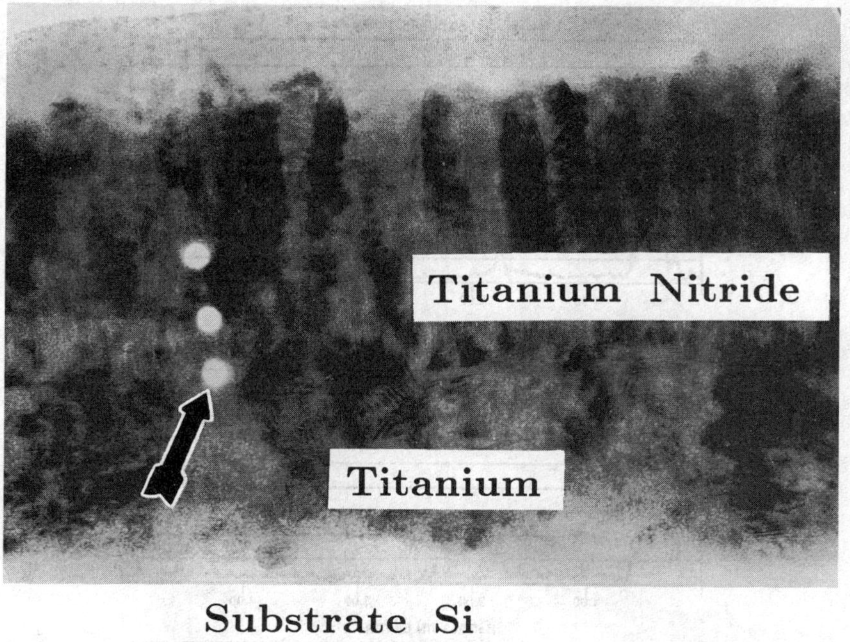

Figure 9-21a. 70Å Electron Probe Diameter for EDS/Diffraction Analysis Across a Barrier Layer

the sputter removal of sequential surface layers of the specimen. Auger depth profiles are obtained by monitoring the intensities of the Auger transitions as a function of sputter time. Figure 9-22 illustrates the use of Auger depth profiling to characterize the thermal reaction between a deposited cobalt layer and a silicon substrate. The profile indicates that a reaction is taking place at the Co/Si interface, resulting in the formation of a series of cobalt silicides of progressively higher silicon content.

The ability of AES to detect thin surface films can be used to solve a number of practical problems. A problem with a silicon nitride removal step in manufacturing, is shown in Figure 9-23. The spectrum obtained on the surface of the sample shows the presence of an oxide layer. This oxide layer was found to be responsible for blocking a phosphoric acid nitride etch step. As a result, a longer hydrofluoric etch, to remove the oxide prior to nitride removal, was successfully used to solve this processing problem.

Other applications of AES include the detection of residual passivation glass on Al bond pads and copper oxidation on silver plated package leads which cause nonsticking of gold wire bonds. Figure 9-23 shows a SEM image of a nonsticking bond pad. Figure 9-24

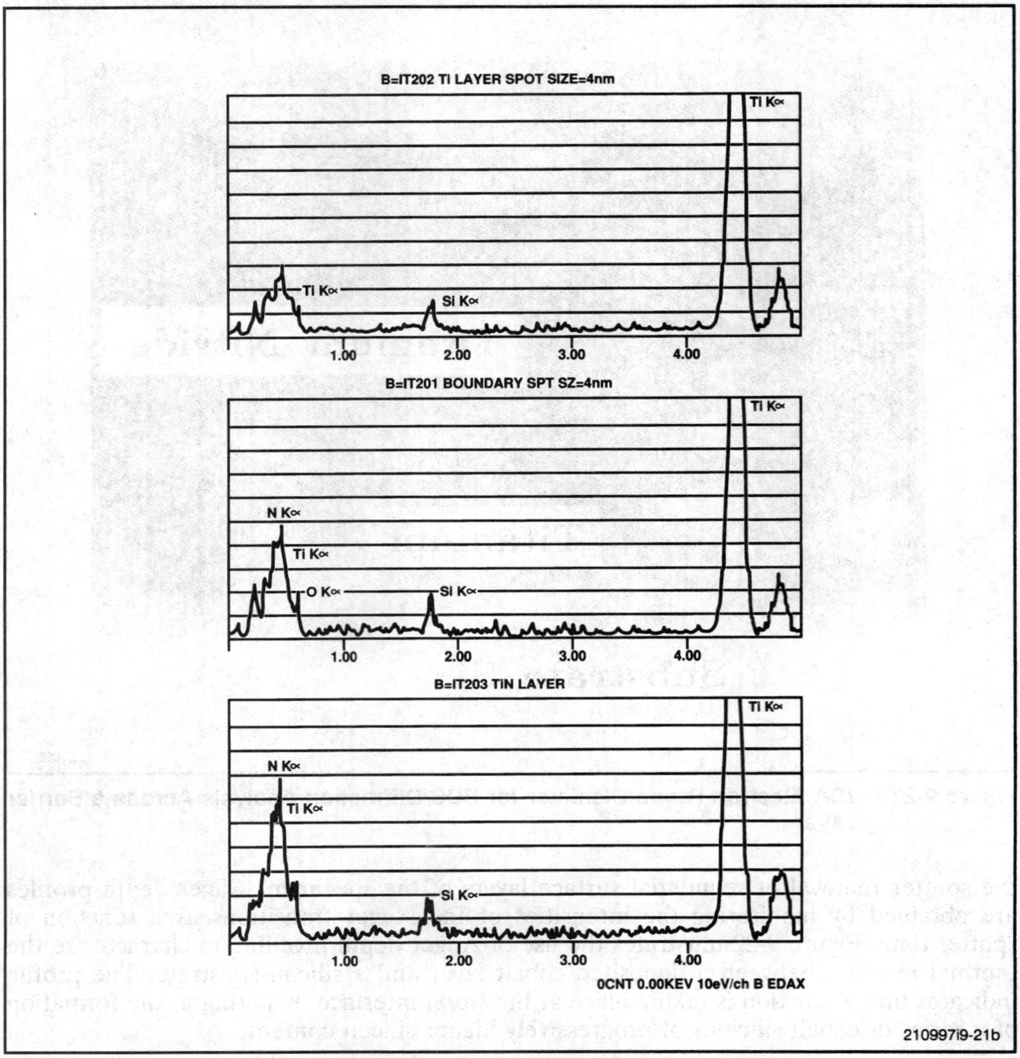

Figure 9-21b. Sample EDX Spectra Results

shows the corresponding AES depth profile analysis detecting passivation glass residues on the pad. The thickness of residual glass on the pad can be estimated to be about 1000Å from this analysis and was traced to incomplete removal at the pad opening step.

Secondary Ion Mass Spectroscopy (SIMS)

Secondary ion mass spectroscopy (SIMS) is used for the ultra high-sensitivity chemical analysis of surfaces, thin films and interfaces of semiconductor material structures. The technique involves irradiating a sample with a medium energy (5-15 KeV) ion beam and

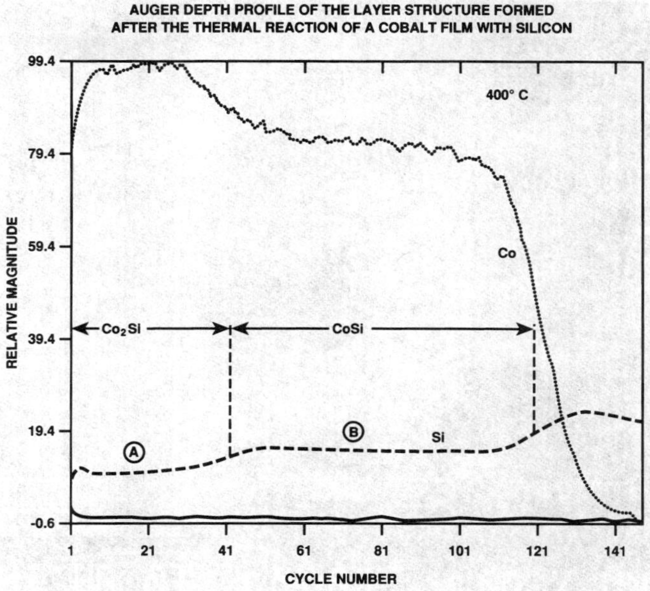

Figure 9-22. Auger Depth Profile

detection of ionized species which are sputtered from the sample surface as a result of the ion irradiation. Elemental detection limits achievable by this technique are in the 10^{13}-10^{15} atoms per cubic cm range (ppm to ppb range) but vary widely depending upon both the element and matrix under investigation. The ultimate lateral resolution of modern SIMS instruments is below 1 μm, while in-depth resolutions of 50-100Å are available through careful control of experimental conditions. Typical applications of SIMS include the determination of dopant profiles and the detection of low-level contaminants within thin-film structures. In addition, SIMS can be used to monitor the stability of thin-film structures during thermal processing. An example of this application, for the case of a bilayer Al/Ti metallization is shown in Figure 9-25a and 9-25b.

Figure 9-25a is a SIMS depth profile obtained from an as-sputter-deposited 1 μm Al-Si/1500Å Ti bilayer metallization. Examination of this profile reveals an abrupt Al/Ti interface with no intermixing of the metallic components. In addition, the Si is segregated in the lower part of the Al layer, corroborating TEM data which had indicated the presence of Si precipitates in this region. A SIMS profile of the same structure following thermal processing at 400°C (Figure 9-26) shows a broadening of the Al/Ti interface, indicating that limited intermixing of the layers has occurred but that the barrier properties of the Ti layer are intact. In addition, a trace level of Ti (50 ppm) has dissolved into the Al bulk and the Si precipitates have dissolved in the Ti layer.

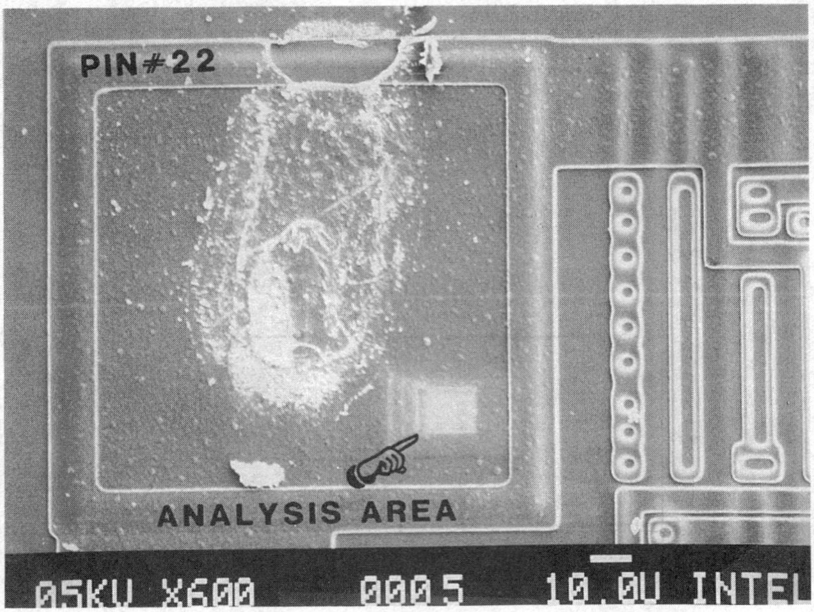

210997i

Figure 9-23. SEM Photo of a Bond Pad Showing the Non-Stick Area of the Wire Bond

SIMS can also be used in the survey mode for high sensitivity detection of surface contaminants. Figure 9-26 illustrates the use of SIMS in the detection of surface contaminants introduced during dry etching.

Rutherford Backscattering Spectroscopy (RBS)

Rutherford Backscattering Spectroscopy (RBS) provides a means for the absolute quantification of thin-film composition and thickness. In RBS analysis, the sample is bombarded with a high-energy beam of alpha particles. As the alpha particles penetrate the sample surface, they monotonically lose energy through collisions with electrons. In addition, there is a probability that the alpha particles will approach sufficiently close to an atomic nucleus and be scattered through a wide angle in a process known as Rutherford backscattering. These backscattered particles are detected in the RBS experiment. The rate of energy loss and the probability of scattering of the penetrating alpha particles have been precisely modeled theoretically. Therefore it is possible, through analysis of the energy distribution of the backscattered alpha particles, to provide quantitative determination of composition and layer thicknesses when the density of the material is known. Figure 9-27 shows a RBS spectrum of a tungsten silicide gate structure, from which the material stoichiometry can be determined.

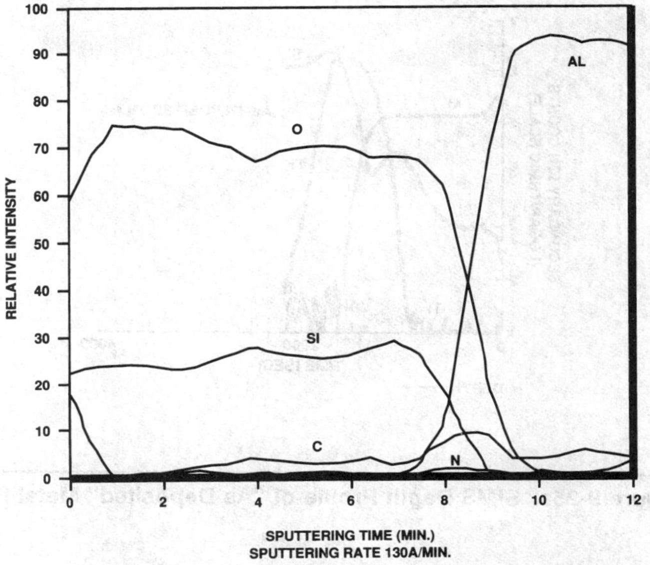

Figure 9-24. AES Depth Profiling Identified Silicon and Oxygen (Glass) on the Surface of the Pad Shown in Figure 9-23 to a Depth of Approximately 1000Å

Fourier Transform Infrared Spectroscopy (FTIR)

Although analysis methods which use photons as probes are not capable of the extremely high spatial resolution that can be obtained with electrons and ion beams, they are essential for certain purposes. In addition to optical microscopy, which is still valuable for initial examination, methods based on selective absorption of photons of particular energies have important applications. Absorption of photons in the infrared is especially useful, since this energy range corresponds to that of common vibrational frequencies of interatomic bonds. The development of Fourier transform infrared spectroscopy (FTIR), which makes possible the rapid acquisition of spectra and modern computer-based data analysis techniques, have made this technique extremely useful for a variety of analytical applications. It is currently used in wafer fabrication for determining oxygen and carbon content in silicon and characterizing various passivation and interlayer dielectric glasses. In the assembly operations, FTIR is used to analyze mold compound formulations, wafer and die coatings, tape/adhesive systems for advanced plastic packages, surface adhesion promoters, plating bath additives and surface contamination.

The analysis of phosphosilicate glass by FTIR is illustrated in Figure 9-28, which shows both the experimental data and the computer-calculated non-linear least squares fit to the data. From the computer analysis, the area associated with the phosphorus-oxygen

9

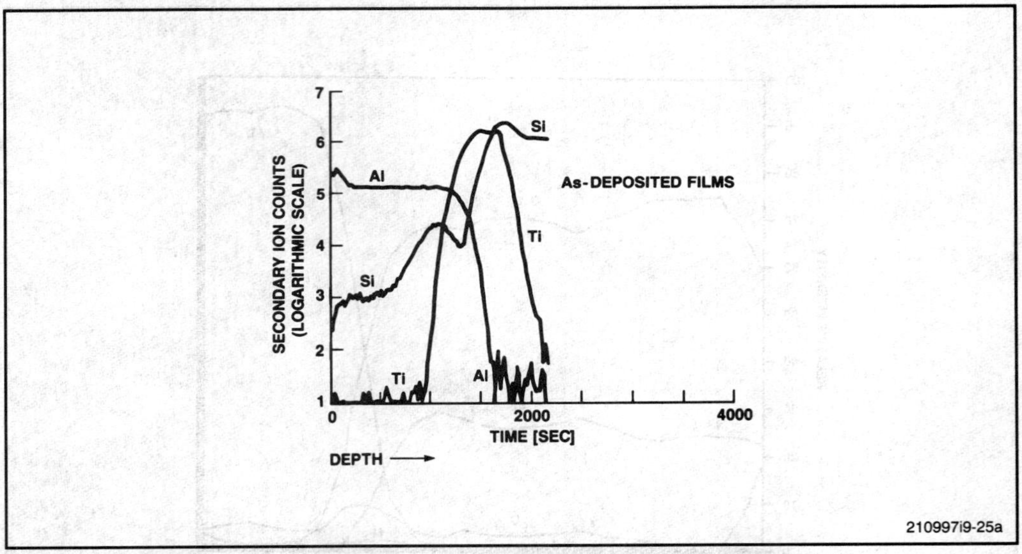

Figure 9-25a. SIMS Depth Profile of "As Deposited" Metal Film

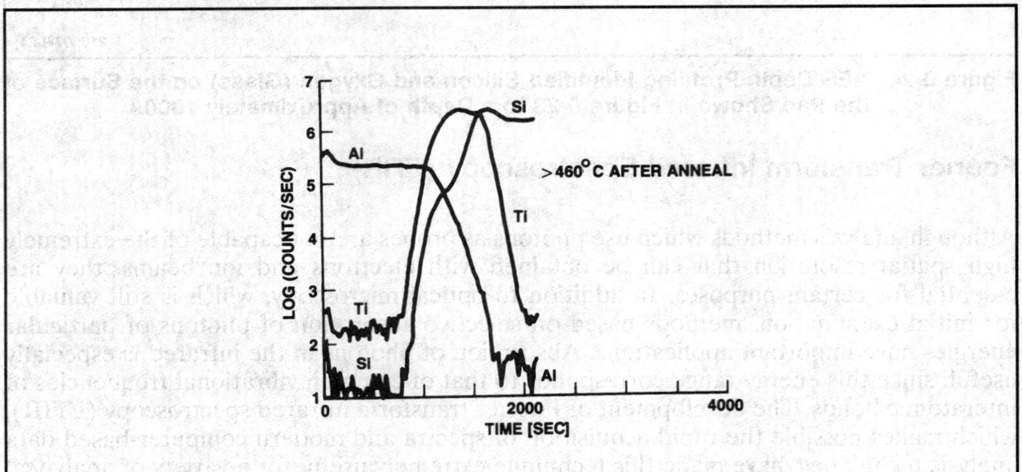

Figure 9-25b. SIMS Depth Profile "After Anneal" Metal Film

(P-O) peak near 1330 cm^{-1} can be accurately determined in spite of the overlap with the much stronger nearby peak, the Si-O bond. From the area of the P-O peaks, the concentration of phosphorus can be obtained for well calibrated cases. Changes in both the position and the area of the P-O peak can be observed and can be used to measure moisture pickup by the glass as a function of moisture content.

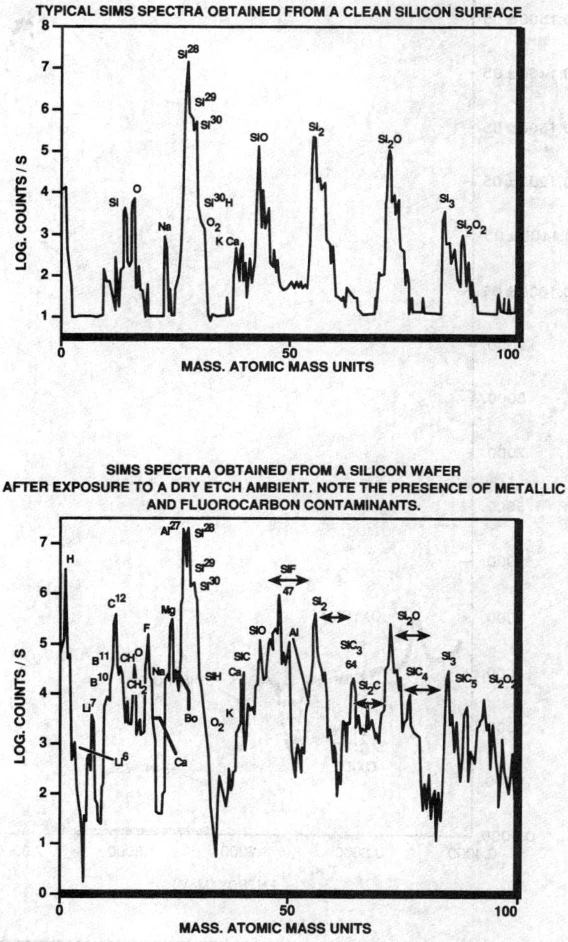

Figure 9-26. Typical SIMS Spectra Before and After Plasma Etch Exposure

The sensitivity of FTIR to chemical bonds, rather than simply to elemental composition, provides molecular structure information which can not be obtained with methods such as energy-dispersive X-ray analysis. The techniques can be extended to borophosphosilicate glass. The boron oxygen (B-O) bond gives rise to a peak near 1400 cm^{-1}, whereas analysis of boron by X-ray methods is impractical as a consequence of the extremely low energy of the boron X-ray.

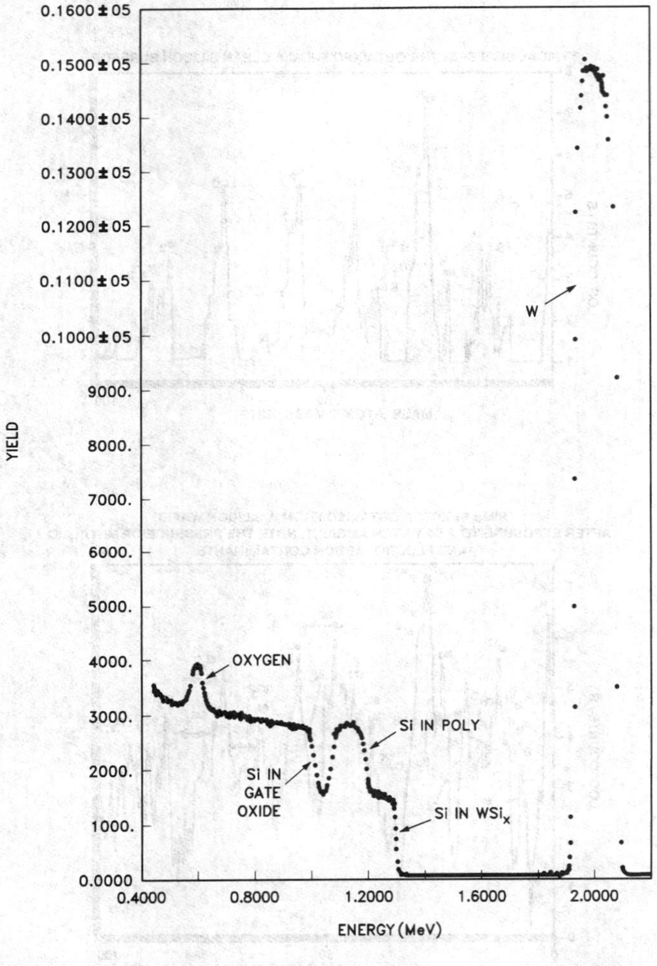

Figure 9-27. RBS Spectrum from a Tungsten Silicide Polycide Gate Structure

FTIR is also useful for characterizing silicon oxide, nitride and oxynitride films. The hydrogen content can be quantified from the peak height of Si-H and N-H bands at 2170 cm^{-1} and 3300 cm^{-1}, respectively.

For die coating applications, FTIR is useful in determining the imidization kinetics of wafer level polyimide coatings by tracking the growth of the 1380 cm^{-1} imide band. Similarly, the hydrolysis of kapton tape/polyimide adhesive, used in certain types of advanced IC packaging, can be quantified during steam exposure by measuring the

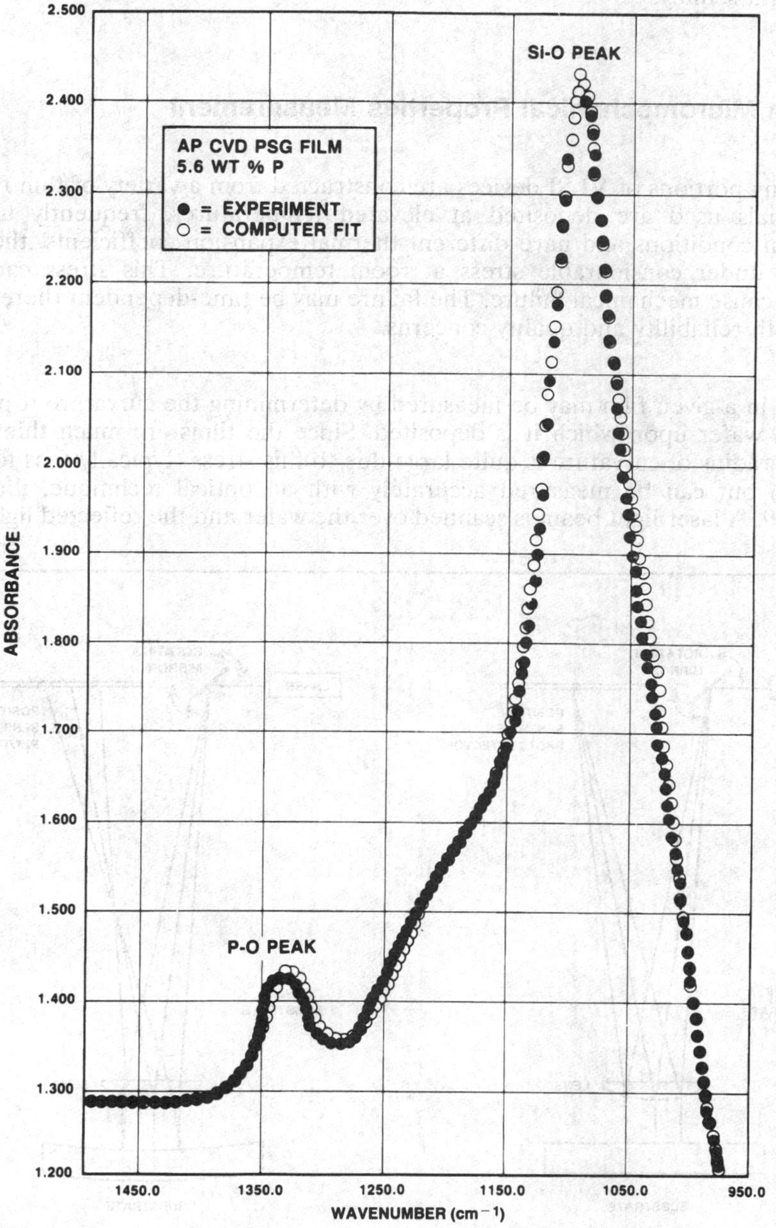

Figure 9-28. FTIR Spectrum of Phosphosilicate Glass

decrease in the 1380 cm^{-1} band. FTIR can also be used in the microspot mode (20 μm spot size microscope) to detect contamination on wire bond pads, a common bondability problem in assembly.

Thin-Film Micromechanical Properties Measurement

The working portions of VLSI devices are constructed from a variety of thin films. Since the materials used are deposited at elevated temperatures, frequently under non-equilibrium conditions and have different thermal expansion coefficients, the films are commonly under considerable stress at room temperature. This stress can be large enough to cause mechanical failure. The failure may be time-dependent therefore; there may be both reliability and quality concerns.

The stress in a given film may be measured by determining the curvature it produces in the silicon wafer upon which it is deposited. Since the films are much thinner than a wafer, the radius of curvature is quite large due to this stress (typically tens to hundreds of meters) but can be measured accurately with an optical technique, illustrated in Figure 9-29. A laser light beam is scanned over the wafer and the reflected light detected

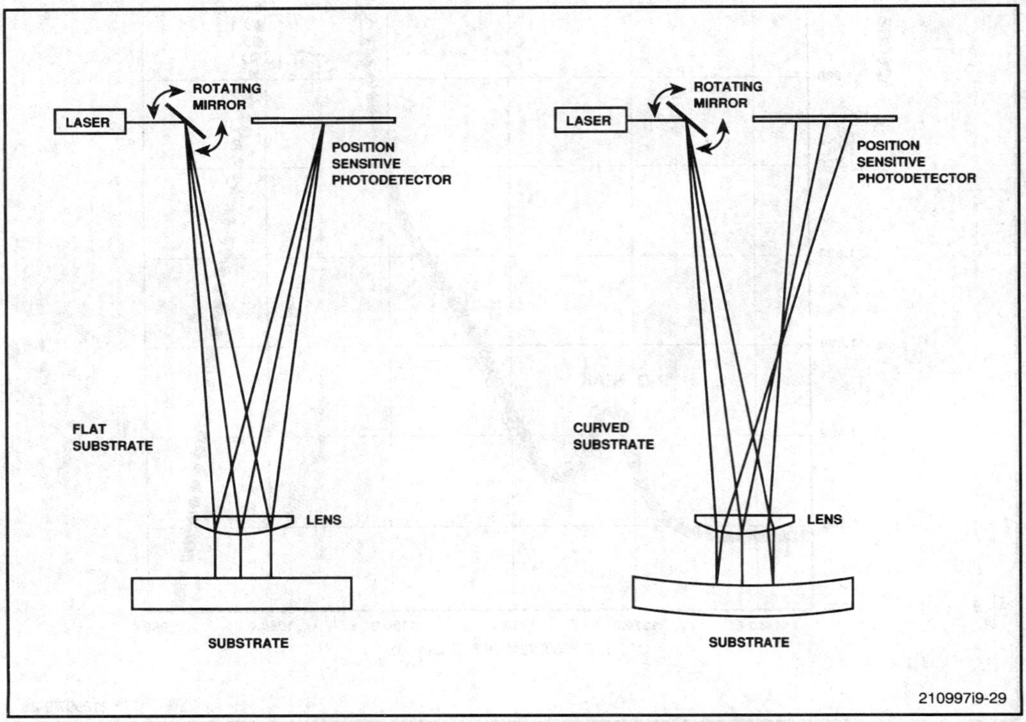

Figure 9-29. Schematic Diagram of the Wafer Curvature Apparatus

by a position sensitive photodetector. For a flat wafer, the reflected beam remains stationary. For a curved wafer, the reflected beam is displaced by an amount proportional to the wafer curvature. The ratio, m, of the diode displacement to the wafer displacement, gives the radius of curvature:

$$r = 2L/m$$

The stress in the film can be calculated from the radius of curvature, the film thickness and the known elastic properties of silicon. The initial curvature of the wafer is corrected for by measuring the displacement curve without the film present (either before the film is deposited or after it is stripped off) and analyzing the difference.

By adding wafer heating capabilities, it is possible to measure film stress as a function of temperature. An example of a stress-temperature curve obtained from an Al-Cu film on silicon is presented in Figure 9-30. The hysteresis observed in this plot is due to recrystallization, relaxation and work-hardening processes occurring in the thin-film metallization.

Microhardness is another important mechanical property used to predict the behavior of metallization and passivation layers under stress or plastic deformation conditions. This technique is being used more frequently in characterization and in failure analysis. For example, the hardness of bond pad metallization and of the silver plating on leadframes can be a factor in successful wire bonding.

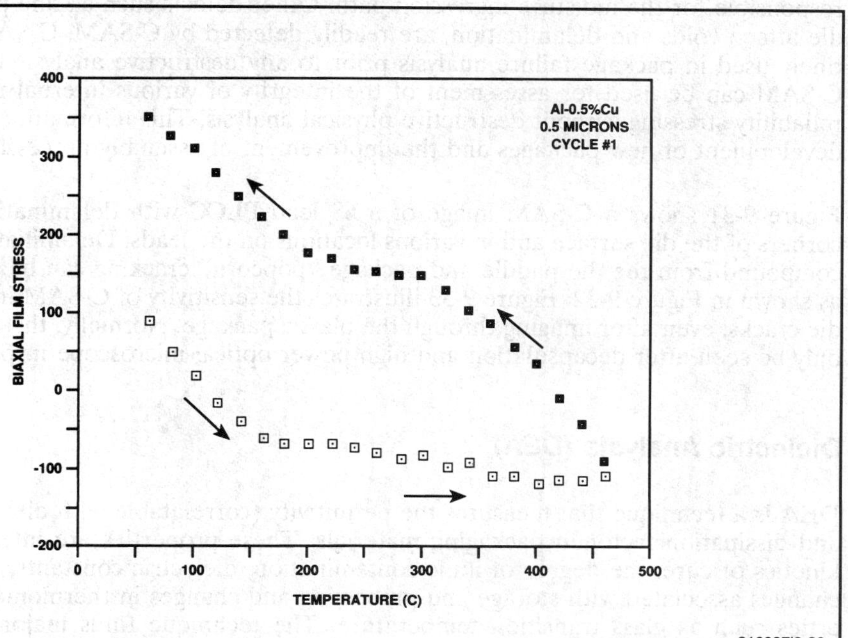

Figure 9-30. Stress Temperature Curve for Al-Cu Film on a Silicon Substrate

TECHNIQUES SPECIFIC TO ASSEMBLY AND PACKAGE ANALYSIS

Scanning Acoustic Microscopy (C-SAM)

The C-mode reflection scanning acoustic microscope (C-SAM) is a powerful new analytical tool for non-destructive evaluation of microelectronic packages. Similar in principle to ultrasound used in the medical field, a focused beam of high frequency sound waves is used to raster scan the package. Reflected waves from various interfaces and defects are reconstructed electronically to form an image of the plane in focus. Resolution and penetration depth in the package are a strong function of the frequency of sound used. Typically, C-SAM uses frequencies between 10 MHz and 200 MHz resulting in a resolution of the order of 500 to 5 μm, respectively and penetration depths in typical molding compounds of 3 mm and 50 μm respectively. Although resolution may have to be compromised for depth penetration in plastic packages, defects an order of magnitude smaller than the resolution limit are detectable due to the ability to image their associated stress field.

C-SAM can detect internal discontinuities and interfaces between materials in ceramic and plastic packages non-destructively. In plastic packages, delamination of the molding compound from the die surface, leads and die paddle is readily detected. Porosity and voids in the plastic mold material as well as mold material variation or property changes due to thermal or moisture exposure, are detected by C-SAM. In hermetic packages, C-SAM can be used to analyze gross leakage failures by determining the discontinuity responsible for the moisture ingression path. Other defects such as fine package cracks, die attach voids and delamination, are readily detected by C-SAM. C-SAM is now routinely used in package failure analysis prior to any destructive analysis technique. The C-SAM can be used for assessment of the integrity of various internal interfaces after reliability stressing without destructive physical analysis. This information speeds up the development of new packages and the improvement of assembly processes.

Figure 9-31 shows a C-SAM image of a 68 lead PLCC with delamination on all four corners of the die surface and in various locations on the leads. Delamination of molding compound from the die paddle and package "popcorn" cracking can be easily detected as shown in Figure 9-32. Figure 9-33 illustrates the sensitivity of C-SAM in detecting fine die cracks, even after imaging through the plastic package. Normally, these defects could only be seen after decapsulation and high power optical microscope inspection.

Dielectric Analysis (DEA)

DEA is a technique that measures the permitivity (correlatable with dielectric constant) and dissipation factor in packaging materials. These properties are interrelated to the kinetics of cure, the degree of ionic contamination, dielectric constants, the rheological changes associated with storage and processing and changes in thermomechanical properties such as glass transition temperature. The technique finds major application in assembly materials/failure analysis of leadframes constructed with tape/adhesive systems, molding compounds, die-attach materials, wafer and die coatings.

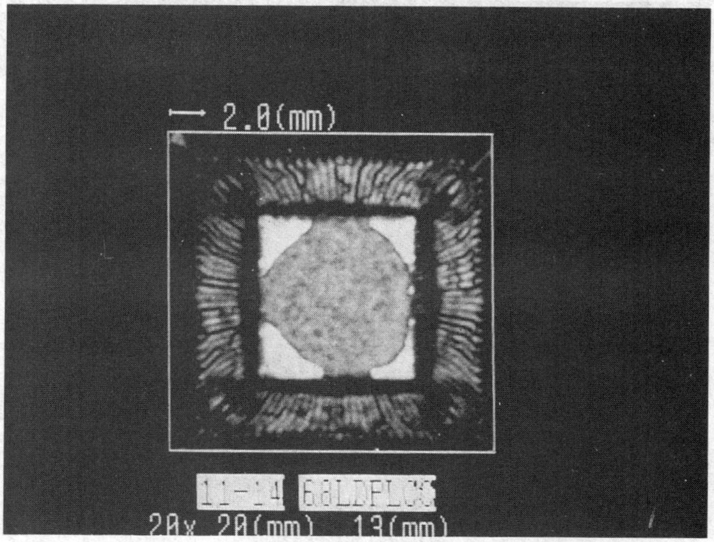

210997i

Figure 9-31. C-SAM Image of Die Surface and Leadframe Plane of a 68-Lead PLCC Package Showing Delamination (White Areas) at Die Corners and Along Several Leads

This method can be used to differentiate between ionic contamination and other contributions to dielectric change. Permittivity is a function of the degree of alignment and strength of dipoles in the material whereas the loss factor is a measure of both dipole motion and conductivity. At low frequencies, conductivity contributions from ionic contaminants predominate; at higher frequencies, dipole contributions predominate.

Differential Scanning Calorimetry (DSC)

DSC measures exothermic or endothermic changes associated with thermomechanical/chemical properties of assembly materials. The types of changes identified and, in some cases, quantified, are crystalline transitions, polymerization, decomposition, cure, catalysis, oxidation/reduction, dehydration and absorption/desorption.

The technique measures changes in either temperature or heat flux of a sample relative to a thermally inert reference such as gold as the sample is uniformly heated or cooled. DSC can detect changes in material properties resulting from stressing and improper handling or processing.

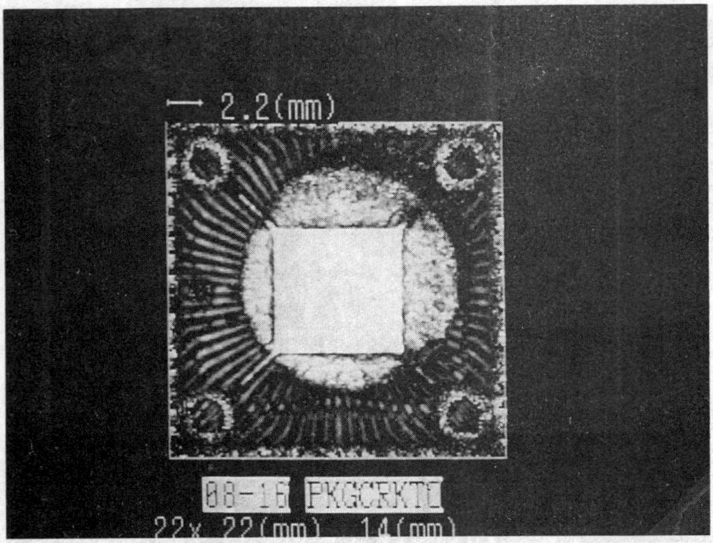

210997i

Figure 9-32. C-SAM Image of Die Paddle Backside Showing Plastic Delamination (White Square Region) on the Paddle and a Circular Package "Popcorn" Crack Emanating from the Paddle Sides.

Thermogravimetric Analysis (TGA)

TGA measures mass change as a function of sample heating. This can be used to quantify and identify (especially when interfaced with FTIR) the out-gassed products associated with incomplete cure and solvent removal of plastics and die attach materials. It is applicable to the study of the decomposition and contamination of assembly/package materials in general. The technique is useful in materials/failure analysis of tape/adhesive systems and mold compounds. The measured mass change (usually loss), occurs on application of a uniform heating rate to a sample in a specific atmosphere.

Thermomechanical Analysis or Dilatometry (TMA)

TGA is used to measure the linear coefficient of thermal expansion of leadframe materials and the softening temperature or glass transition temperature of mold compounds and die-attach materials. Understanding of these properties, is important in materials and failure analysis. The technique measures the change in length or volume of a sample as a function of temperature.

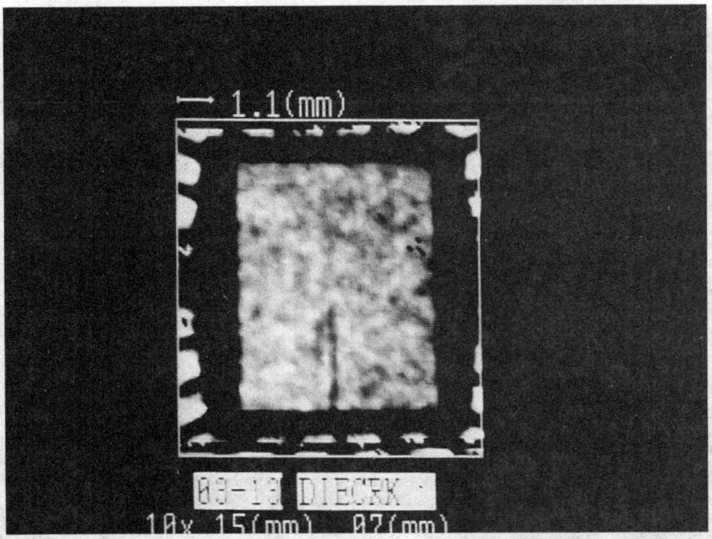

210997i

Figure 9-33. C-SAM Image of the Die Surface of a 40-Lead PDIP Showing a Die Crack (Black Line) in the Middle of the Die

Dynamic Mechanical Analysis (DMA)

DMA measures Young's modulus, and tan δ as a function of temperature. These parameters are useful in determining the glass transition temperature, modelling stress in plastic packages and in identifying assembly materials changes due to stress or misprocessing.

Infrared Microscopy (IRM)

An infrared microscope (IRM) is an optical microscope optimized for use in the IR range. Whereas a normal optical microscope operates in the wavelength region of 0.45 to 0.7 μm, the IRM operates in the near-infrared wavelength region of 0.8 to 1.8 μm giving a useful working resolution of about 2 μm. Since silicon is transparent to wavelengths longer than the silicon absorption edge of 1.06 μm, IR light can pass through the silicon and reflect from all metal surfaces. Thus, this technique lends itself to damage inspection below the bond pad of integrated circuit chips in plastic packages. The device can be examined by carefully grinding into the die from the backside through the package, eliminating the need for full mechanical or chemical decapsulation, thus preserving the integrity of the topside wire bonds and leadframe attachment. Figures 9-34a and 9-34b show a damaged bond pad viewed from below with the IRM and viewed from above with an optical microscope after metal etch.

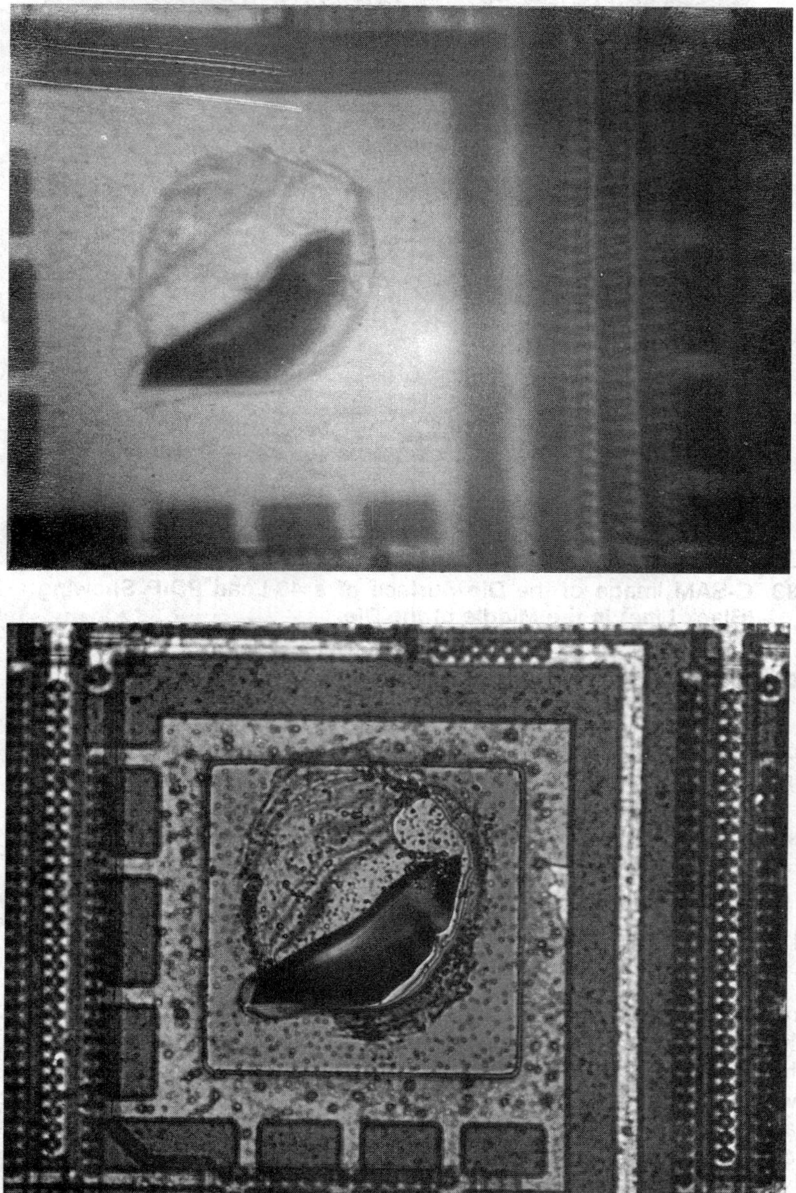

210997i

Figure 9-34. Correlation of IR Microscopy and Metal Etch a) Bottom View by IRM b) Topside View by Normal Optical Microscope

IRM, can be used in assembly-related failure analysis in assisting to identify the following:

- Bond pad or metal line corrosion
- Bond craters (underlying damage in the silicon)
- Silicon damage in general
- Dielectric damage

Bond Shear and Wire-Pull Test

The bond shear test is complementary to the more traditionally used wire-pull test. Wire-pull is widely accepted to assess the strength of gold wire and wedge bonds. However, this method is unacceptable for assisting the strength of most ball bonds since they have an interfacial area about six to ten times the cross sectional area of the wire and the gold at the neck of the wire is annealed during the bonding operation. It is apparent that the wire will break during a pull test long before even a poorly welded ball bond will lift.

The bond shear test is therefore a preferred method to determine the integrity of gold ball bonds, as well as TAB bumps and TAB bonds. During the bond shear test, a shear tool touches the surface of the die next to a ball bond, steps back to a preset tool height and shears the ball. The maximum shear strength and failure mode are then recorded. In order to get a valid shear strength measurement, machine setup parameters are critical. The shear tool must be made of a hard material, usually tungsten carbide, and have a highly polished ram face 3 to 9 mils wide. The tool stepback height must be controlled and remain 0.1 to .33 the height of the ball bond. We typically use a tool height of 0.2 mil. The speed of the shear should also be controlled; if it is too fast, the impact force will be measured instead of the strength of the bond. A shear speed of 300 to 500 μm's per second is recommended. Finally, a planarized die attach pad and secure gripping of the die are necessary to obtain reliable shear test results.

Bond shear can be used along with wire-pull and visual examination in failure analysis in a number of ways:

- Measure the strength of TAB bumps and compare to known "good" bumps.
- Measure the strength of TAB bonds.
- Measure the strength and identify the weakest interface of ball bonds to the die and substrate.
- Detect bond craters and severe cracking in the underlying dielectric and/or silicon.
- Identify improper ball bond parameters.
- Measure strength reduction resulting from residual glass on bond pads.

Glossary

GLOSSARY

A: Symbol for Angstrom, which equals 10^{-8} meters.

A1: Penang Assembly Plant.

A2: Chandler Assembly Plant.

AES: Auger Electron Spectroscopy.

APCVD: Atmospheric Pressure Chemical Deposition of thin films, typically used for interlayer dielectrics and passivation films.

APL: Acceptable Process Limit. If the process average is within a calculable limit, then a very high percentage of the process has a high probability of being within specification.

Align: The operation of exposing a resist covered wafer in a projection printer.

AQL: Acceptable Quality Level. Generally 95 percent confidence that material of the stated AQL will pass sample inspection.

ASIC: Application Specific Integrated Circuits.

BPP: Bias Pressure Pot.

BPSG: Boron-doped Phosphosilicate Glass.

Betascope: Tool used to measure metallization thickness via the measured intensity of backscattered radiation from a beta isotope source.

Bond pads: Exposed aluminum pads on chip, to which wires from package are bonded during assembly.

Bonding: The act of connecting package leads to specified locations on the chip via fine wire.

CAD: Computer-Aided Design.

CAM: Computer-Aided Manufacture.

CD: Critical Dimension. A specific feature on a chip whose width is used to characterize the quality of a given masking step. Typically, a line width, contact opening, or spacing between two features or layers.

CHMOS: Complementary High-Performance MOS technology. Advantages include speed and low power dissipation.

CIM: Computer Integrated Manufacture.

CMD: Chandler Microcomputer Division.

CMOS: Complementary MOS technology combining n and p transistors in the same product. Advantages include low power dissipation.

CPO: Custom Products Operations.

CQ: Conditional qualification.

CQE: Customer Quality Engineer.

CQIP: Continuous Quality Improvement Process.

C of C: Certificate of Conformance.

CR: Chip carrier (package).

CVD: Chemical Vapor Deposition of thin films. Gaseous reactants are brought together over the silicon wafer, depositing required layers.

C/V measurements: Capacitance-Voltage measurement. Typically used to measure dopant distributions and oxide-properties and instabilities.

Cell stress: A special test which occurs in wafer sort to separate out devices with weak oxides.

Chip: One square on a wafer containing a single integrated circuit. The substrate on which all active and passive components of a circuit are fabricated; also called a die.

Class test: Measurement of assembled device performance. Products are categorized by speed/power/performance criteria.

Clean Room: The rooms in a chip fabrication plant in which chips are made. This area features a controlled environment with filtered air that eliminates essentially all of the dust and dirt. Clean rooms for semiconductor manufacture are far cleaner than hospital operating rooms.

Contact: A connection between two conductive layers, e.g., metal-to-silicon contact.

Control limit: A statistically defined limit which determines whether or not a process has changed significantly as compared to past history. A measure of statistical process control.

DC: Document Control.

DCCB: Divisional Change Control Board. The local divisional body that proposes product changes and reviews/evaluates fab and assembly/test process changes to further assess potential customer impact.

DCO: Data Communications Components Operations.

DCAS: Defense Contract Administration Services.

DD: Cerdip (package).

DESC: Defense Electronic Supply Center.

DFI: Dynamic Fault Imaging (a voltage contrast SEM technique).

DFM: Design For Manufacturing.

DI: Deionized water.

DIP: Dual-In-Line Package.

DMPC: Direct Materials Project Committee.

DTS: Dock To Stock.

DPM: Defectives Per Million. 1000 DPM = 0.1 percent defective.

DRC: Design Rule Check.

DTF: Deflash, Trim, Form.

DUT: Device Under Test.

Dep: Deposition.

Depletion transistor: A MOSFET with a permanently "on" channel; requires a negative applied gate voltage to turn off. (See "enhancement transistor".)

Develop: A chemical process that fixes photoresist where it has been exposed and removes it elsewhere (for negative resist) or vice versa (for positive resist).

Develop check: A visual check following dry masking to verify proper resist patterning before etch.

Diffusion: (1) The process of doping silicon by diffusing impurities from the surface into the wafer at high temperature. (2) Any region in the silicon substrate doped by diffusion or by ion implant (e.g., source and drain diffusions).

Die: A single integrated circuit separated from the wafer on which it was made; also called a chip.

Dopant: Any impurity intentionally introduced into silicon to control its electronic behavior (e.g., Boron, Arsenic, Phosphorus).

Dose: In ion implant, a measure of the amount of dopant implanted; usually expressed in ions per square centimeter.

Drain: A highly doped region adjacent to a transistor current carrying channel. It carries electrons out of the transistor to the next circuit element or conductor.

Dry masking: A process segment where a photoresist is spun onto the wafer, soft-baked, exposed, and developed to obtain a desired pattern ready for etch or implant (see "wet masking").

ECO: Embedded Controller Operation.

EDS: Engineering Document System. Also Energy Dispersive Spectroscopy.

EDX: Energy Dispersive X-ray analysis. Normally uses electron beam excitation in the scanning electron microscope.

EEC: Electronic Error Correction.

EER: Engineering Evaluation Report.

ELT: Extended Life Test.

EPROM: Electrically Programmable Read Only Memory. Retains data even if device power is turned off. Is erased by UV light.

E Test: The first electrical test of processed wafers using insitu test patterns. Done after A1 deposition and alloy but prior to passivation.

Enhancement transistor: A MOSFET with a normally "off" channel; requires a positive applied gate voltage to turn on (see "depletion transistor").

Etch rate: The rate at which a given layer is etched off in a given standard acid solution, expressed in A/sec.

Evaporation: Deposition technique for Aluminum, Gold, and Chromium thin films (versus sputtering).

Expose: Expose a photoresist-coated wafer to light through a mask.

F1: Fab 1 Santa Clara, California.

F3: Fab 3 Livermore, California.

F4: Fab 4 Aloha, Oregon.

F6: Fab 6 Chandler, Arizona.

F7: Fab 7 Albuquerque, New Mexico.

F8: Fab 8 Israel, Jerusalem.

F9: Fab 9 Albuquerque, New Mexico Under Construction.

FAA: Failure Analysis Administrator.

FA/CR: Failure Analysis/Correlation Request.

FIT: Failure in Time. The number of device failures in 10^9 device hours.

Flash EPROM: Electrically bulk-erasable device that fills the functionality gap between the traditional byte-alterable EPROM and UV-erasable EPROM.

FMD: Folsom Microcomputer Division.

FPO: Finish Process Order. A lot traveler, which accompanies product through the finish (Mark and Pack and FQA) areas.

FQA: Final Quality Assurance.

FQADB: Final Quality Assurance Database.

FSE: Field Sales Engineer.

FTIR: Fourier Transform Infra-Red Spectroscopy.

Final check: A visual check done at the conclusion of a (dry or wet) masking step.

Gate: Common shorthand for the gate of a transistor.

Gate oxide: Dielectric oxide between the gate and the channel region in the silicon.

GCCB: Geographical Change Control Board. The body, located in each specific Intel geography, which is ultimately responsible for communicating proposed product and process changes to customers and to seek customer approval of such changes.

GCO: Graphic Components Operations.

Gettering: Trapping of contamination atoms (especially alkali ions) to prevent their drift into device regions where they may affect electrical performance.

Glass: The amorphous form of SiO_2, used in various insulating layers on the wafer.

HMOS: High Performance MOS processing.

HMOS I: HMOS introduced via projection printer lithography.

HMOS II: An HMOS I shrink made possible by the introduction of wafer stepper lithography.

HMOS III: An HMOS II shrink made possible by the introduction of wafer stepper lithography.

HTRB: High Temperature Reverse Bias.

Hard bake: A step following dry masking, where the resist is heated to prepare it for wet etch.

IC: Integrated Circuit.

II: Ion Implant. The introduction of impurity atoms into silicon by bombarding its surface with a high-energy beam of dopant ions.

IPP: Intel Policies and Procedures.

ITR: Inspection Trouble Report.

IWS: Intel Workmanship Standards.

K: Kilo, Thousand, 10^3.

LCC: Leadless Chip Carrier.

LIFO: Last In, First Out.

LIMA: Laser Ionization Mass Analysis. A technique for surface analysis by laser vaporization and ionization, followed by time-of-flight mass analysis.

LPCVD: Low Pressure Chemical Vapor Deposition. A process in which reactant gases at subatmospheric pressure are introduced onto hot wafers and react on the hot surfaces to deposit a solid layer. (See "plasma-enhanced LPCVD".)

LRR: Lot Reject Rate.

LSI: Large Scale Integration.

LSM: Logic State Map.

LTO glass: Low Temperature Oxide glass used for interlayer or passivation dielectric. Typically deposited at the same temperature as APCVD-deposited glasses used for passivation, but at low pressure.

LTPD: Lot Tolerance Percent Defective. A sample plan that will reject 90 percent of the lots equal to or worse than the stated LTPD value.

Layout: A magnified, physical representation of an electronic circuitry at the transistor level.

Lead: The connection to an element on the integrated circuit.

Lithography: The portion of the process involving the use of light-sensitive photoresist material for layer definition.

MCCB: Manufacturing Change Control Board. The body that facilitates divisional and customer notification of all proposed process and product changes.

MCD: Memory Components Division.

MCG: Microcomputer Components Group.

ME: Manufacturing Engineering.

MFG: Manufacturing.

MeV: Million electron Volt.

meV: Milli electron Volt.

MOS: Metal Oxide Semiconductor integrated circuit technology.

MPC: Manufacturing Process Control. A group of inspectors who sample and monitor manufacturing to provide rapid feedback to establish process control.

MQ: Materials Quality (Incoming Inspection).

MRB: Material Review Board.

MTBF: Mean Time Between Failures.

MTTF: Mean Time To Fail. Time to 50 percent Cumulative Fail.

Mask: A pattern, usually "printed" on glass, used to define areas of the chip on the wafer for production purposes.

Masking: The lithography portion of the process or physical area where lithography occurs.

Mil: 0.001 inch.

MIL: Military.

NAA: Neutron Activation Analysis. Trace element analysis by inducing radioactivity with thermal neutrons and gamma ray spectroscopy for quantitative analysis.

Nano: 10^{-9}.

NDT: Non Destructive Testing.

NIST: National Institute of Standards and Technology.

NMOS: N channel MOS technology.

nm: Nanometer (1nm = 10A = 10^{-9} meters).

ns: Nanoseconds (10^{-9} seconds).

NTE: New Technology Engineer.

Negative photoresist: A resist material in which unexposed areas are developed away.

Nitride: Silicon Nitride, Si_3N_4.

Nitrox: A sandwich passivation structure consisting of plasma deposited silicon nitride over plasma deposited silicon dioxide.

OEM: Original Equipment Manufacturer.

OTP: One Time Programmable EPROM sold in plastic packaging. No window is provided for UV erasure.

"Oxi": A process whereby thick oxide islands are grown between active device region for better isolation and performance.

Oxynitride: A plasma-deposited passivation or interlayer dielectric film consisting of silicon, oxygen, and nitrogen.

P: Phosphorous.

PAG: Process Area Group.

PC: Process Control.

PCCB: Process Change Control Board. Local factory body that coordinates, forecasts, approves and reports required process change activity.

PDIP: Plastic Dual In-Line Package.

PCO: Peripheral Components Operation.

PE: Plastic Epoxy (package). Product Engineer.

PGA: Pin Grid Array (package).

PLCC: Plastic-Leaded Chip Carriers.

PM: Preventive Maintenance. Routine maintenance performed in the manufacturing operations to avoid equipment and instrument problems. Performed per a predetermined schedule.

PMO: Programmable Memory Operation.

PMOS: P channel MOS technology.

PPR: Positive Photoresist.

PR: Plastic Chip Carrier (package).

Process module: A sequence of process steps which define a key property of the device or circuit. For example the gate oxide module is the portion of the process in which the gate oxide is defined and formed.

PROM: Programmable Read Only Memory.

PSG: Phosphosilicate Glass. A glass containing phosphorus (in the form of P2O5). LTO, Pyrox and Pyroglass are all types of PSG.

PSMC: Plastic Surface-Mount Component.

Package: The container used to hold an active semiconductor device.

Photomask: (1) A patterned chrome on glass photographic plate used to transfer a pattern to photoresist in dry masking. (2) A process segment involving the patterning of a given layer by use of a photomask.

Photoresist: Photoresist, a light-sensitive polymer material which is used as a mask for etching and ion implant steps. See also Negative and Positive Photoresist.

Plasma ash: A process using a gas transformed by an RF field into a reactive plasma.

Plasma deposition: Deposition of thin films using gaseous reactants in the presence of a plasma for lower temperatures.

Plasma etch: An etching process using a gas transformed by an RF field into a reactive plasma.

Poly: Polycrystalline silicon made up of many tiny crystals (as opposed to single-crystal silicon).

Poly Re-ox: Oxidation of the poly after it has been defined. The re-ox provides the interpoly dielectric in a double (two layer) poly process.

Positive photoresist: A photosensitive organic polymer material in which exposed areas are developed away.

Prebake: First step of dry masking, in which the wafers are dried in an oven prior to resist application.

Presort: Sort type electrical test in the fab. Used on sample basis to get early yield data.

Prime: Preparation of the wafer surface for photoresist adhesion.

Projection printer: A machine which projects the photomask onto the resist-coated wafer. The mask is the same size as the wafer and imaged 1:1 on the wafer.

Pyroglass: A type of phosphosilicate glass containing approximately 10 wt Phosphorous.

Pyrox: A type of phosphosilicate glass containing approximately 4.5 wt Phosphorous.

QA: Quality Assurance.

QFD: Quality Function Deployment.

QDF: Qualification Detail Form.

QE: Quality Engineer.

QIP: Quality Improvement Process.

Q&R: Quality and Reliability.

QUIP: Quad In-Line Package.

RBS: Rutherford Back Scattering. A method for non-destructive depth profile analysis of thin films by backscattering of high energy helium ions.

RE: Reliability Engineer.

REDB: Reliability Engineering Database.

RGA: Residual Gas Analysis.

RH: Relative Humidity.

RIE: Reactive Ion Etch.

RMA: Return Material Authorization.

ROI: Return on Investment.

ROM: Read Only Memory.

R&R: Ranking and Rating.

Rear end: The finale of the process flow. Usually includes all steps beyond the final poly re-ox.

Refractive Index: A basic physical property which determines the extent of light bending (refraction) upon entering the surface. Used in thin film process control as an indirect measure of chemistry.

Resist: See Photoresist.

SAM: Scanning Auger Microprobe.

SBS: Strategic Business Segment. A business planning committee.

SCQI: Supplier Continuous Quality Improvement. A program for ensuring top quality in incoming materials.

SCS: Strategic Capability Segment. A capability planning committee.

SER: Soft Error Rate.

SEM: Scanning Electron Microscope. A microscope which makes use of a scanning beam of electrons to image detail less than 100Å in size (surface only).

SET: Summary of Electrical Test. A specification which defines the test flow and current revision of test programs for all products.

SIMS: Secondary Ion Mass Spectroscopy.

SLRP: Strategic Long Range Plan.

SMD: Santa Clara Microcomputer Division.

SPC: Statistical Process Control.

SRAM: Static Random Access Memory. Data is continuously retained in the device, except where the power is turned off. Offers the advantage of high speed access.

SRD: Spin Rinse Dryer. A machine which cleans wafers by spraying various liquids on them while centrifuging the wafers.

SRO: Static Ram Operations.

S-Spec: Specifications Intel uses to customize products to unique customer requirements.

STEM: Scanning Transmission Electron Microscope. An electron microscope using a scanning electron beam. (Surface or transmission.)

Schematic: A computer drawing of an integrated circuit.

Scribe lines: Areas on the wafer separating dice from each other.

Short loop: A special manufacturing monitor or experiment to get early process parameter results which would not normally be available until much more processing had occurred.

Silicon: Metallic element which forms the substrate in most semiconductor devices.

Soft bake: A step preparing freshly spun photoresist for exposure by baking it in an oven (to remove excess solvent).

Sort test: First electrical test of actual devices at the wafer level. All bad dice are thrown out, product yield and performance data are determined.

Source: Equivalent to the drain of a transistor with the exception that electrons leave the source into the channel of the active device.

Spec Limit: Absolute acceptable limit for a process parameter.

Spiking: Deep penetration of aluminum into the silicon substrate below the doped diffusion region of the contact (an undesired effect).

Spin: A process step which coats a spinning wafer with liquid photoresist by dispensing the liquid onto its center.

Sputtering: Deposition of a metal layer by bombarding a metal target with heavy ions from a gaseous (e.g., argon) plasma. Metal atoms are removed from the target and deposited onto the wafer during this process.

T1: Test Plant, Folsom, California.

T3: Test Plant, Penang, Malaysia.

T6: Test Plant, Chandler, Arizona.

T9: Test Plant, Makati, Metro Manila.

T10: Test Plant, Hillsboro, Oregon.

T12: Test Plant, Santa Clara, California.

TCE: Thermal Coefficient of Expansion.

TCO: Telecom Operation.

TD: Technology Development.

TDDB: Time-Dependent Dielectric Breakdown.

Telecom: Telecommunications Operations.

TEM: Transmission Electron Microscope. A microscope used to obtain high resolution images with a transmitted electron beam by electron lens imaging rather than scanning.

THB: Temperature Humidity Bias (85°C/85 percent RH).

TPO: Test Process Order. A lot transfer which accompanies product through the test process.

Test patterns: Special electrical test structures included on production device wafers for monitoring critical parameters.

Thermal oxide: A high quality SiO_2 layer grown by oxidizing the silicon in a furnace (as opposed to externally-deposited glass).

UL: Underwriters Laboratory.

UV: Ultra Violet.

Unit: A package with a die in it.

VCSEM: Voltage Contrast Scanning Electron Microscope. A SEM that is specially modified so that image contrast depends on differences in voltage rather than in topography or composition.

V/I: A monitor measuring voltage and current between probes applied to a semiconductor layer. Measures layer resistivity.

VLSI: Very Large Scale Integration.

Visual: A check of process quality by examination of wafers under a light microscope.

Vt: Transistor threshold voltage. Voltage at which the transistor turns on.

WDX: Wave-length Dispersive X-ray analysis.

Wafer: A thin piece of silicon sliced from a cylinder shaped crystal. It is polished so that the surface is like a mirror. It is most commonly found in 4-, 5-, and 6-inch diameters. The wafer is the base material for most of the world's integrated circuits.

Wafer flat: A flat area ground onto the original silicon ingot from which the wafers are sliced. Gives crystallographic orientation and sometimes additional information if codes are specified.

Wafer sort: Same as Sort Test.

Wafer stepper: A machine which projects the image of a photomask or reticle onto a portion of the wafer, performs the exposure, and then steps to the next region. The mask may or may not be the same size as the image formed on the wafer. Multiple stepping and alignments are required to expose the entire wafer.

Wet masking: Process segment following "dry masking" in which the wafer, covered with the resist pattern, is etched to transfer the resist pattern to the wafer; then the resist is removed. (Includes wet and/or plasma etching.)

Wet etch: Etching in a liquid acid or solution.

Wire bonding: The process of connecting thin wires from the chip's bond pads to the package lead. (This is done at assembly.)

XPS: X-ray Photoelectron Spectroscopy.

XRD: X-ray Diffraction.

XRF: X-ray Fluorescence.

XRT: X-ray Topography.

ZID: Zero Incoming Defects.

ZOD: Zero Outgoing Defects.

ZUD: Zero Unscheduled Downtime.

Index

INDEX

IN

IN

IN

IN

Related Readings

RELATED READINGS

REL

TOTAL QUALITY METHODOLOGY/TECHNOLOGY

"Evolution of VLSI Reliability Engineering," D.L. Crook; 28th Ann. Int'l Reliability Physics Symposium, pp 2-11 (1990).

PROCESS/PRODUCT TECHNOLOGY

"A Critical Review of VLSI Die Attachment in High Reliability Applications," R.K. Shukla and N.P. Mencinger; Solid State Technology, Vol. 28, No. 7, pp 67-74, (1985).

"Building Reliability Into EPROMs," D.A. Baglee, L. Nannemann and C. Huang; 28th Ann. Int'l Reliability Physics Symposium, pp 12-18 (1990).

"Bulk and Surface Conduction in CVD SiO_2 and PSG Passivation Layers," R.B. Comizzoli; J. Electrochem. Soc., Vol. 123, pp 386-391 (1976).

"Control of Package Cracking in Plastic Surface-Mount Devices During Solder Reflow Process," R. Lin, E. Blackshear, G. May, G. Hamilton and D. Kirby; Proc. 7th Ann. Int'l Elec. Packaging Conf., Boston, Mass., pp 995-1010 (1987).

"Design Limits When Using Gold-Aluminum Bonds," E. Philofsky; Proc. 9th Ann. Int'l Reliability Physics Symposium, pp 11-16 (1971).

"Focused Ion Beam Technology and Application," J. Melngailis; Vac. Sci. Technol., Vol. 5(2) Mar/Apr 1987, p 469.

"Improved EPROM Moisture Performance Using Spin-Glass (SOG) for Passivation Planarization," I.S. Gaeta and K.J. Wu; 27th Ann. Int'l Reliability Physics Symposium, pp 122-126 (1989).

"Intermetallic Formation in Gold-Aluminum Systems," E. Philofsky; Solid-State Electronics, Vol. 13, pp 1391-1399 (1970).

"Passivation Material and Thickness Effects On The MTTF of Al-Si Metallization," L. Yau, C. Hong and D. Crook; 23rd Ann. Int'l Reliability Physics Symposium, pp 115-118 (1985).

"P-MOSfet Gate Current and Device Degradation," T.C. Ong; 27th Ann. Int'l Reliability Physics Symposium, pp 178-182 (1989).

"Reliability Performance of ETOX™ Based Flash Memories," G. Verma and N. Mielke; 26th Ann. Int'l Reliability Physics Symposium, pp 158-166 (1988).

"Some New Aspects of Gold-Aluminum Bonds," I.A. Blech and H. Sello; J. Electrochem. Soc., Vol. 113, p 1052 (1966).

"Special Properties of Molding Compounds for Small-Outline Packaged Devices," S. Ito, Y. Uhara, H. Tabata and H. Suzuki; IEEE Trans. Components, Hybrids, Manufac. Technol., Vol. CHMT-9, pp 374-378 (1986).

"Swelling and Glass Transition Relations for Epoxy Matrix Material in Humid Environment," E.L. McKague Jr., J.D. Reynolds and J.E. Halkias; J. Appl. Polymer Sci., Vol. 22, pp 1643-1654 (1978).

"The Electrical Resistance Ratio (RR) As A Thin-Film Metal Monitor," W. Berg, K. Wu, P. Davies, G. Dao and D. Fraser; 28th Ann. Int'l Reliability Physics Symposium, pp 119-123 (1990).

U.S. Patent Application, V.R.M. Rao; Electron Beam Tester.

RELIABILITY PHYSICS

"A Bond Failure Mechanism," T. Koch, W. Riching, J. Whitlock and D. Hall; Proc. 24th Ann. Int'l Reliability Physics Symposium, pp 55-60 (1986).

"Aluminum Corrosion in the Presence of Phosphosilicate Glass and Moisture," R.B. Comizzoli; RCA Rev., Vol. 123, pp 386-391 (1976).

"A Model for EPROM Intrinsic Charge Loss Through Oxide-Nitride-Oxide (ONO) Interpoly Dielectric," K. Wu, C.S. Pan, J.J. Shaw, P. Freiberger and D.A. Baglee; 28th Ann. Int'l Reliability Physics Symposium, pp 145-149 (1990).

"A Review of Corrosion Failure Mechanisms During Accelerated Tests; Electrolytic Metal Migration," J.J. Steppan, J.A. Roth, L.C. Hall, D.A. Jeanotte and S.P. Carbone; J. Electrochem. Soc., Vol. 134, pp 175-190 (1987).

"A Review of the Status of Plastic-Encapsulated Semiconductor Component Reliability," R.W. Lawson; Br. Telecom. Technol. J., Vol. 2 April 1984.

"A Survey of Corrosion Failure Mechanisms in Microelectronic Devices," G.L. Schnable, R.B. Comizzoli, W. Kern and L.K. White; RCA Review, Vol. 40, pp 416-445 (1979).

"Characterization of Electromigration Under Bidirectional (BC) And Pulsed Unidirectional (PDC) Currents," J.A. Maiz; 27th Ann. Int'l Reliability Physics Symposium, pp 220-228 (1989).

"Charge Loss Associated with Program Disturb Stresses in EPROMs," T. Miller, S. Illyes and D.A. Baglee; 28th Ann. Int'l Reliability Physics Symposium, pp 154-158 (1990).

"Chip Corrosion in Plastic Packages," H.M. Berg and W.M. Paulson; Microelectron. Reliab., Vol. 20, pp 247-263 (1980).

"Corrosion of Aluminum IC Metallization with Defective Surface Passivation Layer," R.B. Comizzoli, L.K. White, W. Kern, G.L. Schnable, D.A. Peters, C.E. Tracy and R.D. Vibronek; Proc. 18th Ann. Int'l Reliability Physics Symposium, pp 282-292 (1980).

"Deformation of Al Metallization in Plastic Encapsulated Semiconductor Devices Caused by Thermal Shock," M. Isagawa, Y. Iwasaki and T. Sutoh; Proc. 18th Ann. Int'l Reliability Physics Symposium, pp 82-92 (1980).

"Effect of Bromine in Molding Compounds on Gold-Aluminum Bonds," S. Ahmad, R. Blish II, T. Corbett, J. King and G. Shirley; IEEE Trans. on Components, Hybrids, Manuf. Technol., Vol. CHMT-9, pp 379-385 (1986).

"Electrical Measurements of Moisture Penetration Through Passivation," C.G. Shirley and S.C. Maston; 28th Ann. Int'l Reliability Physics Symposium, pp 72-80 (1990).

"Epoxy Degradation Induced Au-Al Intermediate Void Formation in Plastic-Encapsulated MOS Memories," R.J. Gale; Proc. 22nd Ann. Int'l Reliability Physics Symposium, pp 37-47 (1984).

"ESD on CHMOS Devices Equivalent Circuits, Physical Models and Failure Mechanisms," N. Khurana, T. Maloney and W. Yeh; 23rd Ann. Int'l Reliability Physics Symposium, pp 212-223 (1985).

"Factors Contributing to the Corrosion of the Aluminum Metal on Semiconductor Devices Packaged in Plastic," R.C. Olberg and J.L. Bozarth; Microelectronics and Reliability, Vol. 15, pp 601 (1976).

"Horizontal Die Cracking as a Yield and Reliability Problem in Integrated Circuit Devices," Y.M. Kasem and L.G. Feinstein; Ieee Trans. Components, Hybrids, Manuf. Technol., Vol. CHMT-12, pp 654-661 (1987).

"Interaction Between Phosphosilicate Glass Films and Water," N. Nagasima, H. Suzuki, K. Tanaka and S. Nishida; J. Electrochem. Soc., Vol. 121, pp 434-438 (1974).

"Mechanisms of Temperature Cycle Failure in Encapsulated Semiconductor Devices Caused by Thermal Shock," J. Uebbing; Proc. 18th Ann. Int'l Reliability Physics Symposium, pp 142-156(1981).

"Metallurgical Failure Modes of Wire Bonds," G.G. Harmon; Proc. 12th Ann. Int'l Reliability Physics Symposium, pp 131-141 (1974).

"Metal Migrations Outside the Package During Accelerated Life Tests," P. Dumoulin, J.P. Seurin and P. Marce; Proc. 32nd Electronic Components Conference, pp 229 (1982).

"Moisture Resistance Degradation of Plastic LSIs by Reflow Soldering," I. Fukuzawa, S. Ishiguro and S. Nanbu; Proc. 23rd Ann. Int'l Reliability Symposium, pp 192-197 (1985).

"New Filler-Induced Failure Mechanism in Plastic Encapsulated VLSI Dynamic MOS Memories," H. Matsumoto, M. Yamada, J. Fukushima, T. Kondoh, N. Kotani and M. Tosa; Proc. 23rd Ann. Int'l Reliability Physics Symposium, pp 180-183 (1985).

"On the Porosity Observed in the Kirkdall Effect," F. Seitz; Acta Metallurgica, Vol. 1, pp 355 (1953).

"Plastic Outgassing Induced Wire Bond Failure," R.E. Thomas, V. Winchell, K. James and T. Scharr; Proc. 19th Ann. Int'l Reliability Physics Symposium, pp 182-187 (1981).

"Principles of Corrosion," S.C. Kolesar; Proc. 12th Ann. Int'l Reliability Physics Symposium, pp 155-167 (1974).

"Reliability and Failure Mechanisms of Non-Hermetic Aluminum SICs: Literature Review and Bias Humidity Performance," M. Iannuzzi; IEEE Trans., Vol. CHMT-6, pp 181-190 (1983).

"Reliability Comparison of FLOTOX and Textured-Polysilicon E^2PROMs," N. Miekle, A. Fazio and H.C. Liou; 25th Ann. Int'l Reliability Physics Symposium, pp 85-92 (1987).

"Stress-Induced Deformation of Aluminum Metallization in Plastic Molded Semiconductor Devices," R.E. Thomas; IEEE Trans. on Components, Hybrids, Manuf. Technol., Vol. CHMT-8, pp 427-434 (1985).

"The Cathodic Corrosion of Aluminum," E.P.G.T. van de Ven and H. Koelmans; J. Electrochem. Soc., Vol. 22, pp 1643-1654 (1978).

"The Effect of Impurities on the Corrosion of Aluminum Metallization," W.M. Paulson and R.P. Lorigan; Proc. 14th Ann. Int'l Reliability Physics Symposium, pp 42-47 (1976).

"The Effect of Metal Film Topography and Lithography On Grain Size Distributions and on Electromigration Performance," Y.E. Strausser, B.L. Euzent, R.C. Smith, B.M. Tracey and K. Wu; 25th Ann. Int'l Reliability Physics Symposium, pp 140-144 (1987).

"The Effects of Phosphorous-Doped Passivation Glass on the Corrosion of Aluminum," W.M. Paulson and R.W. Kirk; Proc. 12th Ann. Int'l Reliability Physics Symposium, pp 172 (1974).

"The Influence of Plastic Encapsulants and Passivation Layers on the Corrosion of Thin Aluminum Films Subjected to Humidity Stress," S.P. Sim and R.W. Lawson; Proc. 17th Ann. Int'l Reliability Physics Symposium, pp 103-112 (1979).

"The Mechanisms of Elevated Temperature Property Losses in High Performance Structural Epoxy Resin Matrix Materials After Exposures to High Humidity Environments," C.E. Browning; Polymer Engineering and Science, Vol. 18, pp 16-24 (1978).

"Thin-Film Cracking and Wire-Ball Shear in Plastic Dips Due to Temperature Cycle and Thermal Shock," C.G. Shirley and R. Blish; Proc. 25th Ann. Int'l Reliability Physics Symposium, (1987).

"Zinc Diffusion in Alpha Brass," A.D. Smigelskas and E.O. Kirkendall; Trans AIME, Vol. 171, pp 130 (1947).

ANALYTICAL TECHNOLOGY/METHODOLOGY

"Analysis of Corrosion on Aluminum Double layer Metallization," H. Wada, T. Higuchi and T. Ajiki; J. Electrochem. Soc., Vol. 133, pp 362-366 (1986).

"Analysis of Package Cracking During Reflow Solder Process," M. Kitano, A. Nishimura, S. Kawai and K. Nishi; Proc. 26th Ann. Int'l Reliability Physics Symposium, pp 90-95 (1988).

"Analysis of Product Hot Electron Problems by Gated Emission Microscopy," N. Khurana and C.L. Chiang; 24th Ann. Int'l Reliability Symposium, pp 189-194 (1986).

"A Non-Aging Screen to Prevent Wearout of Ultra-Thin Dielectrics," W.K. Meyer and D.L. Crook; 23rd Ann. Int'l Reliability Physics Symposium, pp 6-10 (1985).

"A Resistance Change Methodology for the Study of Electromigration in AL-SI Interconnects," J.A. Maiz; 26th Ann. Int'l Reliability Physics Symposium, pp 209-215 (1988).

"Breakdown Energy of Metal (BEM)—A New Technique for Monitoring Metallization Reliability at Wafer Level," C.C. Hong and D.L. Crook; 23rd Ann. Int'l Reliability Physics Symposium, pp 108-114 (1985).

"Comprehensive Model for Humidity Testing Correlation," D.S. Peck; Proc. 24th Ann. Int'l Reliability Physics Symposium, pp 45-50 (1986).

"Computer Aided Stress Modelling for Optimizing Plastic Packages Reliability," S. Groothius, W. Schroen and M. Murtuza; Proc. 23rd Ann. Int'l Reliability Physics Symposium, pp 184-191 (1985).

"Detection of Junction Spiking and Its Induced Latch-Up By Emission Microscopy," S.C. Lim and E.G. Tan; 26th Ann. Int'l Reliability Physics Symposium, pp 119-125 (1988).

"Dynamic Imaging of Current Conduction in Dielectric Films by Emission Microscopy," N. Khurana and C.L. Chiang; 25th Ann. Int'l Reliability Physics Symposium, pp 72-76 (1987).

"Electromigration Testing of Ti/Al-Si Metallization for Integrated Circuits," J.A. Maiz and B. Sabi; 25th Ann. Int'l Reliability Physics Symposium, pp 145-153 (1987).

"Failure Mechanism of Die Cracking Due to Imperfect Die Attachment," S.S. Chiang and R.K. Shukla; Proc. 34th Ann. Electronic Components Conference, pp 1-8 (1984).

"Fault Contrast: A New Voltage Contrast VLSI Diagnosis Technique," A.R. Stivers and D.C. Ferguson; Proc. 24th Ann. Int'l Reliability Physics Symposium, pp 109 (1986).

"HAST Applications: Acceleration Factors and Results for VLSI Components," D. Danielson, G. Marcyk, E. Babb and S. Kudva; 27th Ann. Int'l Reliability Physics Symposium, pp 114-121 (1989).

"Highly Accelerated Temperature and Humidity Stress Test Technique (HAST)," J.E. Gunn, S.K. Malik and P.M. Mazumbar; Proc. 21st Ann. Int'l Reliability Physics Symposium, pp 66-72 (1983).

"Investigations of Large PLCC Package Cracking During Surface-Mount Exposure," T.O. Steiner and D. Suhl; IEEE Trans. on Components, Hybrids, Manuf. Technol., Vol. CHMT-10, pp 209-216 (1987).

"Life Estimation for IC Plastic Packages Under Temperature Cycling Based on Fracture Mechanics," A. Nishimura, A. Tatemichi, H. Muira and T. Sakamoto; IEEE Trans. on Components, Hybrids, Manuf. Technol., Vol. CHMT-12, pp 637-642 (1987).

"Measurement of Silicon strength as Affected by Wafer Back Processing," G. Hawkins, H. Berg, M. Mahalingam, G. Lewis and L. Lofgran; Proc. 25th Ann. IRPS proceedings, pp 216-223 (1987).

"Rapid Assessment of the Humidity Dependence of IC Failure Modes by Use of HAST," J.E. Gunn, R.E. Camenga and S.K. Malik; Proc. 21st Ann. Int'l Reliability Physics Symposium, pp 66-72 (1983).

"Shear Stress Evaluation of Plastic Packages," D.R. Edwards, K.G. Groothius and J.E. Martinez; IEEE Trans. on Components, Hybrids, Manuf. Technol., Vol. CHMT-12, pp 618-627 (1987).

"Stress Analysis of Passivation Film Cracking for Plastic Molded LSI Caused by Thermal Stress," S. Okikawa, M. Sakimoto, M. Tanaka, T. Sato, T. Toya and Y. Hara; presented at Int'l Soc. for Testing and Failure Analysis Meeting, Los Angeles, CA, Oct. 1983.

Trans AIMEX, A.D. Smigelskas and E.O. Kirkendall; Vol. 171, pp 130 (1947).

"Use of Advanced Analytical Techniques for VLSI Failure Analysis," I. Banerjee, B. Tracy, P. Davies and B. McDonald; 28th Ann. Int'l Reliability Physics Symposium, pp 61-68 (1990).

"Use of Wetting Angle Measurements in Reliability Evaluations of AuSi Eutectic Die Attach," N.P. Mencinger, M.P. Carthy and R.C. McDonald; Proc. 23rd Ann. Int'l Reliability Physics Symposium, pp 173-179 (1985).

"Wire Bond Integrity Test Chip," R.C. Blisk and L. Parobeck; Proc. 21st Ann. Int'l Reliability Physics Symposium, pp 142-147 (1983).

intel®

DOMESTIC SALES OFFICES

ALABAMA

Intel Corp.
5015 Bradford Dr., #2
Huntsville 35805
Tel: (205) 830-4010
FAX: (205) 837-2640

ARIZONA

†Intel Corp.
410 North 44th Street
Suite 500
Phoenix 85008
Tel: (602) 231-0386
FAX: (602) 244-0446

Intel Corp.
7225 N. Mona Lisa Rd.
Suite 215
Tucson 85741
Tel: (602) 544-0227
FAX: (602) 544-0232

CALIFORNIA

†Intel Corp.
21515 Vanowen Street
Suite 116
Canoga Park 91303
Tel: (818) 704-8500
FAX: (818) 340-1144

†Intel Corp.
300 N. Continental Blvd.
Suite 100
El Segundo 90245
Tel: (213) 640-6040
FAX: (213) 640-7133

Intel Corp.
1 Sierra Gate Plaza
Suite 280C
Roseville 95678
Tel: (916) 782-8086
FAX: (916) 782-8153

†Intel Corp.
9665 Chesapeake Dr.
Suite 325
San Diego 92123
Tel: (619) 292-8086
FAX: (619) 292-0628

†Intel Corp.*
400 N. Tustin Avenue
Suite 450
Santa Ana 92705
Tel: (714) 835-9642
TWX: 910-595-1114
FAX: (714) 541-9157

†Intel Corp.*
San Tomas 4
2700 San Tomas Expressway
2nd Floor
Santa Clara 95051
Tel: (408) 986-8086
TWX: 910-338-0255
FAX: (408) 727-2620

COLORADO

Intel Corp.
4445 Northpark Drive
Suite 100
Colorado Springs 80907
Tel: (719) 594-6622
FAX: (303) 594-0720

†Intel Corp.*
600 S. Cherry St.
Suite 700
Denver 80222
Tel: (303) 321-8086
TWX: 910-931-2289
FAX: (303) 322-8670

CONNECTICUT

†Intel Corp.
301 Lee Farm Corporate Park
83 Wooster Heights Rd.
Danbury 06810
Tel: (203) 748-3130
FAX: (203) 794-0339

FLORIDA

†Intel Corp.
800 Fairway Drive
Suite 160
Deerfield Beach 33441
Tel: (305) 421-0506
FAX: (305) 421-2444

†Intel Corp.
5850 T.G. Lee Blvd.
Suite 340
Orlando 32822
Tel: (407) 240-8000
FAX: (407) 240-8097

Intel Corp.
11300 4th Street North
Suite 170
St. Petersburg 33716
Tel: (813) 577-2413
FAX: (813) 578-1607

GEORGIA

†Intel Corp.
20 Technology Parkway
Suite 150
Norcross 30092
Tel: (404) 449-0541
FAX: (404) 605-9762

ILLINOIS

†Intel Corp.*
Woodfield Corp. Center III
300 N. Martingale Road
Suite 400
Schaumburg 60173
Tel: (708) 605-8031
FAX: (708) 706-9762

INDIANA

†Intel Corp.
8910 Purdue Road
Suite 350
Indianapolis 46268
Tel: (317) 875-0623
FAX: (317) 875-8938

IOWA

Intel Corp.
1930 St. Andrews Drive N.E.
2nd Floor
Cedar Rapids 52402
Tel: (319) 393-5510

KANSAS

†Intel Corp.
10985 Cody St.
Suite 140
Overland Park 66210
Tel: (913) 345-2727
FAX: (913) 345-2076

MARYLAND

†Intel Corp.*
10010 Junction Dr.
Suite 200
Annapolis Junction 20701
Tel: (301) 206-2860
FAX: (301) 206-3677
(301) 206-3678

MASSACHUSETTS

†Intel Corp.*
Westford Corp. Center
3 Carlisle Road
2nd Floor
Westford 01886
Tel: (508) 692-0960
TWX: 710-343-6333
FAX: (508) 692-7867

MICHIGAN

†Intel Corp.
7071 Orchard Lake Road
Suite 100
West Bloomfield 48322
Tel: (313) 851-8096
FAX: (313) 851-8770

MINNESOTA

†Intel Corp.
3500 W. 80th St.
Suite 360
Bloomington 55431
Tel: (612) 835-6722
TWX: 910-576-2867
FAX: (612) 831-6497

MISSOURI

†Intel Corp.
4203 Earth City Expressway
Suite 131
Earth City 63045
Tel: (314) 291-1990
FAX: (314) 291-4341

NEW JERSEY

†Intel Corp.*
Parkway 109 Office Center
328 Newman Springs Road
Red Bank 07701
Tel: (201) 747-2233
FAX: (201) 747-0983

Intel Corp.
280 Corporate Center
75 Livingston Avenue
First Floor
Roseland 07068
Tel: (201) 740-0111
FAX: (201) 740-0626

NEW YORK

Intel Corp.*
850 Crosskeys Office Park
Fairport 14450
Tel: (716) 425-2750
TWX: 510-253-7391
FAX: (716) 223-2561

†Intel Corp.*
2950 Express Dr., South
Suite 130
Islandia 11722
Tel: (516) 231-3300
TWX: 510-227-6236
FAX: (516) 348-7939

†Intel Corp.
Westage Business Center
Bldg. 300, Route 9
Fishkill 12524
Tel: (914) 897-3860
FAX: (914) 897-3125

NORTH CAROLINA

†Intel Corp.
5800 Executive Center Dr.
Suite 105
Charlotte 28212
Tel: (704) 568-8966
FAX: (704) 535-2236

†Intel Corp.
5540 Centerview Dr.
Suite 215
Raleigh 27606
Tel: (919) 851-9537
FAX: (919) 851-8974

OHIO

†Intel Corp.*
3401 Park Center Drive
Suite 220
Dayton 45414
Tel: (513) 890-5350
TWX: 810-450-2528
FAX: (513) 890-8658

†Intel Corp.*
25700 Science Park Dr.
Suite 100
Beachwood 44122
Tel: (216) 464-2736
TWX: 810-427-9298
FAX: (804) 282-0673

OKLAHOMA

Intel Corp.
6801 N. Broadway
Suite 115
Oklahoma City 73162
Tel: (405) 848-8086
FAX: (405) 840-9819

OREGON

†Intel Corp.
15254 N.W. Greenbrier Parkway
Building B
Beaverton 97005
Tel: (503) 645-8051
TWX: 910-467-8741
FAX: (503) 645-8181

PENNSYLVANIA

†Intel Corp.*
925 Harvest Drive
Suite 200
Blue Bell 19422
Tel: (215) 641-1000
FAX: (215) 641-0785

†Intel Corp.*
400 Penn Center Blvd.
Suite 610
Pittsburgh 15235
Tel: (412) 823-4970
FAX: (412) 829-7578

PUERTO RICO

†Intel Corp.
South Industrial Park
P.O. Box 910
Las Piedras 00671
Tel: (809) 733-8616

TEXAS

Intel Corp.
8911 Capital of Texas Hwy.
Austin 78759
Tel: (512) 794-8086
FAX: (512) 338-9335

†Intel Corp.*
12000 Ford Road
Suite 400
Dallas 75248
Tel: (214) 241-8087
FAX: (214) 484-1180

†Intel Corp.*
7322 S.W. Freeway
Suite 1490
Houston 77074
Tel: (713) 988-8086
TWX: 910-881-2490
FAX: (713) 988-3660

UTAH

†Intel Corp.
428 East 6400 South
Suite 104
Murray 84107
Tel: (801) 263-8051
FAX: (801) 268-1457

VIRGINIA

†Intel Corp.
1504 Santa Rosa Road
Suite 108
Richmond 23288
Tel: (804) 282-5668
FAX: (216) 464-2270

WASHINGTON

†Intel Corp.
155 108th Avenue N.E.
Suite 386
Bellevue 98004
Tel: (206) 453-8086
TWX: 910-443-3002
FAX: (206) 451-9556

Intel Corp.
408 N. Mullan Road
Suite 102
Spokane 99206
Tel: (509) 928-8086
FAX: (509) 928-9467

WISCONSIN

Intel Corp.
330 S. Executive Dr.
Suite 102
Brookfield 53005
Tel: (414) 784-8087
FAX: (414) 796-2115

CANADA

BRITISH COLUMBIA

Intel Semiconductor of
Canada, Ltd.
4585 Canada Way
Suite 202
Burnaby V5G 4L6
Tel: (604) 298-0387
FAX: (604) 298-8234

ONTARIO

†Intel Semiconductor of
Canada, Ltd.
2650 Queensview Drive
Suite 250
Ottawa K2B 8H6
Tel: (613) 829-9714
FAX: (613) 820-5936

†Intel Semiconductor of
Canada, Ltd.
190 Attwell Drive
Suite 500
Rexdale M9W 6H8
Tel: (416) 675-2105
FAX: (416) 675-2438

QUEBEC

†Intel Semiconductor of
Canada, Ltd.
1 Rue Holiday
Suite 115
Tour East
Pt. Claire H9R 5N3
Tel: (514) 694-9130
FAX: 514-694-0064

†Sales and Service Office
*Field Application Location

intel®

DOMESTIC DISTRIBUTORS

ALABAMA

Arrow Electronics, Inc.
1015 Henderson Road
Huntsville 35805
Tel: (205) 837-6955
FAX: 205-751-1581

Hamilton/Avnet Computer
4930 I Corporate Drive
Huntsville 35805

Hamilton/Avnet Electronics
4940 Research Drive
Huntsville 35805
Tel: (205) 837-7210
FAX: 205-721-0356

MTI Systems Sales
4950 Corporate Drive
Suite 120
Huntsville 35806
Tel: (205) 830-9526
FAX: (205) 830-9557

Pioneer/Technologies Group, Inc.
4825 University Square
Huntsville 35805
Tel: (205) 837-9300
FAX: 205-837-9358

ALASKA

Hamilton/Avnet Computer
1400 W. Benson Blvd., Suite 400
Anchorage 99503

ARIZONA

†Arrow Electronics, Inc.
4134 E. Wood Street
Phoenix 85040
Tel: (602) 437-0750
TWX: 910-951-1550

Hamilton/Avnet Computer
30 South McKemy Avenue
Chandler 85226

Hamilton/Avnet Computer
90 South McKemy Road
Chandler 85226

†Hamilton/Avnet Electronics
505 S. Madison Drive
Tempe 85281
Tel: (602) 231-5140
TWX: 910-950-0077

Hamilton/Avnet Electronics
30 South McKemy
Chandler 85226
Tel: (602) 961-6669
FAX: 602-961-4073

Wyle Distribution Group
4141 E. Raymond
Phoenix 85040
Tel: (602) 249-2232
TWX: 910-371-2871

CALIFORNIA

Arrow Commercial System Group
1502 Crocker Avenue
Hayward 94544
Tel: (415) 489-5371
FAX: (415) 489-9393

Arrow Commercial System Group
14242 Chambers Road
Tustin 92680
Tel: (714) 544-0200
FAX: (714) 731-8438

†Arrow Electronics, Inc.
19748 Dearborn Street
Chatsworth 91311
Tel: (213) 701-7500
TWX: 910-493-2086

†Arrow Electronics, Inc.
9511 Ridgehaven Court
San Diego 92123
Tel: (619) 565-4800
FAX: 619-279-8062

†Arrow Electronics, Inc.
521 Weddell Drive
Sunnyvale 94086
Tel: (408) 745-6600
TWX: 910-339-9371

†Arrow Electronics, Inc.
2961 Dow Avenue
Tustin 92680
Tel: (714) 838-5422
TWX: 910-595-2860

Hamilton/Avnet Computer
3170 Pullman Street
Costa Mesa 92626

Hamilton/Avnet Computer
1361B West 190th Street
Gardena 90248

Hamilton/Avnet Computer
4103 Northgate Blvd.
Sacramento 95834

Hamilton/Avnet Computer
4545 Viewridge Avenue
San Diego 92123

Hamilton/Avnet Computer
1175 Bordeaux Drive
Sunnyvale 94089

Hamilton/Avnet Electronics
21150 Califa Street
Woodland Hills 91367

†Hamilton/Avnet Electronics
3170 Pullman Street
Costa Mesa 92626
Tel: (714) 641-4150
TWX: 910-595-2638

†Hamilton/Avnet Electronics
1175 Bordeaux Drive
Sunnyvale 94086
Tel: (408) 743-3300
TWX: 910-339-9332

†Hamilton/Avnet Electronics
4545 Ridgeview Avenue
San Diego 92123
Tel: (619) 571-7500
TWX: 910-595-2638

†Hamilton/Avnet Electronics
21150 Califa St.
Woodland Hills 91376
Tel: (818) 594-0404
FAX: 818-594-8233

†Hamilton/Avnet Electronics
10950 W. Washington Blvd.
Culver City 20230
Tel: (213) 558-2458
TWX: 910-340-6364

†Hamilton/Avnet Electronics
1361B West 190th Street
Gardena 90248
Tel: (213) 217-6700
TWX: 910-340-6364

†Hamilton/Avnet Electronics
4103 Northgate Blvd.
Sacramento 95834
Tel: (916) 920-3150

Pioneer/Technologies Group, Inc.
134 Rio Robles
San Jose 95134
Tel: (408) 954-9100
FAX: 408-954-9113

Wyle Distribution Group
124 Maryland Street
El Segundo 90254
Tel: (213) 322-8100

Wyle Distribution Group
7431 Chapman Ave.
Garden Grove 92641
Tel: (714) 891-1717
FAX: 714-891-1621

†Wyle Distribution Group
2951 Sunrise Blvd., Suite 175
Rancho Cordova 95742
Tel: (916) 638-5282

†Wyle Distribution Group
9525 Chesapeake Drive
San Diego 92123
Tel: (619) 565-9171
TWX: 910-335-1590

†Wyle Distribution Group
3000 Bowers Avenue
Santa Clara 95051
Tel: (408) 727-2500
TWX: 408-988-2747

†Wyle Distribution Group
17872 Cowan Avenue
Irvine 92714
Tel: (714) 863-9953
TWX: 910-371-7127

†Wyle Distribution Group
26677 W. Agoura Rd.
Calabasas 91302
Tel: (818) 880-9000
TWX: 372-0232

COLORADO

Arrow Electronics, Inc.
7060 South Tucson Way
Englewood 80112
Tel: (303) 790-4444

Hamilton/Avnet Computer
9605 Maroon Circle, Ste. 200
Engelwood 80112

†Hamilton/Avnet Electronics
9605 Maroon Circle
Suite 200
Englewood 80112
Tel: (303) 799-0663
TWX: 910-935-0787

†Wyle Distribution Group
451 E. 124th Avenue
Thornton 80241
Tel: (303) 457-9953
TWX: 910-936-0770

CONNECTICUT

†Arrow Electronics, Inc.
12 Beaumont Road
Wallingford 06492
Tel: (203) 265-7741
TWX: 710-476-0162

Hamilton/Avnet Computer
Commerce Industrial Park
Commerce Drive
Danbury 06810

†Hamilton/Avnet Electronics
Commerce Industrial Park
Commerce Drive
Danbury 06810
Tel: (203) 797-2800
TWX: 710-456-9974

†Pioneer/Standard Electronics
112 Main Street
Norwalk 06851
Tel: (203) 853-1515
FAX: 203-838-9901

FLORIDA

†Arrow Electronics, Inc.
400 Fairway Drive
Suite 102
Deerfield Beach 33441
Tel: (305) 429-8200
FAX: 305-428-3991

†Arrow Electronics, Inc.
37 Skyline Drive
Suite 3101
Lake Marv 32746
Tel: (407) 323-0252
FAX: 407-323-3189

Hamilton/Avnet Computer
6801 N.W. 15th Way
Ft. Lauderdale 33309

Hamilton/Avnet Computer
3247 Spring Forest Road
St. Petersburg 33702

†Hamilton/Avnet Electronics
6801 N.W. 15th Way
Ft. Lauderdale 33309
Tel: (305) 971-2900
FAX: 305-971-5420

†Hamilton/Avnet Electronics
3197 Tech Drive North
St. Petersburg 33702
Tel: (813) 573-3930
FAX: 813-572-4329

†Hamilton/Avnet Electronics
6947 University Boulevard
Winter Park 32792
Tel: (407) 628-3888
FAX: 407-678-1878

†Pioneer/Technologies Group, Inc.
337 Northlake Blvd., Suite 1000
Alta Monte Springs 32701
Tel: (407) 834-9090
FAX: 407-834-0865

Pioneer/Technologies Group, Inc.
674 S. Military Trail
Deerfield Beach 33442
Tel: (305) 428-8877
FAX: 305-481-2950

GEORGIA

Arrow Commercial System Group
3400 C. Corporate Way
Deluth 30139
Tel: (404) 623-8825
FAX: (404) 623-8802

†Arrow Electronics, Inc.
4250 E. Rivergreen Parkway
Deluth 30136
Tel: (404) 497-1300
TWX: 810-766-0439

Hamilton/Avnet Computer
5825 D. Peachtree Corners E.
Norcross 30092

†Hamilton/Avnet Electronics
5825 D Peachtree Corners
Norcross 30092
Tel: (404) 447-7500
TWX: 810-766-0432

Pioneer/Technologies Group, Inc.
3100 F Northwoods Place
Norcross 30071
Tel: (404) 448-1711
FAX: 404-446-8270

ILLINOIS

†Arrow Electronics, Inc.
1140 W. Thorndale
Itasca 60143
Tel: (708) 250-0500
TWX: 708-250-0916

Hamilton/Avnet Computer
1130 Thorndale Avenue
Bensenville 60106

†Hamilton/Avnet Electronics
1130 Thorndale Avenue
Bensenville 60106
Tel: (708) 860-7780
TWX: 708-860-8530

MTI Systems Sales
1100 W. Thorndale
Itasca 60143
Tel: (708) 773-2300

†Pioneer/Standard Electronics
2171 Executive Dr., Suite 200
Addison 60101
Tel: (708) 495-9680
FAX: 708-495-9831

INDIANA

†Arrow Electronics, Inc.
7108 Lakeview Parkway West Drive
Indianapolis 46268
Tel: (317) 299-2071
FAX: 317-299-0255

Hamilton/Avnet Computer
485 Gradle Drive
Carmel 46032

Hamilton/Avnet Electronics
485 Gradle Drive
Carmel 46032
Tel: (317) 844-9333
FAX: 317-844-5921

†Pioneer/Standard Electronics
9350 Priority Way
West Drive
Indianapolis 46250
Tel: (317) 573-0880
FAX: 317-573-0979

†Certified Technical Distributor

DOMESTIC DISTRIBUTORS (Contd.)

IOWA

Hamilton/Avnet Computer
915 33rd Avenue SW
Cedar Rapids 52404

Hamilton/Avnet Electronics
915 33rd Avenue, S.W.
Cedar Rapids 52404
Tel: (319) 362-4757

KANSAS

Arrow Electronics, Inc.
8208 Melrose Dr., Suite 210
Lenexa 66214
Tel: (913) 541-9542
FAX: 913-541-0328

Hamilton/Avnet Computer
15313 W. 95th Street
Lenexa 61219

†Hamilton/Avnet Electronics
15313 W. 95th
Overland Park 66215
Tel: (913) 888-8900
FAX: 913-541-7951

KENTUCKY

Hamilton/Avnet Electronics
805 A. Newtown Circle
Lexington 40511
Tel: (606) 259-1475

MARYLAND

†Arrow Electronics, Inc.
8300 Guilford Drive
Suite H, River Center
Columbia 21046
Tel: (301) 995-6002
FAX: 301-381-3854

Hamilton/Avnet Computer
6822 Oak Hall Lane
Columbia 21045

†Hamilton/Avnet Electronics
6822 Oak Hall Lane
Columbia 21045
Tel: (301) 995-3500
FAX: 301-995-3593

†Mesa Technology Corp.
9720 Patuxent Woods Dr.
Columbia 21046
Tel: (301) 290-8150
FAX: 301-290-6474

†Pioneer/Technologies Group, Inc.
9100 Gaither Road
Gaithersburg 20877
Tel: (301) 921-0660
FAX: 301-921-4255

MASSACHUSETTS

Arrow Electronics, Inc.
25 Upton Dr.
Wilmington 01887
Tel: (508) 658-0900
TWX: 710-393-6770

Hamilton/Avnet Computer
10 D Centennial Drive
Peabody 01960

†Hamilton/Avnet Electronics
10D Centennial Drive
Peabody 01960
Tel: (508) 532-9838
FAX: 508-596-7802

†Pioneer/Standard Electronics
44 Hartwell Avenue
Lexington 02173
Tel: (617) 861-9200
FAX: 617-863-1547

Wyle Distribution Group
15 Third Avenue
Burlington 01803
Tel: (617) 272-7300
FAX: 617-272-6809

MICHIGAN

†Arrow Electronics, Inc.
19880 Haggerty Road
Livonia 48152
Tel: (313) 665-4100
TWX: 810-223-6020

Hamilton/Avnet Computer
2215 S.E. A-5
Grand Rapids 49508

Hamilton/Avnet Computer
41650 Garden Rd., Ste. 100
Novi 48050

Hamilton/Avnet Electronics
2215 29th Street S.E.
Space A5
Grand Rapids 49508
Tel: (616) 243-8805
FAX: 616-698-1831

Hamilton/Avnet Electronics
41650 Garden Brook
Novi 48050
Tel: (313) 347-4271
FAX: 313-347-4021

†Pioneer/Standard Electronics
4505 Broadmoor S.E.
Grand Rapids 49508
Tel: (616) 698-1800
FAX: 616-698-1831

†Pioneer/Standard Electronics
13485 Stamford
Livonia 48150
Tel: (313) 525-1800
FAX: 313-427-3720

MINNESOTA

†Arrow Electronics, Inc.
5230 W. 73rd Street
Edina 55435
Tel: (612) 830-1800
TWX: 910-576-3125

Hamilton/Avnet Computer
12400 Whitewater Drive
Minnetonka 55343

†Hamilton/Avnet Electronics
12400 Whitewater Drive
Minnetonka 55434
Tel: (612) 932-0600
TWX: 910-576-2720

†Pioneer/Standard Electronics
7625 Golden Triange Dr.
Suite G
Eden Prairie 55343
Tel: (612) 944-3355
FAX: 612-944-3794

MISSOURI

†Arrow Electronics, Inc.
2380 Schuetz
St. Louis 63141
Tel: (314) 567-6888
FAX: 314-567-1164

Hamilton/Avnet Computer
739 Goddard Avenue
Chesterfield 63005

†Hamilton/Avnet Electronics
741 Goddard
Chesterfield 63005
Tel: (314) 537-1600
FAX: 314-537-4248

NEW HAMPSHIRE

Hamilton/Avnet Computer
2 Executive Park Drive
Bedford 03102

Hamilton/Avnet Computer
444 East Industrial Park Dr.
Manchester 03103

NEW JERSEY

†Arrow Electronics, Inc.
4 East Stow Road
Unit 11
Marlton 08053
Tel: (609) 596-8000
FAX: 609-596-9632

†Arrow Electronics
6 Century Drive
Parsipanny 07054
Tel: (201) 538-0900
FAX: 201-538-0900

Hamilton/Avnet Computer
1 Keystone Ave., Bldg. 36
Cherry Hill 08003

Hamilton/Avnet Computer
10 Industrial Road
Fairfield 07006

†Hamilton/Avnet Electronics
1 Keystone Ave., Bldg. 36
Cherry Hill 08003
Tel: (609) 424-0110
FAX: 609-751-2552

†Hamilton/Avnet Electronics
10 Industrial
Fairfield 07006
Tel: (201) 575-3390
FAX: 201-575-5839

†MTI Systems Sales
9 Law Drive
Fairfield 07006
Tel: (201) 227-5552
FAX: 201-575-6336

†Pioneer/Standard Electronics
14-A Madison Rd.
Fairfield 07006
Tel: (201) 575-3510
FAX: 201-575-3454

NEW MEXICO

Alliance Electronics Inc.
10510 Research Avenue
Albuquerque 87123
Tel: (505) 292-3360
FAX: 505-292-6537

Hamilton/Avnet Computer
5659 Jefferson, N.E. Suites A & B
Albuquerque 87109

†Hamilton/Avnet Electronics
5659A Jefferson N.E.
Albuquerque 87109
Tel: (505) 765-1500
FAX: 505-243-1395

NEW YORK

†Arrow Electronics, Inc.
3375 Brighton Henrietta Townline Rd.
Rochester 14623
Tel: (716) 427-0300
TWX: 510-253-4766

Arrow Electronics, Inc.
20 Oser Avenue
Hauppauge 11788
Tel: (516) 231-1000
TWX: 510-227-6623

Hamilton/Avnet Computer
933 Motor Parkway
Haupauge 11788

Hamilton/Avnet Computer
2060 Townline
Rochester 14623

†Hamilton/Avnet Electronics
933 Motor Parkway
Hauppauge 11788
Tel: (516) 231-9800
TWX: 510-224-6166

†Hamilton/Avnet Electronics
2060 Townline Rd.
Rochester 14623
Tel: (716) 272-2744
TWX: 510-253-5470

Hamilton/Avnet Electronics
103 Twin Oaks Drive
Syracuse 13206
Tel: (315) 437-0288
TWX: 710-541-1560

†MTI Systems Sales
38 Harbor Park Drive
Port Washington 11050
Tel: (516) 621-6200
FAX: 510-223-0846

Pioneer/Standard Electronics
68 Corporate Drive
Binghamton 13904
Tel: (607) 722-9300
FAX: 607-722-9562

Pioneer/Standard Electronics
40 Oser Avenue
Hauppauge 11787
Tel: (516) 231-9200
FAX: 510-227-9869

†Pioneer/Standard Electronics
60 Crossway Park West
Woodbury, Long Island 11797
Tel: (516) 921-8700
FAX: 516-921-2143

†Pioneer/Standard Electronics
840 Fairport Park
Fairport 14450
Tel: (716) 381-7070
FAX: 716-381-5955

NORTH CAROLINA

†Arrow Electronics, Inc.
5240 Greensdairy Road
Raleigh 27604
Tel: (919) 876-3132
TWX: 510-928-1856

Hamilton/Avnet Computer
3510 Spring Forest Road
Raleigh 27604

†Hamilton/Avnet Electronics
3510 Spring Forest Drive
Raleigh 27604
Tel: (919) 878-0819
TWX: 510-928-1836

Pioneer/Technologies Group, Inc.
9401 L-Southern Pine Blvd.
Charlotte 28210
Tel: (919) 527-8188
FAX: 704-522-8564

Pioneer Technologies Group, Inc.
2810 Meridian Parkway
Suite 148
Durham 27713
Tel: (919) 544-5400
FAX: 919-544-5885

OHIO

Arrow Commercial System Group
284 Cramer Creek Court
Dublin 43017
Tel: (614) 889-9347
FAX: (614) 889-9680

†Arrow Electronics, Inc.
6238 Cochran Road
Solon 44139
Tel: (216) 248-3990
TWX: 810-427-9409

Hamilton/Avnet Computer
7764 Washington Village Dr.
Dayton 45459

Hamilton/Avnet Computer
30325 Bainbridge Rd., Bldg. A
Solon 44139

†Hamilton/Avnet Electronics
7760 Washington Village Dr.
Dayton 45459
Tel: (513) 439-6733
FAX: 513-439-6711

†Hamilton/Avnet Electronics
30325 Bainbridge
Solon 44139
Tel: (216) 349-5100
TWX: 810-427-9452

Hamilton/Avnet Computer
777 Brooksedge Blvd.
Westerville 43081
Tel: (614) 882-7004
FAX: 614-882-8650

Hamilton/Avnet Electronics
777 Brooksedge Blvd.
Westerville 43081
Tel: (614) 882-7004

MTI Systems Sales
23400 Commerce Park Road
Beachwood 44122
Tel: (216) 464-6688

†Pioneer/Standard Electronics
4433 Interpoint Boulevard
Dayton 45424
Tel: (513) 236-9900
FAX: 513-236-8133

†Pioneer/Standard Electronics
4800 E. 131st Street
Cleveland 44105
Tel: (216) 587-3600
FAX: 216-663-1004

†Certified Technical Distributor

DOMESTIC DISTRIBUTORS (Contd.)

OKLAHOMA

Arrow Electronics, Inc.
4719 South Memorial Dr.
Tulsa 74145

†Hamilton/Avnet Electronics
12121 E. 51st St., Suite 102A
Tulsa 74146
Tel: (918) 252-7297

OREGON

†Almac Electronics Corp.
1885 N.W. 169th Place
Beaverton 97005
Tel: (503) 629-8090
FAX: 503-645-0611

Hamilton/Avnet Computer
9409 Southwest Nimbus Ave.
Beaverton 97005

†Hamilton/Avnet Electronics
9409 S.W. Nimbus Ave.
Beaverton 97005
Tel: (503) 627-0201
FAX: 503-641-4012

Wyle
9640 Sunshine Court
Bldg. G, Suite 200
Beaverton 97005
Tel: (503) 643-7900
FAX: 503-646-5466

PENNSYLVANIA

Arrow Electronics, Inc.
650 Seco Road
Monroeville 15146
Tel: (412) 856-7000

Hamilton/Avnet Computer
2800 Liberty Ave., Bldg. E
Pittsburgh 15222

Hamilton/Avnet Electronics
2800 Liberty Ave.
Pittsburgh 15238
Tel: (412) 281-4150

Pioneer/Standard Electronics
259 Kappa Drive
Pittsburgh 15238
Tel: (412) 782-2300
FAX: 412-963-8255

†Pioneer/Technologies Group, Inc.
Delaware Valley
261 Gibralter Road
Horsham 19044
Tel: (215) 674-4000
FAX: 215-674-3107

TENNESSEE

Arrow Commercial System Group
3635 Knight Road
Suite 7
Memphis 38118
Tel: (901) 367-0540
FAX: (901) 367-2081

TEXAS

Arrow Electronics, Inc.
3220 Commander Drive
Carrollton 75006
Tel: (214) 380-6464
FAX: (214) 248-7208

Hamilton/Avnet Computer
1807A West Braker Lane
Austin 78758

Hamilton/Avnet Computer
Forum 2
4004 Beltline, Suite 200
Dallas 75244

Hamilton/Avnet Computer
4850 Wright Rd., Suite 190
Stafford 77477

†Hamilton/Avnet Electronics
1807 W. Braker Lane
Austin 78758
Tel: (512) 837-8911
TWX: 910-874-1319

†Hamilton/Avnet Electronics
4004 Beltline, Suite 200
Dallas 75234
Tel: (214) 308-8111
TWX: 910-860-5929

†Hamilton/Avnet Electronics
4850 Wright Rd., Suite 190
Stafford 77477
Tel: (713) 240-7733
TWX: 910-881-5523

†Pioneer/Standard Electronics
1826-D Kramer
Austin 78758
Tel: (512) 835-4000
FAX: 512-835-9829

†Pioneer/Standard Electronics
13710 Omega Road
Dallas 75244
Tel: (214) 386-7300
FAX: 214-490-6419

†Pioneer/Standard Electronics
10530 Rockley Road
Houston 77099
Tel: (713) 495-4700
FAX: 713-495-5642

†Wyle Distribution Group
1810 Greenville Avenue
Richardson 75081
Tel: (214) 235-9953
FAX: 214-644-5064

UTAH

Hamilton/Avnet Computer
1585 West 2100 South
Salt Lake City 84119

†Hamilton/Avnet Electronics
1585 West 2100 South
Salt Lake City 84119
Tel: (801) 972-2800
TWX: 910-925-4018

†Wyle Distribution Group
1325 West 2200 South
Suite E
West Valley 84119
Tel: (801) 974-9953

WASHINGTON

†Almac Electronics Corp.
14360 S.E. Eastgate Way
Bellevue 98007
Tel: (206) 643-9992
FAX: 206-643-9709

Hamilton/Avnet Computer
17761 Northeast 78th Place
Redmond 98052

†Hamilton/Avnet Electronics
17761 N.E. 78th Place
Redmond 98052
Tel: (206) 881-6697
FAX: 206-867-0159

Wyle Distribution Group
15385 N.E. 90th Street
Redmond 98052
Tel: (206) 881-1150
FAX: 206-881-1567

WISCONSIN

Arrow Electronics, Inc.
200 N. Patrick Blvd., Ste. 100
Brookfield 53005
Tel: (414) 792-0150
FAX: 414-792-0156

Hamilton/Avnet Computer
20875 Crossroads Circle
Suite 400
Waukesha 53186

†Hamilton/Avnet Electronics
28875 Crossroads Circle
Suite 400
Waukesha 53186
Tel: (414) 784-4510
FAX: 414-784-9509

CANADA

ALBERTA

Hamilton/Avnet Computer
2816 21st Street Northeast
Calgary T2E 6Z2

Hamilton/Avnet Electronics
2816 21st Street N.E. #3
Calgary T2E 6Z3
Tel: (403) 230-3586
FAX: 403-250-1591

Zentronics
6815 #8 Street N.E.
Suite 100
Calgary T2E 7H
Tel: (403) 295-8818
FAX: 403-295-8714

BRITISH COLUMBIA

†Hamilton/Avnet Electronics
8610 Commerce Ct.
Burnaby V5A 4N6
Tel: (604) 420-4101
FAX: 604-437-4712

Zentronics
108-11400 Bridgeport Road
Richmond V6X 1T2
Tel: (604) 273-5575
FAX: 604-273-2413

ONTARIO

Arrow Electronics, Inc.
36 Antares Dr., Unit 100
Nepean K2E 7W5
Tel: (613) 226-6903
FAX: 613-723-2018

†Arrow Electronics, Inc.
1093 Meyerside, Unit 2
Mississauga L5T 1M4
Tel: (416) 673-7769
FAX: 416-672-0849

Hamilton/Avnet Computer
Canada System Engineering
Group
3688 Nashua Drive
Units 7 & 8
Mississuaga L4V 1M5

Hamilton/Avnet Computer
3688 Nashua Drive
Units 9 & 10
Mississuaga L4V 1M5

Hamilton/Avnet Computer
6845 Rexwood Road
Units 7, 8, & 9
Mississuaga L4V 1R2

Hamilton/Avnet Computer
190 Colonade Road
Nepean K2E 7J5

†Hamilton/Avnet Electronics
6845 Rexwood Road
Units 3-4-5
Mississuaga L4T 1R2
Tel: (416) 677-7432
FAX: 416-677-0940

†Hamilton/Avnet Electronics
190 Colonnade Road South
Nepean K2E 7L5
Tel: (613) 226-1700
FAX: 613-226-1184

†Zentronics
1355 Meyerside Drive
Mississauga L5T 1C9
Tel: (416) 564-9600
FAX: 416-564-8320

†Zentronics
155 Colonnade Road
Unit 17
Nepean K2E 7K1
Tel: (613) 226-8840
FAX: 613-226-6352

QUEBEC

Arrow Electronics Inc.
1100 St. Regis
Dorval H9P 2T5
Tel: (514) 421-7411
FAX: 514-421-7430

Arrow Electronics, Inc.
500 Boul. St-Jean-Baptiste
Suite 280
Quebec G2E 5R9
Tel: (418) 871-7500
FAX: 418-871-6816

Hamilton/Avnet Computer
2795 Rue Halpern
St. Laurent H4S 1P8

†Hamilton/Avnet Electronics
2795 Halpern
St. Laurent H2E 7K1
Tel: (514) 335-1000
FAX: 514-335-2481

†Zentronics
520 McCaffrey
St. Laurent H4T 1N3
Tel: (514) 737-9700
FAX: 514-737-5212

†Certified Technical Distributor

EUROPEAN SALES OFFICES

FINLAND

Intel Finland OY
Ruosilantie 2
00390 Helsinki
Tel: (358) 0 544 644
TLX: 123332

FRANCE

Intel Corporation S.A.R.L.
1, Rue Edison-BP 303
78054 St. Quentin-en-Yvelines
Cedex
Tel: (33) (1) 30 57 70 00
TLX: 699016

ISRAEL

Intel Semiconductor Ltd.
Atidim Industrial Park-Neve Sharet
P.O. Box 43202
Tel-Aviv 61430
Tel: (972) 03-498080
TLX: 371215

ITALY

Intel Corporation Italia S.p.A.
Milanofiori Palazzo E
20094 Assago
Milano
Tel: (39) (02) 89200950
TLX: 341286

NETHERLANDS

Intel Semiconductor B.V.
Postbus 84130
3099 CC Rotterdam
Tel: (31) 10.407.11.11
TLX: 22283

SPAIN

Intel Iberia S.A.
Zurbaran, 28
28010 Madrid
Tel: (34) (1) 308.25.52
TLX: 46880

SWEDEN

Intel Sweden A.B.
Dalvagen 24
171 36 Solna
Tel: (46) 8 734 01 00
TLX: 12261

SWITZERLAND

Intel Semiconductor A.G.
Zuerichstrasse
8185 Winkel-Rueti bei Zuerich
Tel: (41) 01/860 62 62
TLX: 825977

UNITED KINGDOM

Intel Corporation (U.K.) Ltd.
Pipers Way
Swindon, Wiltshire SN3 1RJ
Tel: (44) (0793) 696000
TLX: 444447/8

WEST GERMANY

Intel GmbH
Dornacher Strasse 1
8016 Feldkirchen bei Muenchen
Tel: (49) 089/90992-0
FAX: (49) 089/904/3948

Intel GmbH
Abraham Lincoln Strasse 16-18
6200 Wiesbaden
Tel: (49) 06121/7605-0
TLX: 4-186183

Intel GmbH
Zettachring 10A
7000 Stuttgart 80
Tel: (49) 0711/7287-280
TLX: 7-254826

EUROPEAN DISTRIBUTORS/REPRESENTATIVES

AUSTRIA

Bacher Electronics G.m.b.H.
Rotenmuehlgasse 26
1120 Wien
Tel: (43) (0222) 83 56 46
TLX: 31532

BELGIUM

Inelco Belgium S.A.
Av. des Croix de Guerre 94
1120 Bruxelles
Oorlogskruisenlaan, 94
1120 Brussel
Tel: (32) (02) 216 01 60
TLX: 64475 or 22090

DENMARK

ITT-Multikomponent
Naverland 29
2600 Glostrup
Tel: (45) (0) 2 45 66 45
TLX: 33 355

FINLAND

OY Fintronic AB
Melkonkatu 24A
00210 Helsinki
Tel: (358) (0) 6926022
TLX: 124224

FRANCE

Almex
Zone industrielle d'Antony
48, rue de l'Aubepine
BP 102
92164 Antony cedex
Tel: (33) (1) 46 66 21 12
TLX: 250067

Jermyn
60, rue des Gemeaux
Silic 580
94653 Rungis Cedex
Tel: (33) (1) 49 78 49 78
TLX: 261585

Metrologie
Tour d'Asnieres
4, av. Laurent-Cely
92606 Asnieres Cedex
Tel: (33) (1) 47 90 62 40
TLX: 611448

Tekelec-Airtronic
Cite des Bruyeres
Rue Carle Vernet - BP 2
92310 Sevres
Tel: (33) (1) 45 34 75 35
TLX: 204552

IRELAND

Micro Marketing Ltd.
Glenageary Office Park
Glenageary
Co. Dublin
Tel: (21) (353) (01) 856288
FAX: (21) (353) (01) 857364
TLX: 31584

ISRAEL

Eastronics Ltd.
11 Rozanis Street
P.O.B. 39300
Tel-Aviv 61392
Tel: (972) 03-475151
TLX: 33638

ITALY

Intesi
Divisione ITT Industries GmbH
Viale Milanofiori
Palazzo E/5
20090 Assago (MI)
Tel: (39) 02/824701
TLX: 311351

Lasi Elettronica S.p.A.
V. le Fulvio Testi, 126
20092 Cinisello Balsamo (MI)
Tel: (39) 02/2440012
TLX: 352040

Telcom S.r.l.
Via M. Civitali 75
20148 Milano
Tel: (39) 02/4049046
TLX: 335654

ITT Multicomponents
Viale Milanofiori E/5
20090 Assago (MI)
Tel: (39) 02/824701
TLX: 311351

Silverstar
Via Dei Gracchi 20
20146 Milano
Tel: (39) 02/49961
TLX: 332189

NETHERLANDS

Koning en Hartman
Elektrotechniek B.V.
Energieweg 1
2627 AP Delft
Tel: (31) (1) 15/609906
TLX: 38250

NORWAY

Nordisk Elektronikk (Norge) A/S
Postboks 123
Smedsvingen 4
1364 Hvalstad
Tel: (47) (02) 84 62 10
TLX: 77546

PORTUGAL

ATD Portugal LDA
Rua Dos Lusiados, 5 Sala B
1300 Lisboa
Tel: (35) (1) 64 80 91
TLX: 61562

Ditram
Avenida Miguel Bombarda, 133
1000 Lisboa
Tel: (35) (1) 54 53 13
TLX: 14182

SPAIN

ATD Electronica, S.A.
Plaza Ciudad de Viena, 6
28040 Madrid
Tel: (34) (1) 234 40 00
TLX: 42477

ITT-SESA
Calle Miguel Angel, 21-3
28010 Madrid
Tel: (34) (1) 419 09 57
TLX: 27461

Metrologia Iberica, S.A.
Ctra. de Fuencarral, n.80
28100 Alcobendas (Madrid)
Tel: (34) (1) 653 86 11

SWEDEN

Nordisk Elektronik AB
Torshamnsgatan 39
Box 36
164 93 Kista
Tel: (46) 08-03 46 30
TLX: 105 47

SWITZERLAND

Industrade A.G.
Hertistrasse 31
8304 Wallisellen
Tel: (41) (01) 8328111
TLX: 56788

TURKEY

EMPA Electronic
Lindwurmstrasse 95A
8000 Muenchen 2
Tel: (49) 089/53 80 570
TLX: 528573

UNITED KINGDOM

Accent Electronic Components Ltd.
Jubilee House, Jubilee Road
Letchworth, Herts SG6 1QH
Tel: (44) (0462) 670011
FAX: (44) (0462) 682467
TWX: 826505

Bytech Components Ltd.
12A Cedarwood
Chineham Business Park
Crockford Lane
Basingstoke
Hants RG24 0WD
Tel: (0256) 707107
FAX: 0256-707162

Conformix
Unit 5
A1M Business Centre
Dixons Hill Road
Welham Green
South Hatfield
Herts AL9 7JE
Tel: (07072) 73282
FAX: (07072) 61678

Bytech Systems
3 The Western Centre
Western Road
Bracknell RG12 1RW
Tel: (44) (0344) 55333
FAX: (44) (0344) 867270
TWX: 849624

Jermyn
Vestry Estate
Otford Road
Sevenoaks
Kent TN14 5EU
Tel: (44) (0732) 450144
FAX: (44) (0732) 451251
TWX: 95142

MMD Ltd.
3 Bennet Court
Bennet Road
Reading
Berkshire RG2 0QX
Tel: (44) (0734) 313232
FAX: (44) (0734) 313255
TWX: 846669

Rapid Recall, Ltd.
Rapid House
Oxford Road
High Wycombe
Buckinghamshire HP11 2EE
Tel: (44) (0494) 26271
FAX: (44) (0494) 21860
TWX: 837931

Rapid Recall, Ltd.
28 High Street
Nantwich
Cheshire CW5 5AS
Tel: (0270) 627505
FAX: (0270) 629883
TWX: 36329

WEST GERMANY

Electronic 2000 AG
Stahlgruberring 12
8000 Muenchen 82
Tel: (49) 089/42001-0
TLX: 522561

ITT Multikomponent GmbH
Postfach 1265
Bahnhofstrasse 44
7141 Moeglingen
Tel: (49) 07141/4879
TLX: 7264472

Jermyn GmbH
Im Dachsstueck 9
6250 Limburg
Tel: (49) 06431/508-0
TLX: 415257-0

Metrologie GmbH
Meglingerstrasse 49
8000 Muenchen 71
Tel: (49) 089/78042-0
TLX: 5213189

Proelectron Vertriebs GmbH
Max Planck Strasse 1-3
6072 Dreieich
Tel: (49) 06103/30434-3
TLX: 417903

YUGOSLAVIA

H.R. Microelectronics Corp.
2005 de la Cruz Blvd., Ste. 223
Santa Clara, CA 95050
U.S.A.
Tel: (1) (408) 988-0286
TLX: 387452

Rapido Electronic Components
S.p.a.
Via C. Beccaria, 8
34133 Trieste
Italia
Tel: (39) 040/360555
TLX: 460461

intel

INTERNATIONAL SALES OFFICES

AUSTRALIA

Intel Australia Pty. Ltd.
Unit 13
Allambie Grove Business Park
25 Frenchs Forest Road East
Frenchs Forest, NSW, 2086
Tel: 61-2975-3300
FAX: 61-2975-3375

BRAZIL

Intel Semicondutores do Brazil LTDA
Av. Paulista, 1159-CJS 404/405
01311 - Sao Paulo - S.P.
Tel: 55-11-287-5899
TLX: 3911153146 ISDB
FAX: 55-11-287-5119

CHINA/HONG KONG

Intel PRC Corporation
15/F, Office 1, Citic Bldg.
Jian Guo Men Wai Street
Beijing, PRC
Tel: (1) 500-4850
TLX: 22947 INTEL CN
FAX: (1) 500-2953

Intel Semiconductor Ltd.*
10/F East Tower
Bond Center
Queensway, Central
Hong Kong
Tel: (852) 844-4555
FAX: (852) 868-1989

INDIA

Intel Asia Electronics, Inc.
4/2, Samrah Plaza
St. Mark's Road
Bangalore 560001
Tel: 011-91-812-215065
TLX: 953-845-2646 INTL IN
FAX: 091-812-215067

JAPAN

Intel Japan K.K.
5-6 Tokodai, Tsukuba-shi
Ibaraki, 300-26
Tel: 0298-47-8511
TLX: 3656-160
FAX: 0298-47-8450

Intel Japan K.K.*
Daiichi Mitsugi Bldg.
1-8889 Fuchu-cho
Fuchu-shi, Tokyo 183
Tel: 0423-60-7871
FAX: 0423-60-0315

Intel Japan K.K.*
Bldg. Kumagaya
2-69 Hon-cho
Kumagaya-shi, Saitama 360
Tel: 0485-24-6871
FAX: 0485-24-7518

Intel Japan K.K.*
Kawa-asa Bldg.
2-11-5 Shin-Yokohama
Kohoku-ku, Yokohama-shi
Kanagawa, 222
Tel: 045-474-7661
FAX: 045-471-4394

Intel Japan K.K.*
Ryokuchi-Eki Bldg.
2-4-1 Terauchi
Toyonaka-shi, Osaka 560
Tel: 06-863-1091
FAX: 06-863-1084

Intel Japan K.K.
Shinmaru Bldg.
1-5-1 Marunouchi
Chiyoda-ku, Tokyo 100
Tel: 03-201-3621
FAX: 03-201-6850

Intel Japan K.K.
Green Bldg.
1-16-20 Nishiki
Naka-ku, Nagoya-shi
Aichi 450
Tel: 052-204-1261
FAX: 052-204-1285

KOREA

Intel Technology Asia, Ltd.
16th Floor, Life Bldg.
61 Yoido-dong, Youngdeungpo-Ku
Seoul 150-010
Tel: (2) 784-8186, 8286, 8386
TLX: K29312 INTELKO
FAX: (2) 784-8096

SINGAPORE

Intel Singapore Technology, Ltd.
101 Thomson Road #21-05/06
United Square
Singapore 1130
Tel: 250-7811
TLX: 39921 INTEL
FAX: 250-9256

TAIWAN

Intel Technology Far East Ltd.
8th Floor, No. 205
Bank Tower Bldg.
Tung Hua N. Road
Taipei
Tel: 886-2-716-9660
FAX: 886-2-717-2455

INTERNATIONAL DISTRIBUTORS/REPRESENTATIVES

ARGENTINA

Dafsys S.R.L.
Chacabuco, 90-6 Piso
1069-Buenos Aires
Tel: 54-1-334-7726
FAX: 54-1-334-1871

AUSTRALIA

Email Electronics
15-17 Hume Street
Huntingdale, 3166
Tel: 011-61-3-544-8244
TLX: AA 30895
FAX: 011-61-3-543-8179

NSD-Australia
205 Middleborough Rd.
Box Hill, Victoria 3128
Tel: 03 8900970
FAX: 03 8990819

BRAZIL

Elebra Componentes
Rua Geraldo Flausina Gomes, 78
7 Andar
04575 - Sao Paulo - S.P.
Tel: 55-11-534-9641
TLX: 55-11-54593/54591
FAX: 55-11-534-9424

CHINA/HONG KONG

Novel Precision Machinery Co., Ltd.
Room 728 Trade Square
681 Cheung Sha Wan Road
Kowloon, Hong Kong
Tel: (852) 360-8999
TWX: 32032 NVTNL HX
FAX: (852) 725-3695

INDIA

Micronic Devices
Arun Complex
No. 65 D.V.G. Road
Basavanagudi
Bangalore 560 004
Tel: 011-91-812-600-631
011-91-812-611-365
TLX: 9538458332 MDBG

Micronic Devices
No. 516 5th Floor
Swastik Chambers
Sion, Trombay Road
Chembur
Bombay 400 071
TLX: 9531 171447 MDEV

Micronic Devices
25/8, 1st Floor
Bada Bazaar Marg
Old Rajinder Nagar
New Delhi 110 060
Tel: 011-91-11-5723509
011-91-11-589771
TLX: 031-63253 MDND IN

Micronic Devices
6-3-348/12A Dwarakapuri Colony
Hyderabad 500 482
Tel: 011-91-842-226748

S&S Corporation
1587 Kooser Road
San Jose, CA 95118
Tel: (408) 978-6216
TLX: 820281
FAX: (408) 978-8635

JAPAN

Asahi Electronics Co. Ltd.
KMM Bldg. 2-14-1 Asano
Kokurakita-ku
Kitakyushu-shi 802
Tel: 093-511-6471
FAX: 093-551-7861

CTC Components Systems Co., Ltd.
4-8-1 Dobashi, Miyamae-ku
Kawasaki-shi, Kanagawa 213
Tel: 044-852-5121
FAX: 044-877-4268

Dia Semicon Systems, Inc.
Flower Hill Shinmachi Higashi-kan
1-23-9 Shinmachi, Setagaya-ku
Tokyo 154
Tel: 03-439-1600
FAX: 03-439-1601

Okaya Koki
2-4-18 Sakae
Naka-ku, Nagoya-shi 460
Tel: 052-204-2916
FAX: 052-204-2901

Ryoyo Electro Corp.
Konwa Bldg.
1-12-22 Tsukiji
Chuo-ku, Tokyo 104
Tel: 03-546-5011
FAX: 03-546-5044

KOREA

J-Tek Corporation
Dong Sung Bldg. 9/F
158-24, Samsung-Dong, Kangnam-Ku
Seoul 135-090
Tel: (822) 557-8039
FAX: (822) 557-8304

Samsung Electronics
Samsung Main Bldg.
150 Taepyung-Ro-2KA, Chung-Ku
Seoul 100-102
C.P.O. Box 8780
Tel: (822) 751-3680
TWX: KORSST K 27970
FAX: (822) 753-9065

MEXICO

SSB Electronics, Inc.
675 Palomar Street, Bldg. 4, Suite A
Chula Vista, CA 92011
Tel: (619) 585-3253
TLX: 287751 CBALL UR
FAX: (619) 585-8322

Dicopel S.A.
Tochtli 368 Fracc. Ind. San Antonio
Azcapotzalco
C.P. 02760-Mexico, D.F.
Tel: 52-5-561-3211
TLX: 177 3790 Dicome
FAX: 52-5-561-1279

PHI S.A. de C.V.
Fco. Villa esq. Ajusco s/n
Cuernavaca – Morelos
Tel: 52-73-13-9412
FAX: 52-73-17-5333

NEW ZEALAND

Email Electronics
36 Olive Road
Penrose, Auckland
Tel: 011-64-9-591-155
FAX: 011-64-9-592-681

SINGAPORE

Electronic Resources Pte, Ltd.
17 Harvey Road
#03-01 Singapore 1336
Tel: (65) 283-0888
TWX: RS 56541 ERS
FAX: (65) 289-5327

SOUTH AFRICA

Electronic Building Elements
178 Erasmus St. (off Watermeyet St.)
Meyerspark, Pretoria, 0184
Tel: 011-2712-803-7680
FAX: 011-2712-803-8294

TAIWAN

Micro Electronics Corporation
12th Floor, Section 3
285 Nanking East Road
Taipei, R.O.C.
Tel: (886) 2-7198419
FAX: (886) 2-7197916

Acer Sertek Inc.
15th Floor, Section 2
Chien Kuo North Rd.
Taipei 18479 R.O.C.
Tel: 886-2-501-0055
TWX: 23756 SERTEK
FAX: (886) 2-5012521

*Field Application Location

intel®

DOMESTIC SERVICE OFFICES

ALASKA

Intel Corp.
c/o TransAlaska Network
1515 Lore Rd.
Anchorage 99507
Tel: (907) 522-1776

Intel Corp.
c/o TransAlaska Data Systems
c/o GCI Operations
520 Fifth Ave., Suite 407
Fairbanks 99701
Tel: (907) 452-6264

ARIZONA

*Intel Corp.
410 North 44th Street
Suite 500
Phoenix 85008
Tel: (602) 231-0386
FAX: (602) 244-0446

*Intel Corp.
500 E. Fry Blvd., Suite M-15
Sierra Vista 85635
Tel: (602) 459-5010

ARKANSAS

Intel Corp.
c/o Federal Express
1500 West Park Drive
Little Rock 72204

CALIFORNIA

*Intel Corp.
21515 Vanowen St., Ste. 116
Canoga Park 91303
Tel: (818) 704-8500

*Intel Corp.
300 N. Continental Blvd.
Suite 100
El Segundo 90245
Tel: (213) 640-6040

*Intel Corp.
1900 Prairie City Rd.
Folsom 95630-9597
Tel: (916) 351-6143

*Intel Corp.
9665 Chesapeake Dr., Suite 325
San Diego 92123
Tel: (619) 292-8086

**Intel Corp.
400 N. Tustin Avenue
Suite 450
Santa Ana 92705
Tel: (714) 835-9642

**Intel Corp.
2700 San Tomas Exp., 1st Floor
Santa Clara 95051
Tel: (408) 970-1747

COLORADO

*Intel Corp.
600 S. Cherry St., Suite 700
Denver 80222
Tel: (303) 321-8086

CONNECTICUT

*Intel Corp.
301 Lee Farm Corporate Park
83 Wooster Heights Rd.
Danbury 06811
Tel: (203) 748-3130

FLORIDA

**Intel Corp.
800 Fairway Dr., Suite 160
Deerfield Beach 33441
Tel: (305) 421-0506
FAX: (305) 421-2444

*Intel Corp.
5850 T.G. Lee Blvd., Ste. 340
Orlando 32822
Tel: (407) 240-8000

GEORGIA

*Intel Corp.
20 Technology Park, Suite 150
Norcross 30092
Tel: (404) 449-0541

5523 Theresa Street
Columbus 31907

HAWAII

**Intel Corp.
Honolulu 96820
Tel: (808) 847-6738

ILLINOIS

**†Intel Corp.
Woodfield Corp. Center III
300 N. Martingale Rd., Ste. 400
Schaumburg 60173
Tel: (708) 605-8031

INDIANA

*Intel Corp.
8910 Purdue Rd., Ste. 350
Indianapolis 46268
Tel: (317) 875-0623

KANSAS

*Intel Corp.
10985 Cody, Suite 140
Overland Park 66210
Tel: (913) 345-2727

KENTUCKY

Intel Corp.
133 Walton Ave., Office 1A
Lexington 40508
Tel: (606) 255-2957

Intel Corp.
896 Hillcrest Road, Apt. A
Radcliff 40160 (Louisville)

LOUISIANA

Hammond 70401
(serviced from Jackson, MS)

MARYLAND

**Intel Corp.
10010 Junction Dr., Suite 200
Annapolis Junction 20701
Tel: (301) 206-2860

MASSACHUSETTS

**Intel Corp.
Westford Corp. Center
3 Carlisle Rd., 2nd Floor
Westford 01886
Tel: (508) 692-0960

MICHIGAN

*Intel Corp.
7071 Orchard Lake Rd., Ste. 100
West Bloomfield 48322
Tel: (313) 851-8905

MINNESOTA

*Intel Corp.
3500 W. 80th St., Suite 360
Bloomington 55431
Tel: (612) 835-6722

MISSISSIPPI

Intel Corp.
c/o Compu-Care
2001 Airport Road, Suite 205F
Jackson 39208
Tel: (601) 932-6275

MISSOURI

*Intel Corp.
4203 Earth City Exp., Ste. 131
Earth City 63045
Tel: (314) 291-1990

Intel Corp.
Route 2, Box 221
Smithville 64089
Tel: (913) 345-2727

NEW JERSEY

**Intel Corp.
300 Sylvan Avenue
Englewood Cliffs 07632
Tel: (201) 567-0821

*Intel Corp.
Parkway 109 Office Center
328 Newman Springs Road
Red Bank 07701
Tel: (201) 747-2233

NEW MEXICO

Intel Corp.
Rio Rancho 1
4100 Sara Road
Rio Rancho 87124-1025
(near Albuquerque)
Tel: (505) 893-7000

NEW YORK

*Intel Corp.
2950 Expressway Dr. South
Suite 130
Islandia 11722
Tel: (516) 231-3300

Intel Corp.
Westage Business Center
Bldg. 300, Route 9
Fishkill 12524
Tel: (914) 897-3860

Intel Corp.
5858 East Molloy Road
Syracuse 13211
Tel: (315) 454-0576

NORTH CAROLINA

*Intel Corp.
5800 Executive Center Drive
Suite 105
Charlotte 28212
Tel: (704) 568-8966

**Intel Corp.
5540 Centerview Dr., Suite 215
Raleigh 27606
Tel: (919) 851-9537

OHIO

**Intel Corp.
3401 Park Center Dr., Ste. 220
Dayton 45414
Tel: (513) 890-5350

*Intel Corp.
25700 Science Park Dr., Ste. 100
Beachwood 44122
Tel: (216) 464-2736

OREGON

**Intel Corp.
15254 N.W. Greenbrier Parkway
Building B
Beaverton 97005
Tel: (503) 645-8051

PENNSYLVANIA

*†Intel Corp.
925 Harvest Drive
Suite 200
Blue Bell 19422
Tel: (215) 641-1000
1-800-468-3548
FAX: (215) 641-0785

**†Intel Corp.
400 Penn Center Blvd., Ste. 610
Pittsburgh 15235
Tel: (412) 823-4970

*Intel Corp.
1513 Cedar Cliff Dr.
Camp Hill 17011
Tel: (717) 761-0860

PUERTO RICO

Intel Corp.
South Industrial Park
P.O. Box 910
Las Piedras 00671
Tel: (809) 733-8616

TEXAS

**Intel Corp.
Westech 360, Suite 4230
8911 Capitol of Texas Hwy.
Austin 78752-1239
Tel : (512) 794-8086

**†Intel Corp.
12000 Ford Rd., Suite 401
Dallas 75234
Tel: (214) 241-8087

**Intel Corp.
7322 SW Freeway, Suite 1490
Houston 77074
Tel: (713) 988-8086

UTAH

Intel Corp.
428 East 6400 South
Suite 104
Murray 84107
Tel: (801) 263-8051
FAX: (801) 268-1457

VIRGINIA

*Intel Corp.
1504 Santa Rosa Rd., Ste. 108
Richmond 23288
Tel: (804) 282-5668

WASHINGTON

**Intel Corp.
155 108th Avenue N.E., Ste. 386
Bellevue 98004
Tel: (206) 453-8086

CANADA

ONTARIO

**Intel Semiconductor of Canada, Ltd.
2650 Queensview Dr., Ste. 250
Ottawa K2B 8H6
Tel: (613) 829-9714

**Intel Semiconductor of Canada, Ltd.
190 Attwell Dr., Ste. 102
Rexdale (Toronto) M9W 6H8
Tel: (416) 675-2105

QUEBEC

**Intel Semiconductor of Canada, Ltd.
1 Rue Holiday
Suite 115
Tour East
Pt. Claire H9R 5N3
Tel: (514) 694-9130
FAX: 514-694-0064

CUSTOMER TRAINING CENTERS

CALIFORNIA

2700 San Tomas Expressway
Santa Clara 95051
Tel: 1-800-328-0386

MARYLAND

10010 Junction Dr.
Suite 200
Annapolis Junction 20701
Tel: 1-800-328-0386

SYSTEMS ENGINEERING OFFICES

MINNESOTA

3500 W. 80th Street
Suite 360
Bloomington 55431
Tel: (612) 835-6722

NEW YORK

2950 Expressway Dr., South
Islandia 11722
Tel: (506) 231-3300

*Carry-in locations
**Carry-in/mail-in locations